MW00783579

NOTES FOR CLARINETISTS

Notes for Performers

Series Editor
KYLE J. DZAPO

Notes for Flutists
A Guide to the Repertoire
Kyle J. Dzapo

Notes for Clarinetists
A Guide to the Repertoire
Albert R. Rice

Notes for Clarinetists

A GUIDE TO THE REPERTOIRE

Albert R. Rice

OXFORD

UNIVERSITY PRESS

Oxford University Press is a department of the University of Oxford.
It furthers the University's objective of excellence in research, scholarship,
and education by publishing worldwide. Oxford is a registered trade mark of
Oxford University Press in the UK and certain other countries.

Published in the United States of America by Oxford University Press
198 Madison Avenue, New York, NY 10016, United States of America.

© Oxford University Press 2017

All rights reserved. No part of this publication may be reproduced,
stored in a retrieval system, or transmitted, in any form or by any means,
without the prior permission in writing of Oxford University Press,
or as expressly permitted by law, by license, or under terms agreed with
the appropriate reproduction rights organization. Inquiries concerning
reproduction outside the scope of the above should be sent to the
Rights Department, Oxford University Press, at the address above.

You must not circulate this work in any other form
and you must impose this same condition on any acquirer.

Library of Congress Cataloging-in-Publication Data

Names: Rice, Albert R., author.
Title: Notes for clarinetists : a guide to the repertoire / Albert R. Rice.
Description: New York : Oxford University Press, [2017]
Identifiers: LCCN 2016021238 (print) | LCCN 2016023435 (ebook) |
    ISBN 9780190205201 (cloth : alk. paper) | ISBN 9780190205218 (pbk. : alk. paper) |
    ISBN 9780190205256 (oxford scholarly online) | ISBN 9780190205249 (epub) |
    ISBN 9780190205232 (updf)
Subjects: LCSH: Clarinet music—Bibliography.
Classification: LCC ML128.C58 R53 2017 (print) | LCC ML128.C58 (ebook) |
    DDC 788.6/2193—dc23
LC record available at https://lccn.loc.gov/2016021238

*I dedicate this book to my loving family: my wife and editor, Eleanor Montague;
my step-daughter Lorelei Montague, her husband Timothy Judge, and their son Landon Judge;
my step-son Scott Montague, his wife Tamara, and their children Jenson and Catalina.*

From the Series Editor

"Notes for Performers" is a series born of my desire to help musicians connect performance studies with pertinent aspects of scholarship. My favorite theory professor, John Buccheri (Northwestern University), used to say that to know a piece intuitively, technically, and intellectually is to *really* know a piece. While some may argue that one should simply "play from the heart," knowledge can be a powerful tool in strengthening or refining a performer's instincts. Additionally, when musicians are armed with knowledge, they can enhance their audiences' understanding of compositions. Having served as a pre-concert lecturer for the Chicago Symphony Orchestra for more than twenty years, I have had the satisfaction of helping audiences engage more fully with the music they are about to hear. I hope this series will encourage performers to offer written or spoken commentary to enhance their audiences' listening experiences.

While all musicians will gain insights from the books in the series, the writing is intended for undergraduate students, perhaps with a bit of professorial guidance. The selection of pieces is admittedly subjective. Each author is asked to identify the best-known compositions written for the instrument. To gain the broadest selection, only one work of a composer is chosen. It is my hope that instrumentalists will view each volume as a starting point for connecting performance studies with scholarship and that it will encourage them to explore other works in a similar fashion. Many more works are worthy of inclusion in each volume and, in time, perhaps second volumes may be added with additional compositions, including more recent works that have stood the test of time and become part of a given instrument's core repertoire.

There have long been helpful resources available to performers for learning about chamber, orchestral, and operatic works, but similar in-depth information to guide one's understanding of a given orchestral instrument's solo repertoire has thus far been noticeably absent from bookshelves. The goal of this series is to fill that open space on the shelf, and my goal as Oxford's "Notes for Performers" editor is to contribute to the intellectual understanding necessary, as Dr. Buccheri would suggest, for a musician to *really* know a piece.

Kyle Dzapo
Professor of Music
Bradley University

Contents

Preface

NOTES FOR CLARINETISTS: A Guide to the Repertoire, a volume in Oxford University Press's *Notes for Performers Series*, offers in a single resource important historical and analytical information about major solo pieces for clarinet alone, clarinet and piano, and clarinet and orchestra. Clarinetists know that scholarship enriches performance and they are eager to utilize contextual information to prepare and present concerts. Violin, vocal, and orchestral repertoires are well represented with published compilations but clarinetists have never had a comparable source to draw upon. Rather, they are forced to collate information from CD liner notes, journal articles, some dubiously reliable Internet sites, and short references in books. *Notes for Clarinetists* is a comprehensive resource for teachers and professors as well as student, amateur, and professional clarinetists who will glean insights into thirty-five compositions and be able to share those insights with audiences.

Presented is historical information about the composer and the composition; the performer(s) for whom the work was written; and the first, and sometimes, later performances. Detailed musical analysis reveals the organization and harmonic construction of the work. Musical examples illustrate individual measures and illustrations portray instruments and performers behind the history. Some performance advice is included concerning technical challenges, fingering difficulties, and tricky ensemble passages that may need to be worked out in rehearsal, but the chapters are not meant to be master classes.

The clarinet's solo music gradually started with concertos written during the 1720s. With clarinet mechanism and design developments, hundreds of composers wrote concertos during the late eighteenth and early nineteenth centuries. Concertos continued to appear during the twentieth and twenty-first centuries. Sonatas and solo works for clarinet and keyboard began to be written about 1770, becoming more common during the nineteenth century and popular during the twentieth and twenty-first centuries. Works for clarinet alone, initially written during the early nineteenth century, became popular during the twentieth and twenty-first centuries.

In selecting compositions for this volume, the author has, with advice from other clarinetists and teachers, developed a list that includes the best known and most often performed pieces in the instrument's repertoire, including contemporary works that are performed primarily by specialist performers but have become recognized as important parts of the literature. Repertoire choices are also informed by lists of clarinet music studied and performed in colleges, universities, and conservatories, primarily in the United States. While some composers have written two or more well-known works for the clarinet, only one composition is selected to allow a greater variety of composers in the volume. Because there was a limit to the number of compositions in the volume, the choice of repertoire was based on the quality of the work, frequency of performance, and substantial and creative use of the clarinet. Inevitably, several works favored by clarinetists do not appear. Finally, the author has performed the majority of the works for clarinet alone, with piano, and in some cases, orchestra, during a period of about forty years.

There are many interesting facts in this book about when, how, why, and for whom each work was written. In some cases, the composer did not write the work for a specific musician. Of interest is the relationship between the composer and the clarinetist when the work was written for a specific player. Reviews of early performances and the published music provide contemporary insights. Early attitudes toward the playability and style of many clarinet works have changed over time, including the advanced style of Berg's *Four Pieces for Clarinet and Piano*, and the extremely difficult and unplayable (!) music of Francaix's concerto, Martino's *A Set for Clarinet Unaccompanied*, and Nielsen's concerto.

The most important part of the book is the musical analysis. Analyses are based on the author's judgment and study, informed by writings in books, articles, newspapers, dissertations, and theses. The sounding pitch of the piano is the basis of the harmonic analyses; the clarinet parts are discussed in the transposed pitches of B♭ and A. Rather than writing a blow-by-blow analysis, the charts give an overview of the work and include: For each movement, sections with measure numbers, number of measures, and repeated measures, are followed by a colon (:). For some works, meter changes are indicated in the text. Works without a chart are described in the text. Themes or motives are indicated with letters, variations and repetitions on a theme are designated with superscript numbers, and theme fragments are denoted by parentheses. Tonalities, implied tonalities, and tonal centers are specified in major and minor keys; Neapolitan and chromatic chords are identified. Several chapters include note corrections and other indications that are not found in the printed music.

There are many possible ways to analyze a piece of music. As a player, use this and other analyses to inform your approach to a solo—to make it your own. It is important to have the score at hand when following each analysis. This will help to understand the form and how the composer wrote his inspiring and enjoyable music.

I would like to acknowledge the help, encouragement, and suggestions that I received from Kyle Dzapo, editor of the Notes for Performers Series, and author of *Notes for Flutists: A Guide to the Repertoire*; Robert E. Eliason for careful preparation of the musical examples; Jane Ellsworth for many suggestions on the text; and to Michel Arrignon, Michael Bryant, Peter Horton, Jocelyn Howell, Jean Jeltsch, David Kirby, Jean-Marie Paul, Ingrid Pearson, Pamela Poulin, Benjamin Reissenberger, David Ross, Denis Watel, and John Yeh. I am especially indebted to my wife, Eleanor Montague, for careful editing and many stylistic suggestions.

The pitches are notated using the following scheme:

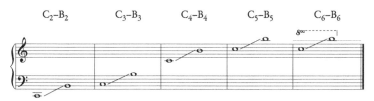

Albert R. Rice
January 2016

Abbreviations

arr.	arranged
ca.	circa, about
chr.	chromatic
dev.	development
diss.	dissertation
ed.	editor, edition, edited
eds.	editors
fig.	figuration, figure
Fig.	Figure
frag.	fragmentary, fragment(s)
ill.	illustration
intro./Intro.	Introduction
m.	measure
mm.	measures
Ms.	manuscript
no(s).	number(s)
rev.	revised
trans.	transition, translator(s), translated
( ) around a theme	partial theme or fragment of a theme
superscript number after a letter	theme or section repeated and/or altered
: after a range of measures	measures repeated

NOTES FOR CLARINETISTS

1 Arthur Benjamin, *Le tombeau de Ravel: Valse-Caprices for Clarinet and Piano*

Date of composition: 1957

First edition/other edition: Arthur Benjamin, *Le tombeau de Ravel: Valse-Caprices for Clarinet and Piano*, London: Boosey & Hawkes, 1958; *The Boosey & Hawkes Clarinet Anthology*, London: Boosey & Hawkes, 2009 (piano and clarinet)

Dedicatee/first performer: Not indicated; Gervase de Peyer, clarinet

Date/place of first performance: 1957 or 1958; London, Wigmore Hall[1]

ARTHUR BENJAMIN (1893–1960) was an Australian composer, conductor, pianist, and teacher. He studied music in Brisbane and completed his training at the Royal College of Music (RCM) in London with Frederick Cliffe (piano) and Charles Villiers Stanford (composition). Benjamin taught at the Sydney Conservatory, 1919–21. In London, he was a music professor at the RCM, 1924–39.[2] Benjamin was the adjudicator and examiner for the Associated Board of the Royal Schools of Music, examining students in Australia, Canada, and the West Indies. During World War II, he settled in Vancouver, British Columbia, where he was conductor of the Canadian Broadcasting Corporation Symphony Orchestra, 1941–46. He was a resident lecturer at Reed College in Portland, Oregon, 1944–45. Benjamin returned to the RCM at the beginning of the 1946

---

[1] John Robert Brown, "Gervase de Peyer in his 80th Year, part II," *The Clarinet* 33, no. 2 (March 2006): 62.

[2] Email correspondence from Dr. Peter Horton, Deputy Librarian, RCM, May 13, 2014.

Christmas term, stopping at the end of the 1953 summer term. One of his piano pupils was Benjamin Britten.[3]

Benjamin's works include operas, ballet music, several film scores, a television production, orchestral works, choral works, songs, chamber music, and piano pieces.[4] Several are recorded and performed. According to Keller, he was instinctively creative and composed quickly; the titles of his works are unconventional, usually referring to musical forms. Benjamin often employs a cyclic design in a single or joined movement.[5]

In 1957, Benjamin wrote *Le tombeau de Ravel: Valse-Caprices*, a virtuoso viola and piano work for the famous violist, William Primrose (1909–1982). Benjamin asked the outstanding clarinetist, Gervase de Peyer (1926–), to review his work. De Peyer found passages that were easily playable by a stringed instrument but very awkward for a clarinet. He told Benjamin who replied, "Good, that is exactly why I asked you to look it over. I want you to adapt the clarinet [part] to suit the instrument and change [the viola part to] whatever you like."[6] According to De Peyer:

> I was somewhat astonished at such an easy-going approach and felt my responsibility with youthful uncertainty. But I need not have worried as Arthur Benjamin was all smiles when I showed him what I had done. This was mainly to straighten out some of those wiggling and curling passages that are much easier on string instruments then [sic] on winds; string [players] can just finger across the strings. Anyway, that was that, and Arthur made no revisions to my revisions, which I played through with him and soon after included in my first recital disc.[7]

Although Benjamin's *Le tombeau de Ravel: Valse-Caprices* can be played by a viola or clarinet soloist, Benjamin notes in the piano part, "So as to make the work characteristic of either the clarinet or viola, it will be noticed that there are many differences (in the passage work especially) between the two. Thus it cannot be said that either is a transcription of the other."[8] The title indicates Benjamin's admiration for

---

[3] Peter J. Pirie and Robert Barnett, "Benjamin, Arthur," *Grove Music Online*; "Benjamin, Arthur," *Baker's Biographical Dictionary of Musicians*, Centennial ed., eds. Nicholas Slonimsky and Laura Diane Kuhn (New York: Schirmer Books, 2001), 1: 286; Herbert Howells, "Arthur Benjamin 1893–1960," *Tempo* 55/56 (Autumn–Winter 1960): 2; "Obituary, Arthur Benjamin," *The Musical Times* 101, no. 1408 (June 1960): 380.

[4] Pirie and Barnet, ibid.

[5] Hans Keller, "Arthur Benjamin and the Problem of Popularity," *Tempo* 15 (Spring 1950): 7–9.

[6] Gervase de Peyer, "Arthur Benjamin's *Le tombeau de Ravel*," *The Clarinet* 18, no. 2 (February–March 1991): 16.

[7] De Peyer, ibid. The recording was released in 1961 as "Gervase De Peyer Recital" with Cyril Preedy, piano, on Éditions de l'Oiseau-Lyre, SOL 60028.

[8] Arthur Benjamin, *Le tombeau de Ravel: Valse-Caprices* (London: Boosey & Hawkes, 1958).

Section:	Introduction	Waltz 1	Waltz 2	Waltz 3
Starts at m.	1 Allegro molto	55 (13 mm. after no. 3)	121 (28 mm. after no. 6, 2nd beat)	224 (21 mm. after no. 11)
No. of mm.	54	66	103	69
Tonalities	f, c	f, c♯, g, f	e	F
Themes	A, trans., A¹	B, B¹	C	D

Section:	Waltz 4	Waltz 5	Waltz 6	Finale
Starts at m.	293 (32 mm. after no. 13, 2nd beat)	359 (14 mm. after no. 16)	426 (28 mm. after no. 19)	479–600
No. of mm.	66	67	53	122
Tonalities	A♭	f	C	f, A, f
Themes	C¹	E	F	A², G, A³

CHART 1.1 Benjamin, *Le tombeau de Ravel: Valse-Caprices for Clarinet and Piano*: Structural analysis.

Maurice Ravel's piano solo, *Le tombeau de Couperin*, although it is more similar to Ravel's piano solo, *Valses nobles et sentimentales*.[9]

The work is unusual in its form: an introduction, six waltzes, and a finale played in one continuous movement. (See Chart 1.1.) It is brilliant and challenging, composed in a Romantic style with flowing melodies, effective changes of tempo, and written out rubato. Technical demands include awkward passages in quick tempos, a high degree of control of dynamics from *ppp* to *ff*, and short and sustained staccato. The beginning of each waltz is numbered in the printed parts. The introduction and all but waltz 2 are about the same length; waltz 2 is much longer; and the finale is about twice as long.

Benjamin's exciting Allegro molto introduction prepares the audience for virtuosic fireworks. It is a fast, repetitive motive of two alternating intervals of a fifth played in the piano's lowest range, answered by the clarinet A theme with rapid *p* arpeggios. This ostinato rhythm propels the music forward and effectively returns in the finale, verifying Keller's observation of Benjamin's cyclic form. Six measures after no. 1, there is a written out portamento with a Meno allegro (little slower) nine-measure passage before returning to Tempo I (Ex. 1.1).

9 Calum MacDonald, "Notes" to Arthur Benjamin, *Violin Sonatina & Viola Sonata*, Hyperion, CDA67979, 2014. [Online] Available: http://www.hyperion-records.co.uk/dc.asp?dc=D_CDA67969. [September 12, 2015]. The late Calum MacDonald mistakenly states in his notes that Benjamin wrote *Le tombeau de Ravel* originally for the clarinet with the viola part second. This is inaccurate. We know from de Peyer that this work was originally written for viola, specifically for Primrose.

EXAMPLE 1.1. Benjamin, *Le Tombeau de Ravel Valse-Caprices for Clarinet and Piano*, mm. 24–32.

Waltz 1, Poco lento, Con espressione di malinconia, is a somber B theme. At no. 4, the piano has two measures of repeated sixteenth notes with the first note slightly lengthened, answered by the clarinet, senza rigore, sempre espressivo, with slurred sixteenth note phrases. The clarinet becomes louder and more passionate, articulating two measures of repeated sixteenth notes with the first note slightly lengthened, and accelerating into a five-measure cadenza that returns to a slow B^1 theme.

Waltz 2, Presto, volante (fast moving), is played lightly in one beat per measure. The *pp* dynamic and thin accompaniment in E minor introduce the C theme, starting on the second beat with four upward slurred eighth notes. Here are passages of light staccato and flowing triplets, with a resemblance to Ravel's style. A short rallentando leads to the slower F major waltz 3, Andante, semplice, at a moderately slow tempo. A plain yet intimate D theme rises to a *ff* central climax, and returns to a bittersweet *pp* melody. Waltz 4, Allegro, Vigoroso, is a transposed Ab major C^1 theme based on theme C from waltz 2, starting on the second beat with four downward slurred eighth notes. It is energetic, with a heavy accent on the first beat, and effective in using clarinet slurred triplets, a staccato section leading to more triplets, a chromatic scale, and a lovely *ppp* arpeggio ending.

Waltz 5, Allegretto, preciso, puts forward an exact, eighth note staccatissimo (marked in the piano part) clarinet E theme, while the sixteenth note theme alternates between piano and clarinet. Waltz 6, Lento, intimo, is an introspective interlude, becoming more sonorous to a *ff* climax, quieting with arpeggios to *ppp*. The finale, Non troppo allegro, begins with staccato eighth notes to a meno allegro F minor A^2 theme, modulating to a Più mosso, giocoso, short A major G theme featuring clarinet triplets and eighth notes, before returning to the meno allegro. This leads back to the F minor introduction with several clarion register trills. The quick A^3 theme closes with a harsh (ruvido) gesture.[10]

Benjamin's piano and clarinet parts resemble Ravel's music in harmonic content, percussive effects, accents, and chromatic inflections. Themes alternate between clarinet and piano in waltzes 1, 2, 5, and 6.[11] A variation using waltzes is unusual, although many nineteenth and twentieth century composers wrote clarinet theme and variation solos based on popular or folk tunes. The most well-known are, Luigi Bassi, *Fantasia di Concerto sopra motivi sull'Opera Rigoletto di Verdi*, Milan: Ricordi, 1865;[12] Louis Cahusac, *Variations sur un air du Pays d'Oc*, Paris: Leduc, 1953; Gioachino Rossini, *Variazioni per Clarinetto,* Florence: G. Cipriani, 1822;[13] Louis Spohr, *Fantaisie et Variations sur un Thême de Danzi*, op. 81, Schlesinger: Berlin, 1814 (clarinet and piano), Berlin: Schlesinger, 1830 (clarinet and string quartet),[14] Heilbronn: C. F. Schmidt, 1900 (clarinet and piano); and Carl Maria von Weber, *Sieben Variationen für Klarinette und Klavier*, op. 33, Berlin: Schlesinger, 1814.[15]

Two notes not corrected in the clarinet part are the third measure of the lento after no. 6, third beat, first eighth note should be A5; and the seventh measure before the lento waltz 6, the downbeat eighth note should be G3. De Peyer suggests three additional corrections: at no. 7, the last two eighth notes should be A$\sharp$3 and B3; two measures before no. 22, the third sixteenth note should be E5; and at no. 24, the third eighth note should be F$\sharp_6$.[16]

Benjamin's *Le tombeau de Ravel* is a major recital work for the clarinet and one of the most brilliant of the twentieth century. It has many challenges: control of a wide dynamic range; technically awkward passages; extended short staccato notes; a variety of different styles to interpret and perform; and endurance, since there are few rests throughout. It will need to be thoroughly learned and rehearsed, and ensemble passages coordinated between clarinet and piano. However, *Le tombeau de Ravel* is easily understood, will go well with either earlier period works or modern pieces, and is only about 12½ minutes.

---

[10] MacDonald, ibid.

[11] MacDonald, ibid.

[12] Adriano Amore, *La letteratura Italiana per clarinetto: Storia, analisi, discografia e curiosità* (Frasso Telesino: Adriano Amore, 2011), 95–96.

[13] Adriano Amore, *Il clarinetto in Italia nell'Ottocento* (Pesaro: Accademia Italiana del Clarinetto, 2009), 150, 167. This is the same work published as *Introduction, Theme and Variations,* ed. Jost Michaels (Hamburg: Sikorsi, 1960).

[14] Folker Göthel, *Thematisch-bibliographisches Verzeichnis der Werke von Louis Spohr* (Tutzing: Schneider, 1981), 135–36.

[15] Wolfgang Sandner, *Die Klarinette bei Carl Maria von Weber* (Wiesbaden: Breitkopf & Härtel, 1971), 101, 113.

[16] De Peyer, "Arthur Benjamin's *Le tombeau de Ravel,*" 16.

2 Alban Berg, *Four Pieces for Clarinet and Piano, op. 5*

Date of composition: May or June 1913[1]

First edition/other editions: Alban Berg, *Vier Stücke: für Klarinette und Klavier, op. 5* (Berlin: Schlesinger'sche Musikhandlung, 1920; Wien: Carl Haslinger, 1920); Alban Berg, *Vier Stücke, für Klarinette und Klavier, op. 5* (Wien: Universal-Edition, 1924) (corrected edition, clarinet and piano printed in one score);[2] Alban Berg, *Vier Stücke op. 5 für Klarinette und Klavier = Four Pieces op. 5 for Clarinet and Piano*, ed. Ullrich Scheideler (München: Henle, 2006) (piano and separate clarinet part)

Dedicatees/first performers: The Society for Private Musical Performances in Vienna (Verein für Musikalische Privataufführungen in Wien) and Arnold Schoenberg; Franz Prem, clarinet, Edward Steuermann, piano

Date/place of first performance: October 17, 1919; Vienna[3]

ALBAN BERG (1885–1935) was an Austrian composer who, before and after World War I, wrote atonal and twelve-tone music with his teacher, Arnold Schoenberg, and fellow student, Anton Webern. The three were later known as the Second Viennese

---

[1] Juliane Brand, Christopher Hailey, Donald Harris, eds., *The Berg-Schoenberg Correspondence: Selected Letters* (New York: W. W. Norton & Company, 1987), 174, note 1 (May); Alban Berg, *Letters to His Wife*, ed., trans., and annotated B. Grun (London: Faber and Faber, 1971), 271 (June). The end of the published score is marked "Frühjahr 1913" (Spring 1913).

[2] Rosemary Hilmar, *Katalog der Musikhandschriften, Schriften und Studien Alban Bergs im Fond Alban Berg und der Weiteren Handschriftlichen Quellen im Besitz der Österreichischen Nationalbibliothek* (Vienna: Universal Edition, 1981), 69–70; Ullrich Scheideler, "Comments," in Alban Berg, *Vier Stücke für Klarinette und Klavier, op. 5* (München: G. Henle, 2006), 12.

[3] Rosemary Hilmar, *Alban Berg: Leben und Wirken in Wien bis zu Seinen Ersten Erfolgen als Komponist* (Vienna: H. Böhlaus, 1978), 137.

School. Berg's music is both modern and romantic.[4] His oeuvre includes operas, stage works, orchestral pieces, chamber works, concertos, string quartets and quintets, works for solo instruments and piano, works for piano two hands, works for piano four hands, songs with orchestra accompaniment, songs with piano accompaniment, and arrangements of several works by Arnold Schoenberg and other composers. He also wrote harmony and counterpoint studies and essays on musical subjects.[5]

Berg learned piano from the family governess, and as a youth, wrote piano duets and almost eighty songs for family performance. In October 1904, his sister and brother replied to a newspaper advertisement and Berg became a student of Arnold Schoenberg. Two years later, his mother inherited money and property, and Berg was able to concentrate on music. He studied harmony, counterpoint, and music theory, 1904–1911; from 1907, composition. In a 1910 letter to his publisher, Emil Herzka, Schoenberg wrote, "Alban Berg is an extraordinarily gifted composer, but the state he was in when he came to me was such that his imagination apparently could not work on anything but lieder. Even the piano accompaniments to them were songlike. He was absolutely incapable of writing an instrumental movement or inventing an instrumental theme." After study with Schoenberg, this flaw was corrected. In 1910, Berg married and moved to Berlin. After finishing his studies, he continued to work for Schoenberg, completing various domestic errands and tasks, and organizing his financial and musical business.[6]

In 1913, during his visit to Berlin, Schoenberg severely criticized either Berg's *Altenberg Lieder, op. 4* (1912), a performance of which caused a scandal in 1913, or the *Four Pieces*. Berg was devastated and wrote a letter in 1915 to Schoenberg stating that he took to heart his criticisms while writing his newest works. Later, Schoenberg seems to have changed his attitude about the *Four Pieces*.[7]

Schoenberg, Berg, and Webern established the Society for Private Musical Performances in Vienna in 1918, to present new works neglected on concert programs, create interest in new composition styles, and educate the audience in recent ideas.[8] Berg's aims for the Society state "In the rehearsal of new works, the performers will be chosen preferably from among the younger and less well-known artists, who place themselves at the Society's disposal out of interest in the cause."[9] Concerts were held in Vienna until the end of 1921 and became a model for similar organizations

---

[4] Douglas Jarman, "Berg, Alban," *Grove Music Online*.

[5] Hilmar, *Katalog der Musikhandschriften*, 207–9.

[6] Jarman, ibid.

[7] Kathryn Bailey, "Berg's Aphoristic Pieces," in *The Cambridge Companion to Berg*, ed. Anthony Poole (Cambridge: Cambridge University Press, 1997), 83–84, 110.

[8] Leonard Stein, "The Privataufführungen Revisited," in *Paul A. Pisk, Essays in his Honor*, ed. John M. Glowacki (Austin: University of Texas Press, 1966), 203.

[9] Society for Private Musical Performances in Vienna, February 16, 1919, trans. Susan Somervell in Laura Diane Kuhn and Nicholas Slonimsky, *Music since 1900*, 6th ed. (New York: Schirmer Reference, 2001), 916–18.

during the 1920s. Schoenberg assigned a director from the Society to rehearse selections for each concert, with as many as thirty rehearsals for certain works. Schoenberg coached the final rehearsals for 113 concerts. A variety of recent chamber works were performed by composers such as Reger, Debussy, Schoenberg, Bartok, Ravel, Scriabine, Mahler, Webern, Stravinsky, Richard Strauss, Berg, Busoni, Szymanowski, Hauer, Zemlinsky, Suk, and others.[10]

After the first performance of the *Four Pieces*, additional performances at the Society concerts occurred on October 24, 1919, with Franz Prem; June 17, 1920, and October 23, 1920, with clarinetist, Karl Gaudriot;[11] June 2, 1921, with clarinetist, Suzie Welty, and pianist, M. J. Guyot, in Paris;[12] February 20, 1923, at the Society for Private Musical Performances in Prague with clarinetist, Victor Polatschek, and pianist, Edward Steuermann;[13] 1923 by an unknown clarinetist in Heidelberg and Mannheim;[14] and on April 23, 1928, with clarinetist, Alfred Ruste, and pianist, Ellen Epstein, in Berlin.[15]

According to Carner, this work, along with the *Altenberg Lieder*, are Berg's only miniatures, similar in short length and expressionist style to Schoenberg's *Six Little Pieces, op. 19* for piano (1911) and Webern's *Six Pieces, op. 6* for chamber ensemble (1911–1913).[16] An outline of the *Four Pieces* shows it is a truncated sonata:

First piece, 12 measures; sonata form exposition, mm. 1–8; condensed recapitulation, mm. 9–12.

Second piece, 9¼ measures; slow movement or adagio.[17]

---

[10] Stein, ibid., 204–5; Bryan R. Simms, "The Society for Private Musical Performances: Resources and Documents in Schoenberg's Legacy," *Journal of the Arnold Schoenberg Institute* 3, no. 2 (October 1979): 128; Joan Allen Smith, *Schoenberg and His Circle: A Viennese Portrait* (New York: Macmillan, 1986), 83.

[11] Smith, ibid., 259, 262–63; Berg, *Letters to His Wife*, 286. Gaudriot was a well-known Viennese clarinetist and band leader.

[12] *Le Ménestrel* 83, no. 23 (June 10, 1921), 244. The reviewer stated that, "It is difficult to make a precise judgment after a single hearing of the *Four Pieces* for piano and clarinet by Mr. Alban Berg." ("Il est difficile de porter un jugement précis après une seule audition sur les *Quatre Pièces* pour clarinette de M. Alban Berg.")

[13] Ivan Vojtech, "Der Verein für musikalische Privataufführungen in Prag," in Ernst Hilmar, ed., *Arnold Schönberg: Gedenkausstellung 1974* (Vienna: Universal Edition, 1974), 89–90. The Prague Society, active 1922–1924, based its charter on Vienna's, used many of the same musicians, and elected Schoenberg honorary president. Alexander L. Ringer, "Schoenbergiana in Jerusalem," *The Musical Quarterly* 59, no. 1 (January 1973): 1–5.

[14] At a Society concert in Salzburg where Berg's *Quartet* was performed, "A clarinet player introduced himself to me enthusiastically. He had played the *Clarinet Pieces* (which he said were beautifully written for the instrument) in Heidelberg and Mannheim, and he would be doing them next in other German cities." Berg, *Letters to his Wife*, 326–27.

[15] Douglas Jarman, *The Music of Alban Berg* (Berkeley: The University of California Press, 1979), 1, note 2.

[16] Mosco Carner, *Alban Berg: the Man and the Work*, 2nd rev. ed. (New York: Holmes & Meier, 1983), 120.

[17] Similarities between the second piece of the *Four Pieces* and Schoenberg's *Sechs kleine Klavierstücke* (1911) are the length of nine measures; slow tempo; very quiet dynamics; a major third in the piano left hand throughout; both works ending with the third that opened the piece; and closing with an augmented triad that can be combined in both works. Bailey, ibid., 106–7.

Third piece, 18⅙ measures; scherzo, mm. 1–4; trio, mm. 9–13; scherzo, mm. 14–18.

Fourth piece, 20 measures; rondo, initial chords return, mm. 11–12; chordal resolution, mm. 17–20.[18]

In the *Four Pieces*, Berg follows Schoenberg's compositional idea that he used since 1909 in various works. Berg explained this idea in a letter to Ferruccio Busoni, "My music must be brief. Succinct!! In two notes: not construction but 'expression'!! […] [Music] must be the expression of a sensation, just as the sensation that brings us into contact with our subconscious is real, and not a changeling of sensation and 'conscious logic.'"[19]

Within a limited structure, Berg uses broad dramatic strokes with enormous dynamic variations for clarinet and piano, from the softest possible dynamics, *p* to *pppp*, to among the loudest, from *f* to *fff*, including many crescendos and diminuendos. The tempos throughout vary twenty times, including written out accelerandos and ritardandos in the clarinet part of Piece I, mm. 5–6, and Piece II, mm. 8–9.[20] Clarinet and piano parts are heavily annotated with tempo and metronome markings and articulations. Performance indications to the performers, mostly in German, include flutter tongue (*quasi Flatterzunge*, Piece I, m. 6); echo tone (*Echoton*, Piece II, mm. 7–8; Piece III, m. 15; Piece IV, mm. 11, 19); pedal until the end (*Pedal bis zum Schluß*, Piece I, m. 10), and without pedal (*ohne Pedal*, Piece II, m. 7).[21] Performance notes in the Universal-Edition score are also printed on pages 4,[22] 5,[23] and 9.[24]

Flutter tongue is achieved by rolling the tip of the tongue against the back of the upper teeth while playing a note or phrase. The result is a purring tone when played softly, and a distorted tone when played loudly. Players whose tongue will not roll use the uvula or back of the throat to make a growling sound.[25] Echo tones are notes played very softly and inwardly to create an echo of notes played in the piano part.

[18] Dennis Nygren, "The Chamber Music of Berg," *The Clarinet* 13, no. 3 (Spring 1986): 26–28; Bruce Archibald, "Berg's Development as an Instrument Composer," in *The Berg Companion*, ed. Douglas Jarman (Boston: Northeastern University Press, 1990), 107.

[19] Ullrich Scheideler, "Preface," in Alban Berg, *Vier Stücke für Klarinette und Klavier, op. 5* (München: G. Henle, 2006), iii.

[20] Archibald, ibid., 107; Arthur Cohn, *The Literature of Chamber Music* (Chapel Hill: Hinshaw Music, 1997), 1:268; Nygren, "The Chamber Music of Berg," 26, 29.

[21] A translation of German terms in Berg's *Four Pieces* is found in Nygren, ibid., 30–31.

[22] Note before piece two, "After each piece provide a plentiful pause; the pieces must not merge into one another!"

[23] "**) The D-flat in the third quarter must be clearly audible without having to be struck anew."

[24] "*) The eighth note of the triplet remains approximately at 88, so at the beginning the dotted quarter note matches the present triplet tied to a quarter note."

[25] Jane Ellsworth, *A Dictionary for the Modern Clarinetist* (Lanham, MD: Rowman & Littlefield, 2015), 45.

Tricky ensemble passages include the first piece, mm. 6–12; second piece, mm. 5–8, 15–18; and fourth piece, mm. 8–10.

Other German terms are, moderate (*Mässig*, Piece I, m. 1); light (*leicht*, Piece I, m. 1); slower (*Langsamer*, Piece I, m. 1); heavier (*schwerer*, Piece I, m. 2); always to the fore (*immer hervortretend*, Piece I, m. 2); more accompanying (*mehr begleitend*, Piece I, m. 5); full of verve (*schwungvoll*, Piece I, m. 7); fleeting (*flüchtig*, Piece I, m. 8); short pause (*kurzer Halt*, Piece I, m. 9); without expression (*ohne Ausdruck*, Piece I, m. 9); hesitating (*zögernd*, Piece II, mm. 2–3); take time (*Zeit lassen*, Piece II, m. 4); still slower (*Noch langsamer*, Piece II, m. 8); very fast (*Sehr rasch*, Piece III, m. 1); rather long (*ziemlich lange*, Piece III, m. 8); slow quarter note (*Langsame Viertel*, Piece III, m. 9); very hasty (*Sehr hastig*, Piece III, m. 14); as fast and light as possible (*so rasch und leise als möglich*, Piece III, m. 14); always still faster (*Immer noch rascher*, Piece III, m. 16); a little hesitating (*ein wenig zögernd*, Piece IV, m. 3); recede (*zurücktreten*, Piece IV, m. 6); short and lightly tongued (*kurz und leicht gestoßen*, Piece IV, m. 9); as at the beginning (*Wie am Anfang*, Piece IV, m. 11); very moving tempo (*Viel bewegteres Tempo*, Piece IV, m. 13); slowly mounting (*langsam steigernd*, Piece IV, m. 14); again very slowly (*Wieder sehr langsam*, Piece IV, m. 17); and quite slow (*ganz frei*, Piece IV, m. 18).

Unusual notation in the first piece (m. 1) is a slur after the clarinet's written F♯5 on the second eighth note, third beat. This suggests a metrical indication that the silence on the first half of beat four must function as a downbeat.[26] The piano part includes special instructions such as hands away (*Hände weg*, Piece III, m. 16), and strike as gently as possible (*so leise also möglich anschlagen*, Piece IV, m. 11).[27] In Piece IV, the clarinet part has a violin phrase mark, an up-bow indication, at the end of m. 4. Perhaps it was intended as a mental preparation for the major seventh slur. The staccato dots under slurs for piano in m. 8 and for clarinet in m. 9 (Piece IV) suggest short up-bows, and are played somewhat short. DeFotis suggests Berg adopted these two indications from his other works, and incorporated them in the *Four Pieces*.[28]

Berg's intention was to avoid old musical ideas, including tonality and the usual theme and motive development. Jarman's analysis notes that the clarinet's mostly unaccompanied opening melody in Piece I presents the important pitch relations that will occur throughout the entire work (Ex. 2.1). There are two phrases or note sets, x and y (set y has one note, A5, in common with x) and a combination of both sets, xy, consisting of six, two, and eight different notes, respectively. Each piece

---

[26] William DeFotis, "Berg's Op. 5: Rehearsal Instructions," *Perspectives of New Music* 17, no. 1 (Autumn–Winter 1978): 132.

[27] Wallace Berry, *Musical Structure and Performance* (New Haven, CT: Yale University Press, 1989), 84–85.

[28] DeFotis, ibid., 136.

opens with a statement using notes from *x, y,* or *xy.* Piece II has an eight note set, starting with the piano's repeated major third of two notes while the clarinet plays six notes. Piece III has an eight note set transposed a major third higher, consisting of six piano notes and two clarinet notes. Piece IV has a six note set of five piano notes followed by the last of the clarinet's three notes.[29]

EXAMPLE 2.1. Berg, *Four Pieces for Clarinet and Piano, op. 5*, piece one, mm. 1–2.

Bailey notes that Berg's most common compositional device is to expand or contract the intervals of the note's cells or sets. This includes a change from a whole-tone scale to a chromatic scale; repetition of larger and smaller intervals; successive intervals in an arpeggio using augmented triads; and major and minor triads. Expansion of notes by adding material on each reappearance occurs in the clarinet part (Piece II, m. 4; Piece IV, mm. 11–12), and in the piano part (Piece IV, mm. 11–12). Piece I has progressively longer note values (mm. 8–9), and Piece III has notated accelerandos in the clarinet part (m. 3) and piano part (m. 16).[30]

Jack Brymer's remarks on the *Four Pieces* are positive and useful: "One of the most rewarding works of the past half-century, it explores not only the rhythmic possibilities of the medium but its immense tonal variety. It requires a really fine piano and should not be attempted in unknown conditions."[31]

Berg's sensitivity to timbre and color is unparalleled. The dynamic contrasts are stunning, as is the earliest use of flutter tongue, unusual sonorities in the piano part, the earliest use of a clarinet echo tone, and the incredible effect of depressing piano keys silently to hear their ghostly vibrations after the *fff* chords played by the pianist's left hand. It is one of the most demanding clarinet works for control of dynamics, articulation, phrasing, and tone colors. Berg's *Four Pieces* is among the most imaginative and innovative works of the early twentieth century.

[29] Jarman, *The Music of Alban Berg*, 23–25; Archibald, ibid., 107. Another good analysis of the *Four Pieces* is by Adorno. It presents a relationship between shorter cells and the clarinet and piano parts in the first piece. See Theodor Adorno, *Alban Berg: Master of the Smallest Link*, trans. Juliane Brand and Christopher Hailey (Cambridge: Cambridge University Press, 1968), 67–71.

[30] Bailey, ibid., 101.

[31] Jack Brymer, *Clarinet* (New York: Schirmer, 1977), 212.

3 Luciano Berio, *Sequenza IXa for Clarinet Solo*

Date of composition: 1980

First edition: Luciano Berio, *Sequenza IX per Clarinetto Solo*, Milano: Universal Edition, 1980.

Dedicatee/first performer: Not indicated;[1] Michel Arrignon, clarinet

Date/place of first performance: April 26, 1980; Paris, Théatre d'Orsay

LUCIANO BERIO (1925–2003) was an Italian composer who was trained by his father and grandfather, both organists. After studying composition with Giorgio Federico Ghedini and counterpoint with Giulio Cesare Paribeni at the Milan Conservatory, Berio married the American soprano, Cathy Berberian. During summer 1952, Berio won a Koussevitzky Foundation fellowship to work at the Berkshire Music Center (Tanglewood), with Luigi Dallapiccola. He was present at the Museum of Modern Art in New York on October 28, 1952, for the first U.S. concert including electronic music written by Otto Luening and Vladimir Ussachevsky. This concert inspired Berio to explore electronic music while working for the RAI, the Italian Radio and Television network. In 1955, he collaborated with Bruno Maderna to establish an electronic music studio, Studio di Fonologia. He later worked with the writer, Umberto Eco.

Berio taught at Mills College, Oakland, California, 1962–1964 and 1965–1966, while simultaneously teaching at Harvard University and the Juilliard School of

---

[1] A 2013 performance in Paris at the Cité de la Musique identifies the dedicatee as Michel Arrignon in "Intégrale des *Sequenze* de Luciano Berio, Dimanche 8 décembre 2013," 18. [Online] Available: http://content.citedela-musique.fr/pdf/note_programme/np_13688.pdf. [September 10, 2015].

Music. He met the psychologist, Susan Oyama, a student at Harvard University. In 1965, Berio was awarded a Ford Foundation grant to work in Berlin. After his divorce, Berio married Oyama, and in 1968 moved to Hoboken, New Jersey. In 1971, he resigned from Juilliard, and in 1975 returned to Radicondoli, a village near Siena, Italy. He married his third wife in 1977, the Israeli musicologist, Talia Pecker. Boulez invited Berio in 1974 to direct the electro-acoustic section of IRCAM (Institut de Recherche et Coordination Acoustique/Musique) in Paris. There, he worked on a major project with the physicist, Giuseppe di Giugno, using the 4X digital system that processed sound in real time. Berio initially used this resource in *Chemins V* (1980) for solo clarinet, which was subsequently withdrawn from his compositions. He stayed at IRCAM until 1980, later establishing a research center, Tempo Reale, in Florence, based in the Villa Strozzi. Berio's works were widely acclaimed, and in 1989 he received the Siemens-Musikpreis. He was Norton Professor of Poetry at Harvard University, 1993–1994, and in 1996 he received the Praemium Imperiale from the Japan Art Association.

Berio's compositions include operas and stage works, orchestra pieces, works for solo voice or choir and orchestra, choir works, pieces for two or more instruments, a set of *Sequenzas* (sequences) for various solo instruments, solo instrumental works, tape recorder works including instruments and chorus, and arrangements of works by other composers.[2] His solo clarinet works include *Concertino* for Clarinet, Violin, Harp, Celesta, and Strings (1949, rev. 1970), *Lied* for Clarinet Solo (1983), an orchestration of Brahms' Sonata, op. 120, no. 1 (1986), and *Alternatim* for Clarinet, Viola and Orchestra (1997).[3] *Sequenza IXa* (1980) is one of a series of eighteen *Sequenzas* written for solo instruments and voice, 1958–2002.[4]

Among the most important unifying elements of the *Sequenzas* are virtuosity, idiomatic writing, and polyphonic listening.[5] Berio describes the last element:

The title *Sequenza* underlies the fact that the construction of these pieces almost always takes as its point of departure a sequence of harmonic fields,

2. David Osmond-Smith, "Berio, Luciano," *Grove Music Online*; Roy Victor Sanderson, "Luciano Berio's Use of the Clarinet in *Sequenza IXa*" (M.A. thesis, California State University, Long Beach, 1986), 6 (partly based on an interview with Luciano Berio while he taught at the California Institute for the Arts, Valencia, California, November 12, 1984).

3. Osmond-Smith, "Berio, Luciano, Works," *Grove Music Online*; David H. Odom, "A Catalog of Compositions for Unaccompanied Clarinet Published between 1978 and 1982, with an Annotated Bibliography of Selected Works" (D.M. diss., Florida State University, 2005), 34.

4. Janet K. Halfyard, ed., *Berio's Sequenzas: Essays on Performance, Composition, and Analysis* (Aldershot: Ashgate, 2007), 297.

5. David Osmond-Smith, ed. and trans., *Two Interviews/Luciano Berio: Rossana Dalmonte; Bálint András Varga* (New York: Marion Boyars, 1985), 90–95, 97.

from which spring, in all their individuality, the other musical functions. In fact almost all the *Sequenzas* have in common the intention of defining and developing through melody an essentially harmonic discourse and, above all when dealing with the monadic instruments (flute, oboe, clarinet, bassoon, trumpet, trombone), of suggesting a polyphonic type of listening, based in part on the rapid transition between different characteristics, and their simultaneous iteration. Here polyphony should be understood in a metaphorical sense, as the exposition and superposition of differing modes of action and instrumental characteristics.[6]

In 1980, Berio worked with Michel Arrignon, clarinetist from Boulez's L'Ensemble Intercontemporain, to study the possibilities of combining the clarinet with a digital sound system. The result was *Chemins V* (1980), performed by Arrignon in 1980 and 1981. Because the computer malfunctioned at the premiere, and after a discussion with Arrignon, Berio eliminated the computer parts, adapting this work for clarinet alone by adding multiphonics, and changing the title to *Sequenza IXa*.[7]

The 1980 publication of *Sequenza IXa* does not include a printed dedication, but Arrignon was given a score of the work with his name inscribed.[8] Berio wrote transcriptions of *Sequenza IXa* published by Universal Edition for alto saxophone as *Sequenza IXb* (1981); bass clarinet as *Sequenza IXc*, ed. R. Parisi (1980; new edition, 1998); materials were reworked and incorporated in the opera, *La vera storia* (1977–1981), part two, scene 7; and for clarinet and saxophone as *Sequenza IX* (1997), premiered April 2008 at Montpellier Conservatory by Phillipe Berrod, clarinet, and Claude Delangle, alto saxophone.[9]

Sequenza IXa is a lyrical work that focuses on a melody presented as a series of notes repeated and transformed using subtly altered harmonic fields and rhythmic patterns. The lyrical nature of the work is noted by the French clarinetist, Paul Meyer:

---

6. Luciano Berio, *Berio Sequenzas*, Ensemble Intercontemporain, Deutsche Grammophon, 1998, CD notes, 18, as quoted by Rebecca Rischin, "The Thinking Clarinet: Berio's *Sequenza* (1980)," *The Clarinet* 40, no. 1 (December 2012): 52.

7. Charles Willett, "A Conversation with Michel Arrignon," *The Clarinet* 16, no. 4 (July–August 1989): 33; Adélaïde de Place, "Luciano Berio," in *Guide de la Musique de Chambre*, eds. François-René Tranchefort, Adélaïde de Place, Pierre-Emile Barbier, Harry Halbreich, et al. (Paris: Fayard, 1989), 120; Rischin, ibid., 51; email from Michel Arrignon and Jean-Marie Paul to the author, May 20, 2014.

8. Email correspondence from Michel Arrignon and Jean-Marie Paul to the author, May 20, 2014.

9. David Osmond-Smith, *Berio* (Oxford: Oxford University Press), 1991, 140; Halfyard, ibid., 297; "Intégrale des *Sequenze* de Luciano Berio, Dimanche 8 décembre 2013," 19, program at the Cité de la musique, Paris. [Online] Available: http://content.citedelamusique.fr/pdf/note_programme/np_13688.pdf. [September 10, 2015]. In 1996, Berio used the music from *Sequenza IXa* to compose a new work, *Récit (Chemins VII)* for alto saxophone and orchestra; Andrea Cremaschi, "Sequenza IX for Clarinet: Text, Pre-Text, Con-Text," in *Berio's Sequenzas*, ed. Janet K. Halfyard (Aldershot: Ashgate, 2007), 153.

It seems to me, and I had the occasion to discuss this with Berio, that this *Sequenza* is perhaps the most melodic of the *Sequenzas*, but especially the most lyrical.... This *Sequenza* should be played like a lyrical song, and the musician should imagine a warm and powerful sonority, all with nuance. It's not a piece of gallantry, but rather a lyrical work. Berio in fact used excerpts from it in his opera, *La vera storia*.[10]

Arrignon adds that Berio asked him to play, "with the most lyricism possible."[11] The ten-page score does not have bar lines, except for two repeated measures at E, and includes many fast grace notes with a melodic significance, single and double grace notes, trills, tremolos, several tempo indications, twenty-eight fermatas or pivot points[12] with their length given in seconds, a wide variety of dynamic indications from *ppp* to *ff*, repetition of microtones with different fingerings, multiphonics with fingerings, and accelerandos.

Cremaschi describes polyphonic listening and transformation in *Sequenza IXa*:

The dialectic contrast between stasis and movement is one of the prominent features of the work. It even acts at the level of the individual parameters, and each one of them, when individually considered, shows constant movement between different degrees of transformation: the *Sequenza* melody can be viewed as the sum of different processes, each having its own duration and involving only one parameter or two at a time. This is the way of listening that Berio defined as polyphonic, which is characteristic of the *Sequenzas*, but which acquires here a particular meaning. It refers not only to the concept of virtual counterpoint between contiguous horizontal events, but also to the internal constitution of these same events, each one of them being the point of intersection of several structural paths.[13]

Arrignon's outline of *Sequenza IXa* reveals a structure in six sections:

Introduction: Beginning until A.
1st section: A until 2 measures after E.
2nd section: 2 measures after E until J, emphasis on virtuosity.
3rd section: J until M, multiphonic section.

---

[10] Meyer email correspondence, March 2, 2012, quoted by Rischin, ibid., 55–56.
[11] Rischin, ibid., 56.
[12] Sanderson, ibid., 20, 27.
[13] Cremaschi, ibid., 155.

4th section: M until R, repeated notes and dramatic moments.

5th section: R to the end, slower tempi with longer notes.[14]

Sanderson divides the work using the fermatas, each section reminding him of melismas, or syllables sung on one note, used in liturgical chants. There are twenty-eight fermatas designated in seconds, except the tenth and thirteenth fermatas; the twelfth fermata (p. 7) ends on a trill, D4–E♭4; and the thirteenth fermata ends on a half rest (end of p. 7). Sanderson suggests a three part structure:

A, first to tenth fermatas: pages 1–3 to line 5.

B, eleventh to thirteenth fermatas: pages 6 to the end of page 7.

C, fourteenth to twenty-eighth fermatas: page 8 to end of page 10.[15]

Cremaschi identifies the notes of the main harmonic or pitch-field (Ex. 3.1), noting a uniform, random, or repetitive use in different sections.[16] He writes that during the introductory section, comprising the first three staves on page 1, the pitch-field is introduced and musical gestures are stated and transformed. At A, a rhythmic pattern is used and varied for the rest of the page, along with a melodic pattern of eleven pitches, almost entirely comprised of the main pitch-field notes (Ex. 3.2). The different lengths of the patterns create a new result. At B, microtones vary the tone colors before returning to the pitch-field notes. These are indicated with a Roman numeral I in a circle with fingerings for each microtone. The metronome change before C leads to a section where the pitches placed in higher octaves are louder, creating tension. A repeating rhythmic pattern results in a gradual loss of tension. A greater variety of notes is introduced on the fifth line of page 3 leading to E, two measures of slurred and staccato chromatic scales, ten and five seconds each, repeated once. This acts as a break before going on to new material with a varied repetition of six pitches and a different rhythmic pattern.

EXAMPLE 3.1. Berio, *Sequenza IXa for Clarinet Solo*, main harmonic notes or pitch-field.

[14] Rischin, ibid., 52.

[15] Sanderson, ibid., 25–29.

[16] Another analysis by Albèra suggests an almost identical pitch-field at A, Philippe Albèra, "Introduction auf Neuf Sequenzas," *Contrechamps* 1 (1983), 117.

EXAMPLE 3.2. Berio, *Sequenza IXa for Clarinet Solo*, rhythmic and melodic patterns at A.

a) Rhythmic pattern

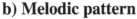

b) Melodic pattern

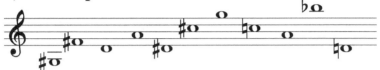

On page 5, microtones on B3 and D4 have fingerings indicated as I and II. Page 6 uses a five-note pattern before introducing three multiphonic fingerings indicated as III and IV, and microtones indicated as 1 and 2. Different melodic and rhythmic patterns are on page 7, and there is a reduction of notes from the main pitch-field to the end of the work. More repetition in the chalumeau register leads to the tremolo at V and greater tension. A number of sustained B♭5s not belonging to the main pitch-field first appear on page 8, used as a gesture to contrast with the melody, contributing to the polyphony. These B♭5s become more important after V, creating a new melodic line and structural element.[17] During the last page, the soft fermatas on B♭5s are integrated into a calm *ppp* ending.[18]

Berio writes multiphonics for a clarinet with a low E♭ key placed for the right little finger, an instrument used by some professional Italian clarinetists. Since many clarinetists do not have such an instrument, other options must be considered. Sanderson suggests humming one of the desired pitches while blowing into the clarinet to produce multiphonics, using a tube to extend the clarinet's length to that of a clarinet with an E♭ key, or selecting other muliphonics.[19] For his recording, Meyer borrowed a Leblanc clarinet with an E♭ key from the Swiss clarinetist, Hans-Rudolf Stalder. Arrignon and Chad Burrow, assistant clarinet professor at the University of Michigan, used their own fingerings. Burrow recommends taking the passages up a half step from J to L. The English clarinetist, Antony Pay, suggests his own fingerings, some of which change the pitches,[20] or extending the clarinet's length using a C clarinet bell with a strip of reusable

---

[17]   Cremaschi, ibid., 159; the B♭5s are noted by Albèra, ibid., 117–18; Sanderson, ibid., 26.

[18]   Meyer considers the B♭5s as central to the work and as pedal notes or accompaniment, Rischin, ibid., 53.

[19]   Sanderson, ibid., 24–25.

[20]   Rischin, ibid., 51, 56.

putty-like pressure-sensitive adhesive placed around the tenon to attach to the bell of his B♭ clarinet.[21]

Berio's *Sequenza IXa* explores the tonal resources of the clarinet and the capabilities of the player extremely effectively. It includes many extremes in dynamics mixed with microtone fingerings, multiphonics, and dramatic outbursts. Among the avant-garde experimental works of the 1980s, it is accessible but challenging to the advanced player. The fingerings for microtones and multiphonics are useable and limited to a few examples. *Sequenza IXa* is an absorbing and intense work open to different interpretations, and a classic of the solo clarinet repertory.

---

[21] Tony Pay, Berio *Sequenza IXa*, Klarinet Archive posting, January 13, 2000. [Online] Available: http://test .woodwind.org/Databases/Klarinet/2000/01/000392.txt. [September 10, 2015]; Antony Pay, "Alternative Fingering for Berio's *Sequenza IXa*." [Online] Available: http://www.woodwind.org/clarinet/Study/Berio .html. [September 10, 2015].

4 Leonard Bernstein, *Sonata for Clarinet and Piano*

Date of composition: August 1941–February 1942

First edition/later edition: Leonard Bernstein, *Sonata for Clarinet and Piano*, New York: M. Witmark & Sons, 1943; Leonard Bernstein, *Sonata for Clarinet and Piano*, rev. ed. based on manuscript sources, eds. Richard Walters and Todd Levy, New York: Boosey & Hawkes, 2012

Dedicatee/first performers: David Oppenheim; David Glazer, clarinet, Leonard Bernstein, piano

Date/place of first performance: April 21, 1942; Boston, Institute of Modern Art, League of Composers' concert[1]

LEONARD BERNSTEIN (1918–1990) was a talented pianist and a particularly versatile musician, successful as a conductor, composer of musical theater and concert works, and a music educator. His first important piano teacher was Helen Coates, assistant to Heinrich Gebhard, and one of Boston's leading piano teachers, with whom he studied at fourteen. She later served as Bernstein's assistant for most of his adult life. He attended Harvard College, majoring in music and studying piano with Gebhard. His music instructors included Edward Burlingame Hill, Tillman Merritt, and Walter Piston. He met and befriended the conductor, Dimitri Mitropoulos, and the composer, Aaron Copland. The latter was a lifelong friend and mentor, and was influential as an informal composition teacher. After graduating in 1939, Bernstein attended the Curtis Institute of Music, where for two years he studied

---

[1] Charles Francis Del Rosso, "A Study of Selected Solo Clarinet Literature of Four American Composers as a Basis for Performance and Teaching" (Doctor of Education diss., Teachers College, Columbia University, 1969), 54; Erika Švalbe, "Looking for David Oppenheim," *The Clarinet* 25, no. 3 (May–June 1998): 44.

conducting with Fritz Reiner, piano with Isabella Vengerova, transposition and sight-reading with Renée Longy-Miquelle, and orchestration with Randall Thompson. During summer 1940, Bernstein attended the first summer school at the Berkshire Music Center (Tanglewood) where he studied conducting with Serge Koussevitzky, who became an important mentor.

In August 1943, the New York Philharmonic Orchestra appointed Bernstein assistant conductor. After substituting at the last moment for an ill Bruno Walter on a November 14, 1943 concert that was broadcast nationally, other conducting opportunities quickly followed. His compositional career was heralded when he conducted his *Jeremiah Symphony* in Pittsburgh in January 1944 and in Boston the next month. The *Symphony* won the New York Music Critics' Circle prize for the season's best symphonic premiere. Jerome Robbins commissioned Bernstein to write the music for his ballet, *Fancy Free*, premiered April 1944 at the Metropolitan Opera House; it was very popular. Bernstein's spectacular debuts as conductor and composer immediately identified him as a prominent and well-known musician.[2] Bernstein's composing efforts include incidental music to plays, musicals, ballets, musical theater, choral and orchestral works, one film score, works for solo voice, and chamber music.[3]

Bernstein was a gifted speaker and enjoyed a lifelong interest in music education, which was directed into his television broadcasts. He wrote dozens of scripts for the television programs *Omnibus* (1954–1961), *Lincoln Presents* (1958–1959), *Ford Presents* (1959–1962), and *Young People's Concerts* (1958–1972). The Young People's Concerts were highly influential on a generation of Americans and musicians. Bernstein adapted the scripts into three popular books, *The Joy of Music* (1959), *The Infinite Variety of Music* (1967), and *Leonard Bernstein's Young People's Concerts* (1970). In 1973, Bernstein was the Norton Professor of Poetry at Harvard University where he presented six scholarly lectures featuring him conducting the Boston Symphony Orchestra. The lectures were later televised, released as video recordings, and published as the book, *The Unanswered Question* (1976).[4]

The *Sonata for Clarinet and Piano* is Bernstein's first published composition, begun in Key West, Florida, during August 1941, and completed in Boston in February 1942.[5] In Key West, Bernstein listened to Radio Havana and composed

---

[2] Paul R. Laird, "Bernstein, Leonard," *Grove Music Online*; Paul R. Laird, *Leonard Bernstein: A Guide to Research* (New York: Routledge, 2002), 2.

[3] David Schiff, "Bernstein, Leonard, Works," *Grove Music Online*.

[4] Laird, "Bernstein, Leonard," *Grove Music Online*.

[5] On a postcard, an arrow points to the right hand window on the top floor reading, "This room is where I worked on my Clarinet Sonata, late August '41, when I was fleeing from Ragweed & total hayfever (2 nights & days by train from Boston). L B." Bernstein to Charles Harmon, undated postcard [1989]; see Nigel Simeone, ed., *The Leonard Bernstein Letters*, (New Haven: Yale University Press, 2013), 567, letter 639, note 55; Joseph B. Carlucci, "An Analytical Study of Published Clarinet Sonatas by American Composers" (D.M.A. diss.,

music for an unfinished ballet, *Conch Town*, a theme of which later became "America" in *West Side Story*. A Cuban influence on the rhythms of the second movement in the *Sonata for Clarinet and Piano* is not important but definitely present.[6] After the premiere by David Glazer and Bernstein, the reviews were mixed, often stating that the piano part was more interesting than the clarinet part, but one review in the *Boston Globe* praised its, "jazzy, rocking rhythms."[7] On February 21, 1943, Oppenheim and Bernstein played the sonata, which was broadcast and recorded on the New York radio station, WNYC, as part of their Festival of American Music.[8] On March 14, 1943, the New York premiere of the sonata was performed at a League of Composers' concert at the New York Public Library with Bernstein and Oppenheim.[9] A mostly positive review by Paul Bowles appeared in the *New York Herald Tribune*; he liked the, "meaty, logical harmony." He comments on Bernstein's writing style, "Through most of this (the andante seemed less real) ran a quite personal element: a tender, sharp, singing quality which would appear to be Mr. Bernstein's most effective means of making himself articulate."[10]

In 1943, the *Sonata for Clarinet and Piano* was published by M. Witmark & Sons in New York. A small publishing company, Hargail Music, had approached Bernstein early in 1943 to publish the score and simultaneously issue a commercial 78 rpm recording. Warner Brothers, which owned the publisher, M. Witmark & Sons, also made an offer to publish the sonata. In April 1943, Bernstein agreed to have Warner Brothers publish the sonata through Witmark, and to have Hargail record it.[11]

Later in April, the sonata was recorded by Oppenheim and Bernstein on one record of a two 78 rpm record set, released in January 1944 by Hargail. The second record has Bernstein's three anniversaries from his *Seven Anniversaries for Piano* (1943).[12] Reviews of the sonata recording were positive. Richard Crooks points out

Eastman School of Music, 1957), 220. At the end of the piano part is, "Key West—Sept. 1941 Boston—Feb. 1942."

[6] Richard Walters in Leonard Bernstein, *Sonata for Clarinet and Piano*, eds. R. Walters and T. Levy (New York: Boosey & Hawkes, 2012), iv.

[7] Lars Erik Helgert, "Jazz Elements in Selected Concert Works of Leonard Bernstein: Sources, Reception, and Analysis" (Ph.D. diss., Catholic University of America, 2008), 121.

[8] Simeone, ibid., Bernstein to Oppenheim, January 15, 1943, 100; Bernstein to Oppenheim, February 1943, 107; Bernstein to Renée Longy-Miquelle, February 20, 1943, 107–108; Oppenheim to Bernstein, March 2, 1943, 109. Bernstein and Oppenheim's recording was re-released on CD as *Aaron Copland and Leonard Bernstein: The composer as performer* (Wadhurst, E. Sussex, England: Pavilion Records, 1997). Interestingly, Oppenheim used considerable vibrato, noted in Bernstein, *Sonata for Clarinet and Piano*, v.

[9] Simeone, ibid., Bernstein to Oppenheim, February 25, 1943, 109.

[10] Helgert, ibid., 123.

[11] Simeone, ibid., Bernstein to Oppenheim, April 17, 1943, 123; Copland to Bernstein, 125.

[12] Simeone, ibid., Bernstein to Oppenheim, July 12, 1943, 133; Harold Newman to Bernstein, June 1, 1944, 160; Amy Shapiro, "Bernstein and the Clarinet: Stanley Remembers Lenny, part 1," *The Clarinet* 33, no. 1 (December 2005): 68.

the influence of Hindemith in the first movement and states, "[T]his sonata, or rather its second movement, is a real contribution to the slim literature for that instrument." Crooks adds, "If this last movement is any indication of Mr. Bernstein's representative style as a composer, we can be sure of having something to look forward to in contemporary American music." Harold Taubman in the *New York Times* states, "Mr. Bernstein writes with zest and with a great deal of relish for the contrasts possible in his instrumental combination. The piano part is especially interesting in its lively rhythms and colorful harmonic effects. Mr. Bernstein is clearly influenced by the generation of American composers that includes Copland and [William] Schuman."[13]

In 1993, the sonata was orchestrated by Sid Ramin, published by Boosey & Hawkes, and premiered in Sapporo, Japan, by Richard Stoltzman and the Pacific Music Festival Orchestra, Michael Tilson Thomas conducting. The same year it was recorded by Stoltzman with the London Symphony Orchestra, Eric Stern conducting.[14]

On December 23, 1945, sixteen-year-old Stanley Drucker, who was then a student at the Curtis Institute of Music, performed the sonata with Shirley Gabis, piano, at the Music Room of the Art Alliance in Philadelphia. Bernstein told him "not to take the piece too seriously. He said it was a student work and I think he felt the first movement shouldn't be played too fast. I think he said it was his Hindemith period and there is a little bit of Hindemith flavor in the first movement, *definitely*."[15] Copland's assessment of Bernstein's music in 1948 is very appropriate for this work, "The most striking feature of Bernstein's music is the immediacy of emotional appeal. Melodically and harmonically it has a spontaneity and warmth that speak directly to an audience.... At its worst Bernstein's music is conductor's music—eclectic in style and facile in inspiration. But at its best it is music of vibrant rhythmic invention, of irresistible élan, often carrying with it a terrific dramatic punch."[16]

The work consists of two contrasting movements marked Grazioso and Andantino which includes a nimble Vivace e leggiero. The first movement is in sonata allegro form.[17] (See Chart 4.1.) It is tonal with predominant chordal patterns using parallel

---

[13] Helgert, ibid., 124–25.

[14] Amy Shapiro, "Bernstein and the Clarinet: Stanley Remembers Lenny, part II," *The Clarinet* 33, no. 2 (March 2006): 66.

[15] Shapiro, "Bernstein and the clarinet, part I," 66–67.

[16] Aaron Copland, "The New School of American Composers," *New York Times Magazine*, March 14, 1948, p. SM18; reprinted in Aaron Copland, *Copland on Music* (Garden City, New York: Doubleday and Co.), 1960, 173.

[17] Carlucci, "An Analytical Study of Published Clarinet Sonatas by American Composers," 221–26.

quintal and quartal harmonies in the piano right hand, and parallel sixths, fifths, sevenths, and ninths in the left hand, from **G** (mm. 78, 82).[18]

The warm, lyrical clarinet A theme is in cut time and consists of four eighth-note pickups to dotted half and quarter notes. This straightforward and expressive theme is developed rhythmically using a hemiola, that is, triplet quarter notes played against two quarter notes by the piano. At **A** (m. 13) the tempo moves forward, Un poco più mosso, *p* and *pp* in the clarinet, *mf* in the piano where the A[1] theme is elaborated. The movement's high point is **L** (m. 108) where the end of the phrase is accented in both the clarinet and piano, and the rhythm returns to the half note pulse of the beginning. The first seventeen measures of the A theme are repeated at **L**, mm. 108–124. This leads to the coda, **N** (m. 133), where the clarinet holds a low E3 and the piano plays the B theme *p* in a higher register in octaves. The last two measures have a small ritardando as the clarinet states a fragment of the A theme with a decrescendo from *pp*.

The second movement is a modified rondo form with several occurrences of the three themes A, B, and C (see Chart 4.2). An introspective twenty-six measure Andantino introduction makes full and sensitive use of the clarinet's registers with dynamic levels as soft as *ppp*. The wide spacing of the piano chords dominates, appearing in the interlude (**J**, m. 151),[19] and five measures before **N** (mm. 174–185), similar to sonorities used by Copland.

Surprisingly, the Vivace e leggiero at **A** (m. 27) begins with a quick 5/8 ostinato of piano eighth notes. The clarinet's A theme begins with an eighth note pickup played short and lightly articulated. The grouping of eighth notes in the 5/8 measures vary; sometimes it is 3 + 2, and sometimes the opposite. This can be challenging to count. The clarinetist should be sure to consult the piano score to determine what the groupings are, mark them in the clarinet part, and practice them slowly until they

Section:	Exposition	Development	Recapitulation	Coda
Starts at m.	1 Grazioso	53 (**E**)	92 (**J**)	133 (**N**)–159
No. of mm.	52	39	41	27
Tonalities	A, E, C	B♭, C, F♯, C, B, trans.	A, E♭	D, A
Themes	A, A[1], B, B[1]	A, B, B[1], A, A, B, A	(A), A	B, B[1], (A)

CHART 4.1 Bernstein, *Sonata for Clarinet and Piano*: Structural analysis, first movement, Grazioso.

[18] Carlucci, ibid., 227–28.

[19] Carlucci, ibid., 230–31.

Section:	Intro.	Ostinato-A	A¹	Episode 1	A	Episode 2	Trans.-B-Trans.	B
Starts at m.	1 Andantino	27 (**A**) Vivace e leggiero	45 (**B**)	59 (**C**)	76 (**D**)	90 (**E**)	100 (**F**)	110 (**G**)
No. of mm.	26	18	14	17	14	10	10	24
Tonalities	D, F	F♯	F♯	G	F♯	B♭, C	F♯	G
Themes	Intro.	A	A¹	A	A	A¹	A¹	B

Section:	Trans.-A	Interlude-Intro. 2	C	C¹	Trans.-Intro. 3	C-Intro.	Trans.-C and A	Episode 1 returns
Starts at m.	134 (**H**)	151 (**J**) Lento molto	157 (**K**) Più Andante	164 (**L**)	170 (1 m. after **M**)	180 (1 m. after **N**) Poco più lento	186 (**O**) Più mosso	192 (**P**) Tempo I
No. of mm.	17	6	7	6	10	6	6	17
Tonalities	G	F♯	D	C¹	F	D	G	A
Themes	A	Intro.	C	C¹	C	C	C, A	A

Section:	A	B	Intro.-Augmented	Episode 2 returns	Episode 2, A & B
Starts at m.	209 (**Q**)	223 (**R**)	239 (**S**)	244 (**T**)	254 (**U**)–273
No. of mm.	14	16	5	10	20
Tonalities	F♯	G	D	B♭, C	B♭, D, F♯, A
Themes	A	B	Intro.	A¹	A, B

CHART 4.2 Bernstein, *Sonata for Clarinet and Piano*: Structural analysis, second movement, Andantino, Vivace e leggiero.

feel natural. This effective, driving 5/8 eighth-note rhythm includes shifting accents six measures before **C** (m. 53), with an eighth-note pickup in the piano, and two measures before **C** in the clarinet.[20] The poco glissando to an eighth note seven measures before **D** (m. 69) and seven measures before **Q** (m. 202) is achieved by tightening the embouchure and quickly sliding the fingers. The string instrument term "détaché" is used three measures after **H** (m. 136) and means slightly less than legato.[21] At **K** (m. 157), a beautiful C theme in the clarion register is accompanied by a piano eighth-note ostinato. The most dramatic part is a passionate, Sostenuto assai section, five measures before **N** (m. 174), followed by the haunting C theme played *pp* dolce, one measure after **N** (m. 180). One measure after **T** (m. 245), the tempo accelerates until the end. Excitement is heightened with the clarinet's subito high F#6 *sffz-p*, five measures after V (m. 270), ending with an emphatic *ff* statement of the B theme.

Bernstein's *Sonata for Clarinet and Piano* is a popular recital piece, easy to listen to, and enjoyable for the performer. The entire work is relaxed and natural sounding, including the 5/8 meter of the second movement with its jazz-inspired theme. The second movement ensemble challenges can be worked out with slow and careful rehearsal. This sonata makes unusually effective use of the clarinet's expressive voice in its melodies, dynamics, and accents, and presents an attractive blend of piano and clarinet.

---

[20] Carlucci, ibid., 235.
[21] Todd Levy in Bernstein, *Sonata for Clarinet and Piano*, vii.

5 Pierre Boulez, *Domaines for Clarinet Alone*

Date of composition: 1961–1968

First edition/other editions: Pierre Boulez, *Domaines pour Clarinette avec ou sans Orchestre*, London: Universal Edition, 1970, 1977, 2003

Dedicatee/first performers: Not indicated; Hans Deinzer, solo clarinet (Ulm); Walter Boeykens, clarinet, with the Association Musiques Nouvelles orchestra, Boulez, conductor (Brussels); revised version, Michel Portal, clarinet, with the Musique Vivante orchestra, Boulez, conductor (Paris)[1]

Dates/places of first performances: September 20, 1968; Ulm, Germany for clarinet solo; December 20, 1968; Brussels, with orchestra; November 10, 1970; Paris, with orchestra

PIERRE BOULEZ (1925–2016), French conductor, writer, pianist, and composer was one of the most important and influential composers of the twentieth and twenty-first centuries. As a young man, Boulez studied music and mathematics, sang in a choir, and played the piano. After school in 1941, he studied higher mathematics in Lyon but continued to study piano and music theory. In 1942, Boulez moved to Paris and, against his father's wishes, entered the Paris Conservatory. After three years of rigorous harmony study with Olivier Messiaen, he won first prize in harmony. Along with some of his contemporaries who were interested in studying outside the Conservatory, he worked privately with Andrée Vaurabourg, the wife of Arthur Honegger. He later studied serial composition with René Leibowitz, a student of Arnold Schoenberg.

---

[1] Dominique Jameux, *Pierre Boulez*, trans. Susan Bradshaw (Cambridge, MA: Harvard University Press, 1991), 146, 343.

In 1946, on Honegger's advice, Boulez assumed the musical directorship of the Compagnie Renaud-Barrault, which influenced his future as a conductor. He wrote theater music and other incidental music that he conducted, but his first substantial and innovative works were the *Second Piano Sonata* (1947–1948) and *Le soleil des eaux* (*The water sun,* 1950), written as a cantata. The first work in total serialization was *Structures I* for two pianos (1951–1952), premiered by Messiaen and the composer. Boulez first gained wide recognition for *Le marteau sans maître* (*The hammer without a master,* 1953–1955) for contralto singer, flute, guitar, vibraphone, percussion, and viola, recognized as one of the most important works of the twentieth century.

Following the success of this work, Boulez was in demand as a composition teacher. He taught at the International Summer Course for New Music in Darmstadt (1954–1956 and 1960–1965); was professor of composition at Basel's Music Academy (1960–1963); was a visiting lecturer at Harvard University (1963); and taught privately. Boulez authored a series of lectures published as *Penser la musique aujourd'hui* in 1964 (*Boulez on Music Today,* 1971). His oeuvre encompasses works for voice and orchestra, chorus, orchestra, chamber music, piano, tape, incidental music, juvenilia, and editions and arrangements of others' works. He wrote numerous books and articles about his compositions and modern music.[2]

In 1954, Boulez founded the Domaine Musical concert series where new works were meticulously prepared and performed, emulated by many later concert series. In 1963, he conducted the first Paris Opéra production of Berg's *Wozzeck* in a very successful performance. He conducted at the 1965 Edinburgh Festival, the 1966 Bayreuth Festival, was guest conductor of the Cleveland Orchestra, with which he made a number of recordings, and in 1971 was appointed principal conductor of the BBC Symphony Orchestra and the New York Philharmonic Orchestra. He left these positions in 1974 and 1977, respectively, and conducted the Ring operas in Bayreuth in 1976 and the first production of Berg's *Lulu* in complete form in 1979. He reduced his conducting activities later, but by the 1990s was conducting and recording again.[3]

Ernest Fleischman (1924–2010) was executive director of the Los Angeles Philharmonic from 1969 to 1999. He worked with Boulez for many years and provides an accurate assessment of his importance as a composer and conductor:

Few living composers are held in such high critical esteem, none have made such a constructive impact on the programs audiences will hear, or indeed on the way in which leading musical institutions are structured, whether in

2. G. W. Hopkins and Paul Griffiths, "Boulez, Pierre," *Grove Music Online.*
3. Hopkins and Griffiths, ibid.

England, in France, in the United States, or in Germany. Be it as a result of playing the music of Boulez, or of rehearsing and performing with him as conductor, musicians everywhere have learnt a great deal about, and have become more open to and skilled in, the performance of music of our time.[4]

Boulez' musical inclinations were affected by the work of the symbolist poet, Stéphane Mallarmé (1842–1898), in the 1950s and 1960s. Mallarmé's unfinished *Livre* utilizes movable sheets that enable several permutations by reading left to right, omitting pages or words, and repeating words or letters in different iterations. The variety of components appealed to Boulez.[5] Mallarmé's influence is reflected in two works written before *Domaines*, the *Third Piano Sonata* and *Pli selon pli*. The American composer, John Cage (1912–1992), with whom Boulez corresponded, 1949–1954, also affected him. Cage pioneered aleatoric music where, by design, chance was determinative, for example in his piano piece, *Music for Changes* (1951). Here, Cage tossed coins to select arrangements from the *I Ching*, a Chinese book of changes, leading to the choice of pitches, durations, and dynamics.[6] In several Boulez' works, aleatoric sounds are used with a rapidly moving or open form where musical events or sections are flexible.

Finnegans Wake (1939) by James Joyce (1882–1941) was also influential on Boulez by Joyce's use of a language similar to Mallarmé's. Joyce uses a cyclic form where the final, incomplete sentence in *Finnegans Wake* leads back to the beginning of the book, a form also used by Boulez.[7] During the late 1950s and early 1960s, Boulez' contemporary, Karlheinz Stockhausen (1928–2007), developed what Stockhausen called moment form in his works, *Kontakte* (1958–1960) and *Momente* (1961). It is similar to Boulez' open form, defined as:

Each individually characterized passage in a work is regarded as an experiential unit, a "moment," which can potentially engage the listener's full attention and can do so in exactly the same measure as its neighbours. No single "moment" claims priority, even as a beginning or an end....[8]

Ernst Fleischmann, "Full of Phantasy, Uncompromising: Boulez the Conductor and Impresario," *Pierre Boulez: eine Festschrift zum 60. Geburtstag am 26. März 1985*, ed. Josef Häusler (Vienna: Universal Edition, 1985), 16.

[5] Jameux, ibid., 92–94.

[6] Robert P. Morgan, "Aleatory Music," *The New Harvard Dictionary of Music*, 4th ed., ed. Don Michael Randel (Cambridge, MA: Belknap Press, 2003), 28–29.

[7] Ian Mitchell, "Toward a Beginning: Thoughts Leading to an Interpretation of *Domaines* for Solo Clarinet by Pierre Boulez," *The Versatile Clarinet*, ed. Roger Heaton, (New York: Routledge, 2006), 113–14.

[8] "Moment Form," *The New Grove Dictionary of Music and Musicians*, London: MacMillan, 1980, vol. 18, 152, as quoted by Mitchell, ibid., 112.

Domaines was written for clarinet alone along with a revised version for clarinet solo with twenty-one instruments divided into six groups, positioned in a circle around the clarinetist.[9] It quickly became a relatively popular work due to its pleasing sonorities and varied virtuoso music that give the listener a feeling of being part of the work. *Domaines* has been called, "one of the most important works for the clarinet in the second half of the twentieth century."[10]

The music is published on twelve large sheets of heavy paper called *cahiers* (sections) labelled A through F. Each sheet contains six cells which vary from a single note to four lines of notes. The first six sheets are marked original; the next six sheets are marked *miroir* (mirror); each may be played in any order, from top or bottom or from left or right. On the mirror sheets, the music is a retrograde reflection of the cahiers (back to front and bottom to top) in respect to notes, tempo, dynamics, and expression. In the left corner of each sheet is a symmetrical grid of Xs corresponding to the position of cells; alongside are two grids with numbers in place of the Xs, suggesting two possible manners of playing the original and mirror versions.[11] The number six takes on a, "unifying significance," six original sheets, six mirror sheets, and six cells.[12] Bar lines are not used in any of the six cells. Each cell usually has two to four options that include different tempi, dynamics (often for each note from *ppp* to *ff*), trills, flutter tongue, vibrato, color fingerings (a note altered by the addition of fingers/and or keys), air sounds, and multiphonics. The clarinet part is well written and most of the quick passages are easily playable, others need practice.[13] Boulez eschews chance to organize the playing of his works, preferring choice.[14] The player can choose between the narrative of the cells' notes and the non-narrative of the moment music, making a connection between individual cells or letting them stand alone.[15] Each performance is unique.

Bradshaw described *Domaines* as, "a series of studies of rhythmic development… The eventual form of the piece, no matter what the chosen route, is that of variations of variations. All its essential material is contained in the six *cahiers* (A–F) of music for solo clarinet, reflected, in reverse, in six corresponding mirror versions."[16]

---

[9] The six groups consist of a trombone quartet (one alto, two tenors, and a bass); string sextet (two violins, two violas, and two cellos); duo (marimba and string bass); quintet (flute, trumpet, alto saxophone, bassoon, and harp); trio (oboe, horn, and guitar); and bass clarinet.

[10] Mitchell, ibid., 109.

[11] Jameux, ibid., 346.

[12] Roger Heaton, "Contemporary Performance Practice and Tradition," *Music Performance Research* 5 (2012): 102. [Online] Available: http://mpr-online.net/Issues/Volume%205%20[2012]/Heaton.pdf [July 13, 2016].

[13] Jameux, ibid., 99–100; Heaton, ibid., 101.

[14] Mitchell, ibid., 115; Jameux, ibid., 102–103.

[15] Mitchell, ibid., 114–15.

[16] Susan Bradshaw, "The Instrumental and Vocal Works," *Pierre Boulez: A Symposium*, ed. William Glock (London: Eulenburg Books, 1986), 198–99.

When the clarinetist performs *Domaines* with six groups of instruments, the arrangement of players is important.[17] The clarinetist and conductor decide the permutations for each sheet and adjust and rehearse the transitions between soloist and groups.[18] The clarinetist plays and moves among each group which plays a response; when all six domains are played, the conductor chooses which groups play their mirror versions, with the clarinet responding and having the last word. There are 518,400 possible outcomes and the structures are linked in several ways.[19] When the clarinetist performs *Domaines for Clarinet Alone*, he or she uses only one music stand rather than six used with instrumental groups. This allows the clarinetist to control the sound, silence, and movements among sections.[20]

The autograph score and the published form are unambiguous and clear, suggesting to the performer that attention to detail and control of multiphonics, color, pace, intensity, continuity, and pauses is vital.[21] (See Figure 5.1.) Cahier A illustrates trills, flutter tongue, multiphonics (marked *harmonique*),[22] and many shades of dynamics. Cahier D illustrates the same techniques with color fingerings (marked + – + –) on various notes. Multiphonics appear on cahiers A, B, C, and E, each specifying various textures and colors with dynamics options offered.

Mitchell listed corrected notes for several mistakes in the 2003 published edition of *Domaines* checked against the composer's manuscript and sketches in the Paul Sacher Foundation archive in Basel, Switzerland.[23]

Ancillary gestures by clarinetists playing *Domaines* are produced by moving the instrument and body during performance. These include lifting the clarinet up and/or down; movement to one side or the other; fast tilt-like gestures; head, waist, and knee movements; and body postures. These movements affect the audience's perception of the music and are seen as either a, "tension or a phrasing judgment." The clarinetist's movements include facial expressions, postures, breathing, and gestures which add to the audience's experience of sound, contributing information to the performance, and transmitting the performer's musical interpretation of the piece.[24]

---

[17] One possible arrangement of the instrumental groups with original and mirror paths is given by Jameux, ibid., 345.

[18] Benny Sluchin and Mikhail Malt, "Open Form and Two Combinatorial Musical Models: The Cases of *Domaines* and *Duel*," *Mathematics and Computation in Music, Third International Conference, MCM 2011, Paris, France, June 15–17, 2011: Proceedings in Lecture Notes in Artificial Intelligence 6726*, eds. Carlos Agon, et al. (New York: Springer, 2009), 262.

[19] Hopkins and Griffiths, ibid.; Jameux, ibid., 147, 344.

[20] Mitchell, ibid., 115.

[21] Mitchell, ibid., 115–16; Heaton, ibid., 103.

[22] Mitchell, ibid., 116–23. Mitchell mentions which multiphonics work best for his performance and provides fingerings on 127–28.

[23] Mitchell, ibid., 115–16, 129–32.

[24] Marchelo M. Wanderley and Bradley W. Vines, "Origins and Functions of Clarinetists' Ancillary Gestures," in *Music and Gesture*, eds. A. Gritten and E. King (Aldershot: Ashgate, 2006), 167, 170, 179–85.

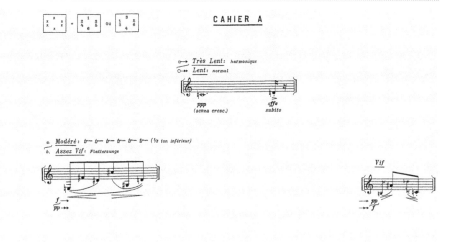

FIGURE 5.1 Boulez, *Domaines for Clarinet Alone, cahier A.*

Boulez's 1971 observation about Anton Webern speaking at the Juilliard School of Music is particularly appropriate to understanding *Domaines*:

> With Webern, one instrument can summarize the world. In that, his world is comparable to Paul Klee's. Klee rarely painted a big painting. The world of Klee can be contained in a drop of water. One can see as many faces in a drop of water as in a large landscape.[25]

Boulez's *Domaines for Clarinet Alone* unfolds as a precise interplay of short cells with a myriad of sounds, articulation, dynamics, color fingerings, and multiphonics

---

[25] Joan Peyser, *To Boulez and Beyond: Music in Europe Since the Rite of Spring* (New York: Billboard Books, 1999), 166.

used in an aleatoric but controlled manner. It remains a paragon of the earliest experimental clarinet solo works of the 1960s. Technically, *Domaines* is very challenging and will be performed by the advanced clarinetist. It is theatrical, analytical, fascinating, and beautiful, and a very important clarinet solo of the late twentieth century.

6 Johannes Brahms, *Sonata for Clarinet and Piano, op. 120, no. 1*

Date of composition: May 17, 1894–July 1894

First edition/other edition: Johannes Brahms, *Zwei Sonaten für Clarinette (oder Bratsche) und Pianoforte, op. 120, no. 1, F moll, no. 2, Es dur*, Berlin: N. Simrock, 1895; Johannes Brahms, *Sonata for Clarinet (or Viola) and Piano, F minor, op. 120, no. 1*, eds. Jost Michaels, Hans-Christian Müller, Emil Seiler, Vienna: Wiener Urtext Edition, 2003

Dedicatee/first performers: Richard Mühlfeld; Richard Mühlfeld, clarinet, Clara Schumann, piano (private performance); Richard Mühlfeld, clarinet, Johannes Brahms, piano (public performance)

Date/place of first private performance/date/place of first public performance: September 22, 1894, Meiningen; January 11, 1895, Vienna, Bösendorfer Saal

JOHANNES BRAHMS (1833–1897) is the most important composer of the last half of the nineteenth century. His oeuvre constitutes works for orchestra, chamber music, piano, piano four hands, two pianos, vocal canons, vocal quartets, vocal duets, accompanied chorus, unaccompanied chorus, solo songs, arrangements of folk songs, and arrangements of vocal, instrumental, and choral works by other composers.[1] Brahms' chamber music comprises twenty-four works, dating 1854–1894, that are arguably the greatest after Beethoven.

In December 1890, Brahms wrote to his publisher and friend, Fritz Simrock, sharing his intention to retire from composing, "With this scrap [I] bid farewell to notes of

---

[1] George S. Bozarth and Walter Frisch, "Brahms, Johannes," *Grove Music Online.*

mine—because it really is time to stop."[2] However, this changed after Brahms was inspired by the playing of the clarinetist, Richard Mühlfeld (1856–1907). Brahms met Mühlfeld during his first visit to Meiningen in autumn 1881. Mühlfeld came from a musical family and was taught violin, clarinet, and piano by his father and older brothers. In 1873, he became a junior violinist in the Meiningen Orchestra at eighteen and was promoted to first violin in 1874. In 1875, he was recruited by Richard Wagner for his Bayreuth Festival Orchestra, and performed in the premiere of Wagner's *Der Ring des Nibelungen* in Bayreuth in 1876. In that year, Mühlfeld settled on the clarinet and occasionally played first clarinet in the Meiningen orchestra. He played through his military service as soloist in the 32nd infantry regiment's band. In 1877, Mühlfeld was soloist with the Meiningen Orchestra, playing Weber's *Concertino*. In 1879, with a letter of recommendation from Richard Wagner, Mühlfeld became first clarinetist of the Meiningen Court Orchestra. A few months later, Hans von Bülow became the Orchestra's director, and shaped it into an excellent ensemble.[3] Shortly after becoming director, Bülow wrote to Duke Georg II that Mühlfeld was the, "most gifted artist among his woodwind players," and in 1881 entrusted Mühlfeld with separate rehearsals for the wind players.[4]

In 1891 Brahms rehearsed the Meiningen Orchestra in his E minor Symphony, performing it several times. In March 1891, Brahms stayed in Meiningen, and requested a private performance of Mozart's *Clarinet Quintet, K. 580* with Mühlfeld and the Fleischhauer String Quartet. It is also possible that Brahms had Mühlfeld play both of the Weber concertos with piano accompaniment.[5] Brahms scheduled Weber's *Concerto in F minor* for the program on March 16, 1891. He enthusiastically remarked to Clara Schumann in his March 17 letter, "There is no way to play the clarinet more beautifully than this Mr. Mühlfeld does."[6] In mid-July Brahms considered composing chamber works expressly for Mühlfeld. By the end of November, Brahms had invited himself to Elisabethenburg, the Meiningen castle, for a private performance of the *Trio for Clarinet, Cello and Piano, op. 114*, and the *Quintet for Clarinet and String Quartet, op. 115*. In July, Brahms wrote Clara joyously, "You cannot imagine a clarinetist like that Mühlfeld. He is the very best wind

---

[2] The "scrap" refers to part of his *String Quintet in G major, op. 111*, David Brodbeck, "Medium and Meaning: New Aspects of the Chamber Music," in *The Cambridge Companion to Brahms*, ed. Michael Musgrave (Cambridge: Cambridge University Press, 1999), 98.

[3] Peter Clive, *Brahms and His World* (Lanham, MD: The Scarecrow Press, 2006), 321; Maren Goltz and Herta Müller, *Richard Mühlfeld der Brahms-Klarinettist, Einleitung, Übertragung, und Kommentar der Dokumentation von Christian Mühlfeld/Richard Mühlfeld*. English trans. Mona Lemmel, *Brahms' Clarinettist: Introduction, Transcription, and Commentary of the Documentation by Christian Mühlfeld* (Balve, Germany: Artivo, 2007), 19.

[4] Goltz and Müller, ibid., 21.

[5] Goltz and Müller, ibid., 29.

[6] Brahms to Clara Schumann, March 17, 1891, Berthold Litzmann, ed., *Letters of Clara Schumann and Johannes Brahms 1853–1896* (London: Longmans, Green and Co., 1927), 2:190; Goltz and Müller, *Richard Mühlfeld der Brahms-Klarinettist*, 37.

player I have ever met. Unfortunately there has been a general decline of them for various reasons. The section in the orchestra in Vienna and elsewhere do well or even very well, but on their own they don't make me very happy."[7] Joachim suggested a performance of the *Trio* and *Quintet* during his string quartet concert series in Berlin, which successfully took place on December 12, 1891, in the Singakademie.[8] The *Trio* and *Quintet* were both well received; the latter more than the former.[9]

In Bad Ischl during summer 1894, Brahms composed the two *Sonatas for Clarinet and Piano, op. 120, nos. 1 and 2*.[10] In August 1895, Brahms sent manuscript copies to Mühlfeld in which he inscribed at the end of *Sonata no. 2*, "To Richard Mühlfeld, the master of his beautiful instrument, in sincerely grateful remembrance, J. Brahms, Ischl in summer 1895."[11] Between September 19, 1894 and the end of February 1895, Mühlfeld and Brahms successfully performed the sonatas from the manuscript about twenty times.[12] As a former violinist, Mühlfeld is known to have had, "a powerful delivery, beautiful tone quality, and generous use of vibrato."[13]

In November Brahms wrote to Clara Schumann, "And now I have to tell you about something which will cause us both a little annoyance. Mühlfeld will be sending you his tuning fork, so that the grand piano to which he is to play may be tuned to it. His clarinet only allows him to yield very little to other instruments."[14] In 1874, Wagner asked Duke Georg II to lower the pitch of the Meiningen Orchestra to the French pitch of 435 Herz so the orchestra members could perform his opera cycle, *Der Ring des Niebelungen*. The Duke did so and all new woodwind and brass instruments were ordered from the Ottensteiner firm in Munich. Two sets of stained boxwood clarinets in A, B♭, and C were shared among the Meiningen orchestra's three clarinetists, Wilhelm Reif, Richard Mühlfeld, and Gottlob Schwarz.[15] These were

[7] Brahms to Clara Schumann, July, 1891, Litzmann, ibid., 2:196–97; Goltz and Müller, ibid., 37, note 59.

[8] Goltz and Müller, ibid., 37.

[9] Goltz and Müller, ibid., 43; Colin Lawson, *Brahms, Clarinet Quintet* (Cambridge: Cambridge University Press, 1998), 35–40.

[10] The sketches were completed May 17–July 1894. Margit L. McCorkle, *Johannes Brahms: Thematisch-bibliographisches Werkverzeichnis* (Munich: G. Henle, 1984), 479; Johannes Brahms, *Sonaten für Klarinette (oder Viola) und Klavier, Neue Ausgabe sämtlicher Werke*, eds. Egon Voss and Johannes Behr, Serie II, Band 9 (Munich: G. Henle, 2010), xxvi.

[11] "Hrn. Richard Mühlfeld / dem Meister seines schönen Instrumentes / in herzlich dankbarer / Erinnerung! / J. Brahms. / Ischl in Sommer 95." Brahms, *Sonaten für Klarinetten*, xxvi; George Bozarth, "Two Sonatas for Clarinet and Piano in F minor and E♭ Major, Opus 120," trans. G. Bozarth in *The Compleat Brahms: A Guide to the Musical Works of Johannes Brahms*, ed. L. Botstein (New York: W. W. Norton, 1999), 102.

[12] Goltz and Müller, *Richard Mühlfeld der Brahms-Klarinettist*, 45.

[13] Lawson, ibid., 68–71.

[14] Brahms to Clara Schumann, end of October 1894, Litzmann, *Letters of Clara Schumann and Johannes Brahms 1853–1896*, 265–66; Lawson, ibid., 40.

[15] Jochen Seggelke, "Richard Mühlfeld's Clarinets" in Goltz and Müller, *Richard Mühlfeld der Brahms-Klarinettist*, 333, 337; Nicholas Shackelton and Keith Puddy, "Mühlfeld's Clarinets," *The Clarinet* 16, no. 3 (May–June 1989): 33–36; Lawson, ibid., 92.

the clarinets used by Mühlfeld when he played for Brahms, and are notable for the smoothness of their transitions from one register to another.[16]

Sonata for Clarinet and Piano, op. 120, no. 1, is in four movements. The themes are written with many leaps throughout, and often slurred. While the technical demands are moderate, a greater challenge is to perform it with control, finesse, tonal beauty, and an understanding of each movement's construction. A sensitive and careful interpretation by clarinetist and pianist is essential.

The first movement, Allegro appassionato, is in sonata-allegro form with an introduction and coda. (See Chart 6.1.) A four measure introduction presents a fervent F minor A theme played by the piano in octaves. It leads directly to the clarinet's equally passionate B theme featuring dramatic leaps (mm. 5–12). The development section from m. 90 in A♭ major is a simple *p* C theme, delicately repeated *pp*, with an expressive chalumeau register solo. An exciting marcato section (mm. 116–129) follows. The retransition is impressive where the piano (m. 130) triumphantly plays the A^3 theme in F♯ minor (mm. 130–135), making a decrescendo before the clarinet states the B^4 theme in the chalumeau register (m. 138) at the recapitulation (Ex. 6.1). Here, the high point is the slurred *f* eighth notes F6–G♯5 and F5–G♯4 (m. 146). A coda, Sostenuto ad expressivo, is subtly developed from the concluding measures of the recapitulation.[17] It features rolled

Section:	Introduction	Exposition	Development-Retransition	Recapitulation	Coda
Starts at m.	1 Allegro appassionato	5	90	138	214–236
No. of mm.	4	85	48	76	23
Tonalities	f	f, D♭, c	A♭, E, c♯, f♯	f	f
Themes	A	B, A¹, B¹, A², B²	C, B³, A³	B⁴, C¹	A⁴

CHART 6.1 Brahms, *Sonata for Clarinet and Piano, op. 120, no. 1*: Structural analysis, first movement, Allegro appassionato[18]

---

[16] Styra Avins, "Performing Brahms's Music: Clues from his Letters," in *Performing Brahms: Early Evidence of Performance Style*, eds. Michael Musgrave and Bernard D. Sherman (Cambridge: Cambridge University Press, 2003), 12, 36–37, note 9. Photographs of Mühlfeld's restored Ottensteiner B♭ and A clarinets in the Meiningen Museum are in Seggelke, ibid., 351–57.

[17] Michael Musgrave, *The Music of Brahms* (Oxford: Clarendon Press, 1994), 254.

[18] Christian Martin Schmidt, *Verfahren der motivisch-thematischen Vermittlung in der Musik von Johannes Brahms, dargestellt an der Klarinettensonate f-moll, op. 120, 1* (Munich: Emil Katzbichler, 1971), 23, 67, chart next to 98, 101, 112, 133; Walter Frisch, *Brahms and the Principle of Developing Variation* (Berkeley: University of California Press, 1984), 147–51; Elisabeth R. Aleksander, "Gustav Jenner's *Clarinet Sonata in G Major, opus 5*: An Analysis and Performance Guide with Stylistic comparison to the *Clarinet Sonatas, opus 120* of his Teacher, Johannes Brahms" (D.M.A. thesis, University of Nebraska, 2008), 105.

EXAMPLE 6.1. Brahms, *Sonata for Clarinet and Piano, op. 120, no. 1*, first movement, mm. 130–140.

piano chords supporting a lyric clarinet solo with triplets and eighth notes, and a memorable ending played sotto voce.

The second movement, Andante un poco Adagio, is a rondo of four parts with a coda, mostly in Ab major, but without clear cadences to confirm the tonality.[19] (See Chart 6.2.) A reflective, improvisatory-like clarinet A theme sounds in the clarion register (mm. 1–22) against a soft piano background while the bass line completes the chord on weak rhythmic halves of the beat, creating a, "hesistant timidity of expression."[20] The B theme (mm. 23–40) introduced by piano sixteenth notes is particularly beautiful and skillfully interwoven with the clarinet's chalumeau and clarion registers. The A³ theme (mm. 49–58) features the clarinet's chalumeau register with a delicate interplay between clarinet and piano,

[19] Musgrave, ibid., 254.

[20] Daniel Gregory Mason, *The Chamber Music of Brahms* (New York: MacMillan Co., 1933), 251.

Section:	A	B	A^1	A^2	Coda
Starts at m.	1 Andante un poco Adagio	23	41	49	71–81
No. of mm.	22	18	8	22	11
Tonalities	A♭	A♭, c♯	E, C	A♭	A♭
Themes	A	B	A^1, A^2	A^3	B^1, A^4

CHART 6.2 Brahms, *Sonata for Clarinet and Piano, op. 120, no. 1*: Structural analysis, second movement, Andante un poco Adagio.

highlighting an intimate atmosphere. An unusual effect at the beginning of this theme is the wide spacing of the piano writing by changing the voicing.[21] A return to the beginning of the second movement is heard with the A^3 theme played in the clarion register (mm. 61–67). In the coda, a poignant B^1 theme emerges (mm. 71–74) before turning to a clarinet *pp* A^4 theme (mm. 75–81), a special moment in the sonata.

The third movement, Allegretto grazioso, is a four-section form of ländler, trio, ländler, coda. The first ländler has five parts and the trio and second ländler have three parts. (See Chart 6.3.) McClelland notes that the first five measures are in E♭ major rather than A♭ major because of a consistent substitution of D♯ for D♭.[22] The movement begins with a comfortable ländler, a Viennese dance or waltz, traditionally played by one or two clarinets accompanied by an accordion. The clarinet A theme is followed by the piano (mm. 1–16) with imitation, inversion, and stretto (mm. 17–46) into section A^2.[23] The trio (mm. 47–62) is heavier, with a chalumeau register C theme and eighth note piano accompaniment shared between the left and right hands. After the piano's fermata on the note F3 (m. 89), the ländler A^3 theme is played, teneramente (tenderly), answered by the piano (mm. 90–98). The remainder of the movement is identical to the first 46 measures of the movement but without the repetition of measures 17–46 in section A^2. The coda begins with clarinet eighth notes alone (mm. 129–130) up to the last six measures marked, calando, suggesting a soft ending.

---

[21] Margaret Notley, *Lateness in Brahms: Music and Culture in the Twilight of Viennese Liberalism* (New York: Oxford University Press, 2007), 138.

[22] Ryan McClelland, *Brahms and the Scherzo: Studies in Musical Narrative* (Farnham, UK: Ashgate, 2010), 260.

[23] Bozarth, ibid., 102.

Section:	A	A[1]	B	B[1]	A[2]	C
Starts at m.	1 Ländler, Allegretto grazioso	9	17	29	39 [17–46:]	47 Trio
No. of mm.	8	8	12	10	68	16
Tonalities	E♭–A♭	E♭–A♭	E♭–A♭	E♭–A♭	E♭–A♭	F, E♭
Themes	A	A[1]	B	B[1]	A[2]	C

Section:	D	C[1]	A[3]	B[2]	A[4]	Coda
Starts at m.	63	79 [68–88]	89 Ländler	107	119	129–136
No. of mm.	16	62	18	12	10	8
Tonalities	E♭–A♭, f	A♭	E♭–A♭	A♭	E♭–A♭	E♭–A♭
Themes	D	C[1]	trans.-A[3]	B[2]	A[4]	coda

CHART 6.3 Brahms, *Sonata for Clarinet and Piano, op. 120, no. 1*: Structural analysis, third movement, Allegretto grazioso.[24]

The fourth movement, Vivace, is in rondo form in four sections, with three parts, five parts, one part, and a coda, respectively.[25] (See Chart 6.4.) The first opening theme begins by the striking of three half-note piano accented F5s, followed by a ferocious series of eighth notes resolving on four half note chords (mm. 1–8). The A theme is carefree and uncomplicated, featuring nimble clarinet staccato,[26] lightly accompanied by the piano (mm. 8–16). The B theme (mm. 42–61) features expansive quarter note triplets played in canon and imitation with the piano, flowing into eighth notes between piano and clarinet, until the clarinet proclaims the half note opening theme[1] answered by the piano (mm. 62–76). The B[1] theme appears in half notes and quarter note triplets (mm. 142–163), gradually building to three repeated clarinet *fp* E♭5s (m. 163) in D♭ major. After a decrescendo to *pp* the clarinet and piano proclaim a *f* reinvigorated opening theme[3] (mm. 174–180). A clarinet *p* A[3] theme follows (mm. 200–206) leading to the coda, statement of the opening theme[4] (mm 207–216), and an electrifying ending.[27]

[24] Schmidt, *Verfahren der motivisch-thematischen*, 112; Aleksander, "Gustav Jenner's *Clarinet Sonata*," 105.

[25] Schmidt, ibid., 133; Aleksander, ibid., 105.

[26] Mason, ibid., 255.

[27] A fascinating study of motivic relationships in both Brahms' sonatas is in Eric Mandat and Boja Kragulj, "Performance Analysis: Intersection and Interaction of Motives in the Brahms Op. 120 Sonatas," *The Clarinet* 40, no. 1 (December 2012): 66–70.

Section:	Opening theme, A	Trans., A^1, opening theme^1	B	Opening theme^2	A^2-trans.
Starts at m.	1 Vivace	17	42	62	77
No. of mm.	16	25	20	15	24
Tonalities	F, a, F,	F	F, C	F	F, a, F
Themes	opening theme, A	trans., A^1, opening theme^1	B, trans.	opening theme^2	A^2, trans.

Section:	Development	C	B^1	Opening-theme^3 trans.-A^3	Coda
Starts at m.	101	119	142	174	207–220
No. of mm.	18	23	32	33	14
Tonalities	d	d	F, C, D♭, A	F, a, F	F
Themes	dev.	C	B^1	opening theme^3, trans., A^3	opening theme^4

CHART 6.4 Brahms, *Sonata for Clarinet and Piano, op. 120, no. 1*: Structural analysis, fourth movement, Vivace.

The *Sonata for Clarinet and Piano, op. 120, no. 1* is written in a serious mood similar to the opening of Brahms' *Quintet* but on a smaller scale. The autograph manuscript, in the Robert Owen Lehman Collection on deposit at the Pierpont Morgan Library, New York,[28] indicates different ideas and changes that Brahms made in the first and second movements. For example, in the first movement, mm. 5–8, he wrote the B theme an octave lower (as he did the B^4 theme at the recapitulation, m. 138), only to restore the melody in the upper octave in mm. 5–8, after playing it with Mühlfeld. Other changes were made at measures 200–203, and at the Sostenuto ed espressivo, deleted in blue pencil. The second movement shows some additional slurring in the clarinet part, written indications of dynamics, the word, "espress.," and a revision of the piano accompaniment in measures 57–71.[29]

---

[28] Notley, ibid., 104, note 81.

[29] Robert Adelson, "The Autograph Manuscript of Brahms' Clarinet Sonatas Op. 120: A Preliminary Report," *The Clarinet* 25, no. 3 (May–June 1998): 62–63; a transcription of the changes made in the sketches are in Johannes Brahms, *Sonaten für Klarinette (oder Viola) und Klavier, Neue Ausgabe sämtlicher Werke*, 185.

Sonata no. 1 is one of the most sophisticated and compelling of Brahms's late chamber works.[30] His clarinet writing is sensitive and expansive, requiring precise control of expression and dynamics. It is tightly constructed with directness of expression, rich in meaningful themes. Like its companion, the *Sonata no. 2*, it is one of the most rewarding sonatas to play over a number of years, and although technically within the grasp of young players, it requires much work with a sensitive pianist to attain a convincing and comprehensive musical presentation. It is the first extended work for clarinet and piano by a major composer since Weber's 1816 *Grand Duo Concertant*.[31]

---

[30] Bozarth and Frisch, ibid.

[31] Lawson, ibid., 41–42.

7 Aaron Copland, *Concerto for Clarinet, String Orchestra, Harp, and Piano*

Date of composition: September 1947–October 1948

First edition/other edition: Aaron Copland, *Concerto for Clarinet and String Orchestra (with Harp and Piano)*, London: Boosey & Hawkes, 1949 (piano and clarinet); Aaron Copland, *Concerto for Clarinet and String Orchestra (with Harp and Piano)*, London: Boosey & Hawkes, 1952 (orchestral miniature score)

Dedicatee/first performer: Benny Goodman; Benny Goodman, clarinet

Dates/places of first performances: November 6, 1950, New York City, NBC Symphony of the Air, Fritz Reiner, conductor (radio performance); November 24, 1950, Philadelphia, Ralph McLane, clarinet, Philadelphia Symphony, Eugene Ormandy, conductor (public performance)

Orchestral instrumentation: First and second violins, violas, cellos, string basses, harp, and piano

AARON COPLAND (1900–1990) was one of the most successful and creative American composers. His *Concerto for Clarinet* is a colorful and evocative work, full of musical and rhythmic challenges. In 1946, Copland received simultaneous requests for works from two famous jazz clarinetists, a concerto for Benny Goodman (1909–1986), and a piece for Woody Herman (1913–1987) and his jazz band. Copland chose the Goodman commission, and asked him for some of his jazz quintet recordings. Goodman wrote Copland on February 5, 1947, from New York, "I'm looking forward in anticipation to the piece."[1] Copland listened to Goodman's

---

[1] Aaron Copland and Vivian Perlis, *Copland: Since 1943* (New York: St. Martin's Press, 1989), 76–77. Goodman's letter is on 87.

recordings, made notes, and brought them with him during the four-month tour of Latin America he took as a goodwill ambassador. He composed the first movement of the concerto in Latin America.[2] Copland wrote to his friend, Victor Kraft, on October 4, 1947, "I badly need a fast theme for part 2. The usual thing. I used the 'pas de deux' theme for part 1, and I think it will make everyone weep."[3] About this time, Copland was asked to write music for a film, *The Red Pony*, based on John Steinbeck's book, and decided he had to accept. On October 18, 1948, Copland wrote to Leonard Bernstein, "Nothing much has been happening. I stayed home a lot and finished my Clarinet Concerto—endlich [finally]! Tried it over for Benny the other day. He had Dave O[ppenheim, the clarinetist, for support]....Seems I wrote the last page too high 'for all normal purposes.' So it'll have to come down a step."[4]

In his biography, Copland states, "I had long been an admirer of Benny Goodman, and I thought that writing a concerto with him in mind would give me a fresh point of view. We did not work together while I was composing the piece, but after it was finished and sent off, Benny wrote to thank me and to say: 'With a little editing, I know we will have a good piece.'"[5] Goodman stated in a telephone interview with Perlis in 1984:

> I made no demands on what Copland should write. He had completely free rein, except that I should have a two-year exclusivity on playing the work. I paid two thousand dollars and that's real money. At that time, there were not too many American composers to pick from—people of such terrific status— as Hindemith and Bartók. I recall that Aaron came to listen when I was recording with Bartók. Copland had a great reputation also. I didn't choose him because some of his works were jazz-inspired.

After several changes in the score, the concerto was to be premiered by Ralph McLane and the Philadelphia Orchestra, but less than three weeks before the

---

[2] The tour included Montevideo, Buenos Aires, Rio de Janeiro, São Paulo, Pôrto Alegre, and many smaller cities. See Copland and Perlis, ibid., 78.

[3] A sketch of the first movement at the Library of Congress is marked "Pas de deux," dated "Feb. 20 [19]46/Aug." Copland and Perlis, ibid., 87, 434, note 43. For this theme, Copland may have relied on sketches from an earlier dance project. Douglas Lee, *Masterworks of 20th-Century Music: The Modern Repertory of the Symphony Orchestra* (New York: Routledge, 2002), 116.

[4] Elizabeth Bergmann Crist and Wayne D. Shirley, eds., *The Selected Correspondence of Aaron Copland* (New Haven, CT: Yale University Press, 2006), 189. At the end of the autograph, Copland wrote, "Snedens Landing Oct 21 1948." See the Juilliard Manuscript Collection, Aaron Copland, "Concerto for Clarinet and String Orchestra (and harp)." [Online] Available: http://juilliardmanuscriptcollection.org/manuscript/concerto-clarinet-string-orchestra-harp-piano/. [September 12, 2015].

[5] Copland and Perlis, ibid., 93.

concert, NBC announced that Goodman would play the radio premiere. McLane performed the first concert performance.[6] Early reviews were lukewarm[7] but after repeated performances by clarinetists in the United States and in other countries, the concerto gained popularity and is now frequently performed. Goodman and Copland made two successful and influential recordings in 1952 and 1963;[8] the second was preferred by Goodman. Although Copland made the piano score simply for rehearsals with Goodman, it was successfully used for some early performances, and Copland requested that Boosey & Hawkes publish it.[9] It is now performed more with piano accompaniment than with full orchestra. Copland's concerto was used in 1951 for the *Pied Piper* ballet choreographed by Jerome Robbins for the New York City Ballet.[10]

The concerto is one continuous work divided into two parts: a slow first movement including an unnumbered but measured cadenza, and a fast second movement. The expressive first movement is written in ternary form, and after a fermata on F♯4 proceeds to a cadenza in the A[1] section. (See Chart 7.1.) A four measure introduction features exquisite sonorities of *pp* harp and strings. The clarinet enters with a slow, tender A theme in 3/4, emphasizing C and D tonal centers. A quarter-note pickup leads to wide slurred leaps, mostly in the clarion register, and a colorful, expressive line that effortlessly moves through several meters. It reminded one reviewer of Satie's "Gymnopédies."[11]

The melody abounds in leaps, as found in many Copland works, and features short, skillfully developed motives.[12] The B section (m. 51)[13] constantly shifts meters, causing displaced accents in the melodic line, providing rhythmic interest.[14] The orchestra plays a striking "Broader" section (m. 73) that is emotional and effective. The elegant A[2] theme (m. 77) has a C tonal center that is the high point of the move-

---

[6] [James Collis], "Copland's Clarinet Concerto," *The Clarinet* 1, no. 3 (Fall 1950): 24; Larry Maxey, "The Copland Clarinet Concerto," *The Clarinet* 12, no. 4 (Summer 1985): 28.

[7] See reviews quoted by Maxey, ibid., 28 and by Aaron Copland and Vivan Perlis, *The Complete Copland* (Hillsdale, NY: Pendragon Press, 2013), 197.

[8] Joann Skowronski, *Aaron Copland: A Bio-Bibliography* (Westport, CT: Greenwood Press, 1985), nos. B78–79, 36.

[9] Copland and Perlis, *Copland: Since 1943*, 97.

[10] Neil Butterworth, *The Music of Aaron Copland*, (London: Toccata Press, 1985), 120.

[11] "Review of Copland, Concerto for Clarinet and String Orchestra," *Music & Letters* 33, no. 4 (1952): 366.

[12] Howard Pollack, "Copland, Aaron," *Grove Music Online.*

[13] Pollock states that this section is from Copland's unpublished work, *The Cummington Story* (1945); Daniel Pollock, *Aaron Copland: The Life and Work of an Uncommon Man* (New York: Henry Holt and Company, 1999), 425.

[14] Charles Francis Del Rosso, "A Study of Selected Solo Clarinet Literature of Four American Composers as a Basis for Performance and Teaching" (Ed.D. diss., Teachers College, Columbia University, 1969), 27; a detailed analysis is given from 23–52.

ment, with an effective subito *p* on high F6 in measure 101. Four measures later, arpeggios in the chalumeau register are expertly used by repeating fragments of the melody throughout. As this section quiets to *pp*, the beginning of a soft, dreamy A³ theme (m. 115) is played freely by the clarinet over sustained strings, just before the cadenza.

There are three dominant motives: three in the cadenza and the same motives, modified and rearranged, in the second movement.[15] The long, athletic cadenza is unusually placed since concerto cadenzas often appear before the conclusion of a movement. Copland's fortunate idea was to have the cadenza introduce material to follow.[16] The first motive is lyrical and songlike (Ex. 7.1a), the second is quick and fleeting (Ex. 7.1b), and the third, incisive and short, played with accents and short articulation (Ex. 7.1c). Goodman identified the second motive in a 1969 taped interview as a phrase from a Brazilian tune heard by Copland in Rio de Janeiro.[17]

EXAMPLE 7.1. a-c. Copland, *Concerto for Clarinet, String Orchestra, Harp, and Piano*, three motives in the cadenza (written in the sounding pitch of the piano).

The cadenza begins tentatively with motive A (Ex. 7.1a), moving twice as fast with a wide ranging group of eighth notes, to a *sf* A6 followed by a low *sf* F#3. Two slow arpeggios lead to the animated Brazilian tune, or motive B (Ex. 7.1b), played three times. The tempo becomes somewhat slower and more languid, then moves back to a fast section of eighth notes that reach a high A6. After a short fermata on low E3, an ad libitum, sixteenth-note run ends on three measures of tied half notes to a quarter note high F#6. This cadenza is demanding and needs to be thoroughly learned.

---

[15] Butterworth, ibid., 121.

[16] Pollock, *Aaron Copland: The Life and Work of an Uncommon Man*, 425.

[17] Del Rosso, ibid., 30.

Section:	A		B	A^1
Starts at m.	1 Slowly and expressively		51	77–115, cadenza (115–120)
No. of mm.	50		26	44
Tonal Centers	C, D, B♭, G, C		E♭	C, E♭, D♭, C
Themes	Intro., A, B, A^1		B^1, trans.	A^2, B^2, (A^3)

CHART 7.1 Copland, *Concerto for Clarinet, String Orchestra, Harp, and Piano*: Structural analysis, first movement with cadenza, slowly and expressively.[18]

The second movement is a "free rondo form—stark, severe and jazzy."[19] (See Chart 7.2.) The twenty-nine measure introduction is rather fast, with strings, piano, and harp stating short, pithy sixteenth-note phrases. At measure 150, a perky A theme (modified C motive, fig. 7.1c) enters with staccatissimo quarter notes, repeated by the piano (mm. 152–154). A transition (mm. 176–186) contains the modified B motive played by clarinet and orchestra in 3/4 (mm. 179–185), and later in 2/4 by the clarinet and orchestra (mm. 324–335). This is followed by a modified A motive (mm. 187–222). Full *ff* orchestra and piano play the A^1 theme (mm. 228–238), and decrescendo before the A^2 theme, with a modified C motive (mm. 239–269), smartly played by the clarinet. In the B^1-transition section, mm. 269–296, the tempo moves a trifle faster, and the string accompaniment becomes more dissonant. The clarinet becomes strident in its highest register with accented E♭$_6$s, two *sf* G$_6$s, ending with accented A$_6$ and F♯$_6$ notes (mm. 274–294). With an eighth-note pickup, the tension is relaxed with a jazz-inspired C theme (C motive, mm. 297–322), accompanied by one stand of string basses playing in slap-bass style, the second time with all strings, and the third time with piano and harp.

During mm. 379–430, the development section has many changing meters and tempos. For the convenience of the clarinetist, Copland adds dotted bar lines to show the beginning of the next measures and their accented down beats.[20] At measure 441, the beginning of the A theme is played by the orchestra and later by the clarinet. The A^3 theme and modified C and A motives are played incisively with accents (mm. 465–473), leading to a transitional B^2 section of clarinet polychordal arpeggios with an ostinato piano bass line (mm. 474–480). The coda A^4 theme begins with constant quarter and eighth notes and accents by the piano. Three *ff*

---

18 Vance Shelby Jennings, "Selected Twentieth Century Clarinet Solo Literature: A Study in Interpretation and Performance" (Ed.D. diss., University of Oklahoma, 1972), 15; a detailed analysis is on 15–18.

19 Copland and Perlis, *Copland: Since 1943*, 93.

20 Pollack, "Copland, Aaron," *Grove Music Online*.

Section:	Intro. A-trans.	B	A¹	B¹-trans.	C
Starts at m.	121 Rather fast	187	228	255	297
No. of mm.	66	41	27	42	82
Tonal Centers	D♭	D, C	G♭, D♭	D♭	F, D♭, B♭, A
Themes	A, trans.	B, B¹	A¹, A²	B², trans.	C, C¹, C, trans., C¹, C, C¹, C

Section:	Development	A²	B²	Coda
Starts at m.	379	465	474	481–507
No. of mm.	86	9	7	27
Tonal Centers	A	C	E♭/C-poly-chordal	A, C
Themes	D, (A)	A³	trans.	A⁴

CHART 7.2 Copland, *Concerto for Clarinet, String Orchestra, Harp, and Piano*: Structural analysis, second movement, rather fast.

ascending eighth notes follow forcefully, playing G6 and A6, both held for 2½ measures, and three more ascending eighth notes to high G♯5 and E♯$_6$, the latter held for 2½ measures (mm. 490–500). Then, several *sff* clarinet eighth notes preceded by grace notes and orchestra play, broadening to *sff* whole notes on F♯5 and A♯5, a dotted quarter note F♯4 and a three beat F♭3, ending with a long glissando, or "smear" in "jazz lingo,"[21] to high D6. The glissando will be most effective if, after an upward run, it starts on B4, slowly raising the fingers and tightening the embouchure.

Copland's appropriation of some jazz idioms was a natural choice since he wrote the concerto for Goodman. There are also specific rhythmic features associated with jazz. For example, in measures 447–473, the clarinet ends nearly every phrase with four descending eighth notes, the last of which is given an accent mark, and the 2/2 meter orchestral accompaniment reinforces the syncopation provided by the accents. Copland inserts dotted lines before the last note of the repeated four note figures (mm. 443–455), apparently intending the note to represent the beginning of a new beat. Quarter notes are grouped into a beat of two eighth notes, followed by three eighth notes grouped into a single beat (Ex. 7.2).[22]

Goodman requested changes in four sections of the concerto. The first was the option of leaving out measures 112–114 because of the problem of endurance.

---

[21] Copland and Perlis, *Copland: Since 1943*, 93.

[22] This is shown in Kleppinger's notation of this passage. Stanley V. Kleppinger, "On the Influence of Jazz Rhythm in the Music of Aaron Copland," *American Music* 21, no. 1 (Spring 2003): 107–8, fig. 23.

EXAMPLE 7.2. Copland, *Concerto for Clarinet, String Orchestra, Harp, and Piano*, second movement, showing the rhythmic grouping of mm. 448–452

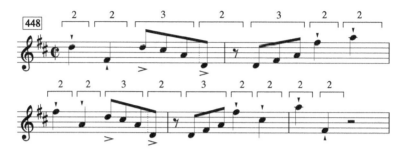

However, this phrase is retained in the clarinet part and a note in the published score states that the soloist may rest after measure 114, the harp playing in three measures while the strings sustain a chord.[23]

The second change was to lower the clarinet notes by a major third toward the end of the cadenza, from B$_6$ and C#7 to G5 and A5. The third change was to simplify the clarinet part that appears in a pencil sketch of measures 441–474 from the development to section B^2 of the second movement. One manuscript page of the coda written by Copland, in the Library of Congress, is marked at the top in pencil, "1st version—later revised—of Coda of Clarinet Concerto (too difficult for Benny Goodman)." The fourth change was to lower by a minor third clarinet notes in measures 503–504, from written A#$_6$ and C#$_7$ to F#$_6$ and A#$_6$.[24] A number of misprints in the clarinet part in the piano-clarinet reduction are noted by Stier.[25]

Copland's *Concerto for Clarinet, String Orchestra, Harp, and Piano* is a brilliant work, written with an intimate knowledge of the clarinet's range and timbre. The beauty of its first movement themes and the challenge and fun of the second movement make it a great pleasure to perform. The greatest hurdles are building stamina and endurance to play the cadenza. There are considerable technical issues in the orchestral string parts, and many sections need to be coordinated with the conductor and soloist when played with orchestra. It remains one of the most expressive and popular twentieth century works.

[23] Copland, Concerto for Clarinet (score), 9, note.

[24] Robert Adelson, "Too Difficult for Benny Goodman: The Original Version of the Copland Clarinet Concerto," *The Clarinet* 23, no. 1 (November–December 1995): 42–45; Copland and Perlis, *Copland: Since 1943*, 92; Copland and Perlis, *The Complete Copland*, 195.

[25] Charles Stier, "Editions and Misprints: Copland Concerto for Clarinet," *The Clarinet* 19, no. 2 (February–March 1992): 48–50.

8 Bernhard Henrik Crusell, *Concerto for Clarinet and Orchestra, op. 5*

Date of composition: 1815 or 1817

First edition/modern editions: Bernard Crusell, *Concerto pour la Clarinette: avec Accompagnement de Grand Orchestra, Oeuv. 5*, Leipzig: Peters, ca. 1818; Bernhard Henrik Crusell, *Concerto F minor for Clarinet and Orchestra, op. 5*, ed. Jost Michaels, Hamburg: H. Sikorski, 1962; Bernhard Henrik Crusell, *Konzert für Klarinette und Orchester op. 5 = Concerto for Clarinet and Orchestra op. 5*, ed. Pamela Weston, Vienna: Universal Edition, 1991 (piano and clarinet); Bernhard Henrik Crusell, *Konsert för Klarinett och Orkester F-moll = Concerto for Clarinet and Orchestra, F minor, op. 5, Monumenta Musicae Svecicae* 16, eds. Fabian Dahlström and Margareta Rörby, Stockholm: Edition Reimers, 1995 (orchestral score)

Dedicatee/first performer: Alexander I, Emperor of Russia;[1] Bernhard Crusell, clarinet

Date/place of first performance: 1815 or 1817; Stockholm, Sweden

Orchestral instrumentation: First and second violins, violas, cellos, basses, flute, two oboes, two bassoons, two horns (F and E♭), two F trumpets, and timpani in F and C

BERNHARD HENRIK CRUSELL (1775–1838) was a Swedish-Finnish clarinetist, composer, and translator. He composed a number of songs, cantatas, and settings for choir; three quartets for clarinet, violin, viola, and cello; three duos for two clarinets;

---

[1] Alexander I (1801–1825) annexed Finland to Russia as an autonomous principality in 1801–1809. The dedication is likely connected to easing tensions sought by French marshall Jean Baptiste Bernadotte. As Carl Johan XIV, Bernadotte succeeded to the Swedish throne in 1810 and entered an alliance with Russia in 1812. Fabian Dahlström, "Preface" to Bernhard Henrik Crusell, *Konsert för Klarinett och Orkester F-moll = Concerto for Clarinet and Orchestra, F minor, op. 5, Monumenta musicae svecicae*, 16, eds. Fabian Dahlström and Margareta Rörby (Stockholm: Edition Reimers, 1995), xvi.

Concertante for Clarinet, Bassoon, Horn, and Orchestra; Introduction et air suédois for Clarinet and Orchestra; and three concertos for clarinet and orchestra. He was well known for solo songs composed for texts from *Frithiof's Saga* by Swedish poet, Esaias Tegnér. His popular opera, *Lilla slavinnan (Small slave, 1824)*, was performed thirty-four times in fourteen years.

Crusell taught himself to play the clarinet. During the 1790s, he studied music theory with the composer, Georg Vogler. In 1798, he studied with the well-known soloist, Franz Tausch, in Berlin. He was a clarinetist with the Swedish Court Orchestra and the Royal Opera Orchestra, 1793–1833. He became an expert soloist, performing concertos and chamber music by Peter von Winter, Ludwig August Lebrun, Louis Emmanuel Jadin, Franz Krommer, Beethoven, Mozart, and others, as well as his own works.[2]

In Stockholm, he met the French minister, Jean-François de Bourgoing. In 1803, Bourgoing was recalled to Paris and invited Crusell to travel with him. During five months in Paris, he studied composition with Henri Montan Berton and François-Joseph Gossec. He met many outstanding musicians, including the violinists, Rodolphe Kreutzer and Pierre Baillot; composers, Luigi Cherubini and Étienne Méhul; and the clarinetist, Jean-Xavier Léfevre, with whom he may have informally studied.[3] Crusell was offered a first clarinet position in the Italian Theater but declined.[4]

In 1811, in Leipzig, Crusell contacted the publisher, Ambrosius Kühnel, to publish several of his clarinet works.[5] About that time, Crusell purchased an eleven-key B♭ boxwood clarinet with ivory ferrules from Heinrich Grenser in Dresden.[6] Several eleven-key clarinets by Grenser have survived,[7] thus, it is reasonable to assume that Crusell wrote all his concertos with an eleven-key instrument in mind, having the

---

[2] Fabian Dahlström, "Crusell, Bernhard Henrik," *Grove Music Online*; John Payne Spicknall, "The Solo Clarinet Works of Bernhard Henrik Crusell (1775–1838)" (D.M.A. diss., University of Maryland, 1974), 13–16; Dahlström, *Bernhard Henrik Crusell: Klarinettisten och hans Store Instrumentalverk* (Helsinfors, Finland: Svenska Litteratursällskapet i Finland, 1976), 93–96, 242–62; Dahlström, "Preface," xiv.

[3] Fabian Dahlström, "B. H. Crusell à Paris en 1803," *Finnish Music Quarterly*, Numéro Spècial en Français (1990): 55–57.

[4] Dahlström, "Preface," xiv.

[5] Pamela Weston, *Clarinet Virtuosi of the Past* (London: R. Hale, 1971), 71. In 1811, Crusell concertized in Berlin, Leipzig, and Dresden; in 1822 in Linköping, Ystad, Sweden, Berlin, Dresden, and Karlsbad; Dahlström, *Bernard Henrik Crusell*, 53, 56.

[6] This instrument has a corp de rechange left hand joint with nine keys, for playing as an A clarinet. It was given to Stockholm's Scenkonst Museet, Swedish Museum of Performing Arts (no. 43554) and photographed in Dahlström, *Bernhard Henrik Crusell*, 313, 315; Dahlström, "Preface," xxi. Crusell's B♭ clarinet with a mouthpiece, but without a corps de rechange, is photographed in Weston, *Clarinet Virtuosi of the Past*, pl. 6.

[7] Phillip T. Young, *4900 Historical Woodwind Instruments: An Inventory of 200 Makers in International Collections* (London: T. Bingham, 1993), 103–4, and additional examples in private collections.

following keys: register, A–B trill, A, G♯, f/c, E♭/B♭, C♯/G♯, B♭/F, A♭/E♭, F♯/C♯, and E/B.[8] Reviews of his playing praised his tone, especially his pianissimo. Most clarinetists played with the reed against the upper lip, the most common method at that time.[9] Dahlström suggests that after about 1810, Crusell played with the reed against the lower lip because it favors playing in a "cantabile manner."[10] Crusell may have played with a lower-lip embouchure, but there is no evidence this reed position encourages cantabile playing.

In Stockholm, Crusell may have played this concerto in a March 1815 concert, since it was praised in a newspaper report as, "very beautiful—especially the Adagio with echoes," matching the second movement echoes of the op. 5 concerto.[11] Crusell mentioned his *Concerto in F minor* in an 1817 letter to Kühnel's successor, Carl Friedrich Peters in Leipzig,[12] who published it as op. 5 about 1818.[13] It is one of the few nineteenth century concertos written in F minor, along with Carl Maria von Weber's *Concerto no. 1* (1811) and Louis Spohr's *Concerto no. 3* (1821).[14] Michaels noted that the dark tone of Crusell's *Concerto op. 5* was due to its soloistic use of the clarinet's low register and the F minor tonality; and at this time, expressive use of the low register was a new technique in clarinet concertos.[15]

An 1818 review of the *Concerto for Clarinet* in the *Allgemeine musikalische Zeitung* praises Crusell and his work:

> For a number of years Mr. C., first chamber musician and clarinetist of the King of Sweden, has earned a distinguished reputation for himself through his compositions for his instrument, not only in Germany but wherever that

---

[8] Heinrich Grenser eleven-key clarinet owned by Bernhard Crusell, Scenkonst Museet, Swedish Museum of Performing Arts, N.43554. [Online] Available: http://instrument.musikverket.se/samlingar/detalj.php?l=sv&iid=288&v=2009-08-25%2014:19:28&str=. [September 17, 2015]. Eric Hoeprich used his copy of Crusell's eleven-key Grenser clarinet in a fine recording of the three Crusell concertos with the Kölner Akademie and Michael Alexander Willens, conductor, Ars Produktion, 2006.

[9] See the evidence from twenty-five German language instructional sources in Albert R. Rice, "The Development of the Clarinet as Depicted in Austro-German Instruction Sources, 1732–1892," in *Tradition und Innovation im Holzblasinstrumentenbau des 19. Jahrhunderts*, ed. S. Werr, 84–85, Augsburg: Wissner, 2012.

[10] Dahlström, "Crusell, Bernhard Henrik," *Grove Music Online*.

[11] "[S]ehr schön–besonders das Adagio mit Eccho" in "Nachrichten," *Allgemeine musikalische Zeitung* 17, no. 27 (July 5, 1815): 451.

[12] As "mein neuster grand Concerto pour la Clarinette, in F-moll," April 25, 1817, letter, Crusell to Peters. Dahlström, *Bernhard Henrik Crusell*, 240–41; Dahlström, "Preface," xvi.

[13] The dating is based on the plate number 1335; see Otto Erich Deutsch, *Musikverlager's Nummern: eine Auswahl von 40 datierten Listen, 1710–1900* (Berlin: Merseburger, 1961), 14.

[14] Albert R. Rice, *The Clarinet in the Classical Period* (New York: Oxford University Press, 2003), 167; Spicknall, "The Solo Clarinet Works of Bernhard Henrik Crusell," 151.

[15] Jost Michaels, "Preface" to Bernhard Henrik Crusell, *Concerto F minor for Clarinet and Orchestra, op. 5* (Hamburg: H. Sikorski, 1962), 2.

instrument is treated with true artistry and where there is a love for substantial instrumental compositions. All who have heard Mr. C. in person also praise him as one of the foremost virtuosos. This work is more likely to increase that reputation than to detract from it, and to confirm that judgment, since attentive perusal of the principal part shows Mr. C.'s knowledge of the instrument in all its essential strengths, and how he turns them to advantage without, however, landing in the peculiarities of other instruments, or in an excessive accumulation of difficulties in execution.[16]

The F minor concerto is written in an early Romantic or nineteenth century style with three movements. Harmonically, it is fairly conservative, modulating to other minor keys, and using the parallel major for the last movement. Diminished chords appear frequently, including Neapolitan and German sixth chords.[17] Technically, it is demanding to play on a modern or eleven-key clarinet, and of the three Crusell clarinet concertos, is arguably the finest and most dramatic.[18]

The first movement is in sonata-allegro form, Allegro, quarter note = 108.[19] It has a long orchestral exposition including several themes played by the strings, individual woodwinds, and brasses. (See Chart 8.1.) Crusell unusually uses the notes of the first four measures as a motive or basic musical idea that is repeated and transformed throughout.[20] The opening motive, played by the orchestral strings, is used later in an elaborate orchestral exposition (mm. 26–27); by strings and woodwinds (mm. 44–45); an augmented version (mm. 48–60); the clarinet's principal exposition motive (mm. 61–62); the continuation of the clarinet motive (mm. 70–73); the clarinet's subordinate motive (mm. 99–102); the second episode (mm. 224–227); and the recapitulation (m. 285).[21] This movement flows with eight attractive themes and shows an intimate understanding of the clarinet's and orchestral instruments' color and techniques.

A fiery A^1 theme played by the clarinet at measure 61 (**C** in the Sikorski edition) features dramatic leaps of two octaves and a sixth (Ex. 8.1). The development's

---

[16] *Allgemeine musikalische Zeitung* 20, no. 31 (August 5, 1818): 560–61, trans. Eric Hoeprich in *The Clarinet* (New Haven, CT: Yale University Press, 2008), 147; the full review is translated and cited in German by Spicknall, "The Solo Clarinet Works of Bernhard Henrik Crusell," 148–51.

[17] Spicknall, ibid., 165–66.

[18] Hoeprich, *The Clarinet*, 147; Hoeprich notes to Bernhard Crusell, *Klarinettenkonzerte*, Ars Produktion, 2006, CD.

[19] Suggested by the author.

[20] Later composers who used this cyclic technique include Berlioz, Schubert, and Schumann. "Cyclic Form," *The Harvard Dictionary of Music*, 4th ed., ed. Don Michael Randall (Cambridge, MA: Belknap Press, 2003), 231.

[21] Spicknall, "The Solo Clarinet Works of Bernhard Henrik Crusell," 155–61; Dahlström, *Bernhard Henrik Crusell*, 121–27.

EXAMPLE 8.1. Crusell, *Concerto for Clarinet and Orchestra, op. 5*, first movement, Allegro, mm. 61–68.

Section:	Orchestral exposition	Solo exposition	1st episode
Starts at m.	1 Allegro	61 (**C**)	138 (**G**)
No. of mm.	60	77	38
Tonalities	f, A♭, D♭, f	f, f, a♭, A♭	A♭, b, E♭, A♭
Themes	A, B, A¹, C, A², D	A, A¹, E, A², F	C

Section:	Development		2nd episode	Recapitulation	Conclusion
Starts at m.	176 (**I**)		224 (**K**)	246 (**L**)	318 (**P**)–329
No. of mm.	48		22	72	12
Tonalities	A♭, c, c		c, G	f, D♭, D♭, F, F	F
Themes	G, H		A, B	A, A¹, A², A³, A⁴	A¹

CHART 8.1 Crusell, *Concerto for Clarinet and Orchestra, op. 5*: Structural analysis, first movement, Allegro

G theme at **I** (m. 176) is lyrical and relaxed, and later elaborated with arpeggios, chromatic scales, triplets, and wide leaps (mm. 188–223). In the recapitulation, a gradual crescendo with several accents leads to a forceful clarinet entrance at **L** (m. 246), modulating to D♭ major and F major, where the A³ theme plays at **N** (m. 284). A short and stylistically appropriate cadenza, added by Michaels, appears at measure 317 and ends on a high G6, at **P** (m. 318). The orchestral conclusion is beautifully written, using martial and lyrical motives for a natural and convincing ending.[22]

---

[22] Spicknall, ibid., 217–19, further analysis is on 152–67; Dahlström, *Bernhard Henrik Crusell*, 121–22.

Section:	A	B	A¹
Starts at m.	1 Andante pastorale	26 (10 mm. after **A**)	38 (**B**)–64
No. of mm.	25	12	27
Tonalities	D♭, b♭, f, D♭	D♭, A♭, E, c♯	D♭
Themes	A, B, C	D, B¹	A¹, C¹, A²

CHART 8.2 Crusell, *Concerto for Clarinet and Orchestra, op. 5*: Structural analysis, second movement, Andante pastorale.

The second movement, Andante pastorale, dotted quarter note = 50,[23] is in ternary form, lightly scored for clarinet and strings. (See Chart 8.2.) It differs from the first movement in its tonality, meter, mood, and sonority.[24] A calm *p* A theme sensitively played in the clarion register (mm. 2–9) is followed by *mf* clarinet G major and F major arpeggios from G3 to D6 and F3 to C6, incorporated into the B theme (mm. 10–17). Crusell's careful and delicate writing reveals his understanding of the clarinet's overtones and fingerings. In measures 31–33, he writes an upward skip from G♭5 to E♭6 played on an eleven-key clarinet with the A♭/E♭ key and a firmer embouchure; on a Boehm-system clarinet by half-holing the first finger hole of the left hand.[25] After a short cadenza, the beautiful A¹ theme plays in the clarino register (mm. 38–45). The C¹ theme follows played *f* in the chalumeau register, and an echo *ppp* phrase in the same register (mm. 46–49). The orchestra plays an expressive four measure phrase at **C** (m. 50), theme A², answered by a *ppp* clarinet echo of the phrase in the chalumeau and clarion registers. The movement ends with alternating orchestral and clarinet phrases played *ppp*.

The third movement, Rondo, Allegretto, quarter note = 96,[26] has a rondo form and coda. (See Chart 8.3.) A relaxed tempo begins with a pickup of two sixteenth notes to a playful A theme in the clarion register (mm. 1–20). Chromatic scales, fast arpeggios, staccato, staccato under a slur, and several leaps are liberally written between the themes. The B theme at measure 60 (nine measures after **B**) is lyrical but liberally sprinkled with sixteenth notes, wide eighth note leaps, arpeggios, and triplet sixteenth notes. The A¹ theme begins at measure 119 (sixteen measures before **F**) and at **F** there is a fermata requiring a short cadenza or Eingang. The solo continues

---

[23] Suggested by the author.

[24] Michaels suggests that a greater contrast is achieved when the string instruments play with mutes. Michaels, "Preface" to Bernhard Henrik Crusell, *Concerto in F minor for Clarinet and Orchestra, op. 5*.

[25] Spicknall, "The Solo Clarinet Works of Bernhard Henrik Crusell," 204–5.

[26] Suggested by the author.

Section:	A	B	A¹	C
Starts at m.	1 Allegretto	60 (9 mm. after **B**)	119	169 (**H**)
No. of mm.	59	59	50	30
Tonalities	f	A♭	f	A♭
Themes	A	B	A¹	C

Section:	B¹	A²	A³	Coda
Starts at m.	199 (Maggiore)	220 (1 m. before **K**)	251 (1 m. before **M**)	271 (più vivo)–285
No. of mm.	21	31	20	15
Tonalities	F	F, B♭, d	F	F
Themes	B¹	A²	A³	figuration

CHART 8.3 Crusell, *Concerto for Clarinet and Orchestra, op. 5*: Structural analysis, third movement, Rondo, Allegretto.

for six measures when the orchestra plays a polonaise-style double-dotted rhythm, seven measures after **F** (m. 141). The clarinet returns with a forceful chromatic scale at **G** (m. 151), developing the A¹ theme. At **H** (m. 169), A♭ major is established with the C theme, and the clarinet answers with wide leaps and arpeggios (mm. 171, 175). At measure 199 in the major tonal section (Maggiore), the clarinet plays the B¹ theme in F major followed by a short orchestral episode. A light A² theme features triplet sixteenth notes and offbeat accents at measure 220 (one measure before **K**). The A³ theme at measure 251 (one measure before **M**) emerges with many sixteenth note triplets. A faster più vivo coda with arpeggios, triplets, and runs to high G6, provides a thrilling ending.

An 1818 *Allgemeine musikalische Zeitung* reviewer mentioned that this movement is written "more or less after the type of finales in Rode's violin concertos."[27] Throughout, Crusell adroitly imitates several solo clarinet phrases with the orchestral flute, oboe, and bassoon. Many arpeggios, chromatic scales, and short trills push the solo clarinet's technique to the level of Weber's concertos, using a range from E3 to G6. Although the solo part is demanding, it is not overtly virtuosic. Crusell's themes are spun out with poignant melodies and dramatic contrasts. The entire chalumeau register is used in solo passages, arpeggios, chromatic scales with a distinctive contrast to the clarion register solos. Some of the fluent sixteenth-note runs resemble

---

27 "[U]ngefähr nach Art der Finalen Rode's in seinen Violinconcerten," "Nachrichten," *Allgemeine musikalische Zeitung* 20, no. 31 (August 5, 1818): 560.

runs in Weber's works but all the themes are uniquely Crusell's. The clarinet writing is self-assured with large leaps, chromatic scales, long lyrical phrases, and staccato passages. Crusell also achieves a careful balance between the orchestra and soloist by reducing the number of orchestral instruments when the clarinet plays in the chalumeau register.[28]

Nineteenth century clarinet articulation offered several options for the player. According to Fröhlich (1812–1813), with reed above articulation, the clarinetist could use tongued or chest articulation, both techniques providing a variety of detached sounds. Chest articulation used the syllable "ha," and facilitated rapid passages and leaps of large intervals. According to Vanderhagen (1785), tongued articulation for notes not marked used voiced consonants, such as the letter "d (du)." Notes indicated with short dots used unvoiced consonants, such as the letter "t (tu)." When slurring notes, the first of each pair is given more emphasis. Notes indicated with a wedge use a short tongue stroke. If articulation is not indicated for a triplet, the first two notes are slurred, and the next is tongued with voiced consonants using the letter "d." Reed below articulation used the tongue, lips, and throat. For tonguing, Müller (1821) suggested using "ti" for tongued notes and "di" for the wedge or shortest strokes.[29]

The scoring of this concerto is carefully done, with a selection of timbres that always suits the musical gestures. While the brass instruments are generally limited to dotted rhythms, the woodwinds play an active role in the melodic dialogs, and occasionally have their own melodies.[30] In Sweden and Finland, Crusell's concertos and vocal works continued to be performed during the nineteenth century, and he is revered in both countries.[31] Crusell's *Concerto, op. 5*, is virtuosic and lyrical, using all the resources of the clarinet with a colorful and thoughtful orchestration. It is an accomplished and rewarding concerto from the early nineteenth century.

---

[28] Spicknall, ibid., 206.

[29] See Ingrid Pearson, "Playing Historical Clarinets," in Colin Lawson, *The Early Clarinet: A Practical Guide* (Cambridge: Cambridge University Press, 2000), 47–51.

[30] Spicknall, "The Solo Clarinet Works of Bernhard Henrik Crusell," 166–67.

[31] Dahlström, "Preface," xvii–xviii.

9 Claude Debussy, *Première Rhapsodie for Clarinet and Piano*

Dates of composition: December 1909–January 1910 (clarinet and piano); 1911 (orchestral version)

First edition/other editions: Claude Debussy, *Première Rhapsodie pour Clarinette et Piano*, Paris: Durand, 1910; Paris: Durand, 1911 (orchestral score); Claude Debussy, *Petite pièce and Première Rhapsodie: Works for Clarinet in B-flat and Piano*, ed. Reiner Zimmermann, Leipzig: Peters, 1971; Claude Debussy, *Première Rhapsodie und Petite Pièce für Klarinette und Klavier*, corrected edition, ed. Ernst-Günter Heinemann and Klaus Schilde, Munich: G. Henle Verlag, 2004

Dedicatee/first performers: Prospère Mimart; Prospère Mimart, clarinet, Marie-Georges Krieger, piano

Date/place of first performance: January 16, 1911; Paris, Salle Gaveau[1]

Orchestral instrumentation: Three flutes, two oboes, English horn, two B♭ clarinets, three bassoons, four F horns, two C trumpets, triangle, cymbal, two harps, solo violin, first and second violins, solo viola, violas, cellos, and basses

DEBUSSY'S *Première Rhapsodie* (*First Rhapsody*) is one of the most beautiful and challenging clarinet solos of the twentieth century. This relatively short work is highly effective in its clarinet-piano version and stunning in its version for clarinet and orchestra.

During the early twentieth century, Claude Debussy (1862–1918) was known as an experimental and avant-garde composer who wrote in an impressionistic style.

---

[1] Reiner Zimmermann, "Concluding Remarks," in Claude Debussy, *Petite pièce and Première Rhapsodie: Works for Clarinet in B-flat and Piano* (Leipzig: Peters, 1976), 50.

He wrote in most genres: orchestral, ballet, vocal or instrumental soloist and orchestra, chamber, solo piano, piano four hands or two pianos, voice and piano, and vocal works.[2] After the 1909 retirement of a music instructor at the Paris Conservatory, the director, Gabriel Fauré (1845–1924), unexpectedly appointed Debussy to this position. Debussy and Fauré had never been friends and Debussy's revolutionary attitudes and concepts seemed in opposition to the traditionally conservative Paris Conservatory. Although Debussy was willing to serve, he criticized the Conservatory's system of public competitions as an unfair evaluation of a student's talent. Despite this, one of his duties was to adjudicate the competitions and to serve as a juror during the 1909 examinations for woodwind instruments.[3] Clearly, Debussy was impressed with Conservatory students. In a letter to the publisher, Jacques Durand, he wrote, "I've just been sitting on the jury for the woodwind competitions…and I can give you good news of the high standards of the flutes, oboes, and clarinets; as for the bassoons, they're admirable.…"[4]

The next year, Debussy agreed to compose two pieces for the clarinet competition. One work was used on the sight-reading test; the other was to be prepared in advance. The first piece was published in 1910 as *Petite Pièce pour Clarinette et Piano.*[5] The second was the *Première Rhapsodie*, dedicated to the accomplished soloist and clarinet professor at the Conservatory, Prospère Mimart (1859–1928).[6] Plans to program this work at a new music series were made quickly. Fauré wrote to Debussy in early May 1910, "As far as the piece for clarinet of which Mimart was so proud and delighted, it will be programmed, if you want, for the next season."[7] July 1910, both works were performed in the examinations. Debussy heard the *Première Rhapsodie* eleven times and wrote to his publisher, Durand, "The clarinet competition [the previous day] went extremely well and, to judge by the expressions on the faces of my colleagues, the *Rhapsodie* was a success.… [O]ne of the candidates, [Maurice] Vandercruyssen, played it by heart and very musically. The rest were straightforward and nondescript."[8] Vandercruyssen and Gustave Hery shared first

---

[2] François Lesure and Roy Howat, "Claude Debussy," *Grove Music Online.*

[3] Dennis Nygren, "The Music for Accompanied Clarinet Solo of Claude Debussy: An Historical and Analytical Study of the *Première Rhapsodie* and *Petite Pièce*," (D.M. diss., Northwestern University, 1982), 1–2.

[4] François Lesure, ed. and trans. Roger Nichols, *Debussy Letters* (Cambridge, MA: Harvard University Press, 1987), 205.

[5] Originally entitled, "Morceau à déchiffrer pour le concours de clarinette de 1910"; James R. Briscoe, *Claude Debussy: A Guide to Research* (New York: Garland Publishing, 1990), 44.

[6] François Lesure, *Catalogue de L'oeuvre de Claude Debussy* (Geneva: Minkoff, 1977), 120.

[7] "Quant au morceau de clarinette dont Mimart est si fier et si heureux ce serait si vous le vouliez bien, pour la saison prochaine." François Lesure, "Deux Lettres de Gabriel Fauré à C. Debussy (1910–1917)" in "Claude Debussy (1862–1962) Textes et Documents Inédites," *Revue de Musicologie* 48 (July–December 1962): 75.

[8] Lesure and Nichols, ibid., 222.

FIGURE 9.1. Prospère Mimart at the piano, with his students at the Paris Conservatory. Mimart at the piano accompanying a student as other students look on, including Daniel Bonade, fifth from the right.

prize.[9] There is a photograph (Fig. 9.1) of Mimart at the piano accompanying a student as other students look on, including Daniel Bonade, fifth from the right.[10]

During 1911, Debussy orchestrated the *Première Rhapsodie.* A performance that year was given in Russia, but it is unknown if the piano or orchestral version was used. Debussy wrote to Durand that the reaction was not entirely positive. In December 1913, Debussy was invited by the Russian conductor, Serge Koussevitsky, to conduct two festivals of his works in Moscow and St. Petersburg. The *Première Rhapsodie* was not performed to Debussy's satisfaction. The Paris performance of the orchestrated *Rhapsodie*, with Gaston Hamelin, soloist, did not occur until May 3, 1919, after Debussy's death.[11] Hamelin later made the first recording of the *Rhapsodie* during the 1920s.[12]

Première Rhapsodie is in ternary form with an introduction and coda. Tonality is often implied. The music is constructed around four motives. Debussy uses these

[9] Philippe Cuper and Jean-Marie Paul, "The Paris Conservatoire Supérieur: 'Solo de Concours' and Prize Winners from the Origins to the Present Day," *The Clarinet* 15, no. 3 (May–June 1988): 44.

[10] The photograph is in Cuper and Paul, ibid., 40. Permission to reproduce it was given by James Gillespie, editor of *The Clarinet.*

[11] Nygren, ibid., 5–7; Lesure, ibid., 120.

[12] On *The French Clarinet School—Revisited*, Grenadilla RGP-1008, CD; Richard Gilbert, *The Clarinetists' Discography III* (Harrington Park, NJ: RGP Productions, 1991), 37, 268.

motives (short musical ideas) to construct phrases rather than longer themes.[13] Each of the four motives uses one of four small cells that continually change and expand throughout the composition.[14] The four cells consist of (1) four notes of a falling chromatic figure (mm. 1–2); (2) a quasi-pentatonic scale of three notes (m. 2); (3) a returning figure of three notes (m. 9); and (4) a minor 3rd and its inversion, a major 6th, in three notes (m. 21, Ex. 9.1).[15] The four motives move within a narrow range and are generally short and rhythmically precise.[16]

EXAMPLE 9.1. Debussy, *Première Rhapsodie for Clarinet and Piano.* Four cells used throughout.

[13] Edward Lockspeiser, *Debussy: His Life and Mind, Vol. II 1902–1918* (New York: Macmillan Co., 1962), 244.

[14] Raymond Roy Park, "The Later Style of Claude Debussy" (Ph.D. diss., University of Michigan, 1967), 33.

[15] Nygren, ibid., 15–16.

[16] Harry Gee, *Clarinet Solos de Concours, 1897–1980: An Annotated Bibliography* (Bloomington: Indiana University Press, 1981), 32.

Debussy included metronome marks in his works only after completing *La Mer* in 1905, but intended them as general guides, not to be strictly observed throughout.[17] In *Première Rhapsodie*, metronome numbers are used only at the introduction and at no. 5. Debussy uses several changes in meter, tempo, acceleration, and deceleration that affect the musical motives and the pacing of material.[18] On the appearance and reappearance of each motive, he changes register, accompaniment, sonority, and emotional intensity.

A dreamily slow, eight measure introduction features an expressive clarinet line with delicate dynamic swells from *p* to *pp*. A *pp* piano two measure introduction with triplets in the right hand and syncopated eighth notes in the left, sets the mood for the clarinet entrance. The A motive (quarter note = 50) at no. 1 (Henle edition, m. 11) is a sweet and penetrating (doux et pénétrant) melody. At no. 3 (m. 40), the A[1] motive is an octave higher, shortened to five measures, and accompanied by thirty-second note arpeggios on the first beat, sounding similar to a harp glissando.[19]

The C motive at no. 5 (m. 58, quarter note = 72), marked moderately animated (Modérément animé), is a yearning melody in the clarinet's clarion register, accompanied by quarter and eighth notes. The sweet and expressive (doux et expressif) B[1] motive (mm. 76–83) is a major second higher than the earlier B motive (mm. 21–24), and a particularly beautiful section. At no. 6 (Modérément animé, mm. 84–91), the C[1] motive is a witty alternation between two groups of clarinet staccato sixteenth notes, answered by the piano's five sixteenth notes. A playful and faster D motive (mm. 96–131, Scherzando), played staccato in the clarinet's chalumeau register, has sustained piano chords changing texture and density when played two octaves higher at no. 7 (m. 112). After a caesura, five measures of the B[2] motive (mm. 124–128) are very softly played in the left hand's tenor register marked, a little more prominent (en peu en dehors). At no. 8 (mm. 132–140), a particularly beautiful moment occurs when the clarinet continues the B[2] motive with charm (avec charme), playing a melody doubled by the left hand an octave below the clarinet.

After gradually slowing (Cédez), the A[1] section, at no. 9 (Tempo I, mm. 152–157), the dreamily slow A[2] motive plays, this time accompanied in the left hand with sextuplets, similar to a tremolo. At no. 10, a brilliant transitional section marked animated

[17] James R. Briscoe, "Debussy and Orchestral Performance," in *Debussy in Performance*, ed. James R. Briscoe (New Haven, CT: Yale University Press, 1999), 83–84.

[18] Richard S. Parks, "Music's Inner Dance: Form, Pacing and Complexity in Debussy's Music," in *The Cambridge Companion to Debussy*, ed. Simon Trezise (New York: Cambridge University Press, 2003), 219–25.

[19] Guy Dangain, "Debussy et la Rhapsodie pour Clarinette," *Journal d'Informations Selmer Paris*, no. 15 (December 2003): supplément, 2. [Online] Available: http://www.selmer.fr/media/action/partitions/Debussy_site.pdf. [September 18, 2015]. In Debussy's orchestration, first and second harps play glissandos during mm. 40–44 as part of the accompaniment.

Section:	Introduction	A	B	A¹	Coda
Starts at m.	1 Rêveusement lent	9 (two mm. before no. 1)	58 (no. 5)	152 (no. 9) Tempo 1	197 Un peu retenu–206
No. of mm.	8	49	94	45	10
Implied Tonalities	Chr.	Gb, Ab, chr., Gb, chr.	A, chr., Ab, chr.	Gb, chr., f, Gb, chr.	G Neapolitan, Gb
Motives	intro.	A, B, trans., A¹, trans.	C, trans., B¹, C¹, trans., D, B²	A², B³, trans., D¹	coda

CHART 9.1 Debussy, *Première Rhapsodie for Clarinet and Piano*: Structural analysis.

(animé, m. 163) features quarter note trills, staccato downward sixteenth notes, thirty-second notes upward and downward, quick alternations between *f* and *p*, and dissonant piano quarter and half notes. A chromatic run of sixteenth note triplets arrives at a very animated eighth-note D¹ motive in the clarion register (plus animé, Scherzando, m. 169) with many crescendos and subito *pp* passages, accompanied by accented quarter, eighth, and sixteenth notes. The clarinet has mid-register sextuplets and chromatic runs with an accented chromatic accompaniment.[20] The coda (mm. 197–206) surprises with its held back (un peu retenu) slow rhythmic pulse, before a brilliant scale and high sustained Eb6, ending with a chord.[21]

Debussy's colorful orchestration is new and imaginative, not a simple transcription of the clarinet-piano version.[22] Some of the instruments are used sparingly for their color, effect, or sound quality, such as the trumpets scored in just twenty-eight measures. The woodwinds, particularly the oboe, English horn, and bassoon play melodic material, sometimes contrasting or exchanging these lines with the solo clarinet. The string instruments vary the sound and texture with accompanying repeated figures, sustained harmonies, arpeggios, figurations, and rhythmic punctuation, often using pizzicato. They produce a number of timbres, ornaments, and articulations by using mutes, artificial harmonics, bowing over the fingerboard, bowed and fingered tremolo, portamento, numerous trills, grace notes, and different resolu-

---

[20] Parks, ibid., 220–21; John Graulty, "Debussy for Clarinet Solo: The Music and the Conservatoire Context," ClarinetFest 2001 Archives.

[21] An interesting and detailed study of *Première Rhapsodie* emphasizing the interactions, chromatic alterations, and closed-open phrasing appears in Eric Mandat and Boja Kraguli, "Performance Analysis: Debussy's *Première Rhapsodie*—Motivic Permutations and Interactions," *The Clarinet* 40, no. 4 (September 2013): 42–46.

[22] Zimmermann, ibid., 50.

tions of chords by simultaneous bowing and pizzicato in the strings. The two harps perform single line melodies, arpeggio passages, harmonic support, and harmonics. The horns have solos, play harmonic and contrapuntal materials, and use muted and stopped sounds. The two percussion parts heighten rhythms and increase crescendo effects.[23]

Debussy does not use all the orchestral instruments together but prefers to select a few instruments at a time. He frequently adds orchestral timbre to the piano score, including English horn, bassoon, and pizzicato strings (mm. 86–89), counterpoint with oboes and horns (mm. 14–17), ornamentation by the strings (mm. 169–172), altered harmony, cross rhythms, and increased rhythmic activity.[24] Debussy rewrote some passages and changed notes in the solo clarinet part from the autograph clarinet-piano and orchestral manuscripts to the corresponding scores published by Durand in 1910 and 1911. These changes are detailed by Nygren and Heinemann.[25] Changes to the piano part and to the parts in the orchestral score are noted by Nygren.[26]

The *Première Rhapsodie* is outstanding among all the Paris Conservatory solos de concours. It requires a mastery of breath control and technique, and a sensitivity to and understanding of its form and construction. It is a masterpiece of the twentieth-century clarinet repertory.

[23] Nygren, ibid., 106–8; Zimmermann, ibid., 50.

[24] Nygren, ibid., 109–14.

[25] Nygren, ibid., 130–33; Nygren, "Debussy's Works for Clarinet—Part I," *The Clarinet* 12, no. 1 (Fall, 1984): 40–42; Nygren, "Debussy's Works for Clarinet—Part II," *The Clarinet* 12, no. 2 (Winter, 1985): 19–21; Heinemann, "Comments," Debussy, *Première Rhapsodie and Petite Pièce* (Munich: G. Henle, 2004), 18–20; Dangain, ibid., III–IV. Clarinetist François Petit recorded Debussy's *Première Rhapsodie* playing the manuscript version for clarinet and piano with Carole Carniel on the recording "Dans le Salon d'Emma Bardac," Ligia, CD, 2010.

[26] Nygren, "Debussy's Works for Clarinet—Part II," 21; Nygren, "The Music for Accompanied Clarinet," 142–44.

10 Gerald Finzi, *Five Bagatelles for Clarinet and Piano, op. 23*

Date of composition: 1938–1943

First edition: Gerald Finzi, *Five Bagatelles for Clarinet and Piano*, London: Boosey & Hawkes, 1945

Dedicatee/first performers: Not indicated; Pauline Juler, clarinet, Howard Ferguson, piano (*Four Bagatelles* without the last movement); Pauline Juler, clarinet, Howard Ferguson, piano (*Five Bagatelles*)

Dates/places of first performances: January 15, 1943; London, National Gallery (*Four Bagatelles*); February 1944; London, National Gallery Concerts (*Five Bagatelles*)[1]

GERALD FINZI (1901–1956) was an English composer who studied music with Ernest Farrar (1915–1916), Edward Bairstow (1917–1922), and counterpoint with R. O. Morris (1925). After moving to London in 1925, he became friends with several musicians including Arthur Bliss, Howard Ferguson, Robin Milford, and Edmund Rubbra, and he met Gustav Holst and Ralph Vaughan Williams. He taught at the Royal Academy of Music (RAM), 1930–1933. In 1933, he married the artist Joyce Black, and in 1935 they moved to Aldbourne in Wiltshire. In 1937, the Finzis found a sixteen-acre site on the Hampshire hills at Ashmansworth, and built a house where they worked. Finzi worked in London at the Ministry of War Transport, 1941–1945. In 1951, he was diagnosed with Hodgkin's Lymphoma. In 1956, he brought Ralph

---

[1] Five clarinet pieces by Gerald Finzi performed by Pauline Juler are mentioned in "Music in the Making: Notes and News about Composers Associated with Boosey & Hawkes," *Tempo* 6 (February 1944): 11.

Vaughn Williams and his family to the church at Chosen Hill, between Cheltenham and Gloucester, where Finzi caught chicken pox from a child, and died shortly after.[2]

Finzi's works include songs with piano, choral works with orchestra, orchestral works, chamber music, arrangements and editions of earlier English composers' works, and incidental music for *Love's Labour's Lost* (1946) for a radio broadcast. Finzi's clarinet music includes a concerto for clarinet and string orchestra (1949) written for Frederick Thurston (1901–1953).[3]

The *Five Bagatelles for Clarinet and Piano, op. 23*,[4] was originally completed in 1943 as a four movement piece for the clarinetist, Pauline Juler.[5] Between December 1941 and May 1942, Finzi sent four of the bagatelles to Howard Ferguson to check for errors, and debate the meanings of movement names.[6] Finzi had some reservations about the first movement, writing to Ferguson, "It has turned out to be rather larger in scale, & more difficult, than the others & I only hope that it's not outside the 'Bagatelle' radius."[7] Leslie Boosey initially wanted to publish the pieces separately but Finzi insisted they be published together, "I'm not accepting unless they agree to do them together," he told William Busch after Juler and Finzi played them for Boosey. After Finzi agreed to add a finale, which was suggested by several people, Boosey agreed to publish the work.[8] On January 17, 1943, Finzi wrote of his surprise to find favorable reviews of the first performance. He wrote to Ferguson, "Well, you know how grateful I am for the good send-off you've given them, and though I've made it clear enough that they are only trifles, the performance has been one of the few things that I've been able to look forward whilst this interminable dreary waste land has to be crossed."[9]

---

[2] Diana McVeigh, "Finzi, Gerald," *Grove Music Online*; Diana McVeigh, *Gerald Finzi: His Life and Music* (Woodbridge: Boydell Press, 2005), 249–50.

[3] Stephen Banfield, *Gerald Finzi: An English Composer* (London: Faber and Faber, 1998), 542–50; Pamela Weston, *Yesterday's Clarinetists: A Sequel* (Haverhill: Panda Group, 2002), 171.

[4] Opus numbers were added to Finzi's works by John C. Dressler in *Gerald Finzi: A Bio-Bibliography* (Westport, Connecticut: Greenwood Press, 1997), 173–74; opus numbers are used in Boosey & Hawkes' list of Finzi's complete works. [Online] Available: http://www.boosey.com/cr/catalogue/ps/powersearch_results.asp?search=Finzi. [October 9, 2015].

[5] Pauline Juler was an English clarinetist who studied with Charles Draper, active during the 1930s and 1940s, playing Howard Ferguson's *Four Short Pieces for Clarinet and Piano* in 1937. In September 1948, Juler married the cellist, Bernard Richards, and retired from playing. Pamela Weston, *Clarinet Virtuosi of the Past* (London: Robert Hale, 1971), 271; Ferguson to Finzi, January 3, 1937; Ferguson to Finzi, September 4, 1948, Howard Ferguson and Michael Hurd, eds., *Letters of Gerald Finzi and Howard Ferguson* (Woodbridge: The Boydell Press, 2001), 141, 257–58.

[6] Finzi to Ferguson, Ferguson and Hurd, ibid., 229–30.

[7] Finzi to Ferguson, June 14, 1942, ibid., 229.

[8] Finzi to Busch, Letter 19430122, Banfield, ibid., 299–300.

[9] Finzi to Ferguson, January 17, 1943, Ferguson and Hurd, ibid., 234.

Trifles indeed! The first edition of the *Five Bagatelles* issued in July 1945 sold out within a year and became a popular recital and examination piece.[10] The movements are Prelude, Romance, Carol, Forlana, and Fughetta. The Carol, begun as a song, and the Romance, were probably completed in June 1941; a third, probably the Forlana, was finished in July; and the Prelude was probably finished in January 1942.[11] Only the Fughetta, written during summer 1943, was new.[12] It is an accomplished and fluent work, "top-drawer Finzi."[13]

Denman describes the effect of the opening as church bells on a Sunday morning that often sound like a scale.[14] The *Times* reviewer of the first performance approved of the Prelude, stating it, "shows that a diatonic scale may still be used as the basis of a vigorous theme."[15] Lockspieser's 1946 music review of the *Five Bagatelles* in *Music & Letters* is complimentary, but also critical:

> It is difficult not to dissociate these pieces from the style of Vaughn Williams and Delius, at any rate the two slow movements and the "Forlana." They contain beautiful passages obviously written with feeling and sincerity, but Mr. Finzi's re-creation of this now well-known lyrical style is really a reproduction: He does not make the style live again in a new and refreshing way. The opening and closing movements reveal a more vigorous aspect of Mr. Finzi's music— vigorous, but unadventurous and essentially conservative.[16]

Not all agreed with Lockspieser's comments. For example, Brymer describes the *Five Bagatelles* as, "a charming work by an English composer whose early death robbed us of much great music. The movements may be used separately, but the final Fughetta—a little masterpiece of craftsmanship—must never be missed."[17] Rees-Davies notes that, "The concerto by Gerald Finzi, who died young, is a thoughtful work, while his Five Bagatelles for Clarinet and Piano are among the most popular of English compositions for that ensemble."[18] Banfield notes that a likely influence on the Prelude was the first movement of the similar sounding *Second Sonata*

---

[10] Finzi to Ferguson, Letter 1942011A, Banfield, ibid., 300.

[11] McVeigh, *Gerald Finzi: His Life and Music*, 134; Banfield, ibid., 275, 299.

[12] Finzi to José Maria de Navarro, March 7, 1946, McVeigh, ibid., 134; Banfield, ibid., 299.

[13] McVeigh, ibid., 134; Banfield, ibid., 300. Boosey & Hawkes published a version of the *Five Bagatelles* in 1984 arranged for clarinet and string orchestra by Lawrence Ashmore.

[14] John Denman, "English Clarinet Music (continued)," *The Clarinet* 8, no. 1 (Fall 1980): 12–13.

[15] *Times,* January 16, 1943, 7; Banfield, ibid., 300.

[16] Edward Lockspieser, review of Gerald Finzi, "Five Bagatelles, for Clarinet and Piano," *Music & Letters* 27, no. 3 (July 1946): 201.

[17] Jack Brymer, *Clarinet* (New York: Schirmer Books, 1976), 214.

[18] Jo Rees-Davies, "The Development of the Clarinet Repertoire," *The Cambridge Companion to the Clarinet*, ed. Colin Lawson (Cambridge: Cambridge University Press, 1995), 88.

Section:	Introduction	Exposition	Development	Recapitulation	Coda
Starts at m.	1 Allegro deciso	4	32 (no. 3) Poco meno mosso	70 (2 mm. before no. 7) Tempo primo	87–92
No. of mm.	3	28	38	17	6
Tonalities	C	C	E, D♭, b♭	C	C
Themes	intro., (A)	A	B, A^1	A^2	A^3

CHART 10.1 *Finzi, Five Bagatelles for Clarinet and Piano, op. 23*: Structural analysis, first bagatelle, Prelude, Allegro deciso.

for Clarinet (1923) by Charles Koechlin, a composer that Finzi thought was underrated.[19]

The Prelude or first bagatelle, Allegro deciso, is written in sonata allegro form with an introduction and coda. (See Chart 10.1.) It begins with a three measure piano introduction, a partial statement of the A theme, followed by the full A theme (mm. 4–10), a C major scale marked with a tenuto line under each note, slurred and tongued played by the clarinetist. A lyrical E major theme (m. 32) in the development features long slurred clarinet phrases of the B theme, and modulates to D♭ major with similarly long phrases, two measures before no. 5. One measure after no. 6, the A^1 theme appears in B♭ minor as a short motive, and, after a caesura, the recapitulation A^2 theme in C major emerges, two measures before no. 7. At the coda, the A^3 theme plays in the original key of C major to convincingly finish the first bagatelle.

The second bagatelle, Romance, Andante tranquillo, a ternary form, begins with a lovely E♭ major clarinet A theme sensitively written with several hairpin dynamics and *ppp* passages. (See Chart 10.2.) A steady quarter note throughout the constantly shifting 3/4 and 4/4 meters nicely shapes the irregular but mainly four measure slurred phrases.[20] Section B shifts the mood with a Poco più mosso, 3/4 tempo. The piano introduces a warm, singing B theme in A♭ major, answered by a clarinet B^1 theme. Using both 3/4 and 4/4 time signatures, the B^1 theme is elaborated, reaching a *f* climax with slurred clarinet phrases, one measure after no. 4 (m. 42). Chromatic alterations in the piano part tend to obscure the tonality. At Tempo primo, one measure after no. 5, the clarinet A^1 theme presents slurred *pp* phrases in A♭, a fourth

---

[19] Banfield, ibid., 300–1.

[20] See also, David Campbell, "Master Class: Five Bagatelles for Clarinet & Piano by Gerald Finzi," *The Clarinet* 26, no. 3 (June 1999): 8–9.

Section:	A	B	A¹
Starts at m.	1 Andante tranquillo	24 Poco più mosso	52 Tempo primo (1 m. after no. 5) to 76
No. of mm.	23	28	25
Tonalities	E♭	A♭	A♭, E♭
Themes	A	B, B¹	A¹, (A)

CHART 10.2 Finzi, *Five Bagatelles for Clarinet and Piano, op. 23*: Structural analysis, second bagatelle, Romance, Andante tranquillo.

higher with a new countermelody in the piano.[21] The last five measures modulate to the original key of E♭. The clarinet plays *ppp*, and with a ritardando, recalling the first two measures of the A theme.

The third bagatelle, Carol, Andantino semplice, in ternary form has the same expressive melodic material in all three sections, written in combined 3/2 and 6/4 meters, and heard as a broadly felt three beat pulse. (See Chart 10.3.) After a one-measure introduction, a six-measure B♭ major clarinet tune is repeated one octave lower at measure 9. In measure 15, the piano plays the A² theme joined by the clarinet playing a counter melody in measure 16, while the piano plays the A theme. The last four measure phrase dies away from *pp* to *ppp*, marked, niente, and the piano strikes a B♭ major chord reminiscent of a "Christmas morning clock."[22]

EXAMPLE 10.1. Finzi, *Five Bagatelles for Clarinet and Piano, op. 23*, grouping of phrasing, third bagatelle, mm. 2–7.

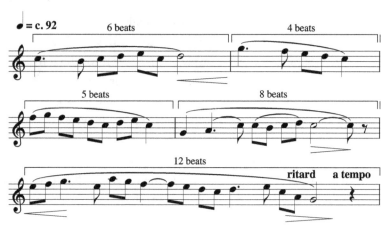

---

[21] Banfield, ibid., 302.
[22] Banfield, ibid., 302.

Finzi uses irregular phrase lengths and slurred clarinet phrases with different dynamics, similar to a wassail or greeting carol, common in many English Christmas carols.[23] Campbell rebarred measures 2–7 according to phrase lengths, the first phrase in six beats; second, four beats; third, five beats; fourth, eight beats; and fifth, twelve beats (Ex. 10.1).[24]

The fourth bagatelle, Forlana, a lively dance in ternary form, varies by changes of tonality in the second section. (See Chart 10.4.) The repeated quarter and eight note rhythm supplies a gently rolling tempo. After a two-measure introduction, the D♭ major clarinet A theme (m. 3) is beautifully expressive with carefully marked dynamics and slurs. In the second phrase at no. 1 (mm. 11–14) the clarinet offers harmonic support in dotted quarter notes, *ppp*. In section B, the F major B theme (m. 27, seven measures after no. 2) resembles a, "simple, common man's folk song,"[25] and includes imitation between piano and clarinet. At the 9/8 measure of no. 4 (m. 41),

Section:	A	A¹	A²
Starts at m.	1 Andantino semplice	8 A tempo	15–28, a tempo
No. of mm.	7	7	14
Tonalities	B♭	B♭	B♭
Themes	A	A¹	A², A

CHART 10.3 Finzi, *Five Bagatelles for Clarinet and Piano, op. 23*: Structural analysis, third bagatelle, Carol, Andantino semplice.

Section:	A	B	A¹
Starts at m.	1 Allegretto grazioso	27 (7 mm. after no. 2)	52 (1 m. after no. 5) to 74
No. of mm.	26	25	23
Tonalities	D♭	F, G, D♭, A♭	D♭
Themes	A	B, B¹	A¹, A², (A)

CHART 10.4 Finzi, *Five Bagatelles for Clarinet and Piano, op. 23*: Structural analysis, fourth bagatelle, Forlana, Allegretto grazioso.

---

23 "Wassail," *The Oxford Companion to Music, Oxford Music Online.*
24 Campbell, ibid., 9.
25 Banfield, ibid., 303; Campbell, ibid., 9.

the piano plays one measure of the B[1] theme answered by a *f* clarinet passage imitating the piano quarter and eighth note rhythm for four measures. At measure 59, two measures before no. 6, the clarinet softly plays the A[2] theme, and after a poco ritardando, five measures of A theme fragments are played on the piano and then the clarinet, *ppp*.

The last bagatelle, Fughetta, Allegro vivace, is a brilliant movement, full of fun, in a ternary form with an introduction and coda. (See Chart 10.5.) Finzi uses the greatest variety of articulation here—staccato, accented eighth notes, slurred staccato, and tenuto—and it is the most technically demanding of the bagatelles.[26] A percussive and exciting six-measure introduction in F major leads directly to the A theme, modified throughout, with imitation between clarinet and piano (mm. 7–15). The fugue subject modulates back to F major at measure 17 (four measures before no. 2) and is passed between the clarinet and both hands of the piano. In section B (m. 26, six measures after no. 2), after two measures of modulation, the clarinet plays the *mp* A[2] theme, transposed down a seventh in G major. The music modulates (mm. 28–38), bringing the clarinet to D♭ major (m. 39). Here a crescendo, two large leaps from F3 to B♭5 and F3 to E♭$_6$, and two B♭ major scales arrive at a climax of the A[3] theme played *ff* beginning on E♭$_6$ (m. 42, two measures after no. 4). The fugal subject is continued as the music modulates, and the A[4] theme is played by the clarinet (mm. 49–52). At the coda, measure 54 (four measures after no. 5), fragments of the fugal A theme appear in the piano's left hand and the clarinet (mm. 55–57). Two measures from the introduction (mm. 5–6) are repeated in the highest clarinet register at no. 6 (mm. 61–62), leading to the A[5] theme, and the final fugue statement between the clarinet and piano (mm. 63–69). The work ends with two humorous *ppp* measures from the A theme for a quick and satisfying ending.

Section:	Intro.–A	B	A[1]	Coda
Starts at m.	1 Allegro vivace	26 (6 mm. after no. 2)	42 (2 mm. after no. 4) a tempo	54 (4 mm. after no. 5) to 71
No. of mm.	25	16	12	18
Tonalities	F, C, F	G, D♭	D♭, A♭	F
Themes	A, A[1]	A[2]	A[3], A[4]	(A), A[5], (A)

CHART 10.5 Finzi, *Five Bagatelles for Clarinet and Piano, op. 23*: Structural analysis, fifth bagatelle, Fughetta, Allegro vivace.

---

[26] Campbell provides a very useful fingering for high G6 that works well in Finzi's scale, Campbell, ibid., 9.

Finzi's *Five Bagatelles* is an exceptional recital work with lovely folk-like melodies in the three inner bagatelles and very effective first and fifth bagatelles. The clarinet writing is skillful, requiring expert control of dynamics, several types of articulation, and specific timbre changes. It is a rewarding work to learn and perform; its popularity is due to Finzi's beautiful themes and directness of expression.

11 Jean Françaix, *Concerto for Clarinet and Orchestra*

Date of composition: 1967–1968

First editions: Jean Françaix, *Concerto pour Clarinette et Orchestre*, Paris: Editions Musicales Transatlantiques, 1968 (clarinet and piano); Jean Françaix, *Concerto pour Clarinette et Orchestre*, Paris: Editions Musicales Transatlantiques, 1968 (orchestral score)

Dedicatee/first performer: Fernand Oubradous; Jacques Lancelot, clarinet

Date/place of first performance: July 30, 1968; Nice, France

Orchestral instrumentation: First and second violins, violas, cellos, basses, two flutes (second flute also plays piccolo), two oboes, two B♭ clarinets, two bassoons, two F horns, C trumpet, timpani, and percussion

JEAN FRANÇAIX (1912–1997) studied composition at the Conservatory in Le Mans and the Paris Conservatory. He was a prolific composer and pianist and wrote over two hundred compositions encompassing operas, dramatic works, film scores, orchestral, chamber, and vocal works, and orchestral arrangements of other composers' works. Françaix wrote the *Quadruple Concerto for Flute, Oboe, Clarinet, Bassoon, and Orchestra* (1935); *Concerto Grosso for Flute, Oboe, Clarinet, Bassoon, String Quartet, and Orchestra* (1976); *Concerto for Fifteen Soloists and Orchestra* (1988); and *Double Concerto* for Flute, Clarinet, and Orchestra (1991).[1] His clarinet concerto was dedicated to the conductor, bassoonist, and chamber music professor at the Paris Conservatory, Fernand Oubradous (1903–1986). The clarinetist, Jacques

---

[1] Muriel Bellier, "Françaix, Jean," *Grove Music Online*; Frédéric Cellier, "La Musique avec Clarinette de Jean Françaix," *Clarinette Magazine*, no. 28 (1998): 11.

Lancelot (1920–2009), premiered it in July 1968 at the International Summer Academy in Nice with the Orchestre des Concerts Symphoniques de Chambre de Paris, conducted by Louis Fourestier, and played it in November in Paris at the Salle Gaveau, with the same orchestra and conductor. Lancelot's recording of the concerto with the Orchestre de Chambre de Nice, conducted by Pol Mule, won the Grand Prix du Disque in 1971.[2]

Françaix had a humorous streak and enjoyed having fun. He delighted in wrong-note music, altering classically balanced phrases, or reworking Haydn's work, as he does in his *Eleven Variations on a Theme of Haydn for wind ensemble and double bass*.[3] He expresses his view of the *Concerto for Clarinet* this way:

> This concerto is, or at least I hope it is, amusing to listen to. It is a kind of aerobatics display for the ear, complete with loops, wing-turns and nose-dives which are fairly terrifying for the soloist, who needs to have a good stomach and several thousand flying hours under his belt. I must say the poor fellow has been given the full treatment, including a slow movement full of phrases with great charm but little time for breathing—rather like a long glide in a plane which is constantly on the verge of stalling. Finally, the pilot starts his noisy engines again, but remains carefree to the point of swapping his air force cap for the revolving wig of a clown.[4]

Françaix wrote the B♭ clarinet part in B major, a previously unheard tonality for a clarinet concerto. The technical requirements are very demanding, and initially the concerto was not embraced outside France. The well-known and experienced British soloist, Jack Brymer, wrote about Françaix's *Concerto for Clarinet* in his 1976 book, *Clarinet*:

> A work for the future, possibly when the instrument has developed further or the human hand has changed. At present, its roulades in the key of B major are beyond almost any player; but the work is a worthwhile challenge, and the A clarinet would probably provide the answer.[5]

[2] Philippe Cuper, "Le Concerto pour Clarinette de Jean Françaix," *Clarinette Magazine*, no. 28 (1998): 12–13; trans. Cuper "Jean Françaix *Clarinet Concerto*," *The Clarinet* 40, no. 3 (June 2013): 42–43; Jean-Marie Paul with Eric Perrier, "Jacques Lancelot: A Tribute," *The Clarinet* 34, no. 1 (December 2006): 45.

[3] Richard Langham Smith, "More Fauré than Ferneyhough: Françaix at 80," *The Musical Times* 133, no. 1797 (November 1992): 556.

[4] Cuper, "Jean Françaix *Clarinet Concerto*," 42.

[5] Jack Brymer, *Clarinet* (New York: Schirmer Books, 1976), 222.

After a few years, with more performances worldwide and recordings, this attitude among clarinetists changed, and it is now considered a repertoire concerto. Since the piano accompaniment often includes a third line indicating the orchestral parts, two pianos are recommended.[6]

Although the concerto is tonal at the beginning and end of the movements, the work is not organized by harmonic construction, but by its recurring themes. Françaix's orchestration is carefully written with felicitous choices of timbre, skillfully mixing flutes, oboes, and first orchestral clarinet with the solo clarinet line. Bassoons often play repeated sixteenth notes in their low register, a comical sound. The first movement, Allegro, follows a modified sonata-allegro form, full of staccato sixteenth note passages, chromatic scales, and arpeggios at a frantic speed (quarter note = 120–126, Françaix's corrected metronome marking).[7] (See Chart 11.1.) After a four-measure orchestral introduction, the clarinet introduces the A theme at no. 1 (m. 5), which is later varied with arpeggios and runs. A sweet clarinet B theme from nos. 5 to 8 (mm. 43–68) charms the listener while the flutes play sixteenth-note scales and figurations. At the development, five measures after no. 8 (m. 73), the A^1 theme is transposed a minor third lower to F major for the oboe, answered by clarinet arpeggios, runs, quintuplets, and triplets leading to the recapitulation at no. 12 (m. 109). The A^2 theme develops *mp* by the clarinet; the full orchestra answers with a two measure fragment of the A theme, played six times in different tonalities, and after a lengthy rallentando, proceeds to a forty-seven measure cadenza, ten measures after no. 13 (m. 130 ex. 11.1.).

This is a tour-de-force, incorporating repeated staccato sixteenth notes, rapid runs, wide leaps, and tremolos. It requires a wide range of dynamics from *ppp* to *fff*

Section:	Orchestral introduction	Exposition	Development	Recapitulation	Coda
Starts at m.	1 Allegro	5 (no. 1)	73 (5 mm. after no. 8)	109 (no. 12)	198–206
No. of mm.	4	68	36	89	9
Themes	intro.	A, fig., B	fig., A^1	A^2, (A), cadenza, trans., B^1, (A^3)	fig.

CHART 11.1 Françaix, *Concerto for Clarinet and Orchestra*: Structural analysis, first movement, Allegro.

[6] Yu-Chien Chen, "An Analytic Interpretation of the Clarinet Concerto by Jean Françaix" (M.M. thesis, California State University, Northridge, 2013), 16.

[7] Cuper, ibid., 42; Aaron Brisbois, "Jean Françaix's Clarinet Concerto: An Examination of Performance Practices" (D.M.A. diss., University of Oklahoma, 2012), 9–11.

and sensitivity to humorous gestures and phrases. Toward the end, string pizzicato quarter notes are answered by clarinet repeated notes in arpeggios three times; the fourth time is a final series of thirty-second-note arpeggios. The cadenza ends with woodwinds and strings playing *pp* trills and a transitional orchestral theme at no. 15 for eight measures. At no. 16 (m. 185), strings play a *pp* B^1 theme while the clarinet adds sixteenth-note flourishes, four measures of the A^3 theme, runs, arpeggios, and a nine-measure coda of *pp* sixteenth notes, to a high $F\sharp_6$ whole note and a quiet ending.

Françaix thought of the second movement, Scherzando, as a little 3/8 waltz (proposed metronome speed, dotted quarter note = 68–72)[8] in ternary form with an introduction. (See Chart 11.2.) The oboes and flutes play a forceful twelve-

EXAMPLE 11.1. Françaix, *Concerto for Clarinet and Orchestra*, first movement, mm. 130–150.

8 Cuper, ibid., 43.

EXAMPLE 11.2 Françaix, *Concerto for Clarinet and Orchestra*, third movement, measures 13–24. The right hand is the first flute part; the left hand is string parts.

measure introduction which includes a fragment of the A theme. The clarinet joins the strings with a pickup of three sixteenth notes (m. 12) to the A theme at four measures after no. 18 (m. 13). Varied staccato notes and slurs are utilized in section A. At no. 20 (m. 58), a *mp* lyrical clarinet B theme is accompanied by *pp* sixteenth notes in the strings. At no. 21 (m. 71), the athletic A¹ theme becomes more insistent and is transposed a half-step lower. Sixteen measures of the A² theme in the original written key of E major at no. 23 (m. 107) quietly leads to a *ppp* E₆. In section B, a

Section:	Introduction	A	B	A
Starts at m.	1 Scherzando	13 (4 mm. after no. 18)	135 (no. 25, 4 mm. before the Trio) to 250 (Da Capo repeat)	13 (4 mm. after no. 18) to 134
No. of mm.	12	122	116	122
Themes	intro., (A)	A, B, A¹, A²	(A), trans., B¹	A, B, A¹, A²

CHART II.2 Françaix, *Concerto for Clarinet and Orchestra*: Structural analysis, second movement, Scherzando.

Section:	Introduction	Theme	Variation 1
Starts at m.	1 Andantino	13 (no. 31)	29 (no. 32)
No. of mm.	12	16	16
Themes	intro.	A	A¹

Section:	Variation 2	Variation 3	Coda
Starts at m.	45 (no. 33)	55 (no. 34)	71 (no. 35)–93
No. of mm.	10	16	23
Themes	A²	A³	coda

CHART II.3 Françaix, *Concerto for Clarinet and Orchestra*: Structural analysis, third movement, Andantino.

fragmented four measure A orchestral theme is a transition to an eight-measure horn solo introducing a playful clarinet B_1 theme, eight measures after the Trio (mm. 147–154). The clarinet theme comprises a biting, recurring triplet sixteenth note followed by a slurred, short eighth and quarter note melody in an effective and amusing way. The orchestral strings intersperse sixteenth notes similar to the A theme with the clarinet B theme, and play straightforward eighth note phrases at no. 26 (m. 163) and throughout the B section, while the clarinet emphatically answers with the B¹ theme. The second A section is repeated as the clarinetist returns to the Da Capo sign at four measures after no. 18 (m. 13), ending with a satisfying diminuendo to a *ppp* E_6 (m. 134).

The third movement, Andantino, proposed metronome speed, quarter note = 68–72),[9] is a theme and three variations, with an introduction and coda. (See Chart II.3.) The clarinet begins with eight measures of a *pp* melody, the strings joining *ppp*

---

[9] Cuper, ibid., 43.

at measure 3. After a short caesura, a four measure *ppp* string orchestral interlude with flute eighth notes precedes a sweet and yearning *pp* clarinet A theme (mm. 13–28), accompanied by one flute and strings (Ex. 11.1). This intimate melody is limited to a small range of an octave and a fifth in the clarion register, B3–F#5. Variation 1 at no. 32 (mm. 29–44) uses the A^1 theme in the orchestra as the clarinet freely embellishes it with sixteenth notes in groups of five, six, and eight, using the entire range of E3 to F$_6$. In variation 2 at no. 33 (mm. 45–54), the clarinet states the A^2 theme in the chalumeau and clarion registers, embellished with thirty-second notes. Variation 3 at no. 34 (mm. 55–70) consists of clarinet embellishments of double grace notes, trills, and sixteenth quintuplets while the orchestra plays the A^3 theme. At the coda, no. 35 (mm. 71–93), the clarinet proffers a chromatic melody similar to the A theme as *ppp* eighth notes, double grace notes, quarter notes, and half notes (mm. 71–73, 79–81), ending (mm. 90–93) with *ppp* quarter notes and a fermata over sustained strings.

The fourth movement, Allegrissimo rondo, includes an introduction, two cadenzas, and a coda. The clarinet begins an excited 6/8 four-measure introduction to a carefree, accented eighth-note A theme (mm. 5–12), varied with sixteenth-note embellishments (proposed metronome speed dotted quarter note = 126–132),[10] (See Chart 11.4.) After an ecstatic *ff* orchestral statement of the A theme at no. 39 (mm. 50–57), the B theme, nine measures after no. 39 (mm. 58–69), features five repeated low notes in the bassoon, answered by the orchestra. The clarinet responds with eighth notes played in the clarion register against violin and bassoon triplets, reappearing in the bassoon and first oboe. Up to measure 110, a hemiola rhythm of two dotted eighths against three eighth notes is predominately heard in the clarinet, and in some orchestral sections. There are clarinet embellishments of sixteenth-note runs and eighth notes, and four orchestral measures until the cadenza begins.

The first cadenza, 13 measures after no. 42 (m. 114), uses fluid sixteenth notes, wide leaps, short and varied staccato, with contrasts between *ppp* and *ff*. The carefree, accented eighth note A^1 theme is emphatically stated *ff* by the orchestra at no. 43 (m. 146). At no. 44 (m. 166), the clarinet introduces the C theme with a recurring, teasing motive in 4/4, eight sixteenth notes followed by four eighth notes with grace notes. At no. 46 (m. 186), a fragment of the first movement's A theme returns briefly in the orchestra answered by the clarinet with sixteenth note triplets. A fragment of the second movement's A theme is quoted by the clarinet in measures 193–194, followed by the second movement's sixteenth note A theme in the clarion and acute registers (mm. 195–197), and fragments of the C theme from the third movement. This leads to a short second cadenza (mm. 202–215) with several comic moments,

---

[10] Cuper, ibid., 43.

Section:	Introduction	A	B		1st cadenza	A¹
Starts at m.	1 Allegrissimo	5 (m. 5)	58 (9 mm. after no. 39)		114 (13 mm. after no. 42)	146 (no. 43)
No. of mm.	4	53	56		32	20
Themes	intro.	A	B		fig.	A¹

Section:	C		2nd cadenza	A²	Coda
Starts at m.	166 (no. 44)		202 (8 mm. after no. 47)	216 (no. 48)	231 (no. 49)–243
No. of mm.	36		14	15	13
Themes	C, (A) 1st movement, (A) 2nd movement, (C) 3rd movement.		fig.	A²	C¹

CHART 11.4 Françaix, *Concerto for Clarinet and Orchestra*: Structural analysis, fourth movement, Allegrissimo.

alternating five *p* eighth notes played affectuoso followed by *fff* riffs in the chalumeau register. Five *mp* eighth notes reach $F\sharp_6$, ascend by half notes to $A\sharp_6$, and provide a whole note crescendo. Theme A^2 is played *pp* by the piccolo and flute at no. 48 (m. 216) for fifteen measures until the coda, no. 49 (m. 231), where the clarinet enters with the C^1 theme, an octave lower, ending with a *fff* F$\sharp$ major arpeggio.

There are a number of misprints in the clarinet part of the 1968 edition, listed by Cuper with the cooperation of Françaix.[11] In 2011, the French clarinetist, Franck Amet, along with the composer's son, Jacques, and daughter, Claude, discovered in Françaix's Parisian apartment the manuscript of his incomplete piano reduction (91 measures of the concerto's first movement). Amet recorded this version with other Paris Conservatory solos.[12]

The Françaix *Concerto for Clarinet and Orchestra* contains many technical and musical hurdles for the clarinetist but is an absolute delight to perform. It requires a nimble and fluid technique, similar to flute music, and uniquely shows off the clarinet's technical and tonal agility. It is one of the most sensitive, challenging, and memorable works of the twentieth century.

---

[11] Cuper, ibid., 42–43.
[12] Franck Amet, "Rediscovery of a Jean Françaix Piano Score," *The Clarinet* 39, no. 4 (September 2012): 61.

12 Paul Hindemith, *Sonata for Clarinet and Piano*

Date of composition: September 21–28, 1939

First edition/other edition: Paul Hindemith, *Sonata for Clarinet in B♭ and Piano*, Mainz: Schott, 1940; Paul Hindemith, *Sonata for Clarinet in B♭ and Piano*, New York: Associated Music Publishers, 1940

Dedicatee/first performer: Not indicated; Not known

Date/place of first performance: Not known; Not known

PAUL HINDEMITH (1895–1963) was a consummate craftsman and one of the outstanding composers of his generation. A versatile musician, he published 247 works for the stage, orchestral works, choral works, solo vocal with piano, ensemble, or orchestra, chamber music, keyboard music, mechanical and electro-acoustic music, incidental music for puppet plays, film scores, radio plays, canons, etudes, teaching pieces, parody pieces, and editions of works by other composers.[1]

Hindemith studied the violin as a child, played professionally, and studied composition in 1912–1913 at the Hoch Conservatory in Frankfurt. In later years, he learned to play several instruments on an amateur level, including the clarinet.[2] In 1927, he taught composition at Berlin's Staatliche Hochschule für Musik. He was considered an important composer at this time.[3] Hindemith also researched early

---

[1] *Paul Hindemith: Werkverzeichnis = List of Works* (Mainz: Schott, 1985); Giselher Schubert, "Hindemith, Paul, Works," *Grove Music Online.*

[2] A caricature of Hindemith playing the clarinet in 1937 by Rudolf W. Heinisch is on the dust cover of Pamela Weston's *Clarinet Virtuosi of Today* (Baldock: Egon Publishers, 1989).

[3] Schubert, "Hindemith, Paul"; Luther Noss, *Paul Hindemith in the United States* (Urbana: University of Illinois Press, 1989), 103.

German folk music and early art music, gaining a broad knowledge and deep appreciation of their value.[4] After the National Socialists came to power in 1933, half of his music was branded "cultural Bolshevism" and was banned. Two years later, he prepared to emigrate. In 1936, all performances of Hindemith's works were banned. He had no performing engagements and did no teaching. In September 1938, Hindemith and his wife emigrated to Bluche, Switzerland, a village above Sion.[5]

In February 1940, after the outbreak of World War II, Hindemith left Switzerland for the United States. He taught at the State University of New York at Buffalo, Cornell University, Wells College, and the Berkshire Music Center (Tanglewood). After a series of guest lectures at Yale University, he became a visiting professor for 1940, and in 1941, accepted a permanent position. At Yale, he taught the history of music theory, founded the Yale Collegium Musicum in 1943, and inaugurated its famous concerts in 1945 which continued until 1948, resuming in 1950 and 1953.[6] In 1950, Hindemith wrote a foreword to a collection of fourteenth century French secular music compiled by Willi Apel. He offers a critical appreciation as an early music performer and an expression of his own musical and personal ideals:[7]

It is rewarding to see those masters struggle successfully with technical devices similar to those that we have to reconquer after periods in which the appreciation of quantity, exaggeration, and search for originality in sound was the most important drive in the composer's mind.... Their unselfish and uninhibited way of addressing the audience and satisfying the performer; the perfect adequacy of poetic and musical form; the admirable balance of composition's technical effort and its sensuous appeal—these are only a few of the outstanding solutions they found in their works.[8]

In 1935, Hindemith began to compose a series of twenty-five sonatas that would eventually include one for nearly every orchestral instrument. Each has a formal structure tailored to the character of the solo instrument and the unique qualities of each individual timbre.[9] The *Sonata for Clarinet and Piano* was completed in Bluche in one week in 1939.[10] It has been called, "a great work which requires more musical

---

[4] Noss, ibid., 1989, 103.
[5] Schubert, ibid.
[6] Schubert, ibid.
[7] David Neumeyer, *The Music of Paul Hindemith* (New Haven, CT: Yale University Press, 1986), 16.
[8] Paul Hindemith, "Foreword" to *French Secular Music of the Late Fourteenth Century*, ed. Willi Apel (Cambridge, MA: Medieval Academy of America, 1950), viii.
[9] Schubert, ibid.
[10] Neumeyer, ibid., 272; Geoffrey Skelton, ed. and trans., *Selected Letters of Paul Hindemith* (New Haven, CT: Yale University Press, 1995), 136, Hindemith to Willy Strecker, September 25, 1939; 140, Hindemith to Willy Strecker, November 29, 1939.

intelligence than technique, and is consequently not as popular as it deserves."[11] It is beautiful and idiomatically written by a composer who was very familiar with the clarinet's possibilities. Hindemith did not dedicate the sonata to anyone but may have had Philipp Dreisbach (1891–1980) in mind. Dreisbach was the principal clarinetist in the Stuttgart Court Orchestra, 1914–1948. In 1922, Dreisbach played Brahms' *Quintet for Clarinet and String Quartet* in Breslau, and in 1923 Hindemith's *Quintet for Clarinet and String Quartet, op. 30* with the Amar Quartet in Winterthur, with Hindemith as violist. Hindemith and Dreisbach remained good friends, often travelling to the Donauschingen Musical Festivals together.[12]

The *Sonata for Clarinet and Piano* consists of four movements. The first, second, and fourth movements are in B♭ major, the third in F major; all exhibit a sense of calm and balance.[13] Throughout, there is extensive imitation, division of duple meter into triple meter, quartal and quintal piano intervals, and the same intervals played melodically by the clarinet.[14] An interesting aspect of the work is Hindemith's use in the second movement of rhythmic techniques characteristic of fourteenth century mensuration.[15] This is not surprising considering his lifelong interest in early music.

The first movement, Moderately, with motion (Mässig bewegt), is in sonata-allegro form with a coda. (See Chart 12.1.) The clarinet flows with a vocal A theme in an arch form, repeated as A² by the clarinet at the beginning of the coda (m. 140). This flow and imitation continues, followed by a canonic stretto[16] (mm. 14–19), where the clarinet repeats a short melodic figure accompanied by quartal harmony (mm. 17–18).[17] The clarinet B theme, one measure after no. 2 (m. 21), plays expressively in the chalumeau register. A plaintive clarinet C theme of minor third quarter and eighth notes, four measures after no. 3 (m. 37), is answered by the piano, followed by repeated piano triplets at no. 4 (m. 46), and a martial clarinet dotted-eighth and sixteenth-note figure. The development D theme begins at no. 5 with a piano

[11] Jo Rees-Davies, "The Development of the Clarinet Repertoire," in *The Cambridge Companion to the Clarinet*, ed. Colin Lawson (Cambridge: Cambridge University Press, 1995), 86.

[12] Geoffrey Skelton, *Paul Hindemith, the Man Behind the Music: A Biography* (London: V. Gollancz, 1977), 73–74; Pamela Weston, "Players and Composers," in *The Cambridge Companion to the Clarinet*, 98–99; Peter Sulzer, *Zehn Komponisten um Werner Reinhart: Ein Ausschnitt aus dem Wirkungskreis des Musikkollegiums Winterthur 1920–1950* (Winterthur: Stadtbibliothek, 1980), 2, 16–18; Pamela Weston, *Yesterday's Clarinettists: A Sequel* (Haverhill: Panda Group, 2002), 62–64, photo of Dreisbach, pl. 9.

[13] Dorothy Katherine Payne, "The Accompanied Wind Sonatas of Hindemith: Studies in Tonal Counterpoint" (Ph.D. diss., University of Rochester, 1974), 11–12.

[14] Payne, ibid., iv, 173, 178–79, 215.

[15] James C. Kidd, "Aspects of Mensuration in Hindemith's Clarinet Sonata," *The Music Review* 38, no. 3 (August 1977): 211–22.

[16] Payne, ibid., 36.

[17] Payne, ibid., 67–68.

Section:	Exposition	Development	Recapitulation	Coda
Starts at m.	1 Mässig bewegt	54 (no. 5)	99 (4 mm. before no. 10)	140 (7 mm. after no. 13) to 173
No. of mm.	53	45	41	34
Tonalities	B♭, C, F, B♭, trans., C♭, F♯	A, D, B♭, E, C, trans.	E♭, E♭/C, B♭/E♭, B♭	D, C, E♭, D♭, B♭
Themes	A, B, C	D	A¹, B¹, C¹	A²

CHART 12.1 Hindemith, *Sonata for Clarinet and Piano*: Structural analysis, first movement, Mässig bewegt.

ostinato,[18] continuing while the clarinet plays a sustained group of quarter notes in fourths, followed by slurred thirds and sixths, two measures after no. 7 (mm. 54–78). At no. 9 (m. 93), the imitation between the clarinet and piano in sixteenth notes becomes more active. The recapitulation has *f* piano tremolos and the A¹ clarinet theme played a fifth higher, four measures before no. 10 (m. 99). The B¹ theme plays expressively at measure 110, four measures before no. 11. The plaintive clarinet C¹ theme appears on the second beat of measure 125, no. 12. A slower, calm section (Langsamer, ruhig) introduced by the clarinet at the coda (m. 140), provides one of the sonata's most beautiful sections (mm. 141–149). The piano moves ahead (Vorangehen) at no. 14 (m. 150) and calms down (Wieder beruhigen, m. 159) to a reflective, very calm (Sehr ruhig, m. 162) ending. Here, the clarinet plays two quarter notes, G3–G4, to a whole note G5 three times, with an underpinning of changing tonalities, ending on a blissful B♭ chord.

The second movement, Lively (Lebhaft), is a scherzo, trio, scherzo three-part form. (See Chart 12.2.) It begins with a light, airy A theme tune accompanied softly by the piano. The B theme, at no. 16, becomes more animated as the piano accents are written in 3/4 meter while the clarinet continues in 4/4. The clarinet begins *mp* and crescendos, accenting the third and fourth beats, as the piano begins *pp* and crescendos. In the next six measures there are few places in which the clarinet and piano rhythmically coincide. If the two parts are grouped according to rhythmic emphasis it becomes clearer as shown in Ex. 12.1. Five measures after no. 16 (mm. 16–19) a clarinet half-note rhythm, after one beat, is placed against a piano dotted-half-note rhythm. Two measures before no. 17 (mm. 20–25) a clarinet half and dotted quarter note rhythm is placed against a piano dotted half note rhythm. Here, Hindemith seems to recall fourteenth-century mensural notation in a modern guise. Four measures before no. 19, a *mp* B¹ piano theme is played with imitation with the clarinet used

18 Payne, ibid., 124.

EXAMPLE 12.1. Hindemith, *Sonata for Clarinet and Piano*, second movement, mm. 12–21.

Section:	Scherzo	Trio	Scherzo
Starts at m.	1 Lebhaft	51 (1 m. before no. 20)	89 (1 m. after no. 23) to 112
No. of mm.	50	38	24
Tonalities	B♭, trans., F/G♭, B♭, trans., F	G♭, trans.	B♭, B♭, B, B♭
Themes	A, B, A¹, B¹	C	A², B²

CHART 12.2 Hindemith, *Sonata for Clarinet and Piano*: Structural analysis, second movement, Lebhaft.

throughout. One measure before no. 20, a C theme in the trio is very effective by using a soft ostinato pattern which gradually crescendos until measure 62 (four measures before no. 21). There are several amusing sections such as sixteenth and eighth note motives alternately answered *f* and *p* by clarinet and piano, from nos. 22–23. The scherzo A^2 at measure 89, one measure after no. 23, alternates between *ff* and *pp* utterances by piano and clarinet. The clarinet B^2 theme plays softly and ends the movement with a single, *p* low B♭.

The third movement, Very Slowly (Sehr langsam), is in ternary form with a coda. (See Chart 12.3.) The first seven measures begin with a serious *f* statement of the A theme in the chalumeau register. The second phrase, in the clarion register at no. 25, is introverted and thoughtful. Seven measures of the hauntingly beautiful *p* A theme is played very quietly (Sehr ruhig) by the clarinet at no. 26, answered by the piano. The fourth eighth note in measure 30, marked a little less movement (Ein wenig fließender), introduces the beautiful B theme. A seven-note ostinato pattern in the piano and clarinet appears at measures 41–45, and is used effectively throughout the rest of the movement.[19] At no. 29, an insistent seven measure C theme arises and, as the clarinet and piano move to a lower range, the piano loses its octave doubling, playing triplets against the clarinet's eighth notes, producing a hemiola, slowing the pace.[20] The A^1 theme at measure 60 uses a dotted rhythm in the piano, adding considerable weight and seriousness. After the theme is repeated in the clarion and high registers, the high point of the movement is reached *ff* at no. 31 (m. 73). A remarkable effect is achieved as the clarinet powerfully crescendos on a low E3, and the piano continues *ff*. The intensity winds down with a long decrescendo. At the coda, no. 32 (m. 85), the hauntingly beautiful A^2 theme begins *p,* gains in intensity to measure 90,

Section:	A	B	A^1	Coda
Starts at m.	1 Sehr langsam	30 (2 mm. before no. 27)	60 (5 mm. before no. 30)	85 (no. 32)–92
No. of mm.	29	30	25	8
Tonalities	F, B, B♭, F	F♯, E♭, G♭, B	B♭, F	F
Themes	A	B, C	A^1	A^2

CHART 12.3 Hindemith, *Sonata for Clarinet and Piano*: Structural analysis, third movement, Sehr langsam.

---

[19] Payne, ibid., 130.
[20] Payne, ibid., 87–88.

Section:	Exposition	Development	Recapitulation	Coda
Starts at m.	1 Kleines Rondo, gemächlich	45 (no. 36)	78 (no. 39)	106 (7 mm. after no. 41) to 119
No. of mm.	44	33	28	14
Tonalities	B♭, trans, F, C♯	A♭, D, B♭, E♭, E	E♭, A, B♭	B♭
Themes	A, A¹, B	A²	A³, B¹	A⁴

CHART 12.4 Hindemith, *Sonata for Clarinet and Piano*: Structural analysis, fourth movement, Kleines Rondo, gemächlich.

and effectively ends the movement. Because of the slow tempo, this movement requires careful breath control and optimum placement of breath marks.

The fourth movement, Small rondo, comfortably (Kleines Rondo, gemächlich), is in sonata-allegro form with a coda. (See Chart 12.4.) It opens with a perky, fifth-based *p* tune accompanied by triads and quintal chords, answered in the piano's highest range, both unusual and effective. The A¹ theme, three measures after no. 33, in the chalumeau register, is followed by a long, slurred B theme, at no. 34. In the exposition, the clarinet sometimes briefly acts as an accompaniment to the piano (mm. 11–13, 33–35). The development A² theme, no. 36 (m. 45), starts with a *mf* statement by the piano in the low register accompanied by the clarinet, followed by a *ff* canonic section, no. 37 (m. 55) to six measures after no. 38 (m. 70). The clarinet A² theme plays alone in the chalumeau register, joined by the piano's right hand in the highest register, seamlessly arriving at the recapitulation at no. 39 (m. 78).[21] The clarinet phrases are expertly shaped, using contrasting chalumeau and clarion registers, from measure 93, six measures after no. 40, to measure 105, six measures after no. 41. The coda at measure 106 turns to the A⁴ theme, accompanied by triads and quintal chords as heard at the beginning and decrescendos to a *pp* and a satisfying ending.

Hindemith's *Sonata for Clarinet and Piano* is not technically difficult but musically it is dense and contains many levels of meaning. The quartal sonorities are unique to Hindemith's style and he writes with a certainty of expression and purpose that exhibits deft craftsmanship. This sonata is a marvel of invention with clever use and transformation of themes, and it is an extremely effective recital piece.

---

[21] Payne, ibid., 139–40.

13 Franz Krommer, *Concerto for Clarinet and Orchestra, op. 36*

Date of composition: 1800–1803

First edition/other editions: Franz Krommer, *Concerto pour la Clarinette avec accompa-gnement d'Orchestra*, Offenbach: J. André, ca. 1803; František Kramář-Krommer, *Konzert Es Dur für Klarinette und Orchester*, ed. Jiří Kratochvíl, Prague: Státní Hudební Vydavatelstiví, 1953, 1985 (piano and clarinet); Franz Krommer, *Konzert Es-dur für Klarinette und Orchester op. 36*, ed. Melinda Berlász, Zürich: Eulenberg, 1975 (piano and clarinet; orchestral score)

Dedicatee/first performers: Monsieur de Marsano;[1] Not known

First modern performer: Jiří Kratochvíl, clarinet, Prague Conservatory Orchestra

Date/place of first modern performance: 1949; Prague[2]

Orchestral instrumentation: First and second violins, violas, cellos, basses, flute, two oboes, two bassoons, two horns (F and E♭), two F trumpets, and timpani in F and C

FRANZ VINCENC KROMMER (František Vincenc Kramář, 1759–1831) was a Czech composer, violinist, and organist. He studied violin and organ from fourteen to seventeen with his uncle, the composer Anton Matthias Krommer (1742–1804), in Turan. In 1785, he became a violinist in the orchestra of the Duke of Tyrum in

---

[1] Written on the title page of a part in the Gesellschaft der Musikfreunde, Vienna, VIII. 2513/i; Melinda Berlász, "Preface" to Franz Vinzenc Krommer, *Konzert Es-dur für Klarinette und Orchester Op. 36*, ed. Melinda Berlász (Zürich: Edition Eulenburg, 1975).

[2] Jiří Kratochvíl, "Koncertantní Klarinet v Českém Klasicismu," *Ziva Hudbá* 9 (1968): 305.

Simontomya, Hungary.[3] After 1810, he was ballet kapellmeister of the Vienna Hoftheater. Two years later, he became musical director. In 1815, he was appointed Kammertürhüter (Imperial Court Usher) to the emperor and in 1818 until his death, succeeded Johann Antonin Kozeluch as the last official director of chamber music and court composer to the Habsburg emperors.[4]

At the turn of the eighteenth century, Krommer was one of the most successful Czech composers in Vienna. He wrote over three hundred works including one hundred sixty published opus numbers in almost all musical genres of the time, with the exception of piano works, lieder, and operas. His output includes several well-written wind octets, twenty marches for ten instruments, seven partitas for eight to ten instruments, and ten wind band pieces or harmonien for nine instruments. They were written in Vienna between 1800 and 1818.[5] Krommer's high reputation is supported by the publication of many compositions in reprints and arrangements by German, Danish, French, English, Italian, and American publishers. He was regarded as a leading composer of string quartets along with Haydn, and as a serious rival to Beethoven. His solo concertos for flute, oboe, and clarinet are considered his most important accomplishments.[6]

Krommer's clarinet works include *Concerto for Two Clarinets and Orchestra, op. 35* (ca. 1802); an arrangement of an oboe concerto, probably by Joseph Küffner, as *Concerto for Clarinet and Orchestra, op. 52* (ca. 1805); *Concerto for Two Clarinets and Orchestra, op. 91* (ca. 1815); and an arrangement of a flute concerto by Küffner as *Concerto for A Clarinet and Orchestra, op. 86* (1819–1820).[7] All were published by Johann Anton André in Leipzig; the opus 36 concerto was also published in Paris by Vernay, ca. 1803 (plate no. 170) and Duhan, ca. 1806.[8]

---

[3] In 1790, Krommer became kapellmeister of Pécs Cathedral; after 1793, he was kapellmeister and composer to Duke Karolyi and later to Prince Antal Grassalkovich. In 1795, he returned to Vienna and probably taught composition before he was appointed kapellmeister to Duke Ignaz Fuchs in 1798. In 1798 he applied, unsuccessfully, as a violinist in the Vienna Hofkapelle. Othmar Wessely, "Krommer, Franz," *Grove Music Online.*

[4] Wessely, ibid.; Bohumír Koukal, "Franz Vincenc Krommer (Kramář) and His Solo Works for Clarinet," *The Clarinet* 12, no. 2 (Winter 1985): 18.

[5] David Whitwell, "Franz Krommer: Early Wind Master," *Journal of Band Research* 10 (Spring 1974): 23.

[6] Krommer received honorary memberships in the Istituto Filarmonico in Venice; the Philharmonic Society in Lujbljana; the Musikverein in Innsbruck; and the conservatories in Paris (1815), Milan (1818), and Vienna (1826). Othmar Wessely, "Krommer, Franz," *Grove Music Online.*

[7] Koukal, ibid., 18; Wessely, ibid.; Louis Vincent Sacchini, *The Concerted Music for the Clarinet in the Nineteenth Century*" (Ph.D. diss., University of Iowa, 1980), 99–105.

[8] Britta Constaple, *Der Musikverlag Johann André in Offenbach am Main: Studien zur Verlagstätigkeit von Johann Anton André und Verzeichnis der Musikalien von 1800 bis 1840* (Tutzing: H. Schneider, 1998), 515; Gomer J. Pound, *A Study of Clarinet Solo Concerto Literature Composed Before 1850: with Selected Items Edited and Arranged for Contemporary Use* (Ph.D. diss., Florida State University, 1965), 65; *Einzeldrucke vor 1800, International Inventory of Musical Sources*, Series A, no. 1 (Kassel: Bärenreiter, 1975–1992), 5: 152–53, 12:356–57; Anik Devriès and François Lesure, *Dictionnaire des Éditeurs de Musique Français* (Genève: Minkoff, 1979), 1:62, 87.

The concerto, op. 36, is written in late Classical style in three movements. Krommer's clarinet writing is idiomatic, using a wide compass, E3–F$_6$, primarily in the clarino register for a five-key clarinet. He writes several chromatic runs that are not difficult and make effective use of arpeggios and runs in the chalumeau register.[9] Unusual for eighteenth century concertos is the lack of cadenzas or places to insert them.[10]

The first movement is in sonata-allegro form with an orchestral exposition, two episodes, and a coda. The solo clarinet sections are lyrical with pleasing themes. In the E♭ major orchestral exposition, the strings proclaim a heroic-sounding A theme (mm. 1–8, Kratochvíl edition) with eighth-note leaps, arpeggios, and wide jumps. The orchestral strings play a lyrical B theme (m. 25) before a cadence is reached at no. 5 (m. 51), using all the orchestral instruments. In the solo exposition, no. 5, the clarinet plays a forthright and assertive A[1] theme (Ex. 13.1)

EXAMPLE 13.1. Krommer, *Concerto for Clarinet and Orchestra, op. 36*, first movement, mm. 51–60.

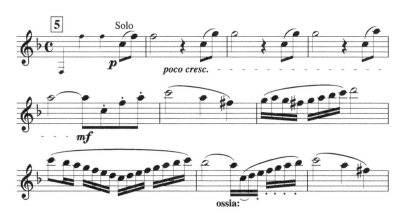

The Allegro, quarter note = 112,[11] A[1] theme arises with two eighth-note pickups on the fourth beat of measure 51, gradually building in intensity and dynamics. (See Chart 13.1.) The chalumeau register is impressively featured in five sixteenth- and thirty-second-note arpeggios from low F3 and low E3 (mm. 63–67). However, much of the melodic material and passage work is in the clarion register. A lyrical B[1] theme at no. 8 (m. 81) begins on a high C$_6$ whole note accompanied by eighth notes in the strings. There are virtuosic moments, such as a fast sixteenth-note arpeggio, A5–F3, and a dramatic three octave downward leap, high F$_6$–F3 (m. 91), at no. 9. The clarinet plays a pensive C minor melody *pp* four measures before no. 10 (mm. 97–107),

[9] Robert A. Titus, *The Solo Music for the Clarinet in the Eighteenth Century* (Ph.D. diss., State University of Iowa, 1962), 391.

[10] Sara Anbari, *The Clarinet Concertos of Franz Krommer* (M.M. thesis, University of Kansas, 1996), 10.

[11] Suggested by the author.

Section:	Orchestral exposition	Solo exposition	1st episode
Starts at m.	1 Allegro	51 (no. 5)	131 (no. 13)
No. of mm.	50	80	37
Tonalities	E♭, c♭, E♭	E♭, c, g, B♭, b♭, B♭, b♭, D♭, B♭, b♭	B♭
Themes	A, B	A¹, B¹, fig.	A², C

Section:	Development	2nd episode	Recapitulation	Coda
Starts at m.	168 (3 mm. before no. 17)	239	254 (4 mm. after no. 25)	329–340
No. of mm.	71	15	75	12
Tonalities	B♭, D♭, b♭, A♭, f, B♭, E♭	A♭, E♭	E♭, c, E♭	E♭
Themes	A³, B²	C¹	A⁴, fig.	B³

CHART 13.1 Krommer, *Concerto for Clarinet and Orchestra, op. 36*: Structural analysis, first movement, Allegro.

modulating to D♭ major and B♭ major at no. 11 (m. 111). Here a number of arpeggios and scales are skillfully written with runs from the chalumeau register up to high G_6.

During the first episode, no. 13, there is an active and varied A² theme and a new vocal C theme played by the strings at measure 147, four measures before no. 15. On beat four, the clarinet begins the development section three measures before no. 17 (m. 168), using an A³ theme in the clarion register with arpeggios and scales up to high F_6 and E_6. B♭ minor and F minor tonalities create drama as well as chromatic scales and repetition of various notes alternating E5–F5 and G♭5–F5 (mm. 227–228, 231–232), between no. 21 and two measures after no. 23.

After the short second episode, the clarinet starts the recapitulation at measure 254, four measures after no. 25, repeating all the A⁴ material until measure 274, four measures after no. 27. A modulation to E♭ major alters the melody, although the phrase patterns remain quite similar. A pensive short phrase plays in C minor at no. 30 (mm. 301–310), and when E♭ major returns, the bravura arpeggios are very effectively written from measure 314, four measures after no. 31, to the end of the recapitulation. Krommer occasionally allows some interplay between the flute, oboe, bassoon, and the soloist as in measures 75–78, 224–227, 233–237,[12] and 278–281. He primarily uses the orchestral strings and winds to sustain chords and move stepwise

---

[12] David H. Evans, *Franz Krommer (1759–1831) and His Music for Clarinet: A Stylistic Analysis and Interpretive Study of Selected Works* (D.M. diss., Indiana University, 1986), 20.

within a restricted range. The orchestral coda concludes the movement with an affirmative statement of the B³ theme.¹³

The second movement, Adagio, quarter note = 56,¹⁴ in ternary form with an eleven measure introduction, has a poignant oboe solo in a brief counterpoint to the bass line, measures 4–8.¹⁵ (See Chart 13.2.) Except for the tutti sections and the last three measures, the clarinet is accompanied only by the orchestral strings played *p*. After the brooding introduction, a romantic A theme begins *p* on the fourth beat of measure 12. It becomes operatic in content, using chromatic runs in the clarion register, extended runs in the chalumeau register, and immediate changes in dynamics from *pp* to *f*. A lyric B theme, five measures before no. 4 (fourth beat of measure 36), cleverly moves from E♭ minor to C minor, passing through B major and G major before arriving at C minor in the A¹ section.¹⁶ The A¹ theme is preceded by nine sixteenth notes and a decrescendo from *mf* to *p* (m. 52, after the third beat, 2 measures after no. 5). It corresponds nicely with the clarinet's closing thirty-second notes and sixteenth-note sextuplets (mm. 60–64, ending on the first eighth note), followed by a *f* three-measure orchestral closing.

The third movement, Rondo, Allegro moderato, dotted quarter note = 88,¹⁷ has six sections and a coda. (See Chart 13.3.) It is in 6/8 throughout, one eighth note pickup leads to two recurring eighth notes; the first tongued, the second slurred, in a sixteen measure dance-like A theme played in the clarion register. The orchestral response is emphatic, repeating a *ff* theme, using sixteenth note runs and a strong cadence. The clarinet responds *p* with two eighth notes (mm. 32–33) answered *f* by

Section:	Introduction	A	B	A¹
Starts at m.	1 Adagio	12 (2 mm. after no. 1)	36 (5 mm. before no. 4)	52 (third beat, 2 mm. after no. 5) to 66
No. of mm.	11	24	16	15
Tonalities	c	c, E♭	e♭, c, B, G	c
Themes	intro.	A	B	A¹

CHART 13.2 Krommer, *Concerto for Clarinet and Orchestra, op. 36*: Structural analysis, second movement, Adagio.

---

¹³ Evans, ibid., 40, 72, 135; Anbari, ibid., 12–38, 79.
¹⁴ Suggested by the author.
¹⁵ Evans, ibid., 47.
¹⁶ Evans, ibid., 54–55.
¹⁷ Suggested by the author.

Section:	A	B	A¹
Starts at m.	1 Allegro moderato	34 (4 mm. after no. 3)	73 (3 mm. after no. 7)
No. of mm.	33	39	17
Tonalities	Eb, c, Eb	c, Eb, c, g, Bb	Eb, c, Eb
Themes	A	B	A¹

Section:	C	A²	D	Coda
Starts at m.	90 (1 m. before no. 9)	134 (4 mm. after no. 13)	165 (6 mm. before no. 17)	230–239
No. of mm.	44	31	65	10
Tonalities	Ab, bb, f, Eb	Eb	eb, bb, Eb	Eb
Themes	C	A², C¹	D, fig.	coda

CHART 13.3 Krommer, *Concerto for Clarinet and Orchestra, op. 36*: Structural analysis, third movement, Rondo, Allegro moderato.

the orchestra. The B clarinet theme in C minor, four measures after no. 3 (m. 34), begins with the last eighth note of the measure tied to a dotted half note, joined to a *p* melody that becomes chromatic. Four measures after no. 5 (m. 54), a modulation goes to Eb major and the clarinet plays arpeggios that make extensive use of the chalumeau register with a bouncing staccato. The timpani and orchestral winds are usually restricted to orchestral passages. However, in one measure before no. 7 (m. 70), the flute answers the clarinet's high eighth notes, two octaves above the clarinet's chalumeau notes.[18] The clarinet seamlessly returns to the A¹ theme with the last eighth note of measure 73 (three measures after no. 7) in a group of two tongued and slurred eighth notes. From one measure before no. 9 (m. 90), an eighth note pickup to the happy C theme (mm. 91–133) contrasts with the A¹ theme by using two slurred eighth notes and dotted quarter notes, including staccato and slurred eighth notes. One measure after no. 12 (m. 122), there are six measures of imitation among the solo clarinet, flute, and first bassoon.[19] The imitation ends at two measures before no. 13 with a series of leaps in the chalumeau register, scales, and roulades in the clarion register (mm. 129–150). The clarinet offers a thoughtful Eb minor D theme with an eighth note pickup to dotted half notes, six measures before no. 17 (m. 165). From no. 17, there is some overlapping of the winds and soloist. At no. 21 (m. 211), Eb major returns with arpeggios, runs, and leaps. The coda (mm. 230–239) brings a triumphant orchestral conclusion.

---

[18] Anbari, ibid., 37.

[19] Evans, ibid., 107.

The majority of clarinetists during the early nineteenth century played with the reed against the upper lip,[20] although several soloists, such as, Josef Beer, Anton Stadler, and Bernhard Crusell, are thought to have played with the reed against the lower lip. Various types of articulation are possible using both reed positions. With reed above articulation, Fröhlich suggests using tongued or chest articulation (1811–1812). For notes not marked, Vanderhagen (1785) suggests separating them with the tongue by using the letter "d." When notes are marked with dots, they are comparable to detached bowing, and are separated with the tongue using the letter "t." When slurring notes, the first of each pair is given more emphasis. If articulation is not indicated for a triplet, the first two notes are slurred and the next note is tongued, using the letter "d." With reed below articulation, Müller (1821) suggests using the tongue, lips, and throat. For tonguing separate notes, "ti" is used and for the wedge and shortest strokes, "di."[21]

Krommer's *Concerto for Clarinet and Orchestra* exploits the clarinet's technical potential and uses expressive themes; it is enjoyable to perform. The clarinet solos are beautifully tailored to the capabilities of a five-key clarinet, and is very attractive on the modern instrument. Musically, its skillful orchestration makes it one of the finest concertos from the late Classical and early Romantic periods.

---

[20] See Albert R. Rice, "The Development of the Clarinet as Depicted in Austro-German Instruction Sources, 1732–1892," in *Tradition und Innovation im Holzblasinstrumentenbau des 19. Jahrhunderts*, ed. Sebastian Werr (Augsburg: Wissner, 2012), 84–85.

[21] Ingrid Pearson, "Playing Historical Clarinets," in Colin Lawson, *The Early Clarinet: A Practical Guide* (Cambridge: Cambridge University Press, 2000), 47–51; Joan Michelle Blazich, *Original Text, English Translation, and A Commentary on Amand Vanderhagen's Méthode Nouvelle et Raisonnée pour la Clarinette (1785) and Nouvelle Méthode de Clarinette (1799): A Study in Eighteenth-Century French Clarinet Music* (Lewiston, NY: Edwin Mellen Press, 2009), 37–38.

14 Jean-Xavier Lefèvre, *Sonata for Clarinet and Bass (Cello), op. 12, no. 1*

Date of composition: ca. 1793–1794

First edition: Jean-Xavier Lefèvre, *Trois Grandes Sonates pour Clarinette et Basse*, Paris: Janet, ca. 1793–1794[1]

Modern editions: Jean-Xavier Lefèvre, *Trois Grandes Sonates pour Clarinette et Basse*, 1793, facsimile ed., eds. Jean Jeltsch and Jean Saint-Arroman, Courlay: J. M. Fuzeau, 1998; Jean-Xavier Lefèvre, *Five Sonatas from Méthode de Clarinette (1802) for Clarinet and Piano*, eds. John Davies and Paul Harris, piano part realized by David Rowland, Oxford: Oxford University Press, 1988; Xavier Lefèvre, *Sonata in B-Flat Opus 12 No. 1 for Clarinet and Piano*, ed. and realized by Georgina Dobrée, London: Oxford University Press, 1973

Dedicatee/first performer: François Simonet; Jean-Xavier Lefèvre, clarinet

Date/place of first performance: Not known; Not known

JEAN-XAVIER LEFÈVRE (1763–1829) was a Swiss clarinetist and composer who studied in Paris during the 1770s with Michel Yost (1754–1786). He played in the French Guard's military band 1778–1795, and performed at the Paris Concert Spirituel as a soloist in woodwind concertos by Yost, Vogel, Devienne, and works of his own, and from 1787, predominantly as a soloist.[2] During the Revolution, on March 1, 1790, he played a

---

[1] Dated by the publisher's address; Anik Devriès and François Lesure, *Dictionnaire des Éditeurs de Musique Français* (Genève: Minkoff, 1988), 2: 234.

[2] Albert R. Rice and Frédéric Robert, "Xavier Lefèvre," *Grove Music Online*; Joseph James Estock, "A Biographical Dictionary of Clarinetists Born Before 1800" (Ph.D. diss., University of Iowa, 1972), 212–13; Jean Jeltsch, "Introduction," *Trois Grandes Sonates pour Clarinette et Basse 1793*, eds. Jean Jeltsch and Jean Saint-Arroman (Courlay: J. M. Fuzeau, 1998), 5; Constant Pierre, *Histoire du Concert Spiritual: 1725–1790* (Paris: Société

quartet for clarinet, two horns, and bassoon at the Salomon concerts in London with the soloists Buch, Duvernoy, and Perret.[3] Lefèvre played with the Paris Opéra Orchestra, 1791–1817, and between 1798 and 1799 with other famous instrumentalists in the Concerts de la rue de Cléry Orchestra.[4] In 1795, he was appointed professor, first class, at the newly opened Paris Conservatory and taught there until 1823.[5]

In 1801, a Conservatory committee asked Lefèvre to write the official clarinet method; in 1802, his *Méthode de Clarinette* was published in Paris. It was the first thorough nineteenth century clarinet instruction book.[6] He was the first to provide a chromatic fingering chart, E_3–C_6, and a trill chart to E_6.[7] In fourteen articles, Lefèvre discussed: the instrument, practical aspects of playing, encouraged nuanced playing based on good taste and an understanding of harmony, and argued that the Adagio was more demanding than Allegro movements.[8] He included twelve duos for clarinet and bass (cello), both parts written in C, with the indication that the clarinet part may be played in B♭, and the bass part transposed a major second lower.[9] For many years, Lefèvre's *Méthode* was the most well-known and frequently consulted clarinet instruction book and was used at the Naples Conservatory di San Sebastiano (now San Pietro a Majella) in 1816, one of the oldest schools in Europe.[10] It remains an essential source for understanding the Classical era five-key clarinet.

Lefèvre worked at the court of Emperor Napoleon, 1804–1806, and he was a member of the Imperial Chapel, 1807–1829.[11] In 1812, he was a member of the Paris

---

Française de Musicologie, 1975), 324, 327–29, 337–39, 341–44; François-Joseph Fétis, "Lefèvre," in *Biographie Universelle des Musiciens et Bibliographie Générale de la Musique,* 2nd ed. (Paris: Didot frères, 1883), 5: 253–54.

3 Simon McVeigh, "The Professional Concert and Rival Subscription Series in London, 1783–1793," *Royal Musical Association Research Chronicle* 22, no. 1 (1989): 81.

4 Adam Carse, *The Orchestra from Beethoven to Berlioz* (Cambridge: W. Heffer & Sons, 1948), 88.

5 Jeltsch, ibid., 5.

6 Xavier Le Fèvre, *Méthode de Clarinette* (Paris: L'Imprimerie du Conservatoire, facsimile ed., [1802], reprint, Genève: Minkoff Reprint, 1974). Later editions were published in French and German in 1805, in Italian about 1833, and in Spanish about 1860. Albert R. Rice, "The Development of the Clarinet as Depicted in Austro-German Instruction Sources, 1732–1892," in *Tradition und Innovation im Holzblasinstrumentenbau des 19. Jahrhunderts*, ed. Sebastian Werr (Augsburg: Wißner, 2012), 90–92.

7 Albert R. Rice, "Clarinet Fingering Charts, 1732–1816," *Galpin Society Journal* 37 (March 1984): 27–28.

8 Le Fèvre, ibid., 1–20. Colin Lawson, "Playing Historical Clarinets," in *The Cambridge Companion to the Clarinet*, ed. Colin Lawson (Cambridge: Cambridge University Press, 1995), 145.

9 Colin Lawson, "The C Clarinet," in *The Cambridge Companion to the Clarinet*, ed. Colin Lawson (Cambridge: Cambridge University Press, 1995), 39–40. Lefèvre's Sonata op. 12, no. 1 could have been intended for public performance or for study purposes to play either at home or for the instructor. A contemporary of Lefèvre, François Devienne, wrote six sonatas for clarinet and bass (late eighteenth century-early nineteenth century) which likely were played with a cello. Robert Austin Titus, "The Solo Clarinet Music in the Eighteenth Century" (Ph.D. diss., State University of Iowa, 1962), 487–88. 496–504.

10 Rice, "The Development of the Clarinet," 90.

11 Estock, ibid., 213; Jeltsch, *La Clarinette à Six Clés, : Un Jeu de Clarinettes du Facteur Parisien Jean-Jacques Baumann* (Courlay: J. M. Fuzeau, 1997), 5–6, 9–10, 22–23, 25–26.

Conservatory committee that evaluated Iwan Müller's thirteen-key clarinet. They concluded that the instrument could be played, "neither accurately, nor quickly" ("ni avec justesse, ni avec vitesse"), and did not want to abandon the corps de rechange because it would deprive composers of the expressive possibilities of instruments pitched in C, B♭, and A.[12] Later, Lefèvre stated that he was not a "supporter of any attempts to perfect the clarinet, believing that the addition of keys damaged the tuning of the instrument;" according to Fétis, "this was an error of old age."[13]

After Lefèvre's death in 1829, among his instruments in the estate was a thirteen-key 1824 boxwood A clarinet made in Louis Lefèvre's Paris instrument workshop (now in the Musée de la Musique, Paris, E. 476).[14] It is in excellent condition, does not appear to have been played much, and is the earliest known dated thirteen-key clarinet by Lefèvre, who copied Müller's clarinet but omitted his thumb keys. In 1814, Lefèvre received the title Chevalier de la Légion d'Honneur. Poor health in 1822 caused him to take leave from teaching and playing at the Chapelle, and his brother, Louis Lefèvre, substituted for him. Lefèvre trained several important clarinetists active in Paris, including César Janssen, Jacques-Jules Boufil, Claude-François Buteux, and Franco Dacosta.[15]

He composed several works for clarinet including, *six concertos for clarinet with orchestra*; two *Symphonie Concertantes for clarinet and bassoon*; a *Symphonie Concertante for oboe, clarinet, and bassoon*; *two quartets for clarinet, violin, viola, and cello*; *eleven duos for clarinet and bassoon*; *six sonatas for clarinet and cello*; *six trios for two clarinets and bassoon*;[16] a *Marche militaire* including two C clarinets;[17] and a collection of marches including two C clarinets.[18] Lefèvre's clarinet sonatas are described as, "particularly attractive."[19]

Lefèvre's *Sonata for Clarinet and Bass, op. 12, no. 1* (Dobrée edition) was written for a five or six-key B♭ clarinet. A second transposed part labelled "Basse" was very

---

[12] "Rapport fait pour la Commission chargée d'examiner la Nouvelle Clarinette Propose par M. Muller, et la Clarinette Alto Perfectionnée par la Même Artiste," *Gazette Nationale, ou le Moniteur Universel* 152 (1812): 593–94; Rice, *The Clarinet in the Classical Period*, 68.

[13] Joseph-François Fétis, "Nécrologie. Notice sur J. X. Lefèvre," *Revue Musicale* 6 (November 20, 1830): 399; Jeltsch, ibid., 7.

[14] Florence Gétreau, *Aux Origines du Musée de la Musique: les Collection Instrumentales du Conservatoire de Paris: 1793–1993* (Paris: Klincksieck, 1996), 657.

[15] Jeltsch, "Introduction," 6–7.

[16] Fétis, "Necrologie," 399.

[17] Constant Pierre, *Le Magasin de Musique à L'usage des Fètes Nationales et du Conservatoire* (Paris: Fischbacher, 1895), 156.

[18] *Recueil de Marches & Pas Redoublés Composé pour L'harmonie à Plusieurs Parties* (Paris: Imbault, ca. 1793), Bibliothèque Nationale, Vm. 7100.

[19] Jo Rees-Davies, "The Development of the Clarinet Repertoire," in *The Cambridge Companion to the Clarinet*, ed. Colin Lawson (Cambridge: Cambridge University Press, 1995), 77.

Section:	Exposition	Development	Recapitulation
Starts at m.	1–62: Allegro moderato	63	111–146
No. of mm.	124	48	36
Tonalities	B♭, F	g	B♭
Themes	A, B	A¹, C	B¹

CHART 14.1 Lefèvre, *Sonata for Clarinet and Bass, op. 12, no. 1*: Structural analysis, first movement, Allegro moderato.

likely a cello, since the first movement includes two notes played at once (mm. 12–15), appropriate for a stringed instrument.[20] It is in three movements, with all the themes played by the clarinet while the bass part gives harmonic and rhythmic support. The first movement, Allegro moderato, quarter note = 112,[21] is in sonata-allegro form with a repeated exposition. (See Chart 14.1.) The clarinet A theme is a sprightly melody written with C major arpeggios that are musical and expressive. The subsequent phrases offer interesting ideas, carefully elaborated in triplets and sixteenth notes, using the entire clarinet range, E3–G$_6$. After a half note fermata (m. 26), where a short Eingang or cadenza may be played, there is the pleasant B theme. It is a smooth, conjunct line (m. 27) and easily leaps, G5–A4. The development skillfully uses a G minor A¹ theme (mm. 63, 77) to introduce a completely different mood with a pensive C theme, featuring half, four eighth, and staccato quarter notes. After an elaboration of the theme in triplets and eighth notes, it ends with a written out Eingang at measure 109. The recapitulation's B♭ major B¹ theme (m. 111) incorporates sixteenth-note passages in measures 126–136. The movement ends convincingly with downward arpeggios, C$_6$–C4.

The second movement, Adagio, quarter note = 52,[22] is in ternary form. (See Chart 14.2.) In his *Méthode*, Lefèvre writes that an Adagio movement is the most difficult movement to play, its character quite different from the Allegro.[23] The clarinet's A theme begins with a sixteenth to a double-dotted quarter note, reminiscent of the French overture style, and states the musical ideas in a direct and disarming manner. This expressive melody modulates to C major (m. 27) and is a collection of small gestures within eight-measure phrases. It includes just the right amount of ornamentation in trills and turns, along with arpeggios, octave leaps, and accented,

---

[20] Jeltsch, ibid., 8. This work, however, may be performed on a keyboard instrument with a realized bass, as found in a few modern editions.

[21] Suggested by the author.

[22] Suggested by the author.

[23] Colin Lawson, "Playing Historical Clarinets," in *The Cambridge Companion to the Clarinet*, ed. Colin Lawson (Cambridge: Cambridge University Press, 1995), 145.

Section:	A	B	A¹
Starts at m.	1–29: Adagio	30	50–73
No. of mm.	58	20	24
Tonalities	f, C	C, c, d	F
Themes	A	A¹	A²

CHART 14.2 Lefèvre, *Sonata for Clarinet and Bass, op. 12, no. 1*: Structural analysis, second movement, Adagio.

Section:	A	B	A¹
Starts at m.	1–8: 9–24 Rondo, Allegro moderato	25–32: 33–53	54–61
No. of mm.	32	37	8
Tonalities	B♭	g	B♭
Themes	A, A¹	B	A²

CHART 14.3 Lefèvre, *Sonata for Clarinet and Bass, op. 12, no. 1*: Structural analysis, third movement, Rondo, Allegro moderato.

short staccato, using mainly the clarion register and only occasionally the chalumeau register (mm. 23–24). The A section is repeated. The B section (m. 30) begins the A¹ theme in C major and in measure 33, descends in an arpeggio to low E3. The theme continues in a sensitive manner in D minor (m. 41), ending with a fermata on a half note trill providing the opportunity for another Eingang (m. 49).[24] The third section A¹ at measure 50 uses the F major A² theme, rhythmically varied with triplet and sixteenth notes. Further careful elaboration includes a sixteenth note G7 arpeggio, from D$_6$ ending on E3, and a leap of two octaves and a third to G5, followed by a chromatic scale in triplets (m. 68). The movement ends with a lovely repeated phrase (mm. 71–73).

The third movement, Rondo, Allegro moderato, quarter note = 88,[25] is buoyant and features a continuous stream of clarinet sixteenth notes from beginning to end. (See Chart 14.3.) Its three-part form has partial repeats in the A and B sections. It begins with an eighth-note pickup and presents an attractive A theme played with light staccato and occasional slurs, the first eight measures repeated once. It requires well-placed breaths that do not disturb the phrases. The clarinet A theme is elabo-

---

[24] Dobrée provides a short and appropriate cadenza, Xavier Lefèvre, *Sonata in B-Flat Opus 12 No. 1 for Clarinet and Piano* (London: Oxford University Press, 1973), 12 (piano score).

[25] Suggested by the author.

rated with a flat sixth step, A♭2; a second eight-measure phrase continues in the clarion register and, after a chromatic scale (m. 16), states the A^1 theme (mm. 17–24). The B theme is elaborated (mm. 33–53) with many staccato sixteenth notes, including a *fz* on the upbeat of the second beat in three measures (mm. 48–50). After a brief chromatic scale, the eight-measure statement of the A^2 theme (m. 54) ends the movement abruptly.

Lefèvre and other French clarinetists during the eighteenth century played with the reed on the upper lip[26] which facilitates a light and crisp staccato. In his clarinet tutor, Lefèvre provided instructions to play notes with different articulations, slurred (coulé), detached (détaché), and staccato (piqué). This was achieved by using an unvoiced consonant "tû."[27]

Lefèvre's *Sonata for Clarinet and Bass, op. 12, no. 1*, is a well-written late-eighteenth-century musical work that makes excellent use of the clarinet's entire compass with arpeggios, runs, trills, and many articulated and slurred notes. Lawson writes that the Lefèvre sonatas and other Classical period works, "have a character that is arguably better suited to the lighter and less cumbersome tone of earlier clarinets."[28] Because of almost nonstop playing, the clarinetist needs a reed-mouthpiece setup that allows a quick and easy response. While technically within the grasp of students, this sonata requires thought, practice, stamina, and imagination. In his method, Lefèvre emphasizes the importance of dynamics and articulation as expressive devices:

> If the composer does not indicate the articulation of passages, the intelligence of the artist should supply it. If a passage is repeated two times, it must be played forte, and then piano, or first piano and then forte, according to the character of the work. If, finally, the passage is repeated more than two times, one may make use of different articulation to add nuance.[29]

In addition, Lefèvre warns in his method that:

> clarinet playing becomes monotonous without nuance of sound and articulation, and where there is neither expression nor panache. It is not enough to read the music and play the notes; one must supply those nuances which suit the character of the music and capture what the composer has not troubled to write down.... Uniformity of execution and articulation means that a certain

---

[26] Rice, "The Development of the Clarinet," 85, 90–91.

[27] Ingrid Pearson, "Playing Historical Clarinets," in Colin Lawson, *The Early Clarinet: A Practical Guide* (Cambridge: Cambridge University Press, 2000), 49–50.

[28] Lawson, "Playing Historical Clarinets," 135.

[29] Eric Hoeprich, *The Clarinet* (New Haven, CT: Yale University Press, 2008), 98.

coldness has often been attributed to the nature of the instrument, whereas in fact this is the responsibility of the performer. The range, variety, and quality of clarinet sound distinguishes it from all wind instruments; it can portray whatever character a composer assigns to it, whether a battle hymn or a shepherd's chant.[30]

Lefèvre's *Sonata for Clarinet and Bass, op. 12, no. 1,* is a charming solo, well written for both instruments, that is musically inventive and interesting to play. It is a short work that will easily fit on many programs and will form an excellent contrast to later works. This sonata is accessible to young players but remains challenging on both technical and musical levels.

---

[30] Lawson, "Playing Historical Clarinets," 145.

15 Witold Lutosławski, *Dance Preludes for Clarinet and Piano*

Dates of composition: December 21, 1954 (clarinet and piano); September 5, 1955 (orchestral score); 1959 (score for nine instruments)

First edition/other editions: Witold Lutosławski, *Preludia Taneczne, na Klarnet Solo, Harfę, Fortepian, Perkusję i Orkiestrę Smyczkową. Dance Preludes, for Clarinet Solo, Harp, Piano, Percussion and String Orchestra*, Kraców: Polskie Wydawn. Muzyczne, 1956 (clarinet and piano); 1957, 1971 (orchestral edition); 1970 (edition for nine instruments)

Dedicatee/first performers: Not indicated; Ludwik Kurkiewicz, clarinet, Sergiusz Nadgryzowski, piano (first clarinet and piano performance); Alojzy Szulc, clarinet, Polish Radio Symphony Orchestra, Jan Krenz, conductor on Polish radio (first orchestral performance); Gervase de Peyer, clarinet, English Chamber Orchestra, Benjamin Britten, conductor (first public performance);[1] Czech Nonet (first performance for nine instruments)

Dates/places of first performance: February 15, 1955; Warsaw (clarinet and piano); ca. 1955; Warsaw (on Polish Radio); June 1963; Snape, Suffolk, England, Aldeburgh Festival (clarinet and orchestra); November 10, 1959; Louny, Czech Republic (nine instruments)

Instrumentation: Eight first violins, eight second violins, six violas, six cellos, four double basses, harp, three timpani, piano, and percussion (orchestral); flute, oboe, clarinet, bassoon, horn, violin, viola, cello, and double bass (nine instruments)[2]

---

[1] Lutosławski, Witold, *Preludia Taneczne, na Klarnet Solo, Harfę, Fortepian, Perkusję i Orkiestrę Smyczkową. Dance Preludes, for Clarinet Solo, Harp, Piano, Percussion and String Orchestra* (Kraców: Polskie Wydawn. Muzyczne, 1956), 2.

[2] Irina Nikolska, *Conversations with Witold Lutosławski (1987–1992)*, trans. Valeri Yerokbin (Stockholm: Melos, 1994), 201; Charles Bodman Rae, *The Music of Lutosławski* (London: Faber and Faber, 1994), 268; Stainsław Będkowski and Stainsław Hrabia, *Witold Lutosławski: A Bio-Bibliography* (Westport, CT: Greenwood Press, 2001), 27–28.

WITOLD LUTOSŁAWSKI (1913–1994) was one of Europe's leading twentieth-century composers. He studied composition and piano at the Warsaw Conservatory but could not study in Paris because of World War II. After the war, he wrote his first major orchestral work, *Symphony no. 1* (1941–1947), influenced by Bartók, Albert Roussel, and Prokofiev. When banned by the Russian authorities in 1949, Lutosławski kept a low profile by writing many songs and small-scale occasional pieces.

After the 1956 Warsaw Autumn Festival, more advanced techniques were accepted, and Lutosławski used ideas in his compositions that he had developed over several years. These include, "vertical and horizontal placement of the twelve pitches of the chromatic scale, controlled chance, and new instrumental techniques, particularly for stringed instruments." Since the 1960s, Lutosławski was internationally recognized and received commissions from many leading artists. In his final decade, Lutosławski created works that share some similarities with Ravel in the song cycle *Chantefleurs et Chantefables* (1990); aspects of Rachmaninov, Chopin, Liszt, and Brahms in the *Piano Concerto* (1987–1988); and eighteenth century procedures in the *Symphony no. 4* (1988–1992).[3] Lutosławski is arguably the greatest Polish composer since Chopin.[4]

From 1945 to 1955, Lutosławski wrote several pieces, including easy piano pieces for music schools, children's songs for radio broadcasts, and pieces for small orchestra. For these, he used simple diatonic melodies, sometimes from folklore material, combined with unconventional harmonies and occasionally nontonal counterpoints.[5] During the 1950s, the violinist and teacher, Tadeusz Ochlewski, suggested that Lutosławski write a cycle of easy works using folk themes for violin and piano for academies attended by gifted children who might later go to a conservatory. After he wrote them, Lutosławski was not satisfied with their suitability for violin and rewrote them for clarinet. The results were good for young clarinetists but quite difficult for the accompanists. However, they were and continue to be popular and are performed in various schools.[6] Brymer agrees with this assessment, "A piece of excellent music by Poland's leading contemporary composer. Not difficult, and effective."[7]

The five movement *Dance Preludes* is based on folk songs from northern Poland but the sources are unknown. It is a finely crafted work, "combining diatonic folk dance tunes with chromatic accompaniments and polychords." Each movement has

[3] Adrian Thomas, "Lutosławski, Witold," in *The Oxford Companion to Music, Oxford Music Online*; Rae, ibid., 224–25.

[4] Charles Bodman Rae, "Lutosławski," *Grove Music Online*.

[5] Zbigniew Skowron, ed. and trans. *Lutosławski on Music* (Lanham: Scarecrow Press, 2007), 98.

[6] Skowron, ibid., 160.

[7] Jack Brymer, *Clarinet* (New York: Schirmer Books, 1977), 216.

a definite tonal center, E♭, F, B♭, G, and E♭. Polymeter is frequently used between the clarinet and the accompaniment, notated in the piano score with separate time signatures and dotted bar lines. Lutosławski called the *Dance Preludes*, "my farewell to folklore forever." It, "closed the difficult, middle period of his creative life." Many of the works of this period contain similar instrumentation, rhythm, and tone color that Lutosławski used in his more mature works.[8]

Each movement is short. The first, Allegro molto, quarter note = ca. 160, is in ternary form, beginning with a playful clarinet accented quarter note F major arpeggio, moving to staccato eighth notes between the interval of a major and minor third, creating tonal uncertainty. (See Chart 15.1.) A similar staccato eighth note B theme, at no. 2 (m. 16), starts on a lowered sixth scale degree, D♭4, immediately playing slurred quarter notes *p* at no. 3 (m. 24). Slurred and tongued eighth notes alternate until the A[1] theme at no. 5 (m. 42). After a ritardando at no. 7 (m. 59), staccato eighth notes begin at the first tempo and accelerate to a crisp conclusion.[9]

Polymeters occur at four measures before no. 3 in the clarinet, in 2/4, and at two measures before no. 3 in the piano, in 3/4, indicated by dotted lines in the piano part. The alternating use of both 2/4 and 3/4 meters does not create rhythmic problems since quarter notes remain constant throughout the movement. The tonal uncertainty in this work is emphasized by added tones, such as a major triad with a flat second step and a minor triad with a flat sixth step.[10] Paja-Stach describes Lutosławski's tonal ambiguity as typical of his early works using, "movement between major and minor" and "coloring chords by added tones."[11]

Section:	A	B	A[1]
Starts at m.	1 Allegro molto	16 (no. 2)	42 (no. 5) to 65
No. of mm.	15	26	24
Tonal Centers	E♭	E♭	E♭
Themes	A	B	A[1]

CHART 15.1 Lutosławski, *Dance Preludes for Clarinet and Piano*: Structural analysis, first movement, Allegro molto.

---

[8] Steven Stucky, *Lutosławski and His Music* (Cambridge: Cambridge University Press), 1981, 59; Steven Stucky, "Change and Constancy: The Essential Lutosławski," in Zbigniew Skowron, ed., *Lutosławski Studies* (Oxford: Oxford University Press, 2001), 130, 132, 159–60.

[9] Rae, ibid., 45–46; Jadwiga Paja-Stach, "The Stylistic Traits of Lutosławski's Works for Solo Instrument and Piano," in Zbigniew Skowron, ed., *Lutosławski Studies*, 271–76.

[10] Stucky, ibid., 146.

[11] Paja-Stach, ibid., 270–71.

Section:	A	B	A¹	Coda
Starts at m.	1 Andantino	22 (6 mm. after no. 2)	35 (4 mm. after no. 4)	47 (1 m. after no. 6) to 51
No. of mm.	21	13	12	5
Tonal Centers	F-f	F-f	F-f	F-f
Themes	A	B	A¹	coda

CHART 15.2 Lutosławski, *Dance Preludes for Clarinet and Piano*: Structural analysis, second movement, Andantino.

The second movement, Andantino (dotted quarter note = ca. 50), begins for the first sixteen measures with a repeated phrase of eighth notes forming a major/minor triad in the piano. The clarinet melody begins with an eighth note pickup that could have been based on a folk song, constantly oscillating between F major and F minor. (See Chart 15.2.) It is written in four sections, ternary form with a coda, beginning with a slow and expressive A theme, described as "a sort of lullaby."[12] The B theme (six measures after no. 2) is a little faster (Un poco più vivo); the rhythm is delineated by articulated *pp* sixteenth notes. Polymeters are written one measure after no. 3, when the clarinet moves from 3/8 to 2/4 and the piano from 9/8 to 3/4. Because eighth notes are counted as the main pulse, the changing meters do not cause any rhythmic problems. After a single measure poco ritardando, the A¹ theme emerges at measure 35. A poco ritardando brings a little slower (poco meno mosso), sorrowful sounding, five-measure coda with a haunting *pp* ending.

The third movement, Allegro giocoso (quarter note = ca. 180), is in ternary form with an introduction and coda. (See Chart 15.3.) A three-measure piano introduction features constant eighth notes and grace notes followed by a clarinet A theme of short eighth notes and grace notes. After a sixteenth-note run at no. 1 (m. 12), the clarinet A theme is repeated an octave higher. One measure before no. 2 (m. 23, Ex. 15.1), the piano plays a *f* eighth-note ostinato in alternating 3/4 and 4/4 measures; two measures after no. 2, the clarinet plays accented off-beats of a *f* B theme in alternating 3/4 and 4/4. This part is technically challenging because of its fast tempo and various polymeters, 2/4 against 4/4, 3/4 against 4/4, and 4/4 against 3/4. It requires counting eighth notes with careful and slow practice between clarinetist and pianist. A climax is reached at no. 5 (m. 45) after a five beat trill on $F\sharp_6$ to G_6. Staccato eighth notes play in a 7/4 measure, gradually softening to the A¹ theme (m. 54), three measures before no. 6. After a rallentando and caesura, the coda at no. 7 (m. 67)

---

[12] Elsa Ludewig-Verdehr, "Master Class: Witold Lutoslawski's *Dance Preludes*," *The Clarinet* 24, no. 4 (July–August 1997): 4.

EXAMPLE 15.1. Lutosławski, *Dance Preludes for Clarinet and Piano*, third movement, mm. 19–28.

Section:	Introduction	A	B	A¹	Coda
Starts at m.	1 Allegro giocoso	4	21 (no. 2)	54 (3 mm. before no. 6)	67 (no. 7) to 74
No. of mm.	3	17	33	13	8
Tonal Centers	B♭	B♭	B♭	B♭	B♭
Themes	intro.	A	B	A¹	coda

CHART 15.3 Lutosławski, *Dance Preludes for Clarinet and Piano*: Structural analysis, third movement, Allegro giocoso.

starts with piano sixteenth-note runs, joined by the clarinet leading to a small crescendo and a *pp* staccato ending.

The fourth movement, Andante (quarter note = ca. 60), is written in a two-part song form with a G major tonal center, "in a mood that evokes a funeral dirge."[13] (See Chart 15.4.) The piano begins with a four-measure staccato quarter-note *p* bass line that melodically pairs semitones and minor thirds in a distinctive manner,[14] accented by three groups of four grace notes. The clarinet melancholy A theme (no. 1, m. 6) is a dotted half note E4 tied to a dotted quarter note followed by repeated legato-tongued E4s, featuring minor and major scale degrees.[15] An expressive B theme played *mf* at

---

[13] Ludewig-Verdehr, ibid., 6.

[14] Rae, ibid., 63–65.

[15] "Reminding one of a cantor singing in a Jewish service, or a monk intoning Gregorian chant." Ludewig-Verdehr, ibid., 6.

no. 2, measure 17, includes three major triads, followed by a minor second in eighth notes, that turn into the A^1 theme. The B^1 clarinet theme is repeated *mf* at no. 3 (m. 25) with a big crescendo to the A^2 theme, an octave and a major third higher at no. 4 (m. 32). A diminuendo follows the statement of the B^2 theme (mm. 32–35), a fifth and minor third higher, until the *mf* clarinet A^3 theme, four measures before no. 5 (m. 36). The piano plays *p* quarter notes, repeating semitone and minor third intervals while the clarinet plays fragments of the melancholy phrase (mm. 47–54), succeeded by two meditative clarinet legato-tongued E4s from measure 55, ending *pp*.

The fifth movement, Allegro molto (quarter note = ca. 190), is set in ternary form with a coda, and centers on an E♭ major tonality. (See Chart 15.5.) It begins in 5/4 with piano quarter notes, the first beat often accented throughout. Polymeters of 2/4 with 5/4, 3/4 and 2/4 are used, and with the fast tempo, may cause rhythmic problems. The clarinet A theme plays *p* in the second measure and is repeated *mp* an octave higher at no. 1 (m. 12), and *p* at the lower octave, four measures after no. 2 (m. 21). It returns an octave higher *mp* at no. 3 (m. 33). After a piano fermata at no. 4 (m. 46), the clarinet B theme plays, poco più tranquillo, repeated a major second higher in canon at no. 5 (m. 54) until no. 6 (m. 65). A climax is achieved for the piano at five measures after no. 6 on the second beat (for the clarinet, six measures after no. 6 on C$\sharp_6$), and diminuendos to the clarinet A^1 theme (m. 74) at four measures before no. 7. The clarinet A^2 theme, an octave higher, is repeated once, and directly flows into the coda (m. 98) at a Presto 3/4 tempo, played one beat per measure. It builds to five separate sforzandos and two caesuras, and triumphantly ends with a downward arpeggio.

The orchestration is a transcription of the piano part with the added color of harp and piano providing articulation and accents in the first movement. In the orchestral score, the metronome number has been changed from the clarinet and piano parts, for all five movements. The first movement metronome speed is increased in the score to quarter note = 168–176. The second movement metronome speed is slightly increased to dotted quarter note = 50–54. Throughout this soft-sounding movement, the number of stringed instruments is reduced for a better balance with the clarinet solo to three violins, three violas, three or four cellos, and three double

Section:	A	B
Starts at m.	1 Andante	36 (4 mm. before no. 5) to 62
No. of mm.	35	27
Tonal Centers	G	G
Themes	A, B, A^1, B^1, A^2, B^2	A^3

CHART 15.4 Lutosławski, *Dance Preludes for Clarinet and Piano*: Structural analysis, fourth movement, Andante.

Section:	A	B	A¹	Coda
Starts at m.	1 Allegro molto	46 (no. 4)	74 (4 mm. before no. 7)	98–116
No. of mm.	45	28	24	19
Tonal Centers	E♭	E♭	E♭	E♭
Themes	A	B	A¹, A²	coda

CHART 15.5 Lutosławski, *Dance Preludes for Clarinet and Piano*: Structural analysis, fifth movement, Allegro molto.

basses. There is a brief first violin solo from one measure after no. 2 (mm. 18–22). A *ppp* snare drum roll starting two measures before no. 3 (m. 20), is barely heard and used for background effect. In the third movement, the metronome speed is increased to quarter note = 192–200. The harp is prominent in the accompaniment, adding color to the string instruments, as does the timpani roll at no. 2 to no. 3. Alternation between pizzicato and arco bowing and the piano adds to the sounds of this movement. The metronome's speed of the fourth movement is changed to quarter note = 66–76, and the harp, piano, and pizzicato double basses are prominent sound elements. The metronome's speed of the fifth movement is increased to quarter note = 200–208, all the string parts are divided, and additional colors are provided by harp, timpani, and percussion.

The third version of the *Dance Preludes* was written for the Czech Nonet consisting of a woodwind quintet (flute, oboe, B♭ clarinet, B♭ horn, and bassoon) and a string quartet (violin, viola, cello, and double bass). It is not as popular as the versions for clarinet and piano or clarinet and orchestra. The same music is used as in the first *Dance Preludes* but the clarinet is primarily an ensemble instrument with solo parts only at the beginning of the second movement until three measures after no. 2, and at the beginning of the third movement until two measures before no. 1.

Lutosławski's *Dance Preludes* is generally light-hearted in the first, third, and fifth movements, and melancholy in the second and fourth movements. It is technically accessible by most undergraduate students, but requires good musical and technical controls and an advanced pianist to work out the rhythmic problems caused by the polymeters. *Dance Preludes* is an excellent program choice and an effective recital work.

16 Donald Martino, *A Set for Clarinet Unaccompanied*

Date of composition: February 7–9, 1954

First edition/other editions: Donald Martino, *A Set for Clarinet Unaccompanied*, New York: McGinnis & Marx, 1954, 1957 (rev. 2nd printing); New York: McGinnis & Marx, 1974 (rev. 3rd printing)[1]

Dedicatee/first performer: Arthur Bloom; Arthur Bloom, clarinet

Date/place of first performance: May 1954; Princeton, New Jersey, Princeton University[2]

DONALD MARTINO (1931–2005) studied clarinet, saxophone, and oboe in high school and played jazz and popular music in bands, jazz combos, and dance bands, and classical music in a local symphony orchestra.[3] He attended Syracuse University and Princeton University where he studied music composition with Ernst Bacon, Roger Sessions, and Milton Babbitt, and during two Fulbright Scholarships (1954–1956), with Luigi Dallapiccola in Florence.[4] In 1956, Martino returned to New York to work club dates and write popular music and jazz under the pen name Jimmie Vincent. In 1957, Martino stopped writing popular music and jazz, concentrating on composition. He did not play or practice, ceasing to perform publically in 1959.[5]

---

[1] Two printed versions exist, both with the 1957 date; the latest includes corrections to three errors in the first movement and changes in the second movement. Phillip Rehfeldt, "Master Class: Donald Martino, *A Set for Clarinet (Unaccompanied)*," *The Clarinet* 23, no. 3 (May–June 1996): 7.

[2] Linda Solow Blotner, ed., *The Boston Composers Project: A Bibliography of Contemporary Music* (Cambridge, MA: MIT Press, 1983), 332.

[3] James Boros, "A Conversation with Donald Martino," *Perspectives of New Music* 29, no. 2 (1991): 215.

[4] Elaine Barkin and Martin Brody, "Martino, Donald," *Grove Music Online*.

[5] Boros, ibid., 217, 222–23.

Martino taught at Princeton University, 1957–1959, and Yale University, 1959–1969. From 1969–1981, he chaired the composition department at the New England Conservatory, and taught at Harvard University in 1971. After teaching at Brandeis University (1980–1983), he again taught at Harvard (1983–1992). Martino's oeuvre consists of orchestral, chamber music, works for solo instruments, vocal works with piano, chamber orchestra and/or chorus, film scores, and a mixed mediocritique. In 1978, Martino founded a publishing company, Dantalian, Inc., to promote music. He received a Naumburg Award in 1973 for *Notturno* for chamber ensemble, for which he also won a Pulitzer Prize in 1974.[6]

While a student at Syracuse, he studied Bela Bartók's music and began to write in Bartók's style using octatonic scales, known in jazz as the "diminished scale."[7] In 1954, with Sessions, Martino worked on a cello concerto but Sessions thought it took too long to compose. With thoughts of impressing Sessions, Martino quickly wrote two solo works, *A Set for Clarinet* and *Quodlibets* for flute.[8] The former was written over three days, while he improvised on the clarinet in his parent's resonant basement.[9]

A Set for Clarinet is technically demanding with unfamiliar fingering patterns at a very fast tempo, using rapid single staccato and enormous leaps of two and three octaves to $B\flat_6$ and B_6. Early opinions include, "Extremely demanding solo clarinet pieces";[10] "It is without doubt, one of the most demanding works in all of the clarinet repertory."[11] "Because Martino feels it is important for a composer to advance the literature…his writing is extremely difficult."[12] David Epstein's 1964 review in *Musical America* of Phillip Rehfeldt's recording states:

> Donald Martino's *Set for Clarinet* achieved that most difficult and elusive goal of solo pieces—making music that is interesting as well as virtuosic. Indeed, these were both, for the writing has some fiendish passages in the technique of the instrument, however, and it exploited to the full the textures and effect of

6 Barkin and Brody, ibid.
7 Boros, ibid., 216.
8 Boros, ibid., 218.
9 John Edward Anderson, "An Analytical and Interpretive Study and Performance of Three Twentieth Century Works for Unaccompanied Clarinet" (Ed.D. diss., Teachers College, Columbia University, 1974), 38; Martin Brody, "Liner Notes," Donald Martino, *A Jazz Set*, New World Records 80518, 1996, 4. [Online] Available: http://www.newworldrecords.org/liner_notes/80518.pdf. [Saturday, October 17, 2015].
10 Barney Childs, "Young Performers & New Music," *Music Educator's Journal* 51, no. 1 (September–October 1964): 42.
11 James E. Gillespie, Jr., *Solos for Unaccompanied Clarinet: An Annotated Bibliography of Published Works*, Detroit Studies in Music Bibliography, 28 (Detroit: Information Coordinators, Inc., 1973), 44.
12 Anderson, ibid., 36–37.

the clarinet. The style was tonal and highly chromatic, with traces of Bartókian mannerisms in the second piece and the drives and rhythms of jazz in the third.[13]

In a 1972 interview, Martino felt that the rapid passages in *A Set* were more unfamiliar than difficult:

All you have to do is practice it just the way you would have practiced any other piece. All your lesson books teach you how to practice, and you forget when you approach the Mozart Quintet or some other traditional piece that seems technically simple that you've been playing arpeggios all your life. So, naturally they are easy. You've been playing scales all your life, so you can play them fluently and quickly. This scale, in *A Set for Clarinet*, you haven't been playing. So you're going to have to practice it just the way you practiced all those other scales until it becomes as natural as any of them. Once it becomes that, you will find that *A Set for Clarinet* is not a difficult piece at all.[14]

A Set for Clarinet was written as a challenge to Martino's childhood friend and rival, Arthur Bloom, who was a Juilliard School student at the time, later to become an important new music clarinetist beginning in the 1960s.[15]

The word "set" does not refer to a twelve-tone set but to a "dance band set" of three pieces. Each movement originally had jazz subtitles, "Tenth Avenue Shuffle" for movement one, "Blues in E♭" for movement two, and "Conservatory Stomp" for movement three. These subtitles were removed from the 1957 publication as Martino felt they were unnecessary and dated the composition.[16] "The first title refers to Arthur Bloom's New York address at the time, but more importantly, to off-beat accents and ends of phrases ending on upbeats, often found in jazz, producing a shuffle."[17]

The first movement is in ternary form with an introduction and coda. Each of the ABA[1] sections has a small aba ternary design. Martino's melodic organization is a result of alternately using two diminished seventh chords melodically, known as octatonic scales (Ex. 16.1).[18] The two scales consist of alternating major and minor seconds, f-f♯-g♯-a-b-c-d-e♭ and f-g-g♯-a♯-b-c♯-d-e. Alternative derivations of the same note

[13] Quoted by Gillespie, *Solos for Unaccompanied Clarinet*, 44, from Epstein's record review in *Musical America* on the liner notes of the LP record, *New Music for Solo Clarinet*, Advance FGR-4, 1964.
[14] John Anderson interview with Donald Martino, Boston, July 6, 1972; Anderson, "An Analytical and Interpretive Study," 62.
[15] Boros, ibid., 225.
[16] Anderson, ibid., 38. In the liner notes for Donald Martino, *A Jazz Set*, CD, New York: New World Records, no. 80518, 1996, the first and third movement titles are interchanged; Brody, "Liner Notes," 4.
[17] Anderson, ibid., 41–42.
[18] Anderson, ibid., 43.

sequence create subsets using a minor third motive, f-f♯-g♯, g♯-a-b, etc., or a major second followed by a minor third, f-g-g♯, g♯-a♯-b, etc.[19] Rebecca Wunch observes that Martino uses many possible subsets of the octatonic scale but one subset is prominent, a tritone and a step interval.[20]

EXAMPLE 16.1. Martino, *A Set for Clarinet Unaccompanied*, first movement, two diminished seventh chords.

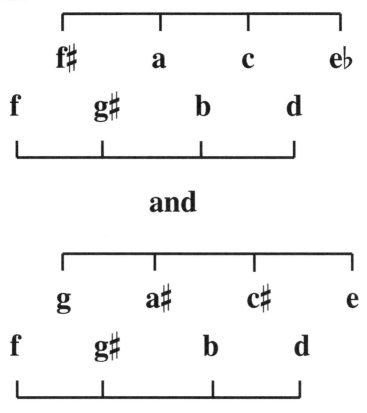

The five measure introductory Allegro flourish (quarter note = 80–76)[21] alternates between major and minor seconds at a dashing speed, highlighted by crescendos and decrescendos. (See Chart 16.1.)[22] A resolution is achieved from the high A₆

[19] Explained to Anderson by Martino; Anderson, ibid., 44. An equally valid approach to analysis using three interwoven diminished seventh chords is described in detail by Rebecca Lynn Wunch, "The Merger of Jazz and Twentieth Century: A Performance Analysis of Donald Martino's *A Set for Clarinet*" (M.M. thesis, Bowling Green State University, 2007), 11–30.
[20] Wunch, ibid., 13.
[21] Martino suggested several changes for Rehfeldt's 1972 recording, including a tempo change of quarter note = 92; Rehfeldt, "Master Class," 6.
[22] Anderson, ibid., 42–62; Wunch, ibid., 31–52.

at the end of measure 5 to a Bb3 at the beginning of the A section (m. 6). Alternating dynamics from *p* to *f*, accents, and crescendos are an important part of the A theme, and the first subsection A (mm. 6–15). A slower tempo (quarter note = 76) and staccato articulation (mm. 20–24) combine major and minor seconds with an accelerando and crescendo to abruptly end on C5. Measure 25 (Tempo I) leads to a tonal center shift from Bb to B, modifying the notes and articulation of the A theme a half-step higher on the note B (mm. 25–32), followed by a minor and major step flourish ending on B3.

The B or development section, marked cantabile (quarter note = 66),[23] presents a pensive, slow melody using minor and major half steps, with larger intervals taken from subsets of the octatonic scales. The fewer repeated notes in the B section (mm. 36–76), makes it more difficult to recognize tonal centers. However, throughout the section there is melodic motion from C# to B, and to E, with cadences on G (mm. 43, 68), suggesting tonal centers on these four notes. After the eighth note fermata, the B[1] theme (mm. 60–76) plays one octave lower, with basically the same pitches and fewer grace notes.[24] The A[1] section (mm. 77–97) on a B tonal center is written with octave and other alterations, and consists of an arch or mirror form with the A[1] theme. The second Tempo I (m. 90) begins on the tonal center Bb but ends on B (m. 96). The introduction reappears at the beginning of the coda (m. 98). The last three measures are an affirming cadence from F3 to Bb3.

The second movement, Adagio, quarter note = 50–54,[25] "Blues in Eb" reflects an introspective, meditative mood. Epstein's "Bartókian mannerisms" mentioned in his 1964 review refer to "Martino's careful use of the tritone and chromatically altered

Section:	Introduction	A	B	A[1]	Coda
Starts at m.	1 Allegro	6	36	77	98–104
No. of mm.	5	30	41	21	7
Tonal Centers	Bb	Bb, B, F, E, Bb, B	C#, B, E, G	B, Bb, F, E, Bb, B	Bb, F, Bb
Themes	intro.	A	B, B[1]	A[1]	coda

CHART 16.1 Martino, *A Set for Clarinet Unaccompanied*: Structural analysis, first movement, Allegro.

[23] Martino suggests a short rest between the A and B sections at measure 35, and a slightly faster tempo; Anderson, "An Analytical and Interpretive Study," 48.

[24] Anderson, ibid., 48–49.

[25] Martino suggests a tempo of quarter note = 42 to enhance the mood and provide a greater change from the first movement, Anderson, ibid., 53; Rehfeldt, "Master class," 6.

Section:	A	B	A¹	Codetta
Starts at m.	1 Adagio	24	39	55–57
No. of mm.	23	15	16	3
Tonal Centers	F, C, F	octatonic	E♭, C, F	octatonic
Themes	A	B	A¹	codetta

CHART 16.2 Martino, *A Set for Clarinet Unaccompanied*: Structural analysis, second movement, Adagio.

notes in an F tonality."[26] Its ternary form with a codetta features a theme of alternating major and minor seconds that, without its three grace notes, is a retrograde of the first scale in the first movement, e♭-d-c-b-a-g♯-f♯-f.[27] (See Chart 16.2.) The A section has small ternary designs, *a* (mm. 1–9), *b* (mm. 10–16), and *a* (mm. 17–23). A more agitated theme begins at measure 10 leading to a *ff* high point at measure 15. A decrescendo brings the clarinet back to the A theme (m. 17) with additional grace notes.

After another *ff* passage at measure 21, a decrescendo brings the clarinet to the B section (quarter note = 76, m. 24), called by Martino a "motivic variation."[28] It represents a development of the octatonic scales in a variation style by using six notes (sextuplets) grouped by slurs in either two or three notes. Random notes without a motivic connection are sounded in the lower register, about two octaves from the majority of the other notes. Martino explained that in this section, a "two-player" concept suggests the upper notes represent one player quickly and softly practicing rapid technique; the lower notes represent a second player practicing loud, low register passages.[29] After a ritardando, there is an A¹ section (mm. 39–54) repeating part *a*, the first part of *b*, and the cadence of part *a*. Measure 52 moves, after two short fermatas, to a cadence on F. The codetta (mm. 55–57) uses a related octatonic scale set, a tritone lower than the B section but without the low notes, ending with a *pp* half step from G♭5 to F5.

The third movement, "Conservatory Stomp," is in a free or through composed form with several sections at different tempos, each having little thematic relationship to the others. The word "stomp" refers to the "jazzy syncopated rhythm and a driving fast tempo."[30] It begins with an A section Allegro, quarter note = 108–112, measures 1–5, featuring off-beat accents, a thirty-second note flourish to A₆, resolving to B♭₆, on

---

[26] Anderson, ibid., 52–53.

[27] Anderson, ibid., 54.

[28] Anderson, ibid., 56. Martino changed the tempo to quarter note = 80 and added "almost inaudible," Rehfeldt, "Master Class," 6.

[29] Anderson, ibid., 56.

[30] Anderson, ibid., 60.

the upbeat of beat four. (See Chart 16.3.) In section B (mm. 6–15), a B♭ tonal center is prominent with a conflict between the notes D♭ and D in the blues scale. This conflict is also found in the third and seventh degrees of a blues scale developed from African melodies that shift around a central tone with quartal and quintal harmony.[31] The fourth beat of measure 17 begins the C section, quarter note = 108–112, where there is a note conflict between E♭ and E. Notes played in the lower register suggest a two-voice setting, leading to a cadence on E♭.[32] The second transition section (mm. 24–27) presents the D and D♭ tonal conflict. A ritardando leads to section B¹, quarter note = 132–138, measures 28–32. This has a similar feeling and tempo as section B, but uses different transitional material leading to a cadenza (mm. 39–43). The cadenza uses the interval of a diminished fifth in three separate passages, B–F, C–F♯, and G–D♭ intervals based on octatonic scales.[33] It continues with trills emphasizing A♯ to B and A♭ to B♭, and rubato sixteenth-note responses. The D section (mm. 44–46) resembles the first part of a first movement phrase (mm. 20–22). At the closing is a thirty-second note octatonic scale from G♯3 to G_6, followed by a two-measure scale that combines octatonic scales ending on a high $B♭_6$.[34]

Three misprints in the score were confirmed by Martino: 1) First movement, m. 72, A♭3 should be a sixteenth note, 2) First movement, m. 96, A♭3 should be a B♭3, and 3)

Section:	A	B	Trans.	C	Trans.
Starts at m.	1	6	16	17	24
No. of mm.	5	10	1	7	4
Tonal Centers	A, B♭	B♭	none	E♭–E, E♭	D–D♭
Themes	A	B	trans.	C	trans.

Section:	B¹	Trans.	Cadenza	D	Closing
Starts at m.	28	33	39	44	47–49
No. of mm.	5	6	5	3	3
Tonal Centers	B♭	none	octatonic	none	octatonic
Themes	B¹	trans.	cadenza	D	ending

CHART 16.3 Martino, *A Set for Clarinet Unaccompanied*: Structural analysis, third movement, Allegro.

---

[31] Gunther Schuller, *Early Jazz: Its Roots and Musical Development* (Oxford: Oxford University Press, 1968), 44–45; as quoted by Anderson, ibid., 58–59.
[32] Anderson, ibid., 60.
[33] Anderson, ibid., 60–61.
[34] Anderson, ibid., 62.

Third movement, m. 2, B♭4 in the second beat should be a sixteenth note.[35] Additional suggestions by Martino to Rehfeldt are 1) First movement, m. 1, add *fp–f–p*; m. 2, add *p–mf–p*; m. 3, add *mp–f–mf*; mm. 4–5, add *mf–ff*; m. 20, play wedge staccatos as "tut" with thirty-second-note rests; mm. 25–26, play slurs as "ta-yut"; m. 35, add above the caesura "brief"; m. 36, think of the phrase as in 1/2 rather than 2/4 connecting them and observing the breath marks; m. 57, add "more intense"; and m. 65, add "broadly in tone"; 2) Second movement, add mesto (sad) and "very intense and passionate"; m. 4, add "intense"; m. 7, add "broadly"; m. 9, add "hesitantly"; mm. 12–15, add "more and more intense"; mm. 13–14, 35–36, end of 38, continue the movement through the rests; m. 16, extend the A♯ into the rest; m. 21, add "pompous"; and m. 42, add "intense"; 3) Third movement, no breaks going into mm. 6, 24; m. 34, add "pomposo"; m. 39, make the caesuras successively shorter as notated, quarter, eighth, and thirty-second; and not too long over the last note.[36]

Martino's *A Set for Clarinet* is an exceptional work for its virtuosity, the manner of composition, its expressive nature, and the enormously effective impact it creates. It is impressive not only for its virtuosity but for its musical depth. A mid-twentieth-century classic of unaccompanied clarinet solos, it serves as an excellent contrast to works for clarinet and piano. This challenging piece is deserving of all the work and effort required to understand and perform it convincingly.

---

[35] Anderson, ibid., 64.
[36] Rehfeldt, "Master Class," 6.

17 Bohuslav Martinů, *Sonatina for Clarinet and Piano*

Date of composition: January 20, 1956

First edition: Bohuslav Martinů, *Sonatina pour Clarinette Sib et Piano*, Paris: Alphonse Leduc, 1957[1]

Dedicatee/first performer: Not indicated; Not known

Date/place of first performance: Not known; Not known

BOHUSLAV MARTINŮ (1890–1959) spent most of his life away from his native Czechoslovakia but is widely regarded, after Leoš Janáček, as the finest Czech composer of the twentieth century. He was a violinist as a schoolboy in Polička in Bohemia, and with funds raised by the village, was sent to the Prague Conservatory where he studied from 1906, but failed the examinations. However, Martinů was attracted to the cultural life of Prague, and passed the state teaching examination in 1912. He composed as early as 1900 and by 1910 wrote piano music, songs, and a work for orchestra. Illness kept him out of World War I. He taught violin and composed. After 1913, he often played as a substitute second violinist in the Czech Philharmonic, traveled with the orchestra, and by 1923 became a full member. At the Prague Conservatory, he wrote several important works and briefly studied in Josef Suk's composition class.

---

[1] The *Sonatina for Clarinet and Piano* was transcribed for bass clarinet and piano and, with Martinů's permission, was given to and performed by Josef Horák. Pamela Weston, *Clarinet Virtuosi of Today* (Baldock: Egon Publishers Ltd., 1989), 134; Guy Erismann, *Martinů, un Musicien à L'éveil des Sources* (Arles: Actes Sud, 1990), 369; Henri Bok, "The Bass Clarinet" in *The Versatile Clarinet*, ed. Roger Heaton (New York: Routledge, 2006), 94.

In 1923, with a small scholarship from the education ministry, Martinů traveled to Paris to study composition with Albert Roussel. He never again lived in Czechoslovakia, although he visited Prague and took several summer holidays in Polička. In Paris, he heard the music of Stravinsky, Les Six, and jazz. His composition teachers were important in developing the techniques of orchestration (Suk) and orchestral timbre (Roussel); he admired Dvořák, and was influenced by Janáček, especially for his Czech language song settings. Two non-Czech composers were influential to him: Debussy and Stravinsky. Jazz was important in the works he composed during the 1920s and 1930s.[2]

His work impressed Koussevitzky, who in 1927, successfully premiered Martinů's *La bagarre* (*The Fight*), with the Boston Symphony Orchestra. By the 1930s, Martinů's style was established and his reputation grew. His works were played in Prague and Brno; the *Cello Concerto no. 1* in Berlin (1931); the *Concerto for String Quartet and Orchestra* in London (1932) and Boston; and the orchestral *Inventions* at the International Society of Contemporary Music Festival in Venice (1934). These compositions show Martinů's interest in Baroque forms, folk music, and the culture of Czechoslovakia.[3]

In 1931, Martinů married the dressmaker, Charlotte Quennehen, in Paris. After the 1939 Nazi invasion of Czechoslovakia, Martinů was named cultural attaché by the Czech opposition and helped many Czech artists travel to Paris as refugees. He was too old for military service and composed music dedicated to the Free Czechoslovak Army Band. The Nazis blacklisted Martinů's music and in 1940, when the Germans entered Paris, he and Charlotte fled to Aix-en-Provence in southern France where he continued to compose. By early 1941, they traveled from Marseilles to Lisbon and on to the United States where Martinů lived in New York City during the war. In the summer of 1942, he taught composition at the Berkshire Music Center (Tanglewood).[4] In America, Martinů was depressed and homesick but kept busy with Koussevitsky's commission of an orchestral work, the *Symphony no. 1* (1942), followed by four more works.

At war's end, Martinů was offered a position as composition professor at the newly founded Prague Conservatory. He asked for an official contract, but because he did not receive it, and because of the political turmoil in Czechoslovakia, he never returned and remained in the United States for the next seven years. Martinů suffered a serious fall while teaching at Tanglewood in summer 1946. His recovery

---

[2] Jan Smaczny, "Martinů, Bohuslav," *Grove Music Online.*

[3] Smaczny, "Martinů, Bohuslav"; F. James Rybka, *Bohuslav Martinů: The Compulsion to Compose* (Lanham, MD: Scarecrow Press, 2011), xix.

[4] During the summer, Martinů traveled to Middlebury, Vermont, Darien and Ridgefield, Connecticut; Cape Cod and South Orleans, Massachusetts.

was slow. After spending summer 1948 in France and Switzerland, Martinů returned to New York to teach at Princeton University and the Mannes School of Music.

He composed several new works including two operas for television and his *Sixth Symphony* (1953). With a Guggenheim scholarship, Martinů returned to Europe in May 1953 and lived in Paris and Nice for two years. He wrote his opera *Miradolina* (1953), and his oratorio *The Epic of Gilgamesh* (1955), then returned to New York in 1955. He wrote several works including the *Sonatina for Clarinet*, but, depressed by New York, he returned to Europe in May 1956 to teach at the American Academy of Music in Rome until summer 1957. At the end of 1958 he developed stomach problems, his health deteriorated, and in August 1959 he entered the hospital at Liestal, Switzerland with stomach cancer; he died on August 28.[5]

In a March 17, 1931, letter to his family, Martinů wrote that he knew he was "sometimes a bit strange, and not everyone understands me at first."[6] In America, Martinů told close friends about his lifelong struggle in socializing. Today we know that Martinů suffered from a developmental disorder called high functioning autism or Asperger's syndrome, which makes socializing difficult.[7]

Martinů was a highly prolific composer with 385 works in his catalog. He wrote music in virtually every instrumental and vocal genre.[8] The composer, Marcel Milhalovici, praised Martinů's work as, "music elevated to a superb spiritual elevation … in a sonorous idiom, simple, direct, accessible."[9]

The *Sonatina for Clarinet and Piano, H. 356*, was composed in New York City during Princeton University's 1955/56 academic year for the Parisian publisher, Leduc.[10] It is in three movements played without pause, influenced by neoclassicism, jazz, Stravinsky, and Czech folk music.[11] The first movement, Moderato, is in ternary form with an introduction, a second introduction before A¹, and a coda. (See Chart 17.1.) No metronome numbers are given; Jennings suggests quarter note = 88;

[5] Smaczny, ibid.

[6] Iša Popelka, ed., trans. Ralph Slayton, English version eds. Martin Anderson and Aleš Březina, *Martinů's Letters Home: Five Decades of Correspondence with Family and Friends* (London: Toccata Press, 2012), 37.

[7] Rybka, ibid., xxvi–xxvii.

[8] Miloš Šafránek, *Bohuslav Martinů: His Life and Works*, trans. R. Finlayson-Samsourová (London: Allan Wingate, 1962), 334–58.

[9] Michael Henderson, "Some Past and Present Reactions to Martinů and His Music," in *Bohuslav Martinů Anno 1981: Papers from an International Musicological Conference, Prague, 26–28 May, 1981*, ed. Jitta Brabcová (Prague: Česká hudební spločečnost, 1990), 260.

[10] A contract identified by Aleš Březina, caretaker for the Bohuslav Martinů Foundation's Study Centre in Prague, was between Martinů and the Paris publisher, Leduc, for two sonatinas, one for clarinet, the other for trumpet; Robert L. Walzel, Jr., "Bohuslav Martinů: An Examination of Selected Chamber Music Involving the Clarinet, with Three Recitals of Selected Works by Rossini, Sutermeister, Castelnuovo-Tedesco, Weiner, Bowen, Beethoven, Brahms, and Others" (D.M.A. diss., University of North Texas, 1997), 47; Harry Halbreich, *Bohuslav Martinů: Werkverzeichnis und Biografie*, 2nd rev. ed. (Mainz: Schott, 2007), 346.

[11] Lawrence McDonald, "Master Class: Sonatina by Bohuslav Martinů," *The Clarinet* 27, no. 1 (December 1999): 4.

Section:	Introduction	A	B	Intro.-A¹	Coda
Starts at m.	1 Moderato	9	67	108	174–191
No. of mm.	8	58	41	66	18
Tonalities	E♭	E♭, d	B♭, d, D, C	E♭	E♭
Themes	intro.	A, trans.	B	intro.-A¹	coda

CHART 17.1 Martinů, *Sonatina for Clarinet and Piano*: Structural analysis, first movement, Moderato.

McDonald, quarter note = 96–104.[12] The piano introduction places the melody on the upbeats in the first four measures, giving a duple feeling rather than the printed 3/4 meter. This is similar to Martinů's 1924 *Quartet for Clarinet, Horn, Cello, and Side Drum*, and reflects Stravinsky's influence.[13] The clarinet A theme (m. 9) is lyrical, and stays in the pleasant clarion register. At the transition, the piano lower register plays off-beat accents (mm. 37–41), followed by clarinet sixteenth-note triplets (mm. 43–45), imitated by the piano (mm. 45–50). Groups of thirty-second notes precede piano trills and arpeggios, first by the clarinet and then clarinet and piano together (mm. 52–66). Jennings suggests quarter note = 76; Macdonald, quarter note = 66–69.[14] These arpeggios and patterns are reminiscent of Czech folk music played on a hammered stringed instrument called a cymbalom.[15] Next is a festive clarinet B theme with mordents and trills (mm. 67–71); a cantabile section featuring a lovely twenty-one measure melody (mm. 76–96); and a serious section of sixteenth note triplets, briefly answered by the piano and ending with the clarinet (mm. 96–107). The Intro.-A¹ section (mm. 108–173) repeats the music from measures 1–66, followed by an exciting coda (m. 174) featuring the clarinet with a rousing eighteen measures of arpeggios and runs.

The short second movement, Andante, is through composed in ternary form with an introduction and coda (Jennings, quarter note = 84; McDonald, quarter note = 63–69).[16] It begins with a slow, introspective piano introduction in D♭ major and, for the first three measures, alternates between the notes D♭ and C with a repetitive, ostinato-like quality. (Chart 17.2.) The clarinet begins on measure 195 with a sorrowful tune in D♭ minor, and at measure 203 imitates the piano. Next, a serious clarinet melody comes to a high point at measure 219. McDonald describes this melodic contour as, "a life-like, even heroic journey, full of struggle and dignity, and ending

[12] Vance Shelby Jennings, "Selected Twentieth Century Clarinet Solo Literature: A Study in Interpretation and Performance" (D.M.A. diss., The University of Oklahoma, 1972), 155; McDonald, ibid., 4.

[13] Walzel, ibid., 48.

[14] Jennings, ibid., 155; McDonald, ibid., 6.

[15] Walzel, ibid., 49.

[16] Jennings, ibid., 156; McDonald, ibid., 8.

Section:	Introduction	A	B	C	Coda
Starts at m.	192 Andante	195	203	210	224–235
No. of mm.	3	8	7	14	12
Tonalities	D♭	D♭	f	E♭	a♭
Themes	intro.	A	B	C	coda

CHART 17.2   Martinů, *Sonatina for Clarinet and Piano*: Structural analysis, second movement, Andante.

with a sense of acquired understanding."[17] The movement closes with a quiet clarinet arpeggio in A♭ minor (written B♭ minor) rather than in the expected dominant key of A♭ major.[18]

The third movement is through composed in a binary form with an introduction and coda. (See Chart 17.3.) The Poco Allegro (Jennings, quarter note = 108; McDonald, quarter note = 120–126)[19] thirteen measure introduction (mm. 236–248) is a prelude to the clarinet 6/8 scherzando A section (mm. 249–287).[20] The A section (Jennings, dotted quarter note = 72; McDonald, dotted quarter note = 80–84)[21] is highly energetic, with syncopation and imitation in the piano part. The exciting B section (m. 288) retains the Poco Allegro tempo; begins with clarinet sixteenth note runs; and includes double grace notes, syncopation, many trills on off beats, and a climax (mm. 330–331) on written G_6.[22] At the coda, Jennings suggests a restrained accelerando from measure 332 to an exciting ending.[23]

One of the earliest performances of Martinů's *Sonatina*, but not the first, was by Benny Goodman, clarinet, and his daughter, Rachel Goodman, piano, on May 2, 1964. The concert was a benefit performance for the Lili Boulanger Memorial Fund, held at the Sanders Theater, Harvard University. Some students at the concert recorded the performance, which included Brahms's *Sonata, op. 120, no. 1* and Weber's *Grand Duo Concertant, op. 48,* and presented the tapes to Goodman. He liked them and had Capitol press the tapes onto a 12" LP record. He gave copies to a few friends.[24]

Martinů's *Sonatina for Clarinet and Piano* is described as a, "discreet jewel, a miniature masterpiece which contains within itself a complete universe of musical

17 McDonald, ibid., 8.

18 Jennings, ibid., 154.

19 Jennings, ibid., 156; McDonald, ibid., 9.

20 McDonald, ibid., 9.

21 Jennings, ibid., 156; McDonald, ibid., 9.

22 Jennings, ibid., 151–64.

23 Jennings, ibid., 156.

24 D. Russell Connor and Warren W. Hicks, *BG on the Record: A Bio-Discography of Benny Goodman* (New Rochelle, NY: Arlington House), 1969, 579–80.

Section:	Introduction	A	B	Coda
Starts at m.	236 Poco Allegro	249	288	332–341
No. of mm.	13	39	44	10
Tonalities	D♭	E♭	C, B♭	B♭
Themes	intro.	A	B	coda

CHART 17.3 Martinů, *Sonatina for Clarinet and Piano*: Structural analysis, third movement, Poco Allegro.

expression."[25] It encompasses an unusual range of styles from flowing cantabile, "prank-filled scherzandi through haunting lyricism, to crackling, whirling virtuoso display."[26] It is a recital piece with accessibility, audience appeal, and is only about ten minutes long. The writing is very idiomatic, and makes excellent use of meter, articulation, and subtle dynamics. There are some problematic fingering passages and rhythmic and ensemble challenges,[27] but with rehearsal and study, these are solved. The *Sonatina for Clarinet and Piano* is an excellent and popular recital piece, and fits well into programs featuring differing styles.

---

[25] McDonald, ibid., 4.
[26] McDonald, ibid., 4.
[27] McDonald, ibid., 6–7, 9; Jennings, ibid., 156, 161–64.

18 Darius Milhaud, *Sonatina for Clarinet and Piano, op. 100*

Date of composition: Summer 1927

First edition: Darius Milhaud, *Sonatine pour Clarinette et Piano*, Paris: Durand, 1929

Dedicatee/first performers: Louis Cahusac; Louis Cahusac, clarinet, Marius-François Gaillard, piano

Date/place of first performance: 1929; Paris, Société Musicale Internationale

DARIUS MILHAUD (1892–1974) grew up in Aix-en-Provence and as a boy studied the violin and played second violin in the string quartet of his teacher, Léo Brugier. After studying Debussy's quartet, Milhaud was so impressed that he bought the score of *Pelléas et Melisande*. The same year, Milhaud took harmony lessons from a local teacher, and despite his success as a violinist, he realized he wanted to compose. In 1909, he went to study at the Paris Conservatory until 1915. His main teachers were Henri Berthelier (violin), Paul Dukas (orchestral playing), Gustave Leroux (harmony), Charles-Marie Widor (fugue), and André Gédalge (counterpoint, composition, and orchestration). Gédalge was his most important influence as Milhaud mastered academic counterpoint, which remained an important part of his technique. He became an excellent orchestrator, a good conductor, and a proficient pianist. In Paris, he discovered the music of Gabriel Fauré, Maurice Ravel, Charles Koechlin, Erik Satie, Ernest Bloch, Albéric Magnard, Albert Roussel, Richard Wagner, Modest Mussorgsky, Igor Stravinsky, and Arnold Schoenberg, among others.

In 1912, Milhaud met the poet, playwright, and diplomat, Paul Claudel, who supplied him with the text for songs, and became a close personal friend. Milhaud was unable to fight in World War I for medical reasons, and instead helped Belgian refugees. In 1916, he worked for the foreign ministry propaganda department. Claudel became minister to Brazil, and Milhaud became attaché for propaganda. In 1917, he traveled to Lisbon and then to Brazil where his official duties were translating coded messages, accompanying Claudel on his travels, and organizing concerts and lectures for the Red Cross. He left Brazil in 1918, traveling through the West Indies and New York, arriving in Paris in 1919. During the 1920s, Milhaud renewed old acquaintances with Koechlin, Honegger, and Poulenc, and made new acquaintances, including Satie. He visited London where he first heard jazz; traveled to Vienna where he met Schoenberg, Berg, and Webern; and completed concert tours in the United States (1922 and 1927) and the USSR (1926). During this time, Milhaud produced many compositions and had many successes.

At decade's end he was an established major composer, particularly with the success of his 1930 opera, *Christophe Colomb*, in Berlin. During the 1930s, Milhaud completed several film scores, incidental music, ballet music, operas, and worked as the music critic for the daily *Le jour* 1933–1937. During this time, he suffered frequent and painful attacks of rheumatoid arthritis which, by 1948, confined him to a wheelchair. Since he was a prominent Jewish artist, in 1940 Milhaud immigrated to the United States. On his way, a telegram from Mills College, Oakland, California, offered a teaching post, which he accepted. Later he taught at the summer school in Aspen, Colorado, and 1948–1951 was honorary director of the Music Academy of the West in Santa Barbara, California. In 1947, he returned to France to become a professor of composition at the Paris Conservatory. He gave up the Mills College position in 1971; the latter part of his life was divided between the two countries. Constant concerts required much travel which Milhaud accepted gratefully. He taught many French and American composers including the jazz pianist, Dave Brubeck.[1] Milhaud was an extremely prolific composer in all genres and all combinations, including his arrangements of works by other composers. His total output is recorded as 443 compositions written 1910–1973.[2]

Colin Mason's 1957 article on Milhaud's chamber music in *The Musical Quarterly* was quite enthusiastic about the *Sonatina for Clarinet and Piano*:

> Like many modern composers, he has also been attracted by the possibilities of the use of wind instruments in chamber music. These works are generally lighter, more divertimento-like in character, than those for strings, but there is a notable exception in the magnificent *Sonatina for Clarinet and Piano* (1927), one of his most exciting and harmonically fierce works of the late 1920's, terse

[1] Jeremy Drake, "Milhaud, Darius," *Grove Music Online*.
[2] Paul Collaer, *Darius Milhaud, with a Definitive Catalogue of Works Compiled from the Composer's own Notebooks by Madeleine Milhaud*, rev., trans., and ed. Jane Hohfeld Galante (San Francisco: San Francisco Press, Inc., 1988), 231–365.

and crisp, in the same mood as the *Concerto for percussion and small orchestra* from the same period, especially in its two outer movements, which, unusually in Milhaud, are thematically related, giving the *Sonatina* the effect of one extended movement with a slow middle section.[3]

Later writers were also complimentary, "In Milhaud's most dissonant style, with some very charming spots in the slow movement, other movements are marked, "très rude."[4] "The *Sonatine* by Milhaud is characterized by spiky wit and quirky rhythms."[5]

The *Sonatina, op. 100*, is written in three movements with a highly chromatic harmony, emphasizing a semitone progression from B to C throughout the work.[6] The similarity of the A themes in the first and third movements and the short slow second movement are relatively unusual for Milhaud.[7] In 1923, Milhaud said the technique of polytonality and atonality was a development of diatonic and chromatic writing, used by Latin and Teutonic composers, and claimed that national traditions were the basis for this music.[8] Milhaud stated that his works' polytonality, combining separate tonal areas, was not a destructive force, but contributed to musical expression. Milhaud did not mention polymodality in this article even though he used diatonic writing, with polytonality and polymodality, in this and other works.[9]

The first movement, Very rude (Très rude), quarter note = 120,[10] (See Chart 18.1) in ternary form with a coda challenges the listener immediately by using a repeated *f* piano sixteenth note motive (F♯, G, A♯, B)[11] to a descending pattern of parallel seventh chords.[12] The clarinet A theme is an accented dotted quarter note, three eighth notes, and a quarter note with a tonal/modal center in Aeolian harmonic minor on B minor.[13] The clarinet answers with a jagged-shaped motive of three sixteenth triplets,

[3] Colin Mason, "The Chamber Music of Milhaud," *The Musical Quarterly* 43, no. 3 (July 1957): 338–39.

[4] Burnet C. Tuthill, "The Sonatas for Clarinet and Piano," *Journal of Research in Music Education* 14, no. 3 (Autumn 1966): 207.

[5] Jo Rees-Davies, "The Development of the Clarinet Repertoire," in *The Cambridge Companion to the Clarinet*, ed. Colin Lawson (Cambridge: Cambridge University Press, 1995), 87.

[6] Deborah Mawer, *Darius Milhaud: Modality & Structure in Music of the 1920s* (Aldershot: Scolar Press, 1997), 206–27; Thomas D. Stirzaker, "A Comparative Study of Selected Clarinet Works by Arthur Honegger, Darius Milhaud and Francis Poulenc" (Ph.D. diss., Texas Tech University, 1988), 12–17, 31–41, 56–59.

[7] Collaer, ibid., 248; Deborah Mawer, ibid., 207.

[8] Darius Milhaud, "Polytonalité et Atonalité," *La Revue Musicale* 4, no. 4 (February 1, 1923): 29–44; as cited by Mawer, ibid., 145; trans. as "Polytonality and atonality," *Pro-Musica Quarterly* 4, no. 1 (October 1924): 11–24.

[9] Barbara L. Kelly, *Tradition and Style in the Works of Darius Milhaud 1912–1939* (Aldershot: Ashgate, 2003), 145–47.

[10] Suggested by the author.

[11] According to Mawer, ibid., 207, this opening is identical to Milhaud's *Fifth Chamber Symphony*.

[12] Stirzaker, ibid., 12.

[13] Mawer, ibid., 208.

Section:	A	B	A/B	Coda
Starts at m.	1 Très rude	35 (6 mm. after no. 2)	57 (no. 4)	87–95 (no. 7)
No. of mm.	34	22	30	9
Tonal/ Modal Centers	Aeolian harmonic minor on B minor	C♯–G♯, C	E♭–c♭, C	B
Themes	A, (A)	B	A/B, B¹	A¹

CHART 18.1 Milhaud, *Sonatina for Clarinet and Piano, op. 100*: Structural analysis, first movement, Très rude.

a quarter note, and a quarter note tied to an eighth note.[14] The *f* dynamic continues until measure 12 when the piano right hand plays an ostinato (mm. 12–15), and the clarinet repeats its initial phrase *mf*. After a decrescendo and cédez, the clarinet plays the first tempo at no. 1 with a *p* slurred and conjunct variation on the A theme. Section B begins on measure 35, six measures after no. 2, with a very sweet (très doux) clarinet melody in the clarion register and *pp* syncopated piano accompaniment. The tonal/modal center is C♯–G♯ major and C major. A piano and clarinet ostinato (mm. 53–56) prepares the listener for the next section. Section A/B begins as a modified recapitulation with four conjunct *ff* clarinet sixteenth notes (m. 57, no. 4) corresponding to the sixteenth note piano arpeggios in the first movement.[15] After two measures, the clarinet plays a sixteenth note motive imitated by the piano (mm. 59–65). A piano *f* ostinato centered on E♭ major-E♭ minor, and C major plays (mm. 72–76) while the clarinet performs the B¹ theme, leading to a rallentando before returning to a *pp* first tempo (m. 77, no. 6). A clarinet crescendo from *f* to *ff* leads to the coda at no. 7 (m. 87), and incorporates the first seven measures of the A¹ theme with a forceful closing.[16]

The slow 9/8 second movement, Lent (dotted quarter note = 52),[17] is in ternary form with a coda (See Chart 18.2), and begins with a sweet, calm repeated piano motive in which the clarinet joins with a long sustained note in the second measure. The A theme (mm. 1–15) is a lovely clarinet melody played in a singing manner (chanté), centered on A♭ major with a Lydian tendency.[18] The piano, measures 14–15, plays a link to section B centered on G♯ major and A♭ major. At no. 8 (m. 16), the B

14 Stirzaker, ibid., 12.
15 Stirzaker, ibid., 33.
16 Mawer, ibid., 208; detailed commentary, 209–15.
17 Suggested by the author.
18 Mawer, ibid., 217.

Section:	A	B	A¹	Coda
Starts at m.	1 Lent	16 (no. 8)	41 (no. 10)	54–58
No. of mm.	15	25	13	5
Tonal/Modal Centers	A♭ (Lydian), A♭-G♯	E, G♯-A♭	A♭	a♭
Themes	A	B	A¹	B¹

CHART 18.2 Milhaud, *Sonatina for Clarinet and Piano, op. 100*: Structural analysis, second movement, Lent.

theme, marked, "a little more slowly" (Un peu moins lent), with a contrasting, dramatic clarinet theme of seven three measure phrases in the chalumeau and clarion registers, is played in imitation with the piano.[19] This builds to a big crescendo at measure 28 (no. 9) and at a high point (mm. 33–35), the piano slows the movement with longer notes, and with a slight slowing (cédez à peine) neatly turns to the A¹ theme, (no. 10, m. 41). Here, the A¹ section's sweet, calm clarinet motive (mm. 41–53) plays. The coda (mm. 54–58) displays a calmly descending clarinet line in dotted quarter notes with a decrescendo from the clarion to the chalumeau registers, while the piano alludes to the dramatic B¹ theme played *pp*.[20]

The third movement, Très rude, quarter note = 120,[21] is a ternary form (See Chart 18.3). It begins with a forceful piano theme of quarter note, four eighth notes, and a quarter note, similar to the first movement's opening theme. It is repeated *f* in the third measure by the clarinet. The loud dynamic is continued until measure 14 where the clarinet introduces a *mf* variation, including three types of tonguing: unaccented, accented, and heavily accented. The tonal/modal center is C, with F♯ and G major, much chromaticism, and a high level of dissonance. Theme B differs from theme A by using slurred clarinet eighth notes (mm. 28–40), played *mp* and *p*

Section:	A	B	A¹
Starts at m.	1 Trés rude	28	61–82
No. of mm.	27	33	22
Tonal/ModalCenters	C, F♯, G	f Phrygian, F♭, f	C
Themes	A	B, B¹	A¹

CHART 18.3 Milhaud, *Sonatina for Clarinet and Piano, op. 100*: Structural analysis, third movement, Très rude.

---

[19] Stirzaker suggests four clarinet motives for this phrase, ibid., 37.
[20] Mawer, ibid., 215, 217; Stirzaker, ibid., 14–15.
[21] Suggested by the author.

that decrescendos to *pp* at measure 40 (one measure before no. 14). A Phrygian modal center in F minor emerges; there is a brief episode on F♭ from measures 36–44 and a return to F minor at measure 47.[22] The clarinet enters *mf* somewhat urgently at measure 51 with the B¹ theme, including different groups of sixteenth notes per beat, gradually increasing in volume to the A¹ theme (mm. 61–82) centered on C.[23] Played *ff* throughout without a rallandando, the work comes to a brilliant and convincing ending.[24]

Milhaud's *Sonatina* reached the furthest point of development in his chamber works of the 1920s. It exhibits a highly chromatic style, extensive modality, and important modifications of the sonata form.[25] The free and agile clarinet writing throughout is in the style of the Paris Conservatory competition works, and requires fine control and a solid technique. The first and third movements are emotionally charged and feature an intense, flippant clarinet part. It is a highly intellectual work with a complex harmonic scheme, yet has sensitively written moments in all three movements. There are some technical issues for the clarinetist, but when solved, it is a remarkably varied work, and a popular recital piece.

[22] Mawer, ibid., 219.

[23] Mawer, ibid., 224–25.

[24] Mawer notes that mm. 5–8 in the first movement of the piano part have five misprints which are corrected in her example 5.5. Mawer, ibid., 359.

[25] Mawer, ibid., 226.

19 Wolfgang Amadeus Mozart, *Concerto for Clarinet and Orchestra, K. 622*

Date of composition: September–October, 1791

First edition: W. A. Mozart, *Concerto pour Clarinette avec accompagnement de 2 Violons, 2 Flutes, 2 Bassons, 2 Cors, Viola, et Basse*, Leipzig: Breitkopf & Härtel, 1801 (solo and orchestral parts)

Modern editions: Wolfgang Amadeus Mozart, *Konzert in A für Klarinette und Orchester, KV 622 = Concerto in A major for Clarinet and Orchestra*, ed. Martin Schelhaas, Kassel: Bärenreiter, 2003; Wolfgang Amadeus Mozart, *Concerto for Clarinet and Orchestra, K. 622*, ed. Pamela Weston, based on the sources and a period arrangement, Vienna: Universal Edition, 1997, for A clarinet or A basset clarinet; Wolfgang Amadeus Mozart, *Concerto for Clarinet and Orchestra*, ed. for clarinet and piano, rev. and ed. Trio di Clarone, Wiesbaden: Breitkopf & Härtel, 1987; Wolfgang Amadeus Mozart, *Concerto for Clarinet and Orchestra*, ed. Hans-Dietrich Klauss, Kassel: Bärenreiter, 1987

Dedicatee/first performer: Anton Stadler; Anton Stadler, basset clarinet

Date/place of first performance: October 16, 1791; Prague

Orchestral instrumentation: First and second violins, violas, cellos, contrabasses, two flutes, two bassoons, and two horns (A and D)

WOLFGANG AMADEUS MOZART (1756–1791) was a superb composer in every type of music performed during his life. His *clarinet concerto* was his last concerto and one of his last instrumental works before his premature death at thirty-five. It is one of dozens of concertos written for the four- or five-key Classical clarinet in Europe since the 1750s. However, it is among only a few written for the A

Section:	Orchestral exposition	Solo exposition	1st episode	Development
Starts at m.	1 Allegro	57	154	172
No. of mm.	56	97	18	55
Tonalities	A	A, a, C, e, E, c♯, e, E	E	E, f♯, D, b, f♯
Themes	A, trans., A¹, A², A³, A⁴	A, B, B¹, Eingang, A, fig.	A¹, A⁴	A⁵ and fig., B³

Section:	2nd episode	Recapitulation	Conclusion
Starts at m.	227	248	343–359
No. of mm.	21	95	17
Tonalities	f♯, e, D	A, a, C, e, d, f♯, A	A
Themes	C, A¹	A, B, B¹, B², Eingang, A, fig.	A², A⁴

CHART 19.1 Mozart, *Concerto for Clarinet and Orchestra, K. 622*: Structural analysis, first movement, Allegro.

clarinet, a more mellow instrument than the brilliant and popular B♭ clarinet. Other repertory concertos for A clarinet are by Louis Spohr, Paul Hindemith, and Carl Nielsen. Mozart's *concerto* is musically outstanding, the finest of the Classical period.

The first movement, Allegro, begins with an orchestral exposition, establishing the key and presenting several themes, later stated, elaborated, and developed by the soloist. (See Chart 19.1.) Mozart's genius produced constantly changing themes and subtle changes that flow effortlessly to create a masterpiece. This *concerto* begins with an engaging theme in A major (mm. 1–9), later restated in canon by the strings (mm. 25–31); the same process occurs again in the solo exposition and recapitulation. The first section orchestral exposition themes are, A (mm. 1–12), A¹ (mm. 16–24), A² (mm. 31–36), A³ (mm. 37–49), and A⁴ (mm. 49–56).

The clarinet in the solo exposition elaborates the themes by using wide-ranging arpeggios and a leap of two-and-a-half octaves (mm. 68–75), expertly moving through a variety of tonalities. Especially striking is the poignant A minor B theme with accompaniment of only the strings and an immediate slowing of the harmonic rhythm with quarter notes and quarter note rests (mm. 78–98). Unusual for a Classical period concerto, this one does not offer an opportunity for a cadenza. Instead, the soloist is expected to play an Eingang (Mozart's own term), a few notes that lead to the next section indicated by a fermata. If the harmony before the fermata includes a tonic 6/4 chord, then a longer cadenza is required; if the harmony is the dominant or a chord

Section:	Exposition	Development	Recapitulation	Coda
Starts at m.	1 Adagio	33	60	83–98
No. of mm.	32	27	23	16
Tonalities	D	D, A	D, D	D
Themes	A, A, A^1, A^1	B, fig., Eingang	A, A^1	A^2

CHART 19.2 Mozart, *Concerto for Clarinet and Orchestra, K. 622*: Structural analysis, second movement, Adagio.

functioning like a dominant, an Eingang is required.[1] The *concerto* has two Eingänge in the first movement (mm. 127, 315) and one in the second (m. 59).

The first episode begins in E major, the dominant, leading to the development (mm. 172–226) that modulates through four different tonalities. It features dramatic contrasts and mood swings with soaring melodies, large leaps, and sustained notes (mm. 194–220). All the themes are varied and sixteenth-note figuration appears in the clarion and chalumeau registers for themes A^5 and B^3. An agitated second episode leads to a brilliant two-octave run from G3 to G5 that comfortably settles back into an A theme recapitulation (mm. 248–252). Alberti sixteenth-note figuration (an octave lower on the basset clarinet) accompanies the two violin melodic parts in duet, and is followed by a number of arpeggios and runs (mm. 324–332) leading to a resounding and satisfying conclusion (mm. 343–359).[2]

The second movement, Adagio in D major, is in sonata-allegro form with a coda. (See Chart 19.2.) The exposition features a solo theme and orchestral response (mm. 1–32), played twice by the clarinetist and the orchestra in eight measure sections. This solo and tutti alternation was used by Mozart in his piano concertos, particularly in the Larghetto of the C minor *Piano Concerto, K. 491*.[3] The simple and evocative *p* A theme consists of two four measure phrases played in the bright clarion register accompanied by strings but without the contrabass (mm. 1–8). The A theme is repeated *f* by the full orchestra (mm. 9–16) followed by the clarinet A^1 theme (mm. 17–24) of three four measure phrases of a dotted quarter and three eighth notes starting on A5, three of which start on a higher note. This theme is repeated *f* by the orchestra (mm. 25–32). It is the most expressive and touching melody in any clarinet concerto. The strings present a somber accompaniment, supported by the

[1] David Whitwell, "Improvisation in Harmoniemusik literature," in *Kongressbericht Abony/Ungarn 1994*, ed. W. Suppan, 438, Alta Musica, vol. 18 (Tutzing: H. Schneider, 1996); Colin Lawson, *Mozart: Clarinet Concerto* (Cambridge: Cambridge University Press, 1996), 62, 64.

[2] Lawson, ibid., 62–66.

[3] Lawson, ibid., 67.

low tessitura of pre-valve horns by their change from A to D horn for this movement, more noticeable when natural horns are played with larger D crooks.[4] The beautiful opening is reminiscent of Mozart's Larghetto second movement from his *Quintet for Clarinet and Strings, K. 581*, where the tempo is slightly faster.

The development section (mm. 33–59) starts with a more dramatic clarinet B theme in the clarion register, brighter in sonority, using a variety of shorter notes and the chalumeau register. These include a thirty-second-note run to low F_3 and a leap to A_5 (mm. 33–36). As is traditional, a short Eingang is adopted (m. 59) from the similar material of the second movement of Mozart's *Quintet* (mm. 49–50), although the player has the option of improvising his or her own Eingang. In the recapitulation (mm. 60–82), the first two strains of the A^1 theme are repeated with the first orchestral response omitted. The second orchestral response (mm. 76–82) is re-harmonized so that the bass line is falling rather than rising in measures 76, 78, 80. The coda transforms the material to include the chalumeau register, an upward leap, and a chromatic run (mm. 88–98). At the end of the movement, a clarinet half note is held alone for one beat, since the orchestra plays a quarter note.[5]

The third movement, Rondo Allegro, presents a blend of sonata and rondo forms with three refrains, three episodes, and a coda. The initial A theme, or refrain of eight measures, lies within an interval of a ninth (written B_4 to C_6) and is lightly scored for clarinet, violins, and violas. (See Chart 19.3.) The A theme is repeated twice as a dialogue between the clarinet and orchestra (mm. 1–16). Scale and arpeggio

Section:	1st refrain	1st episode	2nd refrain	2nd episode
Starts at m.	1 Allegro	57	114	138
No. of mm.	56	57	24	50
Tonalities	A	A, E	A, E	f♯, d
Themes	A, A^1	A^2	A	B, B^1

Section:	3rd episode (recapitulation)	3rd refrain	Coda
Starts at m.	188	247	301–353
No. of mm.	59	54	53
Tonalities	A, a, C, d, a, E	A	A
Themes	A^3	A, A^1	fig., A

CHART 19.3 Mozart, *Concerto for Clarinet and Orchestra, K. 622*: Structural analysis, third movement, Rondo Allegro.

[4] Lawson, ibid., 66.
[5] Lawson, ibid., 66–68.

figures are featured by the soloist leading back to the A theme. Several dialogues occur between the solo clarinet and orchestra using all the wind instruments. The first episode starts with an A^2 theme elaborated by a number of arpeggios and runs (mm. 57–60). An unusual texture is achieved with a flute solo accompanied by the clarinet (mm. 77–81). Clarinet chromatic scales are played from F♯5 to C_6, F♯4 to C5, and F♯3 to C4 all answered by the strings. This is followed by clarinet leaps on dotted quarter notes from C4–C5 to E♭4–F♯5 resolving to G5, held for two measures (mm. 105–111) and the second refrain beginning without a pickup at measure 114. The orchestra modulates to E major (mm. 131–137), when the stringed instruments play each eighth note twice to create an exciting hemiola effect. A lyrical clarinet melody begins the second episode B theme in F♯ minor with an eighth-note pickup (m. 137), repeated by the clarinet one octave lower (m. 145).

The third episode begins with five eighth-note pickups to an A major A^3 theme (m. 188) for eight measures. The music proceeds in A minor where the clarinet and violins are featured in a highly chromatic dialogue (mm. 196–207), the clarinet playing both the melody and a bass line. After modulations to C major and D minor, an usual operatic gesture in A minor occurs where two measures of the main theme are played by upper strings, and answered by the clarinet and lower strings, each statement separated by a fermata (mm. 218–221). The continuation in measures 222–223 has a flute solo and clarinet bass line similar to the earlier orchestration. The third refrain (mm. 247–300) flows into an extended, virtuoso coda developing the rondo theme with striking arpeggios, leaps, trills, and scalar figuration. The coda (mm. 301–353) features clarinet arpeggios and scales. After a final statement of the A theme (m. 334), there is one last display of dotted quarter note leaps, A5–F3 and G3–B5 resolving to C_6. A brief tutti based on the orchestral material (m. 121) resolutely ends the movement.[6]

Lawson observes that many Mozart concertos were written with certain performers in mind, "fashioned for their technique and capabilities."[7] This is particularly true for the *Concerto for Clarinet and Orchestra, K. 622* written for Anton Stadler (1752–1812). In 1779, Stadler and his brother, Johann (1755–1804), moved to Vienna where they played clarinet or basset horn on a freelance basis and were officially appointed to the Court Orchestra and Imperial Wind Octet in 1782.[8] In this orchestra, they performed most of Mozart's operas and chamber works, and works by contemporary composers. The first performance of Mozart's *Serenade, K. 361,* for twelve winds and contrabass was probably at Stadler's benefit concert on March 23, 1784 in Vienna's Burgtheater.[9]

[6] Lawson, ibid., 68–71.

[7] Lawson, ibid., 60–61.

[8] Dorothea Link, *The National Court Theatre in Mozart's Vienna: Sources and Documents, 1783–1792* (Oxford: Clarendon Press, 1998), 209, note 15.

[9] Daniel N. Leeson and David Whitwell, "Concerning Mozart's *Serenade in B♭ for Thirteen Instruments, K. 361 (370a),*" *Mozart Jahrbuch* 1976/1977, 97-130, here, 106-7.

In 1784, Vienna's court instrument maker, Theodor Lotz, first made B♭ and C clarinets for both
Stadlers. Late eighteenth-century clarinets were
usually made of boxwood, a light brown wood, and
had five brass keys.[10] By 1788, Lotz made clarinets
in B♭ and A for both Stadlers with an extended
range of two notes, D3 and C3, below the clarinet's
usual lowest note of E3. These are the same written
notes on contemporary basset horns and must have
been a special request by the Stadlers.

By 1790, Anton Stadler obtained from Lotz a new
clarinet with a chromatic extension including the
notes D♯3, D3, C♯3, and C3, for a total of ten keys. His
instrument had a slightly curved neck, long body, and
an L-shaped joint at the bottom connected to a round
bell with a cylindrical section around the middle. In
October 1791, Mozart completed the *concerto*. He
gave the orchestral parts to Stadler and encouraged
him to perform the piece in Prague, which Stadler
played on October 16, 1791.[11] Stadler requested leave
from his position in Vienna for one year to arrange a
European tour, returning in July 1796.[12] An engraving
of Stadler's basset clarinet was included above the
printed program given in Riga where Stadler performed on March 21, 1794 (Figure 19.1).[13]

Since programs are missing from many of his
concerts, Stadler could have performed Mozart's
concerto in several cities. He continued to perform
on the basset clarinet during the early nineteenth
century and basset clarinets, although rare, continued to be made in various designs during the nineteenth century by a few manufacturers in Germany,

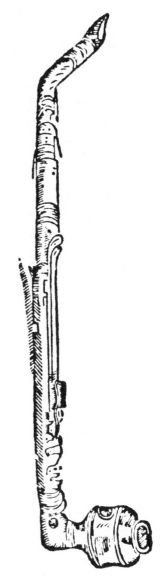

FIGURE 19.1 An illustration of
Anton Stadler's basset clarinet used
for playing Mozart's *Concerto* on
March 21, 1794.

---

[10] Albert R. Rice, *The Clarinet in the Classical Period* (New York: Oxford University Press, 2003), 51–55; Eric
Hoeprich, *The Clarinet* (New Haven, CT: Yale University Press, 2008), 70–74.

[11] See the evidence presented by Lawson, ibid., 35–36.

[12] Pamela Poulin, "Anton Stadler's Basset Clarinet: Recent Discoveries in Riga," *Journal of the American Musical
Instrument Society* 22 (1996): 117, 120–26.

[13] Announcements and newspaper reports of this program were found by Poulin. Poulin, ibid., 122, note 20,
124–25. It is reproduced by kind permission of Pamela Poulin. On March 5, 1794 in Riga, Stadler played a clarinet *Concerto* by Franz Süssmayr, the basset clarinet obligato to "Parto, parto ma tu ben mio" from Mozart's *La
clemenza di Tito*, and Mozart's *Concerto for Clarinet*.

Denmark, Italy, Austria, and Spain for performing Mozart's music and playing in wind bands.[14]

Since the autograph of the *concerto* is missing, the traditional editions have changed the notes of the solo part to fit the normal A clarinet range. Some modern editions of the *concerto* alter notes of the solo part in order to achieve a shape that is likely closer to the original conception.[15] There are several sections where the basset clarinet drops to its lowest register only to continue the melodic line more than two octaves higher. Runs of more than three octaves are very striking when heard with the basset clarinet.

For the student, the question is, is there a difference if Mozart's *Concerto for Clarinet and Orchestra* is played on a basset clarinet rather than a normal A clarinet? After listening to this *concerto* played on a basset clarinet, the player will hear several sections that use the extended low range in arpeggios and other passages, which are musically more logical and convincing than heard with the normal clarinet.[16] In addition, the basset clarinet's low register is fuller and richer because of the additional venting of the lowest keys.[17] If the performer plays Mozart's *concerto* on a basset clarinet, the results are well worth the effort of obtaining a good instrument, and choosing an edition with which the player is comfortable. However, the student can certainly sensitively perform this *concerto* on a normal range A clarinet.[18]

---

[14] Rice, *The Clarinet*, 71, 74–76; Albert R. Rice, "The Basset Clarinet: Instruments, Makers, and Patents," *Instrumental Odyssey: Essays in Honor of Herbert Heyde*, ed. L. Libin (New York: Historic Brass Society, 2016) 157–78.

[15] These editions are: Wolfgang Amadeus Mozart, *Concerto for Clarinet and Orchestra, A major, K. 622*, ed. Alan Hacker (London: Schott & Co., 1974); Wolfgang Amadeus Mozart, *Konzert in A für Klarinette und Orchester*, KV 622, ed. Hans-Dietrich Klaus (Kassel: Bärenreiter, 1987); Wolfgang Amadeus Mozart, *Konzert für Klarinette und Orchester A-Dur, KV 622*, ed. Trio di clarone (Wiesbaden: Breitkopf & Härtel, 1987); and Wolfgang Amadeus Mozart, *Concerto, K622: Edition for Basset Clarinet in A and Clarinet in A*, ed. Pamela Weston (Vienna: Universal Edition, 1997). See Keith Koons, "A Guide to Published Editions of Mozart's Clarinet Concerto, KV622, for Clarinet and Piano," *The Clarinet* 25, no. 3 (May–June 1998): 34–43.

[16] A fine CD recording of Mozart's clarinet concerto on a modern Boehm-system basset clarinet is by Sharon Kam with the Österreichisch-Ungarische Haydn Philharmonie, on Berlin Classics, 0016672BC; two fine CD recordings of Mozart's clarinet concerto played on reproductions of basset clarinets are by Eric Hoeprich with the Orchestra of the Eighteenth Century, Frans Brüggen, conductor, on Philips, 420242-2; and Colin Lawson with the Hanover Band, Roy Goodman, conductor, on Nimbus, N17023.

[17] Modern Boehm-system basset clarinets can be ordered from Buffet Crampon & Cie, the Selmer Co., and Schwenk & Seggelke, Neustadt an der Aisch; Oehler system basset clarinets by Wolfgang Dietz, Leitner & Kraus, and Herbert Wurlitzer all in Neustadt an der Aisch, and Schwenk & Seggelke, Bamberg. Historical basset clarinets are currently available from Steven Fox (Richmond Hill, Ontario, Canada), Schwenk & Seggellke (Bamberg, Germany), Agnès Guéroult (Paris, France), Soren Green (Rotterdam, the Netherlands), and Riccardo von Vitorelli (St. Étienne, Belgium).

[18] See the useful suggestions for altering the original version for a normal clarinet in all three movements by Robert Adelson in "New Perspectives on Performing Mozart's Clarinet Concerto," *The Clarinet* 25, no. 2 (February–March 1998): 50–52, 54–55.

Whether or not the performer plays a modern clarinet, a basset clarinet, or a reproduction of an eighteenth century basset clarinet, it is valuable to be aware of how articulation was approached by players in 1791. Vanderhagen's 1785 *Méthode nouvelle et raisonnée pour la clarinette* was the most widely known and important method at the time. Most players, including Vanderhagen, played with the reed above and when not marked in the music, tongued notes were played by pronouncing the letter "d." Notes indicated with short dots were separated by using the letter "t." The most common articulation for four eighth notes was to slur the first two and tongue the second two. Other typical articulations were, one tongued, three slurred; three slurred, one tongued; and two slurred eighth notes in a pair.[19] Austrian clarinetists such as Anton Stadler, may have played with the reed against the lower lip. Backofen knew both reed positions in his 1803 *Anweisung zur Klarinette*, and wrote that articulation was done with the tongue, lips, or throat, although he preferred the tongue.[20]

Mozart's *Concerto for Clarinet and Orchestra* is a work that is learned and studied by virtually every clarinet student. Slow and careful effort must be made to perform this work with proficiency and understanding. Returning to this concerto after several years of playing is always a delight. It remains one of the great musical creations of the late eighteenth century.

---

[19] Joan Michelle Blazich, *Original Text, English Translation, and a Commentary on Amand Vanderhagen's Méthode Nouvelle et Raisonnée pour la Clarinette (1785) and Nouvelle Méthode de Clarinette (1799): A Study in Eighteenth-Century French Clarinet Music* (Lewiston, NY: Edwin Mellen Press, 2009), 37–38; Ingrid Pearson, "Playing Historical Clarinets," in Colin Lawson, *The Early Clarinet: A Practical Guide* (Cambridge: Cambridge University Press, 2000), 47–51.

[20] Rice, *The Clarinet in the Classical Period*, 89.

20 Robert Muczynski, *Time Pieces for Clarinet and Piano, op. 43*

Date of composition: September 1983

First edition: Robert Muczynski, *Time Pieces for Clarinet and Piano*, Bryn Mawr, Pennsylvania: T. Presser, 1985

Dedicatee/first performers: Mitchell Lurie; Mitchell Lurie, clarinet, Robert Muczynski, piano

Date/place of first performance: August 15, 1984; London, Froebel Institute, International Clarinet Society Congress

ROBERT MUCZYNSKI (1929–2010) was an American composer, pianist, and teacher who studied piano with Walter Knupfer and music composition with Alexander Tcherepnin at DePaul University. He finished a bachelor's degree in 1950 and a master's degree at DePaul in 1952, both in piano performance, although composition had become his main interest. Muczynski taught piano at DePaul, and in 1953, received his first commission for a symphony, which was never performed. However, he did play a piano reduction of the work for the conductor, Fritz Reiner, who critiqued it.[1] In 1958, Muczynski made his New York debut at Carnegie Hall playing a recital of his works. He became head of the piano department at Loras College in Iowa, 1956 to 1959, and from 1963 to 1988 was composer-in-residence at

---

[1] Justin Martin Harbaugh, "The Clarinet B.C. Program Notes for a Masters Clarinet Recital of Works of Brahms' *Clarinet Trio*, Françaix's *Tema con varizioni*, Muczynski's *Time Pieces*, and Carter's *Gra* and *Hiyoku*" (M.M. thesis, Kansas State University, 2009), 22–23.

the University of Arizona, Tucson. His compositions were published by Theodore Presser and include piano solos, works for chamber ensemble, and orchestral works. Most of his music is available on Laurel records, including his performances of solo piano music.[2]

Muczynski's music reflects the influence of Béla Bartók, Samuel Barber, and Leonard Bernstein and is neoclassical with strong neoromantic elements. Simmons states that, "His music is abstract and concise, constructed according to traditional techniques, while avoiding pretense, ostentation, or grandiosity. But it also reveals a concern with mood and emotion, exhibiting a dark, yet gently restrained lyricism, and, in fast movements, strongly accented, irregular meters, which create a vigorous rhythmic drive."[3] His flute, saxophone, and clarinet solos have entered the repertoires for these instruments, and his solo piano and chamber music works for winds are often chosen as competition pieces in the United States, Europe, Asia, and Australia.[4]

Time Pieces was commissioned by Mitchell Lurie, who was formerly principal clarinetist with the Chicago Symphony Orchestra and Pittsburgh Symphony Orchestra, studio clarinetist for many Hollywood films and television shows, and clarinet instructor at the University of Southern California. Lurie explained the reasons for his commission in the liner notes to the recording, *Lurie and Baker Play Muczynski* (1984):

> I knew well and admired Muczynski's *Fantasy Trio for Clarinet, Cello, and Piano*. At student "juries" at semester's end at USC, I was hearing Muczynski's flute sonata played over and over by many flute students. I thought that if he wrote so wonderfully and idiomatically for flute, he would surely compose as brilliantly for clarinet.[5]

In 1984, James Gillespie reviewed the premiere of *Time Pieces* and other performances at the International Clarinet Congress in London for *The Clarinet*:[6]

> Continuing his campaign to introduce new literature to the recital stage, Lurie's program consisted of two world premieres and an early twentieth-century work

[2] Walter Simmons, "Muczynski, Robert," *Grove Music Online*. Theodore Presser Company, Robert Muczynski. [Online] Available: http://www.presser.com/composer/muczynski-robert/. [October 19, 2015].

[3] Simmons, "Muczynski, Robert."

[4] Simmons, ibid.

[5] Quoted in Anne Marie Thurmond, "Selected Woodwind Compositions by Robert Muczynski: A Stylistic and Structural Analysis of Muczynski's Sonata, opus 14, for Flute and Piano, Sonata opus 29, for Alto Saxophone and Piano, *Time Pieces*, opus 43, for Clarinet and Piano, and *Moments*, opus 47, for Flute and Piano" (D.M.A. diss., University of Georgia, 1998), 14–15.

[6] The author was present at this performance.

by the Lithuanian composer Max Laurischkus. The "meat" of the recital, however, was Muczynski's *Time Pieces* which Lurie commissioned. It is a substantial
work with a rhythmic vitality and melodic appeal that mark it as a major addition to the repertoire . . . . Throughout, Lurie played with his characteristic solid
technique, firm tone and musical savvy. American clarinetists in the audience left
the recital knowing that their country could not have been better represented.[7]

A recording of *Time Pieces* was made by Lurie and Muczynski and favorably reviewed in 1985 by Walter Simmons in *Fanfare* magazine:

Time Pieces is one of Muczynski's most recent works, composed within the past
year for Mitchell Lurie, who introduced it in London, with considerable success. It is a welcome contribution to the repertoire of the clarinet and piano,
quite comparable to the Sonata for Flute and Piano composed more than
twenty years earlier. Both pieces display Muczynski's remarkable gift for producing music that may appear on the surface to be conventional neoclassical
gebrauchmusik [functional music], but, on closer inspection, proves to offer
a higher order of musical interest. In pieces like these, tailor-made for the recital needs of any reasonably advanced player, Muczynski extends his diligent
craftsmanship—the type that most composition teachers would consider
"exemplary"—to musical content that is above the routine, while maintaining
an ever-present concern with expressive values. Thus, unified by its own engaging and infectious personality, the music never "just goes through the motions
(which is, after all, the frequent problem with neoclassical chamber music)."
These are the qualities that have made Muczynski's flute sonata a staple of the
repertoire for years and should do the same for *Time Pieces*.[8]

Muczynski described *Time Pieces* in his notes for the recording, *Lurie and Baker
Play Muczynski*:

This composition is a suite of four contrasting pieces, each highlighting
some specific characteristic of the clarinet in terms of range, technical prowess,
color, and expressiveness. . . . The title of the work, *Time Pieces*, has nothing to
do with mechanical clocks or watches. It is not a play on words but rather an

---

[7] James Gillespie, "The International Clarinet Congress London, England: August 12–17, 1984," *The Clarinet* 12,
no. 1 (Fall 1984): 7.

[8] Walter Simmons, record review of "Muczynski, *Time Pieces, for Clarinet and Piano, op. 43. Sonata for Flute and
Piano, Op. 14. Three Preludes for Flute Solo, Op. 18. Six Duos for Flute and Clarinet, Op. 34*," *Fanfare* 8, no. 4
(1985): 265–66.

awareness of the fact that everything exists in time: history, our lives and...in a special way...music.[9]

The first of four movements, Allegro risoluto, quarter note = 112, in ternary form with a coda, exhibits a restless rhythm and continuous momentum. (See Chart 20.1.) The piano sets a strong rhythm with one eighth note, three triplet sixteenths, and two eighth notes in the low register. The clarinet enters in measure 3 with a four measure motive of tongued and slurred sixteenth notes, with an initial accented sixteenth note. Section A has tonal centers of both C and F major. However, the harmony primarily consists of quartal and quintal chords and no specific tonalities are prominent.[10] Throughout the movement, Muczynski uses motives, short musical phrases of four measures or less, to construct the music. The first motive is six sixteenth clarinet notes (m. 3), altered and repeated several times. Throughout the clarinet and piano parts, the upbeats are accented. Each repetition is written a minor second, major second, and minor third higher.[11]

Section B is in four parts, based on motivic material, tonal center, and/or change in tempo. The first part (mm. 24–51), played after a short caesura, develops the motives around the tonal centers of D, F, and D. A second part (mm. 52–74), marked, Subito più mosso, quarter note = 126, begins with the B theme played by the piano; the clarinet enters one octave higher (m. 54), with the tonal centers of F# and E♭. The third part (mm. 75–92) returns to the tempo of section A, and presents a legato, lyrical line until measure 86; the tonal centers are A and C#. A fourth part has the piano in octaves (mm. 89–90) joined by the clarinet with a

Section:	A	B	A[1]	Coda
Starts at m.	1 Allegro risoluto	24	113	134–138
No. of mm.	23	89	21	5
Tonal Centers	C-F	D-F-D, F#-E♭, A-C#, E-A	C-F	C
Themes	A	B, A[1]	A[2]	A[3]

CHART 20.1 Muczynski, *Time Pieces for Clarinet and Piano, op. 43*: Structural analysis, first movement, Allegro risoluto.

[9] Robert Muczynski, *Time Pieces* (King of Prussia, PA: Theodore Press Co., 1985), 1, quoted by Harbaugh, "The Clarinet B.C. Program Notes," 24.
[10] Harbaugh, ibid., 25.
[11] Thurmond, "Selected Woodwind Compositions by Robert Muczynski," 64–65.

marcato A^1 theme (mm. 93–112), a minor sixth lower than its first appearance (m. 107).[12] A sixteenth note clarinet run to a high A♭$_6$ (mm. 98–100) is the high point of the movement; the tonal centers are E and A. The urgent movement continues until an allargando indication, one measure before the A^1 section (m. 112) leading to an "A tempo" and the opening piano ostinato. The coda (mm. 134–138) rewrites material from the A theme for a decisive ending with an allargando at the last two measures.

The second movement, Andante espressivo, quarter note = 52, is in ternary form with a cadenza and coda. (See Chart 20.2.) Each section and its parts have a repetitive rhythm which supports the melodic themes.[13] It begins with two measures of piano half notes to quarter notes, and in the third measure, an expressive *p* legato clarinet A theme. After an allargando (m. 15) there is a three measure piano interlude at a meno mosso tempo, quarter note = 40, before a return of the first tempo and the clarinet A theme (mm. 19–23). The thematic material is based on three note motives and their inversion, retrograde, and variants.[14]

The B section is in three parts marked, Poco più mosso, quarter note = 63. The piano plays an ostinato of constant eighth notes in the low register, and the clarinet follows with two eighth note pickups and a lyrical and legato B theme (mm. 27–29). The second part of the B section is at a meno mosso tempo, quarter note = 40 (m. 36), where the piano plays a sixteenth note ostinato pattern, and after the fourth beat, the clarinet begins with B^1, a variation of the B theme. Harmonically, the notes of the piano right and left hands are based on an octatonic scale. As the clarinet's melody quickens and increases in loudness, it reaches an immediate subito più mosso, quarter note = 52, at the end of measure 41. The second part of the B section includes an elaboration of the melody and a molto ritardando to *pp*.[15]

After a breath, a cadenza begins at Andante, quarter note = 46 (m. 48), and the theme is marked, con rubato, il tema marcato. The cadenza is flexibly played with sixteenth notes that highlight the A theme fragment notes by an upper flag; the accompanying sixteenth notes have a lower flag (Ex. 20.1). In the A^1 section, Tempo primo, quarter note = 52, the piano plays the A^1 theme and the clarinet (mm. 58–61) follows with a partial restatement of the A^1 theme. At the coda, Adagio, quarter note = 42, in D (m. 67), the piano states the B^2 theme in the right hand and the clarinet elaborates with sixteenth notes. The last three Lento measures end on a B♭7th chord, with a mournful clarinet melody that gradually quiets to nothing.[16]

---

[12] Thurmond, ibid., 69–71.
[13] Thurmond, ibid., 74–75.
[14] Thurmond, ibid., 76.
[15] Thurmond, ibid., 76–77, 81.
[16] Thurmond, ibid., 77–79; Harbaugh, "The Clarinet B.C. Program Notes," 31.

EXAMPLE 20.1. Muczynski, *Time pieces for Clarinet and Piano, op. 43*, second movement, cadenza, mm. 48–57.

Section:	A	B	Cadenza	A¹	Coda
Starts at m.	1 Andante espressivo	24 Poco più mosso	48 Andante	58 Tempo primo	67 Adagio to 76
No. of mm.	23	24	10	9	10
Tonal Centers	B♭	B♭-E, Octatonic	B♭-F-D	B♭	D
Themes	A	B, B¹	cadenza (A)	A¹, (A¹)	B²

CHART 20.2 Muczynski, *Time Pieces for Clarinet and Piano, op. 43*: Structural analysis, second movement, Andante espressivo.

The third movement, Allegro moderato, quarter note = 116–120, is in ternary form with a coda. (See Chart 20.3.) It is marked "gracefully," beginning with a lyrical melody and symmetrical phrases, lighter in concept than the previous movements. According to Muczynski, the movement was written earlier with the flute in mind but never used, and it was adapted for the third movement after the other movements had been written.[17] The piano states the A theme, which is restated by the clarinet (mm. 9–17), ending with an incomplete cadence. After a seven measure 6/8 piano introduction to section B (m. 20),[18] the meter changes from 4/4 to 6/8, with a quarter note equal to a dotted quarter note. The clarinet contributes a bounding B theme with many leaps in two four measure phrases (m. 27), further developed in

---

[17] Charles West, "Master Class: *Time Pieces for Clarinet and Piano, op. 43* by Robert Muczynski," *The Clarinet* 26, no. 4 (September 1999): 7.

[18] Thurmond, ibid., 84–85.

Section:	A	B	A¹	Coda
Starts at m.	1 Allegro moderato	20	69 Tempo primo	79–83 Presto subito
No. of mm.	19	49	10	5
Tonal Centers	B Aeolian	F, F-F#, Octatonic	B Aeolian	Octatonic, D♭
Themes	A	B, C, B¹	A¹	(B)

CHART 20.3 Muczynski, *Time Pieces for Clarinet and Piano, op. 43*: Structural analysis, third movement, Allegro moderato.

themes C and B¹ by the piano and clarinet. At measure 66, the piano suddenly plays a sequence of thirty-second note octatonic scales, a molto ritardando, and a fermata, and at the Tempo primo (section A¹) the clarinet brings the A¹ theme (mm. 69–76). The A and A¹ sections are based on a B major tonal center on an Aeolian scale.[19] A short, abrupt coda in 2/4 marked Presto subito (m. 79), ends the movement with a clarinet *ff* octatonic scale and a D♭ chord.[20]

The composer describes the fourth movement in his notes on *Time Pieces* in the recording, *Lurie and Baker play Muczynski*:

> There are moments when the clarinet plays alone, without need of piano accompaniment; i.e., the final movement is introduced by solo clarinet in a brooding, pensive statement that gains in intensity and momentum and leads directly to the "Allegro energico," a dance-like rondo where clarinet and piano are reunited.[21]

The fourth movement, Andante molto, quarter note = ca. 52, incorporates a ternary form adding an introduction, transition, cadenza, and coda. (See Chart 20.4.) The introduction, for clarinet alone in improvisatory style, uses part of an octatonic scale and, from measures 15–19, an embellished version of the first five measures.[22] From measures 23–28, there are 3/8 and 2/8 time signatures until the piano presents a 3/8 accented eighth note rhythm at an Allegro energico, quarter note = 92 (mm. 29–40). A slurred A theme played by the clarinet (mm. 41–53) is followed by an

---

19 An Aeolian B modal scale is B, C#, D, E, F#, G, A, B.
20 Harbaugh, ibid., 38; Thurmond, ibid., 86–87, 89.
21 Thurmond, ibid., 92–93; Harbaugh, ibid., 40.
22 Thurmond, ibid., 92, 94.

Section:	Introduction	A	B
Starts at m.	1 Andante molto	29 Allegro energico	70–83: 84–104
No. of mm.	28	41	49
Tonal Centers	D♭-D-D♭-E♭	C, B♭, C-E, trans.	G-D, F-D, G-D
Themes	intro.	A, A¹	B, B¹

Section:	Transition	A¹	Cadenza	Coda
Starts at m.	105	114	151 Furioso	183–189
No. of mm.	9	37	32	7
Tonal Centers	C	C-B♭	F-C-G-D-C-B♭	C, Octatonic
Themes	transition	A², (A²)	cadenza, (A)	fig.

CHART 20.4 Muczynski, *Time Pieces for Clarinet and Piano, op. 43*: Structural analysis, fourth movement, Andante molto.

articulated and accented A¹ theme (mm. 53–64).[23] The legato clarinet B theme (mm. 70–83) is repeated. A B¹ theme (m. 93) leads to a transition (mm. 105–113) of ferocious sixteenth note runs followed by clarinet runs and accents. This includes a seven measure false recapitulation (mm. 107–113) followed by a 3/8 accented eighth note piano rhythm (section A¹; mm. 114–150) for three measures.[24] The clarinet plays the beginning of the A² theme while the piano leads directly into an accented and emphatic clarinet cadenza marked, Furioso. The cadenza (mm. 151–182) includes fragments from A themes, sixteenth note runs, and written out rubati in ritardandos and accelerandos.[25] An exciting coda includes *ff* piano octatonic scales followed by clarinet runs and octatonic scales (mm. 183–189), ending on a high F₆ marked, allargando.[26]

Charles West, who worked with Muczynski on *Time Pieces* before it was published, states:

> I cannot emphasize enough in discussing this piece the intensity with which [it] must be played—especially in the outer movements, but also in the center sections of the two inner movements as well. This is music of incredible passion, as the composer is a musician of remarkable intensity.... [D]on't program this piece unless you intend to wear every ounce of the emotion that you can muster right out on your sleeve.[27]

---

[23] Thurmond, ibid., 96.
[24] Thurmond, ibid., 98.
[25] Thurmond, ibid., 64-106; Harbaugh, ibid., 25–47.
[26] Thurmond, ibid., 96, 98, 100–102.
[27] West, "Master Class," 8.

Time Pieces appeals to advanced players and is an impressive recital piece. Muczynski develops his ideas with a high degree of technical and musical skill. His clarinet writing is very idiomatic although there are some awkward passages that require practice. The clarinetist and pianist must coordinate several passages carefully, including a wide variety of dynamic contrasts, rhythmic challenges, and tests of endurance. After these challenges are worked out, it is a stunning and effective work.

21 Carl Nielsen, *Concerto for Clarinet and Orchestra, op. 57*

Date of composition: 1928

First edition/later editions: Carl Nielsen, *Koncert for Klarinet og Orkester*, Copenhagen: Samfundet til Udgivelse af Dansk Musik, 1931 (clarinet and piano; orchestral score); Carl Nielsen, *Koncerter = Concertos*, eds. Elly Bruunshuus Petersen and Kirsten Flensborg Petersen, Copenhagen: Wilhelm Hansen, 2002 (orchestral score); Carl Nielsen, *Concerto, op. 57, for Clarinet and Orchestra*, ed. Torben Petersen, Copenhagen: Wilhelm Hansen, 2003 (clarinet and piano)

Dedicatee/first performers (private and public): Aage Oxenvad; Aage Oxenvad, clarinet, Emil Telmányi, orchestra conductor

Date/place of first private performance: September 14, 1928; Copenhagen, home of Carl Michaelsen

Date/place of first public performance: October 11, 1928; Copenhagen

Orchestral instrumentation: First and second violins, violas, cellos, contrabasses, two bassoons, two F horns, and snare drum

CARL NIELSEN (1865–1931) was the most famous Danish composer of the early twentieth century. His *Concerto for Clarinet and Orchestra* was one of his last works and is among the finest twentieth-century concertos. It was written for his close friend, the most accomplished Danish clarinetist of the time, Aage (pronounced Oh-wuh) Oxenvad (1884–1944). In 1909, Oxenvad joined Copenhagen's Royal Chapel Orchestra; he was the first in this orchestra to play the Boehm-system clarinet, and was solo clarinetist until his death.[1] In 1922, Nielsen heard Oxenvad as a member of the Copenhagen Wind Quintet while attending a rehearsal of Mozart's *Sinfonia Concertante for four wind instruments and piano.* The next year, he wrote his famous *wind quintet* for this group, musically portraying the individual quality and character of each player. Nielsen was so impressed with the players that he promised to write a concerto for each.[2] They recorded the *wind quintet* in 1936, and Oxenvad later recorded Nielsen's earlier *Serenata in vano for clarinet, bassoon, horn, cello, and double bass* (1914). There were plans for Oxenvad to record the clarinet concerto but his subsequent illness and death intervened and the French clarinetist, Louis Cahusac, recorded it.[3]

The first public performance in Copenhagen was not well received and its Swedish premier in Stockholm in December was denounced by some critics. The following year, at a performance in Göteborg, the reaction was more favorable.[4] During the composition of the *concerto*, Oxenvad received the manuscript bit by bit as it was written, and the soloist and composer exchanged notes on it. Oxenvad also visited Nielsen to try out specific passages, particularly the long staccato parts in one of the cadenzas.

Nielsen's appreciation of the clarinet was no doubt influenced by the temperament and playing of Oxenvad. Nielsen notes that the clarinet, "can be once warmhearted and completely hysterical, gentle as balm and screaming as a streetcar on ungreased rails."[5] The oboist of the Copenhagen Wind Quintet, Svend Christian Felumb, writes that the clarinet concerto:

> was not only a concerto for clarinet, it was a concerto for Aage Oxenvad. The composer was so deeply inspired by Oxenvad's immersion in the essence of the instrument and by *his* peculiar manner of expressing the soul of the clarinet, that one may safely say that Carl Nielsen would never have written *this* work if he had not heard Oxenvad. No verbal characterization could be more vivid than Carl Nielsen's musical one. It tells everything about Aage and his clarinet.[6]

---

[1] Eric Nelson, "The Danish Performance Tradition in Carl Nielsen's *Koncert for Klarinet og Orkester,* opus 57 (1928)," *The Clarinet* 14, no. 2 (Winter 1987): 30–31; Pamela Weston, *Yesterday's Clarinettists: A Sequel* (Ampleforth: Emerson, 2002), 124–25.

[2] Jack Lawson, *Carl Nielsen* (London: Phaidon Press, 1997), 174–75.

[3] Robert Layton, "Nielsen and the Gramaphone," *The Nielsen Companion,* ed. Mina F. Miller (Portland: Amadeus Press, 1994), 117, 120.

[4] Lawson, ibid., 205–6; Elly Bruunshuus Petersen and Kirsten Flensborg Petersen, "Foreword" to Carl Nielsen, *Koncerter = Concertos,* Series II. Instrumental Music 9, eds. Elly Bruunshuus Petersen and Kirsten Flensborg Petersen (Copenhagen: Wilhelm Hansen, 2002), xxxvii.

[5] Nelson, ibid., 33; Weston, ibid., 125.

[6] S. C. Felumb, "Aage Oxenvad, 16. January 1884–13. April 1944," *Dansk Musik Tidskrift* 19 (1944), 4; cited and trans. Nelson, "The Danish Performance," 31, 35.

According to Tage Scharff, a pupil of Oxenvad, "he played in a late nineteenth century lyrical style with a great deal of rubato and the nuances of passionate playing."[7]

Nielsen's orchestration is small. Because of the lack of other high woodwinds, the clarinet is easily heard. However, its use is atypical; although it predominates in many solo passages, it is unusually paired with the snare drum, and occasionally blends in as an orchestral voice.[8] The drum provides a sense of farce and humor, playing almost always with the clarinet, "coaxing and prodding throughout."[9] The *Concerto for Clarinet and Orchestra* is described as, "angry, with choleric humor, pathos, and kindliness mingled in conflict."[10] Along with passionately tender and lyrical solo passages, "chaos and ecstasy are part of this work."[11] Its sense of conflict is emphasized in the first movement by two tonalities in close proximity, F and E. Unusual for Nielsen, it starts and finishes in the same key, F.[12] When the soloist and orchestra play in different tonal centers, dissonant and polytonal affects are achieved.[13] Thus, tonal relationships are not the primary structure; more importance is placed on a dialogue between the soloist and the orchestra and thematic development.[14]

Set in one continuous movement, the analysis divides the concerto into four movements, each with its own themes and tonal centers, ending with material from the first movement. Nielsen skillfully shapes the themes to reappear in different versions throughout.[15] It is these contrasting themes bound together that shape this compelling concerto.[16]

The first movement, Allegretto un poco, quarter note = 72, is written in sonata-allegro form. (See Chart 21.1.) The haunting fugal opening A theme of cellos and basses is not typical of virtuoso twentieth-century concertos. After sixteen measures, the soloist enters with the A theme early, staying in the background after the orchestra's urgent thirty-second

---

[7] Nelson, ibid., 30–32.

[8] Ann Marie Bingham, "Carl Nielsen's Koncert for Klarinet og Orkester, opus 57 (1928): A Performance Guide" (D.M.A. diss., University of Kentucky, 1990), 9.

[9] David Davenport, "Carl Nielsen's Clarinet Concerto: Specific Interpretation Approach/Part II," *Percussive Notes* 31, no. 5 (June 1993): 52; Daniel Grimley, "Analytical and Aesthetic Issues in Carl Nielsen's Concerto for Clarinet and Orchestra," *Carl Nielsen Studies* 1 (2003): 33, and note 12; Bingham, ibid., 9.

[10] Robert Simpson, *Carl Nielsen, Symphonist* (New York: Taplinger, 1979), 143.

[11] Kjell-Inge Stevensson, trans. W. Jewson, "Carl Nielsen's Clarinet Concerto, Op. 57 (1928)," *The Clarinet* 4, no. 4 (Summer 1977): 29.

[12] Simpson, ibid., 143.

[13] Teresa Waskowska, "Clarinet Concerto Opus 57, FS129," *Carl Nielsen, Mennesket og Musikken = The Man and the Music*, CD-ROM, Denmark: AM Production Multimedia, 1998.

[14] Grimley, ibid., 36–37.

[15] Waskowska, ibid.

[16] Ben Arnold, "Tradition and Growth in the Concertos of Nielsen," in *The Nielsen Companion*, ed. Mina F. Miller, Table 5, Clarinet Concerto, 363–65; Herbert Rosenberg, "The Concertos," *Carl Nielsen: Centenary Essays*, ed. Jürgen Balzer (London: D. Dobson, 1966), 52–55.

Section:	Exposition	Development	Recapitulation
Starts at m.	1 Allegretto un poco	79 (no. 5)	134 (16 mm. before no. 8)–209
No. of mm.	78	55	76
Tonal Centers	F, C, F, cadenza, E, trans., D, cadenza, trans.	C, C, cadenza, trans., trans., cadenza	F, E, E, F, trans., cadenza, E♭
Themes	A	B	(B), A

CHART 21.1 Nielsen, *Concerto for Clarinet and Orchestra, op. 57*: Structural analysis, first movement, Allegretto un poco.

notes at measure 23.[17] The snare drum entry on the third beat, six measures before no. 4 (m. 62), features a duet with clarinet with a high-pitched harsh cry and a driving drum beat. This dies down and at the development section, no. 5 (m. 79), the clarinet introduces, with an intense longing, a slow B theme (Ex. 21.1), A tempo ma tranquillo.

EXAMPLE 21.1. Nielsen, *Concerto for Clarinet and Orchestra, op. 57*, first movement, mm. 79–88.

A short cadenza shifts the mood at no. 6 (m. 96), "when the clarinet starts to take itself too seriously; it suffers rude drum knocks on the head"[18] (mm. 96–97). After a short fermata, four thirty-second notes (m. 102) introduce a gentle clarinet B theme with pizzicato strings and two bassoons (m. 103). This becomes more and more restless up to measure 133, then after a fermata, the clarinet begins a long and athletic

---

[17] Grimley, ibid., 37.
[18] Davenport, ibid., 52.

cadenza, *pp* in the chalumeau register. At the recapitulation, Allegro non troppo, Tempo primo (m. 134), the two bassoons begin with a fragment of the B theme, while the lower strings play the A theme, and the clarinet enters eight measures later with background flourishes. At no. 8 (m. 150), the clarinet states the A theme and the tempo accelerates with a frenzy of dissonant orchestral sixteenth notes leading to a staccato-laden cadenza at no. 10 (m. 189), the orchestra answering *ff* then slowing and quieting down.

The second movement, Poco Adagio, quarter note = 69,[19] is in ternary form. (See Chart 21.2.) It begins with a solemn C theme (m. 210) played by horns and bassoons and beautifully repeated a major sixth higher by clarinet and strings at no. 12 (m. 218).[20] At the B section, Più mosso, no. 14 (m. 244), a dotted rhythm violin phrase appears with sixteenth-note sextuplets (second violins) and sixteenth notes (violas). Over these figures, the clarinet announces an exuberant D theme, five measures after no. 14 (m. 248).[21] This continues to an exciting *ff* brilliant cadenza for snare drum and clarinet (mm. 269–276). A fragment of the C theme is quietly presented by horns and bassoons at no. 18 (m. 283), answered by strings. The ensuing clarinet C theme includes enormous expression and longing, five measures after no. 18. A brief and relaxed cadenza of dotted eighth and sixteenth notes ushers in the third movement.

The third movement, Allegro non troppo, eighth note = 144, is in ternary form. (See Chart 21.3.) At no. 20 (m. 305), a fourteen measure quiet horn introduction in 3/8 leads to a scherzo-like E theme by the strings (m. 319); the clarinet joins at no. 21 (m. 335). Abruptly, "Bartókian imitative scales" alternate between strings and clarinet (m. 347),[22] leading to the orchestral *f* E theme at no. 22 (m. 353). An outburst by

Section:	A	B	C
Starts at m.	210 (8 mm. before no. 12) Poco Adagio	244 (no. 14) Più mosso	283 Poco Adagio (no. 18)–304
No. of mm.	34	39	22
Tonal Centers	E-c, C-a, frag., frag.	C, cadenza, E	G♭, C♯-a, cadenza
Themes	C, (A)	D, trans., (A)	(C), C

CHART 21.2 Nielsen, *Concerto for Clarinet and Orchestra, op. 57*: Structural analysis, second movement, Poco Adagio.

---

[19] Suggested by the author.
[20] Arnold, ibid., 363–64; Rosenberg, ibid., 53.
[21] Rosenberg, ibid., 53.
[22] Arnold, ibid., 364.

Section:	A	B	C
Starts at m.	305 (no. 20) Allegro non troppo	377 (no. 23) Meno	457 (no. 29) Un poco più mosso–519
No. of mm.	72	80	63
Tonal Centers	C♯-a, G♯, D, B, trans., cadenza	C, c, F	F, cadenza
Themes	intro., E, trans.	F, trans.	fugue theme

CHART 21.3 Nielsen, *Concerto for Clarinet and Orchestra, op. 57*: Structural analysis, third movement, Allegro non troppo.

drum and clarinet (m. 365) introduces a slower, softer rhythm at Meno, no. 23 (m. 377) with a flowing and expressive F theme of clarinet and strings. This leads to an agitated section between clarinet and strings (mm. 389–392) that is fiercely cantabile and expressive for both clarinet and string orchestra. This reverie is interrupted by a clarinet/drum duo starting two measures after no. 27 (m. 433). Accompanied by pizzicato *pp* strings, the bassoon states the fugue theme with, "comic swagger,"[23] six measures from no. 29 (m. 457), Un poco più mosso, eighth note = 126.[24] The clarinet answers with the fugue theme at no. 30 (m. 485). Rapid thirty-second-note triplets accompanied by pizzicato strings, snare drum, and bassoon proceed to a long and demanding cadenza (m. 519). At the end of a rallentando, a breath is taken before six chalumeau notes before proceeding to the fourth movement.

A two measure Adagio section (m. 520) launches the fourth movement with an inverted fragment of the clarinet A theme played in the chalumeau register, accompanied by strings. This is followed by a short, lightly tongued cadenza of thirty-second notes and a thirty-second note run. (See Chart 21.4.) A passionate orchestral outburst of the A theme at no. 33 (m. 524), Adagio, quarter note = 69,[25] joins an intensely expressive clarinet response. There is a gradual diminuendo and slowing so that soft sixteenth notes lead directly to a fermata on A♭5 held as the drum plays two measures of eighth notes at the 2/4, Allegro vivace, quarter note = 144,[26] eight measures before no. 34 (m. 538). A simple clarinet tune is answered with a violent orchestral response with accented eighth notes at no. 34 (m. 546). The clarinet responds with a series of angry sixteenth-note runs. The tempo immediately slows a bit at the Pesante, no. 37 (m. 592), where the orchestra plays accented triplets. At the Molto

---

[23] Grimley, ibid., 38.
[24] Suggested by the author.
[25] Suggested by the author.
[26] Suggested by the author.

Section:	A	B	Coda
Starts at m.	520 (4 mm. before no. 33) Adagio	665 (no. 41) Poco Adagio	673 Allegro (9 mm. after no. 41)–719
No. of mm.	145	8	47
Tonal Centers	A, D, A, trans., D, A, trans.	B♭	A, g-F
Themes	(A), cadenza, A, G, trans., G, (F)	G (in diminution)	G, A

CHART 21.4 Nielsen, *Concerto for Clarinet and Orchestra, op. 57*: Structural analysis, fourth movement, Adagio.

tranquillo, quarter note = 112,[27] no. 38 (m. 609), the clarinet plays an expressive melody against an orchestral triplet accompaniment. Twelve measures before no. 39 (m. 622), the orchestral accompaniment changes to eighth notes, and at measure 625 the clarinet enters on a sustained high $E\flat_6$. At no. 39 (m. 634), Tempo primo, Allegro vivace, quarter note = 144, the orchestra plays a harsh *ff* G theme in eighth notes against an accompaniment in quarter triplets to form a hemiola, and a fragment of the F theme reappears with a sustained clarinet high F_6 (m. 645). The hemiola rhythm continues its conflict but slows with softer dynamics for a memorable eight-measure *p* statement of the G theme at no. 41 (m. 665), Poco Adagio, eighth note = 144. This directly enters the coda, Allegro, quarter note = 144 (m. 673), with a *p* restatement of the A theme leading to a heated sixteenth note *f* imitation between orchestra and clarinet. As the frenzied clarinet sixteenth notes and accented upbeats by drum and strings die down, the A theme reappears, a fifth lower in the chalumeau register, elaborated at Poco meno, no. 43 (m. 701). The sound fades and the musical flow quiets, ending the concerto with string chords, harmonics, and an eerie, sustained clarinet low A♭3.[28]

Nielsen's *Concerto for Clarinet and Orchestra* is unique, with powerful and soul-searching themes, a formidable work for advanced and professional players. It presents problems of technique, endurance, and ensemble playing with one or two pianos or with a full orchestra. It is one of the most awe-inspiring and impressive solo concertos and, without question, one of greatest clarinet works of the twentieth century.

---

[27] Suggested by the author.

[28] Rosenberg, ibid., 54–55. Corrections in the clarinet part in the full score pertain to written indications, not notes, and listed by David S. Lewis, "Nielsen's Concerto for Clarinet: Discrepancies between Part and Score," *The Clarinet* 2, no. 1 (December 1974): 9–10.

22 Krzysztof Penderecki, *Three Miniatures for Clarinet and Piano*

Date of composition: 1956

First edition: Krzysztof Penderecki, *3 Miniatures per Clarinetto e Pianoforte*, Melville, New York: Belwin Mills, 1959

Dedicatee/first performers: Władysław Kosieradzki; Władysław Kosieradzki, clarinet, Zbigniew Jażewski, piano

Date/place of first performance: November 17, 1958; Kraków, Polish Composers' Union concert[1]

KRZYSZTOF PENDERECKI (1933–) is a prominent Polish avant-garde composer. In his later works (choral, operatic, and instrumental) he used eighteenth and nineteenth century techniques to challenge previous ideas about contemporary music. He is also a well-known conductor.

In 1951, Penderecki privately studied music theory with Franciszek Skołyszewski and violin with Stanisław Tawroszewicz in Kraków, Poland. He studied philosophy with Roman Ingarden and classical philology with Tadeusz Sinko before choosing music composition as his field. Skołyszewski was a mathematician, physicist, music theorist, and pianist, and an exacting counterpoint and composition instructor. He was a significant and inspiring influence on Penderecki.[2] From 1954 to 1958, he studied with Artur Malawski and Stanisław Wiechowicz at the State Higher

---

[1] Ray Robinson, *Krzysztof Penderecki: A Guide to His Works* (Princeton, NJ: Prestige Publications, Inc., 1983), 15.
[2] Regina Chłopicka, "Stylistic Phases in the Works of Krzysztof Penderecki," *Studies in Penderecki* 1 (1998): 52.

School of Music in Kraków. A successful student work, *Three Miniatures for Clarinet and Piano* (1956), was later published, and reflects Bartók's influence on the work's harmony and rhythm. This work was dedicated to Władysław Kosieradzki, professor of clarinet at the Kraków Academy of Music. In 1958, Penderecki was awarded such a high grade in his final diploma that he was asked to teach a class in composition.[3]

His first major success was in 1959 when he was awarded the top three prizes at a music competition organized by the Union of Polish Composers for *Strophes*, *Emanations*, and *Psalms of David*. He later met two figures that were influential in bringing his music to audiences outside Poland: the publisher, Hermann Moeck, and the music division director of the South West German Radio, Heinrich Strobel. Strobel commissioned several works, and Penderecki earned a reputation as a creative composer for his experimental notation, concept of time, and progressive techniques for instruments, particularly string bowing. Lukas Foss invited him to be composer-in-residence of the Buffalo Philharmonic Orchestra during the 1968–1969 season. This led to performances of Penderecki's works in Buffalo; Rockport, Massachusetts; and New York City. Commissions came from the LaSalle String Quartet (1961), the American Wind Symphony in Pittsburgh (1967), the United Nations (1971), and the Chicago Lyric Opera (1973).[4]

His awards include: a UNESCO prize for *Threnody "To the Victims of Hiroshima"* (1961); Westphalia and Italia Prizes for *St. Luke Passion* (1966, 1967); Sibelius Gold Medal (1967); Polish State Prize, first class (1968); Honegger Award (1977) for *Magnificat*; Grammy award for *Concerto for Cello and Orchestra no. 2* (1988); Austrian medal for Science and Art (1992); Prince of Asturias Award for the Arts Category (2001); and the Gold Medal of the Armenian Ministry of Culture (2009).[5] Penderecki received honorary doctorates from the Music Academy of Gdansk, University of Washington, and Yale University, as well as universities in Rochester, Pittsburgh, Buenos Aires, London, Glasgow, Leuwen, Bordeaux, Madrid, Rome, Leipzig, Belgrade, Berlin, Poznań, Moscow, St. Petersburg, and Beijing, among others.[6]

---

[3] Adrian Thomas, "Penderecki, Krzysztof," *Oxford Music Online*; Wolfram Schwinger, *Krzysztof Penderecki: His Life and Work; Encounters, Biography and Musical Commentary*, trans. W. Mann (London: Schott, 1989), 19.

[4] Ray Robinson, "Penderecki's Reception in the United States of America" in *The Music of Krzysztof Penderecki: Poetics and Reception; Studies, Essays, and Materials*, eds. Mieczysław Tomaszewski and Władysław Chłopicki (Kraków: Akademia Muzyczna, 1995), 173–77.

[5] Thomas, ibid.; Felix Constantin Goldbach, "'Prelude' for Solo Clarinet (1987) by Krzystof Penderecki," in *Recent Researches in Mechanics, Transportation and Culture, Vouliagmeni, Athens, Greece, December 29–31, 2010*, 63, note 4. [Online] Available: http://www.wseas.us/e-library/conferences/2010/Vouliagmeni/MECH/MECH-08.pdf. [October 20, 2015]; Penderecki Awards. [Online] Available: www.music-unites.com/krzysztof_penderecki/awards/. [October 20, 2015].

[6] Goldbach, ibid., 63, note 5.

Penderecki taught composition classes in Essen at the Volkwang Hochschule für Musik (1966–1968), in Berlin for the Deutscher Akademischer Austauschdienst (1968–1970), and at Yale University (1973–1978). In 1972, he was appointed rector of Kraków Academy, a position he held for fifteen years. Festivals have been held in Kraków and at his manor house in Lusławice. Penderecki pursued conducting in 1972, recording seven of his own works for EMI. He conducted mainly in the United States and throughout Europe, specializing in Shostakovich and his own works. He was artistic director for the Kraków Philharmonic Orchestra, 1987–1990, and in 1988 became principal guest conductor of the North German Radio Symphony Orchestra, Hamburg.

Penderecki wrote in many genres including music for film, theater, puppet theater, electronic instruments, instrumental chamber ensembles, orchestral, vocal and instrumental ensemble, chorus, and opera.[7] In addition to the *Three Miniatures*, Penderecki wrote three clarinet works, *Prelude for Solo Clarinet* (1987), *Quartet for Clarinet and Strings* (1993), and *Sextet for Clarinet, Horn, String Trio, and Piano* (2000).[8] The *Three Miniatures* has been called, "elegant virtuoso pieces."[9] A reviewer of a performance by the Milwaukee Contemporary Chamber Ensemble had trouble with the middle movement:

> [T]he *Three Miniatures* is replete with motivic repetitions that stress a strong quick beat. They are run-on, foot-tapping works, full of constant motion and counterpoint—at least the two outer movements. The middle one is slow and reflective yet the rhythm is constant and uneventful.[10]

The *Three Miniatures* for Clarinet and Piano is written in three short movements and uses chromatic harmony without any tonal implications throughout. The first movement, Allegro, quarter note = 144,[11] is thirty measures in two parts. (See Chart 22.1.) It is modeled after a Scarlatti keyboard sonata movement and begins with a colorful, funny, keyboard ostinato, each of the first three measures played *f*, *p*, and *pp*. The unceasing rhythmic drive, with a mix of clarinet slurs and sharp staccato, continues throughout. This movement uses several time signatures, 4/4 to 9/8 to

---

[7] Cindy Bylander, *Krzysztof Penderecki: A Bio-Bibliography* (Westport, CT: Prager, 2004), 44.

[8] Peter Stoll, "Penderecki … by Penderecki!" *The Clarinet* 37, no. 4 (September 2010): 56–60; Peter L. Cain, "A 'Farewell' to his past: Krzysztof Penderecki's Clarinet Quartet and Sextet" (D.M.A. diss., University of Cincinnati, 2012), 2–3.

[9] Schwinger, ibid., 19.

[10] Vincent McDermott, "Current Chronicle, United States, Milwaukee," *Musical Quarterly* 54, no. 4 (October 4, 1968): 524.

[11] Metronome indication used by Stoll, who performed for Penderecki; Stoll, "Penderecki … by Penderecki!" 58.

Section:	A	B
Starts at m.	1 Allegro	14–30
No. of mm.	13	17
Themes	A	A¹, A²

CHART 22.1 Penderecki, *Three Miniatures for Clarinet and Piano*:
Structural analysis, first movement, Allegro.

7/8, using an eighth-note pulse, and 4/4 to 2/4 to 3/4 using a quarter note pulse. The clarinet's entrance (m. 3), is marked scherzando. Penderecki relies on a Baroque-era technique of continuous writing. For example, at measure 5, the clarinet theme is four measures followed by canonic imitation between piano and clarinet (mm. 7, 11). The last three piano staccato eighth notes in measure 14 energetically begin the A¹ theme. The A² theme appears in measure 22 and, after much imitation between piano and clarinet, comes to an abrupt end.[12]

The second movement, Andante cantabile, eighth note = 72,[13] is in ternary form. (See Chart 22.2.) It is a contrast to the outer active movements, with sustained piano chords against a smoothly slurred and expressive *pp* clarinet solo line. There are several meter changes from 5/8 to 6/8 to 9/8, using an eighth note pulse. The nine measure A theme consists of a piano accompaniment of a repeated ostinato of two fifths in the low register, accompanying a clarinet *pp* introspective theme (m. 2). A new piano ostinato group in the high register begins *p* in measure 7 and with two clarinet eighth note pickups in measure 9, the four measure B theme (mm. 10–13) is played *p* with a decrescendo at the end. This leads to the A¹ theme an octave lower at the a tempo (mm. 14–18), played against an ostinato consisting of triads and sevenths which gradually slows and fades. Penderecki asks for a quasi attaca so the performers immediately start the third movement.[14]

Section:	A	B	A¹
Starts at m.	1 Andante cantabile	10	14 a tempo–18
No. of mm.	9	4	5
Themes	A	B	A¹

CHART 22.2 Penderecki, *Three Miniatures for Clarinet and Piano*:
Structural analysis, second movement, Andante cantabile.

[12] Gerhard Nestler, "Dreimal Penderecki," *Melos* 35, no. 12 (December 1968): 469.
[13] Metronome indication used by Stoll in "Penderecki…by Penderecki!" 58.
[14] Stoll, ibid., 58.

Section:	A	B	A¹
Starts at m.	1 Allegro ma non troppo	20	42–46
No. of mm.	19	22	5
Themes	A	B	A¹

CHART 22.3 Penderecki, *Three Miniatures for Clarinet and Piano*: Structural analysis, third movement, Allegro ma non troppo.

The third movement, Allegro ma non troppo, quarter note = 144,[15] is in ternary form, beginning with a *f* piano ostinato of chords in both hands, consisting of fourths, fifths, and seconds. (See Chart 22.3.) There are several meter changes from 5/8 to 2/4 to 3/8, using an eighth-note pulse. The clarinet enters con vigore *mf* in measure 3, with the A theme featuring a dotted-sixteenth and thirty-second-note rhythm, to a trill (mm. 3–9). A con passione staccato *f* run of sixteenth notes leads to a repetitive *mp* series of notes in the chalumeau register and trills, accompanied by piano triplet sixteenth and eighth notes (mm. 11–17). This is followed by a clarinet trill and piano chords consisting of fourths and thirty-second note runs (mm. 18–19) ending the A section. Section B begins with a subito *p* and constant clarinet sixteenth notes accompanied by piano staccato sixteenth notes, accents, and trills. The tempo moves faster, with a stringendo to a four measure Più vivo section (mm. 38–41) in the clarion register. A brief A¹ theme is played (mm. 42–46), then a crescendo, double tonguing on sixteenth notes to a half-note trill on high F♯₆, and a triple grace note to a *sf* accent on G♯3 for an exciting conclusion.[16]

In preparation for a performance in 2010, Peter Stoll asked Penderecki about questionable notes and rhythms in the *Three Miniatures*. The following are corrections: second movement, measure 10, the D5 with a line over it should be re-articulated. Third movement, measure 10, a very slight rallentando is permissible. In measure 14, second beat, four measures after the con passione, the clarinet's rhythm is two sixteenths followed by an eighth note and should be corrected in the piano part. In measure 35, three measures before Più vivo, the third note should read C♯5.[17]

Penderecki's *Three Miniatures* is a challenging and effective recital work with rhythmic and musical difficulties to master. The first and third movements include parts with much repeated staccato, while the second movement has more introspection and expression. It provides an excellent contrast for earlier and more conservative works, and is short enough that it may be used as an encore. It is enjoyable to hear and perform.

---

15 Metronome indication used by Stoll, ibid., 58.

16 Nestler, ibid., 469–70.

17 Stoll, ibid., 58–59.

23 Francis Poulenc, *Sonata for Clarinet and Piano*

Date of composition: Summer 1962

First edition/revised edition: Francis Poulenc, *Sonata for Clarinet in B-flat and Piano*, London: Chester Music, 1963; Francis Poulenc, *Sonata for Clarinet and Piano*, rev. ed., ed. Millan Sachania, London: Chester Music, 2006.

Dedicatee/first performers: To the memory of Arthur Honegger; Benny Goodman, clarinet, Leonard Bernstein, piano

Date/place of first performance: April 10, 1963; New York, Carnegie Hall[1]

FRANCIS POULENC (1899–1963) was a French composer, pianist, and an outstanding melodist in his vocal and instrumental works. He was a piano student of Ricardo Viñes in Paris, 1914–1917, who became his spiritual mentor after the death of Poulenc's parents. Poulenc stated that it was Viñes' influence that directed his career as a pianist and composer. Through Viñes, Poulenc met other musicians, such as Georges Auric, Erik Satie, and Manuel de Falla, and through his childhood friend, Raymonde Linossier, he became familiar with a number of poets and writers and their work.

Poulenc's 1917 debut as a composer was with *Rapsodie nègre*, dedicated to Satie, and performed at a concert of avant-garde music. Igor Stravinsky took notice and got Poulenc's first works published by Chester in London. Poulenc continued to compose in the army (January 1918–January 1921). His works were performed at the studio of the painter, Emile Lejeune, along with music by Darius Milhaud, Georges

---

[1] Performed at the "Composer's Showcase Francis Poulenc Memorial Concert," Carl B. Schmidt, *The Music of Francis Poulenc (1899–1963): A Catalogue* (Oxford: Clarendon Press, 1995), 508.

Auric, Arthur Honegger, Germaine Tailleferre, and Louis Durey. This led to "Les Six" in 1920. These six composers did not share the same approach to music but enjoyed a firm friendship.

In 1921 Poulenc studied piano, counterpoint, and choral writing with Charles Koechlin. He received a commission from Sergei Diaghilev for the ballet *Les Biches (The Does)*, first performed in 1924. During the 1930s, Poulenc formed a duo with the baritone, Pierre Bernac, and composed his first religious work. Poulenc concertized with Bernac, 1934–1959, for whom he wrote about ninety songs for their recitals. His life had two foci: concertizing and composing. During World War II, Poulenc lived in German-occupied Noizay. He composed and wrote his first opera, *Les mamelles de Tirésias* (*The Breasts of Tirésias*), premiered at the Opéra-Comique in 1947. The next year he had his first concert tour in the United States, returning regularly until 1960.[2] Poulenc wrote about 200 works in almost all genres: operas, ballets, incidental music, film scores, orchestral, choral, solo voice with ensemble or orchestra, voice with piano, two voices with piano, a melodrama, chamber and solo instrumental works, and piano solos.[3]

On August 23, 1957, Poulenc wrote his London publisher, R. Douglas Gibson of J. & W. Chester, "I have started working on a sonata for bassoon and piano and envision two others for oboe and piano, and clarinet and piano. Eventually I would like to group together these sonatas with my trio and sextet."[4] This is the first mention of Poulenc's intention to write a *clarinet sonata*,[5] likely prompted by a commission from Chester for these three works.[6] Poulenc wrote to Gibson on August 10, 1959, "I composed the Andante [later called Romanza] for the Sonata and was trying to complete the work but for the moment I am involved in my Gloria for the Boston

[2] Myriam Chimènes, "Poulenc, Francis," *Grove Music Online*.

[3] Chimènes, ibid.

[4] "J'ai commence une Sonate pour bassoon et piano et j'en envisage deux autres pour hautbois et piano, clarinette et piano. Bien entendu je desire grouper le tout à l'ombre de vos Sonates et au Trio et Sextuor." Carl B. Schmidt, *The Music of Francis Poulenc (1899–1963)*, 508–509.

[5] Carl B. Schmidt, *Entrancing Muse: A Documented Biography of Francis Poulenc* (Hillsdale, NY: Pendragon Press, 2001), 433.

[6] It was not commissioned by Benny Goodman as is sometimes suggested. John Albert Snavely, "Benny Goodman's Commission of New Works and their Significance for Twentieth-Century Clarinetists" (D.M.A. diss., University of Arizona, 1991), 28. There is no association of Poulenc's *sonata* with Goodman in Leonard Bernstein's letters, or mention of it in two thorough biographies of Goodman. But it does seem likely that Poulenc wrote the *sonata* with Goodman in mind. Nigel Simeone, ed., *The Leonard Bernstein Letters* (New Haven, CT: Yale University Press, 2013); James Lincoln Collier, *Benny Goodman and the Swing Era* (New York: Oxford University Press, 1989); Ross Firestone, *Swing, Swing, Swing: The Life & Times of Benny Goodman* (New York: Norton, 1993); Henri Hell, *Francis Poulenc: Musicien Français* (Paris: Fayard, 1978), 303; Francis Poulenc, *Selected Correspondence, 1915–1963: Echo and Source*, trans. and ed. Sidney Buckland, research consultant Patrick Saul (London: Victor Gollancz Ltd., 1991), 417, letter 349; Doda Conrad, *Dodascalies: Ma Chronique du XXᵉ siècle* (Arles: Actes Sud, 1997), 411.

Symphony."[7] Other works delayed the *Sonata for Clarinet*, but he continued to work on it during May 1962.[8] The *sonata* was completed, edited, and recopied by November 8, 1962.[9] On November 17, Poulenc wrote to the bass singer and concert organizer, Doda Conrad (1905–1998), to say that both the clarinet and oboe sonatas were to be performed on April 10, 1963, in New York, and on April 27 in Chicago.[10] On December 9, Poulenc wrote from Venice to the soprano, Rose Dercourt-Plaut, in New York, "I think the program for 10 April is well conceived.... The other day I played my sonata for clarinet. It sounds good. So does the one for oboe."[11] On January 18, 1963, Poulenc sent the *Sonata for Oboe* to Gibson in London announcing that the *clarinet sonata* would follow in eight days.[12]

On January 30, 1963, Poulenc died suddenly of a heart attack in Paris. The composer, Virgil Thomson, knew of Poulenc's upcoming American tour and wrote on February 11 to Yvonne Giraud, the Marquise de Casa Fuerte:

> We are all very much shaken by Poulenc's death. A grand memorial is being prepared for April at the time when [Thomas] Schippers will conduct his [Poulenc's *Sept Répons des*] *tenebraes* service in four concerts with the Philharmonic. There will also be a concert in Philharmonic Hall where Benny Goodman and Leonard Bernstein will play the new Clarinet and Piano Sonata.[13]

The concert was the first of three organized by Conrad and there were several tributes to Poulenc in publications worldwide.[14] A review of the concert briefly mentioned the sonata in a very positive light, "This uncomplicated piece is filled with charming ideas, typical of Poulenc's boulevardier side at its most delightful."[15]

The *Sonata for Clarinet* is a neoclassical work in three movements. Its first movement, Allegro tristamente (sadly), was originally a tempo marking used for the second movement. It is also marked Allegretto, quarter note = 136, written in ternary

---

[7] "J'ai fait l'andante d'une Sonate pour clarinette. Je vais tâcher de mener à bien le reste mais pour l'instant je suis plongé dans mon *Gloria* pour le Boston Symphony." Schmidt, *The Music of Francis Poulenc*, 509; Schmidt, *Entrancing Muse*, 433.

[8] Schmidt, *Entrancing Muse*, 457.

[9] Schmidt, *The Music of Francis Poulenc*, 509.

[10] Schmidt, ibid., 509; Schmidt, *Entrancing Muse*, 460, 502.

[11] Poulenc, *Selected Correspondence*, 297; Schmidt, *Entrancing Muse*, 476.

[12] "Vous allez recevoir, par le même courier, le Sonate pour hautbois. Celle pour clarinette suivra dans 8 jours." Schmidt, *The Music of Francis Poulenc*, 512; Schmidt, *Entrancing Muse*, 462.

[13] Tim Page and Vanessa Weeks Page, eds., *Selected Letters of Virgil Thomson* (New York: Summit Books, 1988), 314.

[14] Schmidt, *Entrancing Muse*, 463–64.

[15] Robert Jacobson, "Recitals," *Musical America* 83 (June 19, 1963): 28–29, quoted by George R. Keck, *Francis Poulenc: A Bio-Bibliography* (New York: Greenwood Press, 1990), 196.

form with an introduction and codetta. (See Chart 23.1.)[16] It begins with eight measures of *ff* clarinet accented sixteenth note groups answered by quick eighth note
piano chords, staccato clarinet sixteenth notes, and a minor third tremolo; no clear
tonal center is established.[17] It is a flippant prologue to one of the most imaginative
sonatas in the repertoire.

Alternating eighth note Cs in the piano[18] accompany a ten measure A theme of
upward slurred clarinet quarter notes from F3 (fourth beat of m. 9) to F5, followed
by three sixteenth notes to a half note G4. Clarinet thirty-second notes (m. 22) gal-
vanize a buoyant, flute like theme. At one beat before no. 2 (m. 18), the theme is restated in a more angular fashion with a dotted eighth and sixteenth note pickup
used throughout as a motive. Poulenc uses symmetrical and asymmetrical phrases in
this work.[19] Theme B[1] begins with a dotted eighth and sixteenth note pickup (fourth
beat of m. 26, one measure before no. 3), but is subtly changed (mm. 27–32); including theme B[2], a fourth higher (mm. 31–39), beginning on the fourth beat before
no. 4. Breath marks often separate new phrases. For example, a breath mark precedes
no. 5 (mm. 40–44), a short, five measure connecting phrase, with one measure

Section:	Introduction	A	B	A[1]	Codetta
Starts at m.	1 Allegro tristamente, Allegretto	10 (no. 1)	67 Très calme (no. 8)	106 Tempo Allegretto (no. 11)	123–133
No. of mm.	9	57	39	17	11
Tonal Centers	none	C, g, e, c, b, e	a♭, a, E, a	C, b, d	B
Themes	intro.	A, B, B[1], B[2], B[3], (intro.)	trans., C, C[1], C[2], C[3], D	A[2], B[4]	intro., codetta

CHART 23.1 Poulenc, *Sonata for Clarinet and Piano*: Structural analysis, first movement,
Allegro tristamente, Allegretto.

---

[16] Thomas Stirzaker, "A Comparative Study of Selected Clarinet Works by Arthur Honegger, Darius Milhaud,
and Francis Poulenc" (Ph.D. diss., Texas Tech University, 1988), 18–25, 41–52, 60–67; Janice L. Minor, "'Were
They Truly Neoclassic?' A Study of French Neoclassicism through Selected Clarinet Sonatas by 'Les Six'
Composers: Arthur Honegger, Germaine Tailleferre, Darius Milhaud, and Francis Poulenc" (D.M.A. diss.,
University of Cincinnati, 2004), 80–98.

[17] Stirzaker, ibid., 18, 42.

[18] Alternating octaves were used in the song *Tel jour, tel nuits* (1937) and in *Dialogues des Carmélites* (1957);
Wilfred Mellers, *Francis Poulenc* (Oxford: Oxford University Press, 1993), 165.

[19] Minor, ibid., 82.

played very lightly (très leger), over an eighth note piano accompaniment. A dotted eighth to sixteenth note pickup to the B^3 theme is played a minor second lower (fourth beat of m. 44, one measure before no. 6), followed by dramatic thirty-second note runs and an accented quarter note piano accompaniment. The A section closes with music from the introduction, including thirty-second note runs in the clarino register (mm. 59–66),[20] and ends abruptly (m. 66).

The B section at no. 8, Très calme, quarter note = 54, begins with sedate piano quarter notes, très doux, with an A♭ minor tonal center. The clarinet joins the piano with a quarter note pickup for four measures (mm. 72–75), and six *pp* piano chords modulate to an A minor section at no. 9. The clarinet part is marked, "always without pushing" ("surtout sans presser"), and the eighth note piano accompaniment is, "sweetly monotone" ("doucement monotone"). The clarinet C theme (mm. 78–85) uses a *p* double dotted eighth note followed by two upward sixty-fourth note arpeggios to high notes, $F\sharp_6$ and E_6, sixty-fourth note downward runs to eighth notes,[21] and a cadence on E major in the chalumeau register. The clarinet theme C^1 (no. 10, m. 86) consists of a *pp* arpeggio, B5, D_6, $F\sharp_6$, B_6, as a double dotted eighth note, followed by three sixty-fourth notes, the last held as a quarter note tied to a double dotted eighth note. The entire eight measure phrase (mm. 86–93) is played in an accompanying manner, moodily repetitive, and answered by a contrasting piano two measure phrase. Theme C^2 is a delicately repeated *pp* (mm. 94–101). A short D theme (mm. 102–105) ends section B. The A^1 section in C major immediately begins with piano octaves on *pp* C with the A^2 theme at no. 11 (mm. 106–112), followed by the B^4 theme (fourth beat of m. 116, one measure before no. 12). A codetta begins with the clarinet four sixteenth pickup notes on the fourth beat (m. 122), repeating the sixteenth note motive from the introduction. The piano answers with *f* intervals (mm. 127–130), while the clarinet timidly replies with *pp* sixteenth notes, ending the movement with a clarinet tremolo from C♯4 to E4.[22]

The second movement, Romanza, Très calme, quarter note = 54, is in ternary form with an introduction and codetta. (See Chart 23.2.) It begins unusually with a two measure *pp* clarinet solo answered by a *f* quasi-cadenza with one short and one long fermata, supported by a *mf* G minor piano chord. A *pp* four measure introductory

---

[20] Stirzaker, ibid., 43.

[21] Poulenc wrote the same double-dotted arpeggiated theme an octave higher as an opening clarinet motive in his *Gloria for Soprano Solo, Chorus, and Orchestra* (1959–1960), Keith W. Daniel, "Poulenc's Choral Works with Orchestra," in *Francis Poulenc: Music, Art, and Literature*, eds. Sidney Buckland and Myriam Chimènes (Aldershot: Ashgate, 1999), 69–70. This motive and others are used in the flute and oboe sonatas; Keith W. Daniel, *Francis Poulenc: His Artistic Development and Musical Style* (Ann Arbor, MI: UMI Research Press 1982), 128–30.

[22] Stirzaker, ibid., 44–45.

Section:	Introduction	A	B	A¹	Codetta
Starts at m.	1 Romanza, Très calme	11	25	63	71–76
No. of mm.	10		14	38	8	6
Tonal Centers	g	g	b, a, g, b, b♭, b, b♭, g	g	g
Themes	intro.	A	B, B¹, B², A¹, B³, A², bridge	A³	codetta

CHART 23.2 Poulenc, *Sonata for Clarinet and Piano*: Structural analysis, second movement, Romanza, Très calme.

phrase of quarter notes (mm. 5–8) introduces dotted eighth notes followed by sixty-fourth notes, ornamenting the melody. A delicate and expressive clarinet A theme (mm. 11–18) consists of an upward moving quarter note with double dotted eighth notes followed by two sixty-fourth notes. Stated *pp*, very sweetly with melancholy *(très doux et mélancolique)*, it builds to a *mf* crescendo. On the first beat of no. 2, a dramatic *f* sixty-fourth note scale races to the second beat; highly effective (m. 19); and repeated at measure 21. The piano B theme (mm. 25–28) joined by the clarinet (mm. 29–30), is similar to the A theme but with quarter notes descending and a double dotted motive. The B² theme modulates to B♭ minor (mm. 41–46). A *pp* clarinet A² theme plays a sixth higher in the clarion register (mm. 47–54). In section A¹, the opening six measure A³ theme plays *pp* (mm. 63–68), followed by a *ppp* echo of the first two measures. At no. 7 (m. 71), the codetta starts with an immediate *mf* half step thirty-second note figure, $D\sharp_6$ to E_6, similar to the quasi-cadenza at the beginning (m. 3). The movement ends quietly, with an emphatic closure using *mf* thirty-second chalumeau notes to a low sustained E3 (mm. 74–76).

The third movement, Allegro con fuoco, is in ternary form with a codetta, Très animé, quarter note = 144. (See Chart 23.3.) There are three distinct themes. The A theme (mm. 1–7) begins with accented eighth notes in a rapid, "hammer" rhythm[23] common to music heard at the "circus" or "music hall."[24] The clarinet dominates with an accented second beat, a whirlwind of notes, and three thirty-second notes to a high accented $F\sharp_6$. After the partial A¹ theme, a breath mark separates the next five measure *f* B theme at no. 2 (mm. 13–17). Another breath mark separates the *f* phrase of the C theme at no. 3 (mm. 18–25), with short staccato eighth and sixteenth notes similar to a teasing can-can melody. The C¹ theme plays a fourth higher at no. 4 (mm. 26–34). A high point is reached with dissonant piano chords and *f* clarinet sixteenth note arpeggios from measures 34–41. After a two measure cédez and a

Section:	A	B	A^1	Codetta
Starts at m.	1 Allegro con fuoco, Très animé	44 a tempo subito (no. 6)	80 (no. 10)	116 (no. 13)–128
No. of mm.	43	36	36	13
Tonal Centers	C, E♭, e♭, a♭	b, G	C, b♭, C	c, C
Themes	A, (A^1), B, C, C^1	D, D^1	A^2, C^2, D^2, A^3, trans.	codetta

CHART 23.3 Poulenc, *Sonata for Clarinet and Piano*: Structural analysis, third movement, Allegro con fuoco, Très animé.

breath mark, the B section, a tempo subito, reveals a contrasting clarinet D theme at no. 6 (mm. 44–58), of long held notes with an impressive cascade of piano arpeggios beginning at no. 7 (m. 52). At no. 9 (m. 69), the piano enjoys a syncopated accompaniment while the clarinet plays eighth and sixteenth notes, leading into Section A^1 at no. 10. The clarinet jumps right into the A^2 theme with excitement (mm. 80–83), then turns to the C^2 theme (mm. 83–92). After a breath mark before no. 11 (m. 90) and a three measure interlude, the sweeping and expressive D^2 theme emerges along with a clarinet trill on low G3. At no. 12 (m. 106), the clarinet states the A^3 theme with transitional phrases (mm. 112–115), from the exposition of the first movement (mm. 13–17). The codetta, no. 13 (mm. 116–124) presents some new cleverly placed clarinet arpeggios and staccato eighth notes, leading to a driving, repeated rhythm using dissonant seconds against the tonic C, and the final exciting sixteenth note run to high G$\sharp_6$, and two eighth notes, F$\sharp_6$ and F$\sharp$3.[25]

In the third movement, after no. 3, the clarinetist must be careful to use proper breath support to play the high E$_6$s, G$_6$s, and F$_6$s accurately and in tune. Depending on the tuning of your clarinet, special fingerings should be employed.

Benjamin Britten and Peter Pears characterize Poulenc's music as, "typical of French composers: witty, daring, sentimental, naughty."[26] These attributes are embodied in the sonata and contribute to this musically clear and attractive work. It is the most popular *clarinet sonata* at present and has been reprinted by Chester Music in sixteen editions. Because of Poulenc's sudden death, there were many notation ambiguities in the first edition (1963).

The French clarinetist, André Boutard (1924–1998), worked with Poulenc for several months on the *sonata* during the latter half of 1962. Since it was published in

---

[25] Minor, ibid., 90, 94, 96.

[26] Philip Reed, "Poulenc, Britten, Aldeburgh: A Chronicle," in *Francis Poulenc: Music, Art, and Literature*, eds. Sidney Buckland and Myriam Chimènes (Aldershot: Ashgate, 1999), 360.

London, Boutard's knowledge of the piece was lost in the first edition, but orally passed on to his colleagues at the Paris Conservatory, and incorporated in the fourth edition (1968). The fifth edition was more extensively revised in 1973 by the English clarinetists, Thea King and Georgina Dobrée, but a number of inaccuracies remained. The fifteenth edition (2000) by Dr. Millan Sachania corrected these errors and used Poulenc's copy of the sonata with further clarification of slurs, ties, and corrections of misprints in Sachania's sixteenth edition (2006).[27]

Poulenc's *Sonata for Clarinet and Piano* remains as fresh and novel today as it was in 1963. It presents a refreshing contrast to many other repertoire works by immediately capturing the attention of the audience with a fascinating panorama of musical ideas. It is a technical and musical challenge demanding a high degree of control of dynamics, articulation, and breath control. For many clarinetists, Poulenc's *sonata* will remain a favorite recital piece.

---

[27] Millan Sachania, "Preface," in Francis Poulenc, *Sonata for Clarinet and Piano*, rev. ed., ed. Millan Sachania (London: Chester Music, 2006); David Kirby, "The Extraordinary Life of the *Sonata for Clarinet and Piano (1962)* by Francis Poulenc," 2011 International Clarinet Association Presentation at California State University, Northridge. Mr. Kirby edited the seventeenth edition for Chester, not yet published.

24 Max Reger, *Sonata for Clarinet and Piano, op. 107*

Date of composition: February 20, 1909

First edition: Max Reger, *Sonata B-dur für Klarinette und Klavier*, Berlin: Bote & Bock, 1909

Dedicatee/first performers: Grand Duke Ernst Ludwig von Hessen; Julius Winkler, clarinet, Max Reger, piano

Date/place of first performance: June 9, 1909; Saalbau, Darmstadt, Second Chamber Music Festival

MAX REGER (1873–1916) was a German composer whose chromatic musical style used Baroque and Classical forms. He was a successor to late-nineteenth-century German Romanticism and a precursor to early-twentieth-century modernism.

Reger took piano lessons in 1884 with Adalbert Lindner, and learned the works of Beethoven and Brahms. When Reger saw Wagner's *Die Meistersinger von Nürnberg* and *Parsifal*, he decided on a musical career. He was not interested in opera, but valued Wagner's polyphonic style and chromaticism, although Wagner's influence on Reger's musical style was minimal. In 1890, Reger studied with Hugo Riemann in Sondershausen and Wiesbaden, and continued to compose chamber works, lieder, and piano pieces. In 1898, Reger became ill and returned to Wieden where he concentrated on the organ, composed many large scale works, and gave private lessons.[1]

In 1904, Reger contracted with the publisher Josef Aibl, and he also married Elsa von Bercken. His compositions were not liked by Liszt and Wagner proponents, and his work was frequently criticized in the press. Reger was a vocal critic of Wagner's

---

[1] John Williamson, "Reger, Max" *Grove Music Online*.

supporters, such as Max von Schillings. The first critical support of Reger's career in reviews came during his four years in Leipzig (1907–1910).[2]

In 1911, Reger became director of the Meiningen Court Orchestra. His health was compromised by his conducting, nonstop composing, and drinking. In 1915, he resigned from Meiningen to retire at Jena with his wife and two adopted daughters; he supported his family by his compositions and concerts. In 1916, Reger suffered a fatal heart attack in Leipzig. He completed more than 150 works including orchestral, choral, chamber, solo vocal, piano, organ, and editions and arrangements of works by others.[3]

Reger wrote four clarinet solo works, *Sonata for Bb Clarinet and Piano, op. 49, no. 1* (1900); *Sonata for A Clarinet, op. 49, no. 2* (1900); *Album Leaf and Tarantella for Clarinet and Piano* (1902); and the *Sonata for Clarinet and Piano, op. 107* (1907, or viola or violin).[4] Kroll wrote about the origins of the clarinet sonatas:

> [T]he director of the municipal orchestra [at Wieden], Johann Kürmeyer, was also a brilliant clarinetist and Reger heard a performance by him and Adalbert Lindner of Brahm's *F minor Sonata*. "Lovely," said Reger. "I also will write two of these things." Within three weeks he had written the two Sonatas. His next clarinet work, the great *Sonata Opus 107 in Bb major*, immediately followed the *Symphonic Prologue* He excitedly told his friend Max [Karl] Straube about finishing the Sonata, op. 107.[5]

Despite being forty minutes long, Reger described it as, "a very light, friendly work, not too long, so that the tonal character of the woodwind does not get tiresome."[6] The sonata was a critical success when performed in German cities. A review by Arthur Somlian of a Leipzig concert on March 13, 1910 with clarinetist, Heinrich Bading, and pianist, Reger, observed:

> The sonata has a sensitive and fairly calm counterpoint and light harmonies. In the first movement, which has a beautiful main theme in artistic and fascinating interpretation, we could gladly overlook the many typically Regerian interjections

[2] Williamson, ibid.

[3] Williamson, ibid.

[4] Fritz Stein, *Thematisches Verzeichnis der im Druck erschienenen Werke von Max Reger einschließlich seiner Bearbeitungen und Ausgaben* (Leipzig: Breitkopf & Härtel, 1953), 69–70, 260–61, 378.

[5] Oskar Kroll, *The Clarinet*, rev. Diethard Riehm, trans. Hilda Morris, trans. and ed. Anthony Baines (New York: Taplinger, 1968), 82; letter to Karl Straube, Max Reger, *Briefe eines deutschen Meisters: ein Lebensbild*, ed. Else von Hase-Koehler (Leipzig: Koehler & Amelang, 1928), 206. Adalbert Lindner, *Max Reger: Ein Bild seines Jugendlebens und künstlerischen Werdens* (Stuttgart: J. Engelhorns Nachf., 1922), 227.

[6] "[W]ird ein gar lichtes, freundliches Werk, gar nicht lang, damit der Klangcharakter des Blasinstruments nicht ermüdet!" Letter to Henri Hinrichsen, December 28, 1908, in Reger, *Briefe eines deutschen Meisters*, 200. This letter is translated by Dan Sparks, "Max Reger: A Brief Look at his Life and Clarinet Works," *The Clarinet* 10, no. 2 (Winter 1983): 33.

and sporadic exaltations because of the good-sounding and expressive main sections. In the Adagio songs interspersed in the clown-like Vivace [second movement] we saw again the composer's talent for grotesque humor. The relatively simple, not too profound Adagio [third movement] was pleasant and the Finale, which had reminders of the first movement, delighted with an amusing interpretation of a Negro-dance-type Rondo theme and warm song-like theme.[7]

In the *Sonata for Clarinet and Piano, op. 107*, Reger uses, "motivic variation for development, free tonality, and effectively repeated altered motives throughout."[8] Harmonically, the exposition has the standard progression of tonic B♭ major to dominant F major, but between the opening and closing chords, "the cadences are unconventional."[9] The seven motives of the first movement are presented in four examples by Scott (Ex. 24.1), motives used recurrently and varied throughout the movement. Motives 1a–c are the beginning of the clarinet part (first occurrence, mm. 1–2), with descending minor third and minor second intervals, ascending perfect fifths, rhythmic changes, and dotted quarter, eighth, and quarter notes. Motive 2a (first occurrence, mm. 4–5), begins with a piano quarter note, proceeds to downward

EXAMPLE 24.1. Reger, *Sonata for Clarinet and Piano, op. 107*, first movement, seven motives.

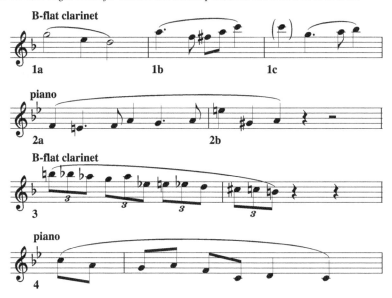

[7] *Leipziger Zeitung* 59, no. 1 (March 14, 1910), quoted in Ottmar Schreiber, *Max Reger in seinem Konzerten. Teil 3. Reger konzertiert* (Bonn: Dümmler, 1981), 245; trans. in Shannon M. Scott, "Two Late Clarinet Works by Max Reger: Historical Perspective, Analysis and Performance Considerations" (D.M. diss., Northwestern University, 1994), 86.

[8] Christopher Robert Nichols, "138 years of the Clarinet: Program Notes for a Master's Clarinet Recital of Works by Reger, Smith, Donizetti, Muczynski, and Schumann" (M.M. thesis, Kansas State University, 2007), 3; Scott, ibid., 160.

[9] Scott, ibid., 166.

minor seconds and an upward minor sixth, and is resolved by a minor second. Motive 2b (first occurrence, clarinet part, m. 6), has a downward major sixth and is a bridge passage. Motive 3 (first occurrence, m. 13, beats 4–6; m.14, beat 1) consists of clarinet chromatic triplets within one octave. Motive 4 (first occurrence, m. 22, beat 6; m. 23, beats 1–4), played by the piano and elaborated by the clarinet, ends the first movement, and is a link to the third and fourth movements.[10]

The first movement, Moderato, quarter note = 72–76, is in sonata-allegro form with a coda (See Chart 24.1.)[11] It begins *pp*, the first phrase played, sempre dolcissimo. Both the piano and clarinet have expressive parts, with continuous dynamic swells from *pp* to *mf*, immediate changes of dynamics up to *ff*, many ritardandos, and three Molto tranquillo sections, each leading to ritardandos and diminuendos of *ppp* and *pppp*. Between these *p* sections, a powerful outburst occurs of full piano *f* chords in measures 12–16.

The end of the exposition section is marked with a double bar; the development begins with a thoughtful piano phrase of half and quarter notes (m. 45), expressively answered by the clarinet with a variant of motive 4. Between *p* and calm lyrical measures are powerful *f* outbursts in full piano chords (mm. 65–72), answered by an agitated *f* clarinet. The movement's high point is the clarinet's high F_6 and $E\flat_6$ (m. 64) in the *ff* animato section while the piano accompanies with accents and marcato notes. At the end of the development section the piano plays a *pppp* motive 4 in octaves ending with a fermata on a chord (m. 78). The recapitulation repeats the first eleven measures of the exposition (mm. 79–89) before altering the notes and harmony. A gorgeous Molto tranquillo section (m. 112) precedes the coda (m. 116) which starts *pp* and is particularly quiet and delicate for both clarinet and piano. From measure 119, the clarinet is *ppp*, sempre dolcissimo. The movement ends with the clarinet's motive 4 played *ppp*, swelling and fading to *pppp*, almost nothing.

The second movement, Vivace, quarter note = 126–132, is in ternary form with a coda. (See Chart 24.2.) Each section has a different tempo. Six motives, different

Section:	Exposition	Development	Recapitulation	Coda
Starts at m.	1 Moderato	45	79	116–128
No. of mm.	44	34	37	13
Tonal Centers	B♭, C, F	C, F	B♭	B♭
Themes	A	B	A¹	coda

CHART 24.1 Reger, *Sonata for Clarinet and Piano, op. 107*: Structural analysis, first movement, Moderato.

---

[10] Scott, ibid., 162–64.
[11] Nichols, ibid., 3, 10, 17, 21.

from those in the first movement, appear throughout the second movement. 1a is a clarinet phrase of quarter, eighth, and two sixteenth notes (first occurrence, mm. 1–2); 1b is the piano right hand accompaniment of eighth and sixteenth notes (first occurrence, mm. 1–2); 2a is the clarinet phrase of quarter and sixteenth notes (first occurrence, mm. 3–4); and 2b is the piano's four eighth notes (first occurrence, mm. 3–4). Motive 3 is triplets corresponding to the clarinet part (first occurrence, mm. 3–4). Motive 4 is eighth notes corresponding to the piano's right hand (first occurrence, mm. 3–4).[12]

In mood, section A is like a scherzo. The clarinet begins with a slightly ponderous and unusual tune that mixes duple and triple sixteenths in the piano against duple clarinet writing. At measure 64, a two measure ritardando arrives at an Andante (m. 66), and a six measure ritardando and diminuendo feature staccato eighth note piano chords supporting a clarinet opening phrase, one octave lower, of quarter and half notes to a low E3 *ppp* fermata.

Section B, Adagio, eighth note = 56–60, begins after an eighth note rest with an expressive, chorale-like piano A theme (mm. 72–79) joined by an equally expressive clarinet melody with a notable leap to C$_6$ at the high point of the phrase.[13] The B theme begins on the second beat of measure 79 with *pp* piano chords answered by an expressive clarinet response. The section ends with more *pp* piano chords, answered by the clarinet ending with a crescendo (m. 91), ritardando, and *ppp* fermata on B3. The A^1 Vivace opening phrase and seven episodes (mm. 93–155) closely resemble the Vivace A section but with ingenious changes and elaboration. After a fermata, the Quasi adagio coda, eighth note = 56–60, begins with the slow and brooding A^2 piano theme including three measures of the B section, Adagio (mm. 2–4). A partially chromatically descending *pp* clarinet solo from E5 (mm. 161–167) has a diminuendo

Section:	A	B	A^1	Coda
Starts at m.	1 Vivace, Andante	72 Adagio	93 Vivace	156 Quasi adagio–167
No. of mm.	71	21	63	12
Tonal Centers	D	G♭	D	d
Themes	opening phrase, 7 episodes, opening phrase^1	A, B, A^1	opening phrase^2, 7 episodes	A^2, closing

CHART 24.2 Reger, *Sonata for Clarinet and Piano, op. 107*: Structural analysis, second movement, Vivace.

12 Scott, ibid., 172–73; Nichols, ibid., 11.
13 Nichols, ibid., 16.

Section:	A	B	A¹	Coda
Starts at m.	1 Adagio	14	28	40–48
No. of mm.	13	14	12	9
Tonal Centers	E♭	B♭	E♭	E♭
Themes	A	B	A¹	coda

CHART 24.3 Reger, *Sonata for Clarinet and Piano, op. 107*: Structural analysis, third movement, Adagio.

and ritardandos, ending on an E4 *ppp* fermata, similar to the closing passage an octave higher than the Andante closing of section A (mm. 66–71).[14]

The third movement, Adagio, eighth note = 58–60, is written in ternary form with a coda. (See Chart 24.3.) Three motives, different from the motives in the first and second movements, appear throughout the third movement: the clarinet's ascending fourths (first occurrence, mm. 1–2); a three-note scale pattern, the upper notes of the piano's right hand chords (first occurrence, mm. 6–7); answered by the clarinet beginning on the second beat of measure 7 and first beat of measure 8.[15] Each section presents several poignant clarinet melodies of great depth, interspersed with ritardandos. Section A makes skilled use of the clarinet's adroit dynamic control from *pp* to *f*, and back to *p* within five measures. Theme A presents many nuances of sound and meaning. In the B section, tonal artistry is demonstrated with a dramatic leap of a fifth from F5 to C$_6$ (m. 16), and characterizes one of the high points in the movement, ending with a decrescendo, ritardando, and diminuendo to a *pp* F3 fermata. At section A¹ (m. 28), the clarinet plays the A¹ theme (based on this movement's A theme, but with changes) always very expressively. The coda ends with the clarinet's last two measure phrase (mm. 47–48), including an ascending fourth, played an octave lower than the opening to a C4 *ppp* fermata.

There are six motives in the fourth movement, used throughout: 1) a lightly played clarinet solo (first occurrence, mm. 1–2); 2) clarinet quarter, eighth, and quarter notes (first occurrence, mm. 6–7); 3) ascending and descending clarinet quarter notes (first occurrence, mm. 18–19); 4) clarinet solo (first occurrence, mm. 28–30); 5) piano quarter and half notes (first occurrence, mm. 56–59); and 6) clarinet half, quarter, and dotted half notes (first occurrence, mm. 82–84).[16] Motive 6 has a melody similar to the first movement's motive 4, but written in quarter and half notes.

The fourth movement is in sonata-allegro form with a coda, Allegretto con grazia, dotted half note = 60–69. (See Chart 24.4.) It is the lightest movement in mood,

---

14 Nichols, ibid., 16.
15 Scott, ibid., 179–80; Nichols, ibid., 17–18.
16 Scott, ibid., 187–88; Nichols, ibid., 22–24.

Section:	Exposition	Development	Recapitulation	Coda
Starts at m.	1 Allegretto con grazia	63	107	163 (fourth beat) Adagio–175
No. of mm.	62	44	56	13
Tonal Centers	Bb, F, a, Gb, Bb	Bb, g	Bb, g, d, Cb, Eb	Eb, B
Themes	A, B, A¹, B¹, C	A², D	A³, B², A⁴, B³, C¹	3rd movement theme A, motive 4 from 1st movement, m. 43

CHART 24.4 Reger, *Sonata for Clarinet and Piano, op. 107*: Structural analysis, fourth movement, Allegretto con grazia.

marked *pp*. Most of the clarinet solo is slurred, with some amusing passages of staccato quarter and eighth notes, and staccato piano passages. The exposition begins with a light clarinet *pp* two measure A theme answered by a two measure piano *f* repetition of these two measures. After accented *f* runs in the clarinet and piano parts and staccato clarinet quarter notes, there is a scherzo mood (mm. 1–24). This mood continues until after a ritardando (mm. 25–27) followed by an eight measure, more serious B theme (mm. 28–35) of a slurred dotted whole note, to quarter and half notes. At measure 37, the staccato and slurred *pp* A¹ theme (mm. 37–45) is presented, then a ritardando, followed by the B¹ theme a half step higher (mm. 46–56). A C theme proceeds with piano quarter and half notes, briefly answered by the clarinet (mm. 55–62).[17]

The development section (m. 63), starts in Bb major, launches with eighteen measures of the exposition modified by several changes and, by measure 82, is in G minor. Reger writes a rhythm (mm. 82–94) similar to this movement's motive 5. At the end of the development section, motive 5 is altered by using piano quarter notes in octaves and a ritardando (mm. 105–106).

The recapitulation (mm. 107–162) is musically similar to the exposition but includes a number of different tonalities and rhythmic changes. At measure 125, the clarinet plays two measures of this movement's motive 3 to avoid tonal repetitions with the exposition. Reger places the motives in different measure locations, creating variety. For example, in the recapitulation, the clarinet plays motive 4 (mm. 134–137) and the piano plays motive 5 (mm. 157–159). The coda (fourth beat of m. 163), quarter note = 48–52, uses the A theme from the beginning of the third

17 Scott, ibid., 185–96; Nichols, ibid., 21–27.

movement. The last three measures (mm. 173–175) use motive 4 from the first movement, ending on a C4 *ppp* fermata.[18] The cyclic nature of the ending is memorable.

Clarinetists' receptions of all three Reger sonatas were positive. For example, Eric Simon wrote in 1955:

> Measured by the standards of an accomplished clarinetist, the technical difficulties are modest. The musical requirements, however, are exacting. As it is often the case, the lack of popularity of the sonatas can be traced to performances that did not exhaust the musical depth of these beautiful pieces, and therefore which left audiences cold, or at best lukewarm. The tempo relationships and the correct amount of the very frequent ritenutos and accelerandos can only be discovered through a great deal of thought and time.[19]

The clarinetist Burnet Tuthill writes highly of Reger's sonatas:

> The three by Reger, though they presented a challenge when they appeared in the first decade of this century, have been shown with the passage of time and with much playing to be late romantic music of extraordinary beauty and musical interest, although still they do not always appeal on the first reading. They require a fine pianist. The clarinet parts offer no technical problems, but call for a high degree of tone control and musicianship.[20]

Reger's Sonata op. 107 is among the great clarinet sonatas and an excellent choice to end a recital. The greatest problems are endurance and many musical challenges that must be carefully worked out between clarinetist and pianist. The constant shifts of tempo, dynamic gradations between *mp* and *p*, and the slow endings of movements at a dynamic of *ppp* and *pppp* are difficult but playable. There is great satisfaction in learning and performing this work.

---

[18] Scott, ibid., 185–96; Nichols, ibid., 21–27.

[19] Eric Simon, "The Clarinet Works of Max Reger," *The Clarinet*, no. 20 (Fall 1955): 13.

[20] Burnet C. Tuthill, "Sonatas for Clarinet and Piano: Annotated Listings," *Journal of Research in Music Education* 20, no. 3 (Fall 1972): 309–310.

25 Gioachino Rossini, *Introduction, Theme, and Variations for Clarinet and Orchestra*

Date of composition: ca. 1819

First edition/early editions: Giovacchino Rossini, *Varazioni per Clarinetto Composte e Dedicate al Sig. Allesandro Abate dal Sig. Giaocchino Rossini*, Firenze: G. Cipiriani, ca. 1822;[1] Gioacchino Rossini, *Variations pour la Clarinette: avec accompagne de l'Orchestre ou de Pianoforte*, Leipsig: Breitkopf & Härtel, ca. 1824;[2] Gioachino Rossini, *Variations: pour la Clarinette: avec accompagnement d'Orchestre ou de Pianoforte*, Paris: Richault, 1827[3]

Modern editions: Gioacchino Rossini, *Introduction, Theme and Variations for Clarinet and Orchestra*, ed. Jost Michaels, Hamburg: Hans Sikorski, 1960; Gioacchino Rossini, *Introduction, Theme and Variations, for B♭ Clarinet and Piano*, eds. David Glazer and Ralph Hermann, New York: Oxford University Press, 1970; Gioacchino Rossini, *Introduction, Theme, and Variations: for Clarinet and Piano*, eds. David Hite and Jean Knox, San Antonio: Southern Music Co., 1991; Gioacchino Rossini, *Andante and Variations for Clarinet and Orchestra or Piano*, ed. Siegfried Beyer, Winterthur: Amadeus, 1993; Gioacchino Rossini, *Introduction, Theme and Variations: For Clarinet*, ed. Charles Neidich, Maryland Heights, Missouri: Lauren Keiser Music, 2012

---

[1] Rossini's first name was spelled in various ways on published music; his own spelling was Gioachino. Herbert Weinstock, *Rossini: A Biography* (New York: Alfred A Knopf, 1968), xviii. The plate number 274 indicates a date ca. 1822, Bianca Maria Antolini, "Cipriani," in Bianca Maria Antolini, ed., *Dizionario degli Editori Musicali Italiani 1750–1930* (Pisa: Edizioni ETS, 2000), 125.

[2] Dated by plate number 3978; Otto Erich Deutsch, *Musikverlags Nummern: Eine Auswahl von 40 datierten Listen 1710–1900*, 2nd ed. (Berlin: Merseburger, 1961), 9.

[3] Dated by plate number 1653; Anik Devriès and François Lesure, *Dictionnaire des Éditeurs de Musique Français* (Genève: Minkoff, 1988), 2:369.

Dedicatee/early performers: Allesandro Abate; Baroni, clarinet, Abramo Basevi, piano

Date/place of early performance: March 27, 1852; Florence, Italy, home of Ferdinando Giorgetti[4]

Orchestration: First and second violins, violas, cellos, string basses, flute, two oboes, bassoon, and two E♭ horns[5]

GIOACHINO ROSSINI (1792–1868) was the most important and influential composer of the first half of the nineteenth century and a significant opera composer. He was born in Pesaro where his father was a horn player, his mother a singer. Both parents were active performers and when they moved to Bologna, Gioachino's ability as a singer was recognized by admission into the Accademia Filarmonica. He studied privately with Father Angelo Tesei, and in 1806 entered the Liceo Musicale, to study singing, cello, piano, and counterpoint under Father Stainslao Mattei. In Bologna, Rossini worked as a harpsichord player in local theaters, and occasionally wrote a new aria for use as a replacement aria in an opera. His opera career began with a commission from the Teatro S. Moisè in Venice for an opera based on Rossi's *La cambiale di matrimonio*. Up to 1829, Rossini wrote thirty-nine operas. He decided to retire as an opera composer because of poor health, personal financial security, and changes in government support in Paris where Rossini and his wife lived. Rossini lived for another thirty-nine years and composed many more works, but no operas. His works include operas, adaptations of operas, masses, sacred music, cantatas, hymns, choruses, vocal solos with piano or orchestra, orchestral works, chamber music, and works for military band.[6]

Rossini composed three solos for clarinet, *Variazioni a Clarinetto o Oboe e Orchestra* (ca. 1810) written for C clarinet,[7] a popular instrument during Rossini's last year (1810) as a student at the Lyceum in Bologna;[8] *Variazioni per Clarinetto in B♭ and Orchestra* (ca. 1819),[9] written for B♭ clarinet while Rossini was living in

---

[4] Mentioned in a March 29, 1852, letter from Ferdinando Giorgetti to Rossini. Fabbri, "Ignoti momenti Rossiniani: Contributo all'indagine sul 'lungo silenzio' di Rossini e alla conoscenza dell' attività creative minore del Maestro; Le segrete confessioni a Ferdinando Giorgetti e le sconosciute 'Variazioni' per Alessandro Abate (1817)," *Chigiana* 25 (1968)," 266–68.

[5] Fabbri, ibid., 278; Louis Vincent Sacchini, "The Concerted Music for the Clarinet in the Nineteenth Century" (Ph.D. diss., University of Iowa, 1980), 358.

[6] Philip Gossett, "Gioachino Rossini," *Grove Music Online*.

[7] Gioacchino Rossini, Variations for Clarinet and Piano, trans. and arr. John Neufeld, ed. Mitchell Lurie (Los Angeles: Western International Music, 1967).

[8] Weinstock, *Rossini: A Biography*, 20; Elio Peruzzi, "Preface," Gioacchino Rossini, Variazioni per Clarinetto e Pianoforte (Padova: G. Zanibon, 1968), 1.

[9] Date of composition suggested by Adriano Amore, *Il clarinetto in Italia nell'Ottocento* ([Perugia]: Accademia Italiana del Clarinetto, 2009), 167.

Naples[10] (*Variazioni per Clarinetto* is widely known from the Sikorski publication as *Introduction, Theme, and Variations*);[11] and *Fantaisie in Eb for Clarinet in Bb and Piano* (1829).[12]

The *Variazioni per Clarinetto in Bb* was dedicated to Allesandro Abate, a clarinet professor in Naples.[13] Abate was the first clarinetist of the Teatro "La munizione" in Messina 1815–1816 and was active as a clarinetist and conductor in various regimental bands in Naples.[14] The melody of the introduction appeared earlier in 8½ measures of Rossini's clarinet solo in the introduction to the aria, "La pace mia smarrita," in act two of *Mosè in Egitto* (*Moses in Egypt*), premiered in Naples on March 5, 1812.[15] Rossini used it again in a horn solo in the aria, "Vorrei vedere lo sposo," in *Ciro in Babilonia* (*Ciro in Babylon*), first produced in Ferrara on March 12, 1812.[16] The melody of variation 1 is from the aria, "Oh quante lagrime," at the end of the cavatina, "Elena, oh tu che chiamo," in his *La donna del lago* (*The Lady of the Lake*), produced in Naples on September 24, 1819.[17]

The form of the piece is an introduction, theme, and five variations.[18] (See Chart 25.1.) It was written to showcase the clarinet's tonal beauty but primarily for virtuoso display. The 6/8 introduction, Andante, eighth note = 88,[19] has a dominant solo clarinet part heard throughout the work; the orchestral part is predominately an accompaniment. Strings begin with three crisp sixteenth notes to dotted quarter notes on the tonic, subdominant, and dominant chords (drawing the audience's attention), calmly answered in quarter notes and chords by the woodwinds and then

---

[10] Amore, ibid., 167.

[11] Fabbri, "Ignoti momenti Rossiniani," 279–85. Fabbri was the first to show that Rossini wrote this work, but his 1968 article was not widely known outside Italy. Subsequently, Newhill reported that Rossini very likely wrote the *Variations* because he found a Cipriani edition of the *Variations* in the library of the clarinetist, Hans-Rudolf Stalder. John P. Newhill, "Further Information on Rossini's Works for Clarinet," *The Clarinet* 11, no. 3 (Spring 1984): 2.

[12] Newhill, "Rossini's Works for Clarinet," 23–25. Modern editions, Gioacchino Rossini, *Fantasia, per Clarinetto e Pianoforte*, eds. Maria Rosa Bodini and Ezio Zappatini (Milan: Zerboni, 1972); Gioacchino Rossini, *Fantaisie per Pianoforte e Clarinetto*, ed. Günther Joppig (Milano: G. Ricordi & C., 1989).

[13] Title page reproduced by Fabbri, "Ignoti momenti Rossiniani," between 272 and 273; Luis Rossi, "Clarinetto alla Italiana," *The Clarinet* 28, no. 4 (September 2001): 67; Adriano Amore, *Il clarinetto in Italia*, 150.

[14] Amore, ibid., 167, note 614.

[15] Gioachino Rossini, *Mosè in Egitto, Edizione critica della opera di Gioachino Rossini*, ed. Charles S. Brauner (Pesaro: Fondazione Rossini, 2004) 24: 437–39.

[16] Amore, *Il clarinetto in Italia*, 167.

[17] Gioachino Rossini, *La Donna del Lago, Edizione critica della opera di Gioachino Rossini*, vol. 2, ed. H. Colin Slim (Pesaro: Fondazione Rossini, 2002), 29:280–92; Amore, *Il clarinetto in Italia*, 167; Amore, *La Letteratura Italiana per Clarinetto: Storia, Analisi, Discografia e Curiosità*, ([Perugia]: Accademia italiana del clarinetto, 2011), 340.

[18] The Sikorski edition is used for this analysis.

[19] Kathy Pope, "Master Class: Introduction, Theme and Variations by Giocchino Rossini (1792–1868)," *The Clarinet* 31, no. 4 (September 2004): 6.

the strings. The orchestra is small, appropriate for the small opera pits and stages available in the 1820s.

In the introduction, the clarinet begins with the last eighth note (m. 7), stating the E♭ major A theme (mm. 7–17) in a tranquil style similar to a coloratura aria. There are beautiful flowing phrases and brilliant runs, primarily in the clarinet's upper register, with a wide range from F3 to A$_6$. The A theme's mood is exceedingly sweet, and the strings modulate to B♭ major, just before the clarinet has an eighth note pickup on the last eighth note (m. 17), to an equally sweet B theme. Additional ornamentation (m. 24), such as turns, a two octave run, and a leap of two octaves and a minor third from D4 to F$_6$ follow. After a bold entrance by the full orchestra and a four measure tune by the strings, there are four chords that cadence on a dominant seventh chord. The clarinet answers with the last eighth note (m. 38), playing the E♭ major A^1 theme an octave higher. After a fermata on C5, a cadenza includes a scintillating run to high A$_6$ down to G4, repeated thirty-second notes, a chromatic scale to G$_6$ down to a thirty-second-note elaboration of the theme, an arpeggio from F3 to A$_6$, and a joyous conclusion.

The theme section, in 4/4, Allegretto, quarter note = 112,[20] begins with three staccato eighth note pickups (m. 53) followed by an eighth and off-beat accented quarter notes. It is amusing to play and fun to hear with its accents and short sixteenth note runs. The orchestral strings accompany with a typical repeated Rossini rhythm of an eighth note rest, three eighths, and a quarter note. The clarinet ends the C theme with two measures of clarion register sixteenth note runs and arpeggios, to a quarter note C5. In six measures (mm. 73–78), the orchestra concludes with a teasing, light hearted D theme by the first violins, an octave lower than the flute, and a crescendo to the end of the section.

Each of the five variations starts with pickup notes. Variations 1–3 and 5 have two sets of measures repeated by the clarinet, followed by an unrepeated set of measures played by the orchestra.[21] Variation 4 has no repeats. Each of the C^1–C^4 themes is altered by writing them as triplets or sixteenth notes, and with various slurs and staccato articulation. The short orchestral responses, themes D^1–D^4, incorporate either the triplet or sixteenth note patterns of the clarinetist into each theme's light hearted and precise endings. Orchestral themes are effectively played by the violins, and the flute doubles the clarinet in fast passage in the variations.

Variation 1, Più mosso, quarter note = 120,[22] is played faster than the theme section. The first repeat (second part of m. 78–first part of m. 86) begins with five

---

[20] Pope, ibid., 6.

[21] Two measures on Chart 25.1 are counted twice, mm. 145, 166, and eleven measures on Chart 25.1 are counted three times, mm. 78, 86, 94, 99, 107, 115, 122, 130, 138, 174, and 182, because of the way the music is written.

[22] Pope, ibid., 7.

triplet eighth notes. (The first portion of measure 78 ends the theme section.) Variation 1 presents the C^1 theme melody as a constant flow of triplets, carefully marked with slurs and staccato dots that delight the listener. In measures 82–84, in the first repeat, the clarinet is doubled at the octave by the flute, adding an accent and emphasis to the C^1 theme. The second repeat (second part of m. 86–first ending of m. 94) begins with five triplet eighth notes that flow into a series of triplets with a variety of slurs and staccato dots. The orchestra concludes with the triplet D^1 theme (second ending of m. 94–first part of m. 99).

Variation 2 features sixteenth notes as the C^2 theme. The first repeat (second part of m. 99–first part of m. 107) begins with a pickup measure of six sixteenth notes. It incorporates the theme melody as a constant flow of sixteenth note runs, wide leaps to G_6, and arpeggios, carefully marked with slurs and staccato dots. The second repeat (second part of m. 107–first ending of m. 115) starts with six sixteenth notes,[23] and continues in sixteenth notes with leaps, arpeggios, and staccato slurred passages. The orchestral conclusion to variation 2, theme D^2 (second ending of m. 115–first part of m. 122), uses sixteenth notes rather than triplets, producing an ending sounding similar to variation 1. Variations 1 and 2 are quite virtuosic with wide leaps and skips throughout (Ex. 25.1).

Variation 3, quarter note = 120[24] continues to feature sixteenth notes as the C^3 theme. The first repeat (second part of m. 122–first part of m. 130) begins with six sixteenth notes and features staccato and slurred sixteenth notes in arpeggios up to G_6 and chromatic passages, creating a brilliant effect. The second repeat (second part of m. 130–first part of m. 138) starts with six downward flowing sixteenth notes, adding chromatic scales, leaps, several staccato upward arpeggios, and a staccato scale from C_6 to C4. The orchestral response, theme D^3 (second ending of m. 138–first part of m. 145) is identical to the light hearted ending of variation 2.

Variation 4 (second part of m. 145–m. 165) in B♭ minor is a slow and expressive Largo Minore, quarter note = 60.[25] Rossini cleverly uses the first three eighth notes of the C theme (m. 145) presenting a highly ornamented minor version of the C^4 theme. The clarinet plays coloratura like chromatic scales, grace notes, short trills, turns, dotted sixteenth and thirty-second notes, mordents, and two chromatic scales, before ending on a half note C5. The orchestral ending (mm. 162–165) is a dramatic continuation of the C^4 theme. Here, violins play tremolo like passages beginning *pp* with a gradual crescendo until reaching a *ff*, and the full orchestra plays heavy chords ending in B♭ major.

---

[23] Pope, ibid., 7.
[24] Pope ibid., 7.
[25] Pope, ibid., 7.

EXAMPLE 25.1. The beginning of the clarinet part for variations 1 and 2.

Variation 5, Maggiore, più mosso, quarter note = 120,[26] is in B♭ major. The first repeat (m. 166–first part of m. 174) begins with clarinet pickup notes of six mixed tongued and slurred sixteenth notes (m. 166). Variation 5 showcases clarinet sixteenth notes with arpeggios, accents, mixed slurs and staccato, brilliantly tongued scales, and leaps. Six slurred sixteenth pickup notes start the second repeat (second part of m. 174–first ending of m. 182). After a four measure orchestral interlude, the clarinet C⁵ theme plays scale like passages (mm. 186–191, having entered the final range of unrepeated measures, second ending of mm. 182–211), answered by the orchestra with four measures of light-hearted melody. The clarinet continues with more sixteenth-note passages and several scales up to A_6, and a two-octave slurred and tongued scale, from G4 to G_6 (m. 202). This is followed by a chromatic scale cadenza from G3 to quarter note G_6, a dotted quarter note Ab_6, and eighth notes to C_6, ending with a brief and brilliant five-measure orchestral conclusion.[27]

---

[26] Pope, ibid., 8.

[27] Pope proposes a cadenza before the last chromatic scale and suggests ideas regarding rhythm, notation, and fingerings; Pope, ibid., 6–9. Neidich provides a cadenza in his edition.

Section:	Introduction	Theme	Var. 1	
Starts at m.	1 Andante	53–78 Allegretto	78–86: Più mosso 86–94: 94–99	
No. of mm.	52	25	37	
Tonalities	E♭, B♭, E♭	B♭	B♭	
Themes	A, B, A¹	C, D	C¹, D¹	

Section:	Var. 2	Var. 3	Var. 4	Var. 5
Starts at m.	99–107: 107–115: 115–122	122–130: 130–138: 138–145	145–165 Largo Minore	166–174: Maggiore, più mosso 174–182: 182–211
No. of mm.	39	39	20	61
Tonalities	B♭	B♭	b♭, B♭	B♭
Themes	C², D²	C³, D³	C⁴	C⁵, D⁴

CHART 25.1 Rossini, *Introduction, Theme, and Variations for Clarinet and Orchestra*: Structural analysis. Between the theme and repeats in the variations, the repeated measures are split.

During the nineteenth century, the most popular type of variation was the melodic form where a theme is either decorated with additional notes or replaced by a close version of the original.[28] Many substantial instrumental variations were written, including thousands on popular operatic tunes or national songs with technically brilliant variations. Variations along with more serious sonatas, concert pieces, and concertos were staples of the nineteenth century repertoire.[29] Contemporary programs illustrate the popularity of variations played by travelling virtuosi,[30] as well as by amateurs at home, including operatic fantasias with variations on melodies from Rossini's operas.[31]

The *Introduction, Theme, and Variations* was originally written for an accomplished clarinetist who, at the time, played a clarinet with at least eleven keys, such as the eleven-key clarinet in the University of Edinburgh Musical Instrument

---

[28] Timothy Rhys Jones, "Variation Form," *The Oxford Companion to Music, Oxford Music Online.*

[29] Rey M. Longyear, *Nineteenth-Century Romanticism in Music*, 2nd ed. (Englewood Cliffs, NJ: Prentice-Hall, 1973), 52; Jones, "Variation Form," *Grove Music Online.*

[30] See William Weber in *The Great Transformation of Musical Taste: Concert Programming from Haydn to Brahms* (Cambridge: Cambridge University Press, 2008), between 144 and 145, and throughout the volume.

[31] Diane Carolyn Cawein, "A Comparative Study of Nineteenth-Century Works for Clarinet Based on Motives from the Operas by Vincenzo Bellini" (D.M. diss., Florida State University, 1999), 2–3; Madeline LeBaron Johnson, "An Examination of the Clarinet Works of Luigi Bassi" (D.M.A. diss., University of North Texas, 2007), 3–6; Gossett, "Gioachino Rossini," *Grove Music Online.*

Collection by the Milan maker, Pietro Piana.[32] During the 1810s, instruments with twelve keys or more were introduced to Italy by Austrian and German makers.[33] On the modern Boehm-system clarinet, this work is a great pleasure to play and an impressive virtuosi piece.

Rossini's *Introduction, Theme, and Variations for Clarinet and Orchestra* remains a favorite recital work because of its brilliance, clarity of form, and appealing music.[34] The greatest challenges for the clarinetist are the many leaps and rapid tongued passages. It is very effective on almost any program and may be used as an encore.

[32] Heike Fricke, *Catalogue of the Sir Nicholas Shackleton Collection: Historic Musical Instruments in the Edinburgh University Collection*, ed. Arnold Meyers (Edinburgh: Edinburgh University Collection of Historic Musical Instruments, 2007), 595, no. 4840.

[33] Albert R. Rice, "The Development of the Clarinet as Depicted in Austro-German Instruction Sources, 1732–1892," in *Tradition und Innovation im Holzblasinstrumentenbau des 19. Jahrhunderts,* ed. Sebastian Werr (Augsburg: Wissner, 2012), 95–97.

[34] Sacchini, "The Concerted Music," 141.

26 Archduke Rudolph of Austria, *Sonata for Clarinet and Piano, op. 2*

Date of composition: 1812–1813

First edition/first modern edition: *Sonate für Pianoforte und Clarinette von R.E.H.*
[Rudolph ErzHerzog] [op.] II dem Grafen Ferdinand Troyer gewidmit, Vienna: Steiner und
Comp., ca. 1822;[1] Archduke Rudolph of Austria, *Sonata for Clarinet and Piano*, ed. Himie
Voxman, London: Musica Rara, 1973

Dedicatee/first performer: Count Ferdinand von Troyer; Not known

Date/place of first performance: Not known; Not known

JOHANN JOSEPH RAINER RUDOLPH, Archduke of Austria (1788–1831) was an
Austrian music patron and composer. In 1792, he went to Vienna when his eldest
brother, Archduke Franz, became emperor, and he became archduke. His thorough
education included music instruction from the court composer, Anton Teyber. By
fifteen, Rudolph was an accomplished pianist and during 1803–1804, Beethoven
became his teacher, first in piano and music theory, and later in composition.[2] They
became close friends and Beethoven respected him as a person and a musician, as
shown by his ninety-five letters to Rudolph and the dedication of thirteen works to
him. Among these are the fourth and fifth piano concertos, the piano sonata "Les
Adieux," the "Archduke" trio, the "Hammerklavier" sonata, and the *Missa solemnis*.[3]

---

[1] Susan Kagan, *Archduke Rudolph, Beethoven's Patron, Pupil, and Friend: His Life and Music* (Stuyvesant, NY: Pendragon Press, 1988), 184, 329.

[2] Susan Kagan, "Rudolph, Archduke of Austria," *Grove Music Online*; Kagan, *Archduke Rudolph*, 2–3, 5.

[3] Otto Biba, "Afterword," in Erzherzog Rudolph, *Variationen über ein Thema von Rossini für Klarinette und Klavier*, ed. Otto Biba (Vienna: Dobliner, 1981); Kagan, "Rudolph, Archduke of Austria," *Grove Music Online*.

In 1809, the archduke, with Prince Kinsky and Prince Lobkowitz, created a lifetime annuity for Beethoven, with the only requirement that he remain in Vienna. On later occasions, Rudolph used his influence on Beethoven's behalf, including advocating in litigation involving his nephew, Karl.[4]

In 1805, at seventeen, Rudolph took holy orders possibly because of his fragile health.[5] In 1819 he became cardinal and a few weeks later, was named Archbishop of Olmütz (Olomouc) by Pope Pius VII. For over twenty years, Beethoven taught composition to Rudolph.[6] Under Beethoven's instruction, the Archduke completed twenty-seven works for piano and piano four hands, chamber music, songs, and one orchestral piece. An additional thirty-five works are incomplete, including a *trio for clarinet, cello and piano*.[7] Rudolph wrote *Introduction, Theme, and Variations in E♭ for Clarinet and Piano* (1822) (the theme taken from Rossini's 1821 opera, *Zelmira*);[8] and *Variations on "To jsou koně"* ("These are the Horses"), for Basset Horn and Piano (ca. 1822), dedicated to Count Ferdinand Troyer.[9] Three works were published in Vienna during the Archduke's lifetime: *Forty Variations on a Theme by Beethoven*, op. 1 (Steiner, 1818–1819); *Fuga on a Theme of Diabelli* (A. Diabelli, 1819–1820); and *Sonata for Clarinet in A and Piano, op. 2* (Steiner, 1822).[10] The *clarinet sonata* was dedicated to Troyer, chamberlain to the archduke since 1814, and an accomplished amateur clarinetist who taught clarinet to the archduke.[11] At least three composers dedicated clarinet works to the archduke: Carlo Paessler, *Concerto in B♭ Major for Clarinet and Orchestra* (1818); Eduard von Lannoy, *Grand Trio for Clarinet, Cello, and Piano, op. 15* (1820); and Philipp Jacob Riotte, *Septet in E♭, op. 39 for Clarinet, Two Horns, Strings, and Piano* (1820s).[12]

---

[4] Kagan, "Rudolph, Archduke of Austria," *Grove Music Online*.

[5] Kagan, ibid.

[6] Kagan, ibid.; Biba, "Afterword."

[7] A modern completed edition is Archduke Rudolph, *Trio for Clarinet, Cello & Piano*, eds. Dieter Klöcker and Werner Genuit (London: Musica Rara, 1969).

[8] Described by Kagan, *Archduke Rudolph*, 152–64. Modern edition, Archduke Rudolph of Austria, *Variationen über ein Thema von Rossini: für Klarinette und Klavier*, ed. Otto Biba (Vienna: Doblinger, 1981).

[9] Described by Kagan, ibid., 164–67. Modern edition, Archduke Rudolph, *Varations, Adagio and Polonaise for Basset Horn (or Clarinet) and Piano*, eds. Luigi Magistrelli and Carlo Ballarini (Bradfield, Berkshire, England: Rosewood Publications, 2002).

[10] Kagan, ibid., 322–23, 329. Two contemporary works for A clarinet and piano were written: Franz Anton Hoffmeister, *Six Duos* (1807–1812), and Karl Arnold, *Sonate* (1816). Lyle Merriman, "Early Clarinet Sonatas," *The Instrumentalist* 12, no. 9 (April 1967): 28. Modern editions: F. A. Hoffmeister, *Sonata for Clarinet in A and Piano*, eds. Dieter Klöcker and Werner Genuit (London: Musica Rara, 1970); Karl Arnold, *Sonate for B♭ Clarinet and Piano*, op. 7, ed. Lyle Merriman (Delaware Water Gap, PA: Shawnee Press, 1982).

[11] In 1824, Troyer commissioned the *Octet, op. 166, for winds and strings* from Franz Schubert. Joseph James Estock, "A Biographical Dictionary of Clarinetists Born before 1800" (Ph.D. diss., University of Iowa, 1972), 349–50; Pamela Weston, *Clarinet Virtuosi of the Past* (London: Robert Hale, 1971), 172–73.

[12] Heribert Haase, *ClarLit Clarinet Bibliography Version 2012E*, 3rd update, ([Germany]: The Author, 2012, CD-ROM.

Kagan suggests that the *sonata* was composed during 1812–1813 and later reworked for publication. In one of the three manuscript copies in the Gesellschaft der Musikfreunde, in Vienna, Beethoven provided about three dozen small corrections in the piano part, one suggestion in the clarinet part, and several metronome indications written in the nearest margins.[13] Metronome numbers were included in the first edition for most of the movements, using the early metronomes patented and improved by Johann Nepomuk Maelzel in 1815.[14] The first page of this manuscript is in the hand of Wenzel Schlemmer, Beethoven's favorite copyist; the remaining pages, by one of Schlemmer's students. Unusually, the clarinet part is written for the A rather than the usual B♭ clarinet.

The first movement is in sonata-allegro form with a coda. (See Chart 26.1.) It is marked Allegro moderato, quarter note = 144. The A theme begins with an upward A major piano scale. This leads to a cadence on a dominant E major chord, and a pleasant piano prelude to the clarinet melody in A major (m. 14). There is a delicate interplay between the clarinet and piano, both having equally important parts. The B theme (mm. 47–61) in E major features the clarinet with large leaps of one or two octaves or more.[15]

The B^1 theme plays in E minor and C major (mm. 62–69), followed by the A^1 theme (mm. 70–78) in E major; following this is the B^2 theme (mm. 79–95) and elements of the A theme in A major. The exposition is repeated from measures 2–95. In the development, the C theme (mm. 96–112) consists of a rhythmic piano motive of three eighth notes in octaves to a half note, answered by the clarinet with a quarter and half note and elaborated with arpeggios and scales (mm. 96–112). Rudolph

Section:	Exposition	Development	Recapitulation	Coda
Starts at m.	1–95, 2–95 Allegro moderato	96	158	261–280
No. of mm.	189	62	103	20
Tonalities	A, trans., E, e, C, E, A	E, f♯, F♯, B♭, E	A, trans. f♯, A	E, F, A
Themes	A, trans., B, B^1, A^1, B^2, (A)	C, trans.	A^2, trans., B^3, B^4	A^3

CHART 26.1 Archduke Rudolph, *Sonata for Clarinet and Piano, op. 2*: Structural analysis, first movement, Allegro moderato.

---

[13] Some of these specific corrections by Beethoven are given by Kagan, *Archduke Rudolph*, 199–204.

[14] Alexander Wheelock Thayer and Dixie Harvey, "Maelzel, Johann Nepomuk," *Grove Music Online*.

[15] In the two-octave leaps downward from G5 to G3 and B5 to B3 (mm. 49–52), Meredith hears the influence of Mozart in the large leaps in the third movement of the Clarinet Concerto (mm. 161–164), William Meredith, "Sound Recording Essay-Review: Archduke Rudolph's Sonata for Clarinet and Piano and Trio for Clarinet, Cello, and Piano," *The Beethoven Journal* 12, no. 1 (Spring 1997): 24, ex. 2.

deftly brings the listener through several tonalities. The transition to the recapitulation occurs with a ritardando to a one measure Adagio (m. 154), with four quarter notes, the last a fermata on which an Eingang or short cadenza may be played. After two measures of piano scales, and clarinet arpeggios and a trill, Rudolph's immediate return to the first tempo (m. 156) is a device also used by Beethoven for dramatic effect.[16]

The recapitulation (mm. 158–260) uses the A^2 theme and a transition, followed by the B^3 theme in F♯ minor, and the B^4 theme in A major. It features virtuosic piano octaves and a chromatic scale (mm. 201–202) to a half note fermata on the third beat of measure 203. The piano continues with a whole-note trill and a chromatic scale ushering in the clarinet with two two-octave downward leaps. At the end of the B^4 theme, the clarinet is given a fermata on a G5 whole note (m. 260), where an Eingang may be played. The coda (m. 261) builds to an exciting ending by starting *pp*, varying the dynamics greatly from measure to measure, and firmly closing with a *fff* ending.

Kagan is critical of the length of this first movement, about thirty-five minutes, describing it as a "sprawling sonata form" and finds the main themes, "discursive."[17] Meredith finds the first movement, "subtle and interconnected" in "the opening gesture, the identity of the opening ten measures, the anticipation of a minor key repeat of the B^1 theme, and the construction of the B theme with its wide downward clarinet leaps."[18]

The second movement, Tempo di Menuetto, begins in E major in ternary form with a coda, quarter note = 112.[19] (See Chart 26.2.) It is fascinating for the many textures achieved between the clarinet and piano and the shifts of mood among the four sections. An expansive and lovely melody begins with a *fp* in the clarinet and *fz*

Section:	A	B	A^1	Coda
Starts at m.	1 Tempo di Menuetto–16: 17–75	76 Trio–91, 92–106: 107–115	1 Tempo di Menuetto–75	116–125
No. of mm.	91	55	75	10
Tonalities	E, F♯, b, E, E♭, E	A, a	E, F♯, b, E, E♭, E	A
Themes	A, A^1	B	A^2	coda

CHART 26.2 Archduke Rudolph, *Sonata for Clarinet and Piano, op. 2*: Structural analysis, second movement, Tempo di Menuetto.

16 Kagan, *Archduke Rudolph*, 189–90.
17 Kagan, ibid., 186, 191.
18 Meredith, "Sound Recording Essay-Review," 23–24.
19 Suggested by the author.

in the eighth note piano accompaniment. At measure 5, the off-beat accent, dotted rhythm, and staccato clarinet line are unexpected, and continue with a conjunct lyrical melody. In the A section, measures 1–16 are repeated once. Rudolph modulates from E major to F♯ major (m. 17), through B minor (m. 25), E major (m. 27), E♭ major (m. 31), and to E major (m. 34). After a brief *pp* clarinet solo (mm. 50–53), and a short fermata on the third beat, the A¹ theme with a sixteenth-note pickup is stated (m. 54). The section B trio (mm. 76–115) in A major communicates a completely different mood, a simple clarinet B theme accompanied by a piano rhythmic figure of a dotted quarter, two sixteenths, and a quarter note, similar to a polonaise rhythm. Measures 92–106 are repeated. At the end of section B, a Da Capo sign signals the clarinetist and pianist to go back to the beginning of the Tempo di Menuetto (mm. 1–75) and play the A² theme, but without a repeat of the first sixteen measures. At the end of the A¹ section, a second ending proceeds to the brief coda (mm. 116–125) featuring clarinet arpeggios with a crescendo to a *ff* D₆ (m. 122), ending wistfully with a *pp* clarinet two measure phrase to a G5 dotted half note, and an accented piano third beat (m. 125).[20]

The third movement is a short, expressive Adagio, eighth note = 84, in two parts, with a mournful clarinet melody. (See Chart 26.3.) In section A, Rudolph uses a limited compass of C4 to A♭5 in A minor, playing *p* and *pp*. In section B, a crescendo is made to *f*, and the compass is extended downward to G3. Rudolph moves the tonality briefly into F major (mm. 17–19), back to A minor (m. 23), and modulates to A major (m. 28). At the end of the B section (mm. 42–44), the clarinet plays *pp*, fading away (calando), with a ritardando to a fermata and a brief Eingang. There is a short fermata on an eighth note, before a dotted-sixteenth and thirty-second-note pickup leading directly into the A major fourth movement. Kagan notes the structural similarity between Rudolph's *sonata* and Beethoven's *Sonata in A for Cello and*

Section:	A	B
Starts at m.	1 Adagio	17–44
No. of mm.	16	28
Tonalities	a	F, a, A
Themes	A	B, A¹

CHART 26.3 Archduke Rudolph, *Sonata for Clarinet and Piano, op. 2*: Structural analysis, third movement, Adagio.

---

20 Meredith, ibid., 24; Kagan, *Archduke Rudolph*, 193–94.

Piano, op. 69 in which the scherzo and slow movement are reversed from the traditional order, and the solo cello and clarinet are written in a similar manner.[21]

The fourth movement, Andantino, quarter note = 108, is written as a theme with nine short variations, offering the opportunity for virtuoso display by the clarinet and piano. (See Chart 26.4.) The expressive *p* A theme (mm. 45–60) consists of two eight measure phrases both of which are repeated. It is primarily in the clarion register and includes sforzandi, crescendos, and short, wedge shaped articulation. Variation 1 (mm. 61–68) consists of eighth notes and in its second half (mm. 69–76) includes eighth–note large leaps from G5 to E3 to C$_6$, and E5 to C4 to G5. Variation 2 (mm. 77–92) incorporates triplets and thirty-second notes. Variation 3 (mm. 93–108), Più mosso, quarter note = 134, presents a *p* melody, leaps, staccato, and *fz* accents. Variation 4 (mm. 109–124), Andantino, Tempo I, quarter note = 108, begins *pp* with accents and *fp* accents. Variation 5 (mm. 125–148), Più mosso, quarter note = 144, utilizes triplets with crescendos and a wide range of G3 to C$_6$. Variation 6 (mm. 149–168), Tempo di Marcia comodo, quarter note = 144, displays a predominately dotted-eighth and sixteenth-note piano rhythm. The clarinet plays smooth eighth notes, triplets, and the dotted rhythm. Variation 7 (mm. 169–190), Moderato e dolce, quarter note = 104, is lyrical and includes clarinet accompaniment to the piano's melody with sixteenth notes and arpeggios. After a short fermata on F5 and a sixteenth note pickup, variation 8, Minore, Adagio espressivo, eighth note = 76, begins with a slow melody in A minor. It includes two clarinet fermatas where Eingänge may be played, a short piano cadenza, a clarinet melody with a highly ornamented piano accompaniment, and two clarinet cadenzas. Its range encompasses a downward arpeggio from B5 to G3, followed by ad libitum arpeggios from G3 to B$_6$ and G3 to G$_6$, among the highest notes in the clarinet's range. Variation 9, Maggiore, Allegretto, dotted quarter note = 84, is in 6/8 in A major, beginning with a lovely *pp* piano melody repeated by the clarinet from measure 238. A poco presto section (mm. 255–270) adds more virtuoso piano writing, quieting down to *pp* and stopping with a piano fermata on the first beat. On the second beat, Presto, dotted quarter = 138, the clarinet quickly ends with *f* eighth notes in four measures.

In the second half of variation 1 (mm. 69–76), Rudolph writes slurred phrases that have large leaps quite similar to Mozart's writing in the fourth movement of his *Quintet for Clarinet and Strings, K. 581* (mm. 25–32) (Ex. 26.1).[22] This is not surprising since Rudolph owned many of Mozart's concertos and chamber music, transcribed a number of others as composition exercises for Beethoven, and in 1808 played a Mozart *piano concerto in B♭* (either K. 450 or K. 456) at a concert in

[21] Kagan, ibid., 193–94; Meredith, ibid., 25.
[22] Kagan, *Archduke Rudolph*, 184–85, 197–99.

Section:	Theme	Var. 1	Var. 2	Var. 3	Var. 4	Var. 5
Starts at m.	45 Andantino to 52: 53–60:	61–68: 69–76:	77–84: 85–92:	93 Più mosso–100: 101–108:	109 Tempo I–116: 117–124:	125 Più mosso–140: 141–148:
No. of mm.	32	32	32	32	32	48
Tonalities	A	A	A	A	A	A
Themes	A	A^1	A^2	A^3	A^4	A^5

Section:	Var. 6	Var. 7	Var. 8	Var. 9
Starts at m.	149 Tempo di Marcia–156: 157–164: 165–168	169 Moderato e dolce–176: 177–184: 185–190	191 Adagio espressivo–230	231 Allegretto–275
No. of mm.	36	38	40	45
Tonalities	A	A	a	A
Themes	A^6	A^7	B	A^8

CHART 26.4 Archduke Rudolph, *Sonata for Clarinet and Piano, op. 2*: Structural analysis, fourth movement, Andantino.

Schönbrunn.[23] Another example of homage to his teacher is the piano figuration in the poco presto section of variation 9 (mm. 255–261), similar to that used by Beethoven in his *Piano Sonata in E♭, op. 81a* (m. 39) and in his *Piano Concerto no. 5 in E♭, op. 73* (m. 144). Rudolph's debt to the music of Mozart and Beethoven is obvious in this movement.[24]

EXAMPLE 26.1. Archduke Rudolph, *Sonata for Clarinet and Piano, op. 2*, fourth movement, mm. 69-76; Mozart, *Quintet for clarinet and strings, K. 581*, fourth movement (mm. 25-32).

Ex. 1. Archduke Rudolph, *Sonata for clarinet and piano, op. 2*, fourth movement (mm. 69-76).

Mozart, *Quintet for clarinet and strings, K.581*, fourth movement (mm. 25-32).

By 1822, a number of advanced clarinets were available in Vienna. These include Heinrich Grenser's eleven-key clarinets (1810s); Stephan Koch's twelve-key clarinets (1817); and Ivan Müller's thirteen-key clarinet (1820s), some with two additional thumb keys and some without.[25] Count Troyer may have performed Archduke Rudolph's works with any of these clarinets. In fact, as Kagan points out, Troyer may have owned a set of B♭ and A basset clarinets, with an extended lower range, for playing Mozart's works.[26]

Archduke Rudolph's *Sonata for Clarinet and Piano, op. 2*, is one of his finest works and provides a more careful balance between the piano and clarinet parts than in his variations for clarinet and basset horn.[27] It is also the only clarinet sonata known in

[23] Kagan, ibid., 28, 57, 60–61.

[24] Kagan, ibid., 197–99.

[25] Albert R. Rice, "The Development of the Clarinet as Depicted in Austro-German Instruction Sources, 1732–1892," in *Tradition und Innovation im Holzblasinstrumentenbau des 19. Jahrhunderts*, ed. Sebastian Werr (Augsburg: Wissner, 2012), 95–103.

[26] Kagan, *Archduke Rudolph*, 186, note 3. For examples of nineteenth century basset clarinets, see Albert R. Rice, "The Basset Clarinet: Instruments, Makers, and Patents," *Instrumental Odyssey: Essays in Honor of Herbert Heyde*, ed. L. Libin (Historical Brass Society, 2016), 157–78.

[27] Kagan, ibid., 204.

which Beethoven made important contributions, and one of the most interesting of the early Romantic period. It requires careful work by both clarinetist and pianist in playing the many shades of dynamics and the careful phrasing written in this work. Although the clarinet part has some virtuosic writing, it requires sensitive playing and analysis.

27 Camille Saint-Saëns, *Sonata for Clarinet and Piano, op. 167*

Date of composition: May–June 1921

First edition/later editions: Camille Saint-Saëns, *Sonate pour Clarinette avec accompagnement de Piano, op. 167*, Paris: Durand & Cie, 1921; Camille Saint-Saëns, *Sonata for Clarinet and Piano, op. 167*, ed. Paul Harvey, London: Chester, 1980; Camille Saint-Saëns, *Sonata for Clarinet and Piano, op. 167*, ed. from the first edition, ed. Yvonne Morgan, Winterthur: B. Päuler, 2007

Dedicatee/first performer: Auguste Périer; Not known

Date/place of first performance: Not known; Not known

CAMILLE SAINT-SAËNS (1835–1921) was a French composer, pianist, organist, and writer. He was very prolific and a fine craftsman who wrote all types of music, and as a child performer, was often compared to Mozart. During the late nineteenth century, he was one of the leaders of French music.

Saint-Saëns' parents died soon after he was born, and he was raised by his mother's aunt, Clémence Masson. At three he was taught to play the piano by Mrs. Masson and was recognized as a child prodigy.[1] At four, he played a Beethoven sonata with the Belgian violinist, Antoine Bessems, in the salon of Madame Violet. A writer for the *Moniteur Universel* was sufficiently impressed to compare his playing to Mozart's.[2]

---

[1] Daniel M. Fallon and Sabina Teller Ratner, "Saint-Saëns, Camille," *Grove Music Online*.
[2] Brian Rees, *Camille Saint-Saëns: A Life* (London: Chatto & Windus, 1999), 33.

Saint-Saëns later wrote a sonata for violin for Bessems at six.[3] At ten, he made a formal début at the Salle Pleyel playing Beethoven's *Piano Concerto in C minor* and Mozart's *Concerto in Bb, K. 450*, performing his own cadenzas. In addition to music, Saint-Saëns was interested in a number of general subjects, and studied the French classics, religion, Latin, Greek, mathematics, astronomy, archaeology, and philosophy. He entered the Paris Conservatory in 1848, studied organ with François Benoist, and won the first prize in 1851. He studied composition and orchestration with Fromental Halévy and took lessons in accompaniment and singing. In 1852, his *Ode à Sainte-Cécile* won first prize in a competition organized by the Société Sainte-Cécile, Bordeaux. He wrote several songs for voice and piano, the *Piano Quintet, op. 14*, and the *Symphony Urbs Roma*, which won another competition organized by the Société Sainte-Cécile in 1857. He contributed to the complete edition of Gluck's works and subsequently contributed to editions of works by Beethoven, Liszt, Mozart, Rameau, and Couperin. In 1913, he was awarded the Cross of the Legion of Honor. He concluded his career as a pianist with a concert on August 6, 1921 in Dieppe, where he played seven works to celebrate seventy-five years of public performances.[4]

Saint-Saëns composed over a period of about eighty years, writing 286 works.[5] His oeuvre includes operas; stage works; sacred works; works for chorus; songs for one voice and piano; orchestral works; solos with orchestra for piano, flute, violin, horn, cello, harp, and organ; works for military band; chamber works; works for piano two hands; and cadenzas, transcriptions, and arrangements of other composers' music.[6] His chamber works for clarinet comprise *Le Carnavel des Animaux* (*The Carnival of Animals*, 1886) *for two pianos, flute, clarinet, violin, cello, string bass, xylophone, and harmonica* (a keyboard with steel bars); *Caprices sur des Air Danois et Russes*, op. 79 (*Caprices on Danish and Russian Airs*, 1887) *for piano, flute, oboe, and clarinet*; and *Sonata for Clarinet and Piano, op. 167* (1921), discussed here.[7]

On September 17, 1920, Saint-Saëns wrote his friend, the composer Gabriel Fauré, "As for me I am writing nothing more. . . . But I have no other plans for composition in my head. The grape harvest is over! At 85, one has the right to be silent and perhaps

---

[3] Elizabeth R. Harkins, "The Chamber Music of Camille Saint-Saëns" (Ph.D. diss., New York University, 1976), 18.

[4] Fallon and Ratner, ibid.

[5] Jacques Gabriel Prod'homme, "Camille Saint-Saëns," *Musical Quarterly* 8, no. 4 (October 1922): 471; Sabina Teller Ratner, *Camille Saint-Saëns, 1835–1921: A Thematic Catalogue of his Complete Works, Vol. 1, The Instrumental Works* (Oxford: Oxford University Press, 2002), 524.

[6] Fallon and Ratner, ibid.

[7] Harkins, ibid., 100–115, 129–34.

the duty."[8] However, in 1921, the publisher, Durand, asked Saint-Saëns to write sonatas for oboe, clarinet, and bassoon. Saint-Saëns started them while in Algiers and completed them in Paris during May and June 1921. According to Bonnerot, they were written, "since the repertoire of these valuable instruments is so poor."[9] Durand paid Saint-Saëns 10,000 francs for the three sonatas scheduled to appear in late August; the *clarinet sonata* was published in November.[10] They are among his last works, and according to Harding, Saint-Saëns had plans to write a *sonata for English horn and piano*.[11]

The four-movement *Sonata for Clarinet and Piano, op. 167* was dedicated to Auguste Périer (1883–1947), clarinet professor at the Paris Conservatory. Later in the twentieth century, this sonata became a favorite recital work. Tuthill observes that it was "light, effective. Good for concert performance."[12] Cohn notes how perfectly the music fits the clarinet:

Thus: lyrical, legato-curved lines in the first movement, tonally conjunct passages plus wide skips in the animated second movement, and kinetic scalar sweeps in the final (fourth) movement. In the last a cyclic tie is made by recapitulating the Allegretto beginning of the first movement. Thereby, the tempoed relaxation of the sonata's ending takes over from the final movement's Molto allegro. The third movement, a somber Lento, is the dramatic peak of the Sonata. It is described by Georges Servièvres as "the most moving music perhaps produced by Saint-Saëns."[13]

The first movement, Allegretto in 12/8, quarter note = 72,[14] is in ternary form (Durand edition). (See Chart 27.1.) It begins with a quiet, rolling piano accompaniment in eighth notes while the clarinet states an elegant and tender A theme.

[8] Camille Saint-Saëns to Gabriel Fauré, September 17, 1920, Jean-Michel Nectoux, ed., J. Barrie Jones, trans., *The Correspondence of Camille Saint-Saëns and Gabriel Fauré: Sixty Years of Friendship* (Aldershot: Ashgate, 2004), 129.

[9] Letter from Saint-Saëns to Durand, June 14, 1921, Harkins, ibid., 45; Rees, ibid.; "instruments si précieux et dont le repertoire est si pauvre," Jean Bonnerot, *C. Saint-Saëns (1835–1921), Sa Vie et son Oeuvre*, new ed. rev. and augmented (Paris: A. Durand et fils, 1923), 215.

[10] Contracts between Durand et Cie. and Saint-Saëns dated August 23, 1921, Harkins, ibid., 46; Sabine Teller Rattner, ibid., 238.

[11] James Harding, *Saint-Saëns and his Circle* (London: Chapman & Hall, 1965), 224.

[12] Burnet C. Tuthill, "Sonatas for Clarinet and Piano: Annotated Listings," *Journal of Research in Music Education* 20, no. 3 (Fall 1972): 324.

[13] "…le plus ému peut-être que le maître ait jamais écrit," Georges Servières, *Saint-Saëns* (Paris: Félix Alcan, 1923), 117; Arthur Cohn, *The Literature of Chamber Music* (Chapel Hill, North Carolina: Hinshaw Music, 1997), 4:2404.

[14] Suggested by the author.

Section:	A	B	A^1
Starts at m.	1 Allegretto	23	55 a Tempo (no. 2)–84
No. of mm.	22	32	30
Tonalities	E♭	f, C♭, c, A♭, d	c, E♭
Themes	A	B	A^1, A^2

CHART 27.1 Saint-Saëns, *Sonata for Clarinet and Piano, op. 167*: Structural analysis, first movement, Allegretto.

Section:	A	B	A^1	B^1
Starts at m.	1 Allegro animato	38½ (no. 1)	65½ (no. 2)	99½–109
No. of mm.	37½	27	34	10½
Tonalities	A♭	A♭	A♭	A♭
Themes	A	B	A^1	B^1

CHART 27.2 Saint-Saëns, *Sonata for Clarinet and Piano, op. 167*: Structural analysis, second movement, Allegro animato.

Saint-Saëns had a keen sense of the clarinet's timbre in its different registers, and he made thoughtful and sensitive choices throughout. The harmony remains squarely in E♭ throughout the A section (mm. 1–22). At section B, Saint-Saëns advances, "through a series of gentle harmonic twists"[15] and various tonalities. At measure 34, no. 1, two clarinet arpeggios in E♭ major and F minor and a *mf* expansive phrase lead to *f* triplet arpeggios in A♭ major and a high point on B♭5 (m. 45, 10 measures before no. 2). A poco ritardando and diminuendo (m. 54) bring the clarinet back to the A tempo section and the A^1 theme at measure 55, no. 2, in C minor. At measure 72 (18 measures after no. 2), Saint-Saëns returns to E♭ major and the expressive A^2 theme, ending with a satisfying *pp* clarinet F major arpeggio from high C$_6$ to low F3, and two *pp* piano chords.

The second movement, Allegro animato, quarter note = 100,[16] is written in 2/2, in a double bipartite form. (See Chart 27.2.) At the end of each short section is a double bar. Each of the sections, except the last, cadence after the first half of the measure; sections B, A^1, and B^1 start on the second half of the measure. The harmony briefly touches several diverse chords but stays within A♭ major throughout.

---

[15] Stephen Studd, *Saint-Saëns: A Critical Biography* (London: Cygnus Arts, 1999), 285.

[16] Suggested by the author.

It is a light-hearted romp, presenting a technical challenge for the clarinetist, with several quick, staccato upward and downward arpeggios. The clarinet writing is not virtuosic and always idiomatic. Saint-Saëns shows his intimate knowledge of the clarinet's technique by writing rapidly articulated twelfths from C5 to F3 at no. 1 (m. 33, 3rd beat to m. 34); 5 measures after no. 1 (m. 37, 3rd beat to m. 38); 17 measures after no. 1 (m. 49, 3rd beat to m. 50; 6 measures before the end (m. 104); and from D#5 to G#3 13 measures before no.2 (m. 53, 3rd beat to m. 54). This movement is colorful with an ending of a sparkling *pp* staccato G minor arpeggio from G3 to B♭5.

The third movement, Lento, half note = 56,[17] is written 3/2 in a double bipartite form. (See Chart 27.3.) The slow and sorrowful E♭ minor A theme (mm. 1–25) reminds one of a funeral lament. The *f* A section (mm. 1–25) is written in half notes, in the lowest registers of the piano and the clarinet. It is heavy in sound and serious in intent. Dotted whole note *ff* piano arpeggios in section B act as a transition passage (mm. 26–32). These comprise seven measures of arpeggios in E♭ minor, F minor, E♭ minor, D♭ major, G♭ minor, D♭ major, and E♭ minor; and at no. 1 (m. 33), six repeated *pp* quarter note E♭3s, deftly bring the clarinet to the next part. The A¹ section (mm. 34–57) *pp* A¹ theme plays two octaves higher in the clarinet's clarino register, with the piano accompaniment in the highest registers, ending in *ppp*. It is lighter than section A, beautiful in tone but serious. Section B¹ (mm. 58–65) has a series of nine *pp* piano quarter note triplets outlining minor chords for six measures, E♭ minor, D♭ major, G♭ minor, D♭ major, A♭ minor, E♭ minor, and F major, all sustained with the pedal. This ethereal ending is impressive. After two quarter note rests and a short fermata, the pianist directly segues into the fourth movement. Harding writes about this movement:

Section:	A	B	A¹	B¹
Starts at m.	1 Lento	26	34	58–65
No. of mm.	25	8	24	8
Tonalities	e♭	none	e♭	none
Themes	A	arpeggios	A¹	arpeggios

CHART 27.3 Saint-Saëns, *Sonata for Clarinet and Piano, op. 167*: Structural analysis, third movement, Lento.

---

[17] Suggested by the author.

Section:	A	B	A¹		Coda
Starts at m.	1 Molto allegro	28 (no. 1)	118 (18 mm. before no. 4)		136 (no. 4)–159
No. of mm.	27	90	18		24
Tonalities	E♭, f, F	A♭, E♭, E, c	g		E♭
Themes	A	B	A¹		1st movement
					A theme

CHART 27.4 Saint-Saëns, *Sonata for Clarinet and Piano, op. 167*: Structural analysis, fourth movement, Molto Allegro.

[O]ne is hardly prepared to meet with passages (especially in the sonata for clarinet) which are written with more feeling than anything else in the rest of his work. The characteristic lucidity and smoothness are there, of course, but so too is a deeper, intimate emotion that he had rarely allowed to intrude upon his music before.[18]

Saint-Saëns' choice of dynamics and registers is appropriate and evocative. This movement requires careful and sustained breath control throughout.

The fourth movement, Molto allegro, quarter note = 132,[19] is in ternary form, with a fourth part as a coda, consisting of twenty-four measures of the A theme from the first movement. (See Chart 27.4.) The A section begins with a soft piano introduction of three measures of sixteenth note tremolos, followed by a clarinet *p* F3 half note, F major arpeggios and scales, and a series of aggressive arpeggios and scales touching various tonalities, ending on a high F_6 eighth note (m. 12). The clarinet continues with sixteenth notes and eighth note triplets, quickly moving from E♭ major to F minor, to F major. In section B, no. 1 (m. 28), after an accented downbeat, the dynamic immediately changes to *p* and the accompaniment is thinner with dyads in the right hand against a syncopated, repeated single note in the left hand. After a poco ritardando (mm. 34–35), the aggressive tempo continues with trills, triplets, and sixteenth notes. A passionate *f* section ensues with triplets and accents (mm. 52–71); the thin texture returns (mm. 72–79) with a two measure ritardando until an A tempo at measure 80. The agitated movement continues with triplets and sixteenth notes; a subito *p* and gradual crescendo bring the music to a high A_6 eighth note at measure 105 (17 mm. after no. 3). A diminuendo (m. 109), and *p* eighth notes lead to section A¹ (mm. 118–135) with piano sixteenth-note tremolos and clarinet

18 Harding, ibid., 223.
19 Suggested by the author.

arpeggios and scales, to measure 126, in G minor. The clarinet and piano are abruptly *pp* and the clarinet, by itself, ends the section with a diminuendo and ritardando to a fermata on a whole note A3. After a fermata whole note rest, the 12/8 Allegretto, dotted quarter note = 72, first movement A theme returns at no. 4 (m. 136), with the identical piano accompaniment. It is a touching section, enveloping the player and the audience with a feeling of conclusion and unity.[20]

Saint-Saëns' *Sonata for Clarinet and Piano, op. 167* is one of the most interesting and absorbing sonatas of the repertoire. It is beautifully written for the clarinet, takes full advantage of the characteristic timbres in the low and high registers, and requires fine control of dynamics and articulation. After learning this work with a sensitive pianist, it is one of the most satisfying in the repertoire to perform.

---

[20] Studd, ibid., 285.

28 Robert Schumann, *Fantasy Pieces for Clarinet and Piano, op. 73*

Date of composition: February 11–13, 1849

First edition/modern editions: Robert Schumann, *Fantasiestücke für Pianoforte und Clarinette (ad libt. Violine od. Violoncell.)*, Kassel: C. Luckhardt, 1849; Robert Schumann, *Fantasiestücke Opus 73 für Klarinette und Klavier*, ed. Ernst Herttrich, Munich: G. Henle Verlag, 2005; Robert Schumann, *Fantasiestücke für Klarinette (Violine, Violoncello) und Klavier op. 73*, ed. Joachim Draheim, Wiesbaden: Breitkopf & Härtel, 2006

Dedicatee/first performers: Not indicated; Müller, clarinet, Dentler, piano

Date/place of first performance: January 14, 1850; Leipzig, Leipzig Musicians' Association

ROBERT SCHUMANN (1810–1856) was a German composer and music critic. He made important contributions to all types of music of the nineteenth century and to historically informed music criticism. Schumann was a talented pianist during his youth. In 1829, he studied piano in Leipzig with Friedrich Wieck and met Clara Wieck, his nine-year-old daughter, already an accomplished pianist. In 1830, he returned from Heidelberg to live at the Wiecks' home and practiced the piano seven hours a day. In 1831, he studied music theory and composition with Heinrich Dorn and began composing. In 1832, Schumann permanently injured his hand by using a device he invented to keep his fourth finger immobile when he practiced. In 1831, he contributed articles to German newspapers and wrote about Chopin's talent. In 1834, he founded the *Zeitschrift für Musik* which he edited for ten years, sometimes writing and composing as fictional characters he invented which he called the Davidsbund (League of David). Schumann called himself Florestan for his impetuous identity and Eusebius for his contemplative identity, dimensions of his personality apparent in his music.[1]

In 1840, he married Clara Wieck over her father's objections. He wrote many lieder and several song cycles, taught composition at Leipzig Conservatory, and in 1844 toured Russia with Clara. When he returned, he was severely depressed. In 1845 and 1846, he lived in Dresden and composed several important works. He met the twenty-year-old Brahms, whom he admired in his article, "New Paths" (1853). In 1853, Schumann's mental health ebbed and he entered an asylum, so as not to harm Clara. He tried to drown himself in the Rhine River but was rescued and returned to the asylum. He lived two years, dying of dementia, possibly caused by syphilis.[2]

Schumann is primarily known for his piano and vocal works, lieder, and song cycles. He wrote symphonies, chamber works, theatrical works, works for chorus and orchestra, and part songs for voices.[3] His solo clarinet pieces are *Fantasiestücke* (*Fantasy pieces*) *for Clarinet and Piano, op. 73* (1849) and *Drei Romanzen* (*Three Romances*) *for Oboe, Violin or Clarinet and Piano, op. 94* (1851).[4] For each of the clarinet works, publishers included substitute parts for violin or cello to increase sales. It is likely that Schumann authorized these alternate parts, but in the case of the *Three Romances*, Schumann wrote the publisher, Simrock, protesting publication of a substitute clarinet part stating he "meant oboe when he wrote oboe and did not consider it a clarinet piece."[5]

The *Fantasy Pieces* was originally called *Soiréestücke für Clarinette und Clavier* (*Evening Party Piece for Clarinet and Piano*) and consists of three movements. According to Schumann's household diary, he wrote the first two movements on February 11, 1849, and the third on February 13.[6] Four days later, February 17,

---

[1] John Daverio and Eric Sams, "Schumann, Robert," *Grove Music Online.*

[2] "Schumann, Robert," *The Oxford Dictionary of Music, Oxford Music Online*; Daverio and Sams, ibid.; John Worthen, *Robert Schumann: Life and Death of a Musician* (New Haven, CT: Yale University Press, 2007), 395–96.

[3] "Schumann, Robert," ibid.

[4] Daverio and Sams, ibid.

[5] Hans Kohlhase, *Die Kammermusik Robert Schumanns* (Hamburg: Wagner Musikalienhandlung, 1979), 1: 9; John Herschel Baron, *Intimate Music: A History of the Idea of Chamber Music* (Stuyvesant, NY: Pendragon Press, 1998), 317–18.

[6] "2 Stücke f. P[iano] f[or]te u. Clarinette in A"; "3tes Stück f. Clari[nette]" notations in Robert Schumann, *Tagebücher, Band III Haushaltbücher, Teil 2 1847–1856*, ed. Gerd Nauhaus (Leipzig: Deutscher Verlag für Musik, 1982), 3, pt. 2: 484. The autograph movements are dated, first, "12 Febr. 49"; second, "13ten. Febr. 49"; and third, "13 Febr. 1849"; Margit L. McCorkle, *Thematisch-Bibliographisches Werkverzeichnis*, ed. Robert-Schumann-Gesellschaft Düsseldorf, *Robert Schumann Neue Ausgabe sämtlicher Werke*, Serie VIII: Supplement Band 6 (Mainz: Schott, 2003), 318.

Schumann wrote in his diary, "Early [rehearsal] with Kotte" and on February 18, "Early rehearsal of clarinet pieces with Kotte,"[7] and Clara wrote of her, "great enjoyment."[8] Johann Gottlieb Kotte (1797–1857) was solo clarinetist in the Royal Orchestra in Dresden. Schumann heard and met Kotte in 1837 in Leipzig on three occasions.[9] Kotte is pictured about 1830 in an engraving (fig. 28.1) holding a clarinet. At the rehearsal he was playing one of the finest instruments available, an eleven-key clarinet (not all keys visible in the lithograph), made in the workshop of Carl Theodor Golde of Dresden.[10] On March 9, 1852, Clara Schumann and the violinist, Ferdinand David, played the pieces after dinner at the Leipzig home of Prince Reuss, and Schumann noted, "David's splendid playing with Clara, Sonata (in A) [= op. 105] and [the] Fantasy pieces."[11] The *Fantasy Pieces* received very positive responses in concerts and in the press. A second, "new, revised edition" published by Luckhardt about 1852 included metronome numbers, probably by Schumann.[12] In 1885, the *Fantasy Pieces* were published in Schumann's complete works edited by Clara Schumann.[13]

Later writers commented on several differences between the autograph in the Bibliothèque Nationale, Paris, M. 321 and Clara Schumann's edition, such as a name change from *Soiréestücke* to *Fantasiestücke*; elimination of a repeat (mm. 2–18) in the first movement; and addition of two chords at the end of the second movement.[14]

---

[7] Translation by Ernst Herttrich, "Preface," in Robert Schumann, *Fantasiestücke Opus 73 für Klavier und Klarinette*, ed. Ernst Herttrich (Munich: G. Henle, 2005), IV. "Früh bei Kotte"; "Früh Probe d. Clarinettst. [Stücke] m.[it] Kotte," Schumann, *Tagebücher*, 3, pt. 2: 484.

[8] "[M]it großem Vergnügen" cited by Berthold Litzmann, *Clara Schumann: Ein Künstlerleben, nach Tagebüchern und Briefen, Zweiter Band Ehejahre 1840–1856*, 3rd expanded ed. (Leipzig: Breitkopf & Härtel, 1907), 2: 183.

[9] Benjamin Reissenberger, "Schumann und die Klarinette," *Rohrblatt* 25, no. 2 (June 2010): 64; Litzmann misread Kotte's name as Kroth. Litzmann, ibid., 2: 183. This error is repeated by Pamela Weston, "Players and Composers," *The Cambridge Companion to the Clarinet*, ed. Colin Lawson (Cambridge: Cambridge University Press, 1995), 95; Weston, *Yesterday's Clarinettists: A Sequel* (Haverhill: Panda Group, 2002), 91; and Eric Hoeprich, *The Clarinet* (New Haven, CT: Yale University Press, 2008), 365, note 66.

[10] William Waterhouse, *The New Langwill Index: A Dictionary of Musical Wind-Instrument Makers and Inventors* (London: T. Bingham, 1993), 140. The author thanks Benjamin Reissenberger for a copy of the engraving of Kotte.

[11] Herttrich, ibid., IV.

[12] Joachim Draheim, "Preface," in Robert Schumann, *Fantasiestücke für Klarinette (Violin, Violoncello) und Klavier op. 73*, ed. Joachim Draheim (Wiesbaden: Breitkopf & Härtel, 2006), 3.

[13] *Robert Schumann's Werke, serie V für pianoforte und andere Instrument*, ed. Clara Schumann (Leipzig: Breitkopf & Härtel, 1885), 2–15.

[14] Herttrich, ibid., III–IV; Eric Simon, "Robert Schumann's *Fantasy Pieces, Op. 73*: Remarks about the Composer's Manuscript…Suggestion Regarding Interpretation, and Some Thoughts," *The Clarinet* 11, no. 1 (Fall 1983): 11; A. Hacker and R. Platt, "Preface," in Robert Schumann, *Soiréestücke for Clarinet and Piano, opus 73* (London: Faber Music, 1985), critical comments, 21–22. Draheim states that because the Hacker and Platt edition use the autograph with part of the first edition, it does not represent Schumann's intentions. Draheim, ibid., 3, note 6.

FIGURE 28.1 Schumann, *Fantasy Pieces for Clarinet and Piano, op. 73*. Johann Gottlieb Kotte holding a clarinet, Eliasfriedhof, Dresden, no. 1981/k 1115. With permission, Städische Galerie Dresden.

Many more differences between the autograph, the first edition, and Schumann's personal copy of the first edition with comments and corrections are noted by Herttrich in the Henle edition.[15]

Although Schumann wrote for the A clarinet, some clarinetists, such as Eric Simon, prefer to play the *Fantasy Pieces* on the B♭ clarinet, believing it results in a, "much smoother performance of the first and second pieces, while the difficulty of the last piece, in A major, is only moderately increased"; and in Simon's opinion, "The difference between the sound of the A and B♭ [clarinets] is marginal" and "The middle section of the second piece, in G instead of A♭, becomes much easier."[16] Not all clarinetists agree. Reissenberger notes that the autograph of the *Fantasy Pieces* includes a clarinet part in C, but the most practical and best solution is to play the

---

[15] An interesting comparison of Clara Schumann's edition with the edition by Hacker and Platt is given by Christopher Robert Nichols in "138 Years of the Clarinet: Program Notes for a Master's Clarinet Recital of Works by Reger, Smith, Donizetti, Muczynski, and Schumann" (M.M. thesis, Kansas State University, 2007), 67–85.

[16] Simon, ibid., 11.

A clarinet, which matches the tonality of the piano accompaniment.[17] The author prefers the A clarinet's greater depth of timbre and finds, if the instrument is in good working order, the work can be played very smoothly.

Schumann's *Fantasy Pieces for Clarinet and Piano, op. 73*, is in three movements that are closely related in tonality, primarily in A minor for the first movement and A major in the second and third.[18] Daverio describes this work and others of the period as, "cycles of poetic miniatures each joined by a main tonic, appropriate for playing at home."[19] The close relationship between movements is emphasized by immediately playing from one movement to the other, indicated by the instruction, "attacca," and several thematic similarities among the movements. For example, the first movement's opening melody between the piano and clarinet (mm. 1–3) is similar to the second movement's melody (mm. 1–2) played in piano triplets. The third movement skillfully incorporates the first movement's clarinet A theme (m. 13), and the second movement's opening clarinet material (mm. 2–4) is restated at the beginning of the coda (mm. 68–70).[20] Eduard Bernsdorf enthusiastically and accurately reviewed the published *Fantasy Pieces*:

> Rapturous agitation, now infused with a hint of melancholy, now building up to outbursts of joy—this is clearly the predominant character of the present *Fantasy Pieces*. The three pieces are self-contained; nevertheless, the composer wishes them to be linked more closely through an attacca. This, along with a number of other elements in the development of each piece, e.g., the prevailing triplet motion and the use of the same key and meter in all three pieces…consolidates them into a whole and endows them with a unity of atmosphere that seems to derive from a definite intent. With a composer such as Schumann, it is obvious that this uniformity does not lead to monotony. It almost seems as if he were trying to exploit as fully as possible every psychological moment within them—and he has truly succeeded. The great variety and freedom of the ideas are all the more admirable as they move about within self-imposed boundaries, as mentioned above. And then there is the splendid manner in

---

[17] Reissenberger, ibid., 64. In the autograph, the second and third movements are written for the C clarinet, with the words, "für A—Clarinette zu transponieren" (to transpose for A clarinet); Schumann, *Soiréestücke* Op. 73, critical commentary, 22.

[18] A. E. F. Dickinson, "The Chamber Music," in *Schumann: A Symposium*, ed. Gerald Abraham (Oxford: Oxford University Press, 1952), 172.

[19] John Daverio, *Robert Schumann: Herald of a "New Poetic Age"* (New York: Oxford University Press, 1997), 394, 412.

[20] Daverio, ibid., 412–14; John Daverio, "'Beautiful and Abstruse Conservations': The Chamber Music of Schumann," in *Nineteenth-Century Chamber Music*, ed. Stephen E. Hefling (New York: Schirmer Books, 1998), 226–29.

Section:	A		B	A¹
Starts at m.	1 Zart und mit Ausdruck		29	38–69
No. of mm.	28		9	32
Tonalities	a		a	a, A
Themes	A		B	A¹

CHART 28.1 Schumann, *Fantasy Pieces for Clarinet and Piano, op. 73*: Structural analysis, first movement, *Zart und mit Ausdruck*.

which the piano and the clarinet share their statement of the ideas, how they complement one another; how neither one is the absolute lord or servant of the other. One will see that Schumann has once again created a work that occupies a worthy place among the many beautiful works with which he has endowed art.[21]

The first movement, delicate and with feeling (Zart und mit Ausdruck), quarter note = 80,[22] is in ternary form. It is in A minor throughout, except the last three measures which modulate to A major, and the last two A major chords. It begins with a prominent triplet piano accompaniment, followed by the A theme (mm. 1–10) played with a clarinet quarter-note pickup on the fourth beat of the first measure. The remaining phrases almost always begin on the fourth beat. This passionate clarinet melody is primarily in the clarion register with an overall compass of B♭3 to E♭6. There are several small crescendos and decrescendos, written as graphs in the clarinet part requiring, "careful and unexaggerated use of expression."[23] At the high point of two phrases there are two impressive *f* octave clarinet leaps from E♭5 to E♭6 (mm. 17, 53). The A¹ theme is played *pp* expressively in A minor (mm. 59–69) with a satisfying ending in A major.

The second movement, lively, light (Lebhaft, leicht), quarter note = 138, is in ternary form with a coda. (See Chart 28.2.) The A major piano introduction features a melody as part of its triplets, joined by a *p* clarinet theme emphasizing wide quarter note leaps of sevenths and ninths. The clarinet is predominant throughout the

[21] E[duard] Bernsdorf, "Für Pianoforte und Clarinette, Rob. Schumann, Op. 73. Phantasiestücke für Pianoforte und Clarinette (ad libitum Violine oder Violoncell.)," *Neue Zeitschrift für Musik* 32, no. 13 (February 12, 1852): 59–60; trans. Draheim, "Preface," in Robert Schumann, *Fantasiestücke* für Klarinette, 3.

[22] Nichols suggests a slightly faster tempo of quarter note = 100 to avoid a dragging tempo, the author agrees. Nichols, ibid., 86.

[23] Mitchell Lurie, "Master Class: Robert Schumann's *Fantasiestücke*, Op. 73," *The Clarinet* 22, no. 1 (November–December 1994): 6–7.

Section:	A	B	A¹	Coda
Starts at m.	1–26 Lebhaft, leicht	27–34:	51–63	64–73
		35–50:		
No. of mm.	26	48	13	10
Tonalities	A	F, C, a	A	A
Themes	A	B	A¹	coda

CHART 28.2 Schumann, *Fantasy Pieces for Clarinet and Piano, op. 73*: Structural analysis, second movement, Lebhaft, leicht.

movement, and includes *sfp* accents and forte passages. A passage that may pose a technical problem is the E♭5 grace note in measure 30, section B, before the second beat. Lurie suggests that using a soft "d" articulation helps to clarify the grace note.[24] The F major B theme begins as a clarinet *p* chromatic scale of triplets with a crescendo. A delicate and graceful clarinet modulates to C major and A minor in both repeats (mm. 27–34, 35–50).

In section A¹ (m. 51), the A major A¹ theme of wide clarinet leaps continues until measure 63. The coda, little by little more calmly (Nach und nach ruhiger), is a peaceful and gorgeous ending in A major. The last two arpeggiated eighth note A major chords were added in Clara Schumann's edition of Schumann's *Complete Works* as published by Breitkopf & Härtel. They may be left out, but according to Hacker and Platt, they provide a greater dramatic transition between the second and third movements.[25] Herttrich includes these chords in the Henle edition and notes that the two arpeggiated chords are missing in the autograph.[26] The movement's fast tempo, wide leaps, and awkward fingering in the F minor B section (for the A clarinet) are technically challenging, even though the compass is limited from C4 to E♭6.

The third movement, quick and with passion (Rasch und mit Feuer), quarter note = 160, is in ternary form with a coda. (See Chart 28.3.) It is a very passionate movement with crescendos, sforzandos, and accents, particularly in the first nine measures. It begins with an eighth-note rest, then a clarinet eighth note upward passage against triplets in a downward piano passage to a *f* half note, resolving on a quarter note. The accents in the piano and clarinet parts, and the doubling of the clarinet eighth notes in the left hand with a doubling effect of a sixteenth note later in the

---

[24] Lurie, ibid., 6.

[25] Hacker and Platt, ibid., iii; the autograph of the end of the second movement is reproduced as fig. b.

[26] Herttrich, ibid., 19 (no. 2, measure 72).

Section:	A		B	A¹	Coda
Starts at m.	1 Rasch und mit Feuer–9, 10–24:		24–31: 32–45:	45–67	68–98
No. of mm.	39		44	23	31
Tonalities	A		a	A	A
Themes	A		B	A¹	coda

CHART 28.3 Schumann, *Fantasy Pieces for Clarinet and Piano, op. 73*: Structural analysis, third movement, Rasch und mit Feuer.

right hand, give this movement an intensity and excitement not heard in any other clarinet solo. The second part of section A (mm. 10–24) is repeated and after the two *f* cadence notes, begins a *p* phrase with urgency and angst. The tone quality of the high F₆ quarter note (m. 15) provides a striking timbre appropriate to the excited mood. A B section in A minor presents a more relaxed but still tense clarinet B theme (mm. 24–31 and mm. 32–45 are both repeated), with two *sf* piano melodies (mm. 36–37) that intensify the theme. The dramatic A¹ theme plays for twenty-two measures (mm. 46–67). At the coda, the piano accompaniment switches to six-teenth notes while the clarinet performs the melody in the high register to high F₆. The tempo picks up twice in the faster (Schneller) sections (mm. 76, 91) adding more and more excitement until its brilliant end. This is technically the most de-manding movement because of the fast tempo and accelerando sections in the coda. As in the other movements, the greatest difficulty is one of musical expression, which must be worked out carefully with the pianist.

Kotte, the Dresden court clarinetist, played the *Fantasy Pieces for clarinet and piano, op. 73* on a stained or dark brown boxwood clarinet with a slightly lighter and sweeter sound than the modern instrument. Though not as loud and powerful as a modern instrument, nineteenth century clarinets, or copies of them, are capable of every expression, dynamic, and tone color required of them. Kotte's clarinet in the engraving (fig. 28.1) has the mouthpiece and reed turned to press against the lower lip, as many German professional clarinetists played during the early nine-teenth century.

Schumann's *Fantasy Pieces for Clarinet and Piano, op. 73* is one of the finest nine-teenth century works for clarinet and piano, along with Brahms's sonatas. It has great musical depth and intrinsic interest to players and listeners alike, and never fails to please on a recital. Schumann writes several *fp* indications and demands a flexibility of dynamics from *pp* to *f.* The A clarinet part is accessible to students, although there are some awkward fingerings. It poses a problem of endurance since the clarinet is constantly playing and Lurie suggests leaving out the repeats in the second and third movements.[27] This work requires an excellent player with fine control of expression and dynamics, and a schedule of thorough and careful rehearsals.

---

[27] Lurie, "Master Class," 6.

29 William O. Smith, *Variants for Solo Clarinet*

Date of composition: 1963

First edition: William O. Smith, *Variants for Solo Clarinet*, Vienna: Universal Edition, 1967

Dedicatee/first performer: Not indicated; William O. Smith, clarinet

Date/place of early performance: March 13, 1964; New York City

WILLIAM OVERTON SMITH (1926–) is an America composer and clarinetist. He began studying the clarinet at ten; during his teens he led a jazz orchestra and performed with the Oakland Symphony. He studied music composition with Darius Milhaud at Mills College and Roger Sessions at the University of California, Berkeley, and clarinet with Ulysse Delécluse at the Paris Conservatory and Arthur Christman at the Juilliard School. He taught at the University of California, Berkeley, the San Francisco Conservatory, the University of Southern California, and the University of Washington, Seattle, as well as directing the Contemporary Group, 1966–1997. He is an active jazz and avant-garde musician known as Bill Smith in jazz and William O. Smith in classical music. He is lauded as a virtuoso clarinetist with an astonishing technique. As a jazz performer, he is an adventurous and important soloist.[1]

Smith's oeuvre is about 131 pieces for chamber groups and jazz ensembles, including 106 that include the clarinet.[2] Fifty selected clarinet works are listed on his

---

[1] Ian Mitchell, "Smith, William O.," *Grove Music Online*; Phillip Rehfeldt, *New Directions for Clarinet*, rev. ed. (Berkeley: University of California Press, 1994), 95. Excerpts of reviews. [Online] Available: http://faculty .washington.edu/bills/wos_excerpts.html. [October 24, 2015].

[2] See the lists of Smith's compositions in Phillip Rehfeldt, "William O. Smith," *The Clarinet* 7, no. 3 (Spring

website.[3] Probably the best known is his excellent *Five Pieces for Clarinet Alone* (1963).[4] His contributions to the clarinet's technique, timbre, and sound capabilities are immense. Mitchell writes, "I know of no other person who has exploited the potential of an instrument to such an extent."[5] Clarinetist and composer, Eric Mandat, writes, "To merely state that Bill Smith has done more and continues to do more to develop the musical possibilities of the clarinet's technical possibilities than any other clarinetist/composer in our instrument's history only scratches the surface of his vibrancy."[6]

From 1946, Smith worked with Dave Brubeck at Mills College, was a cofounder of the Dave Brubeck Octet, and was responsible for many of the group's arrangements. His *Schizophrenic Scherzo* (1947) is, "one of the first successful integrations of modern jazz and classical procedures, a style which later became known as third stream."[7] Smith began experimenting with unusual clarinet sonorities after hearing double stops (now known as multiphonics) in Luciano Berio's *Sequenza for Solo Flute*, performed by Severino Gazzelloni on May 10, 1960, at the Monday Evening Concerts in Los Angeles.[8] The same year, he was invited by Otto Luening to work at the Columbia-Princeton Electronic Music Studio in New York. The result was *Improvisation for Clarinet and Recorded Clarinet* which explored transformations of clarinet sounds electronically or acoustically. Smith's first composition using these effects was *Five Pieces for Flute and Clarinet* (1961), but since the techniques were so new, he did not include written fingerings in the published score.[9] During his second Guggenheim Fellowship in Rome in 1960, Smith compiled a card file of 262 multiphonic sounds, fingerings, and level of difficulty, the earliest listing of clarinet multiphonics.[10] Smith provided useful comments about them in a January 1976 letter to Rehfeldt:

1980): 42–44; Linda L. Pierce, "William O. Smith I.C.S. 1987 Commission," *The Clarinet* 14, no. 4 (Summer 1987): 28; Rehfeldt, *New Directions for Clarinet*, 96–98.

[3] William O. Smith, Bill Smith. [Online] Available: http://faculty.washington.edu/bills/published.html. [October 24, 2015].

[4] William O. Smith, *Five Pieces for Clarinet Alone*, London: Universal Edition, 1963.

[5] Ian Mitchell, "An American Attitude of Adventure," *Clarinet and Saxophone* 21, no. 3 (1996): 41.

[6] Kathryn Hallgrimson Suther, "Two Sides of William O. 'Bill' Smith," part II, Interview Conclusion and Admirer Tributes, *The Clarinet* 25, no. 1 (November–December 1997): 47.

[7] Rehfeldt, ibid., 95.

[8] Barbara Joan Seitz, "The History and Significance of the Concert Series Evenings on the Roof, 1938–1954" (M.M. thesis, Indiana University, 1971), 98; William O. Smith, "Contemporary Clarinet Sonorities," *Selmer Bandwagon*, no. 67 (1973), 12; Deborah F. Bish, "A Biography of William O. Smith: The Composition of a Life" (D.M.A. diss., Arizona State University, 2005), 50.

[9] Bish, ibid., 52.

[10] William O. Smith, "Master Class: *Variants for Solo Clarinet*," *The Clarinet* 28, no. 3 (June 2001): 4; Bish, ibid., 51; Rehfeldt, *New Directions for Clarinet*, 99. A copy of the card file of Smith's multiphonics, with fingerings when necessary and comments, is reproduced in Rehfeldt, ibid., 100–21.

I've never been sure how many of the multiphonics I've found were practical for other clarinet players. For some reason the mulitphonics over a low E seem very difficult for others to play and I've sometimes wondered if my jazz background (especially throat control in the use of glissandi, etc.) has given me a set of peculiar characteristics (especially in terms of throat flexibility) that are not typical of those clarinetists trained only in the classical tradition. I've found that a new and not-too-hard reed facilitates the production of multiphonics, in general, and those which contain high notes, in particular. The mouthpiece I use has a slightly more open lay than most classical players use, but is quite a bit narrower than I would use if I were playing jazz exclusively.[11]

Smith's first composition using avant garde techniques is *Variants for Solo Clarinet*. It is a set of six miniatures highlighting different tone colors by utilizing two or more techniques per movement. Smith's performance of *Variants* in New York amazed the critic, Eric Salzman:

William O. Smith's unbelievable (literally) *Variants for Solo Clarinet*…, played by himself, must be heard to be believed—double, even triple stops; pure whistling harmonics; tremolo growls and burbles; ghosts of tones, shrill screams of sounds, weird echoes, whispers and clarinet twitches; the thinnest of thin, pure line; then veritable avalanches of bubbling, burbling sound. Completely impossible, except that it happened; with that kind of playing, who needs electronic music?[12]

The score of *Variants* is written in proportional notation without bar lines or time signatures. The duration of its notes is specified by their spacing, and the tempo and mood of each movement are reflected in the movement title. "The rhythm of the notes is unspecified, allowing the performer as much freedom as possible."[13] A preface, in English and German, provides essential explanations about techniques: key vibrato; interrupted tones using legato tonguing; cork in the bell for muted notes; color changes using cork mute; key clicks; air sounds; lip glissandi, tremolos, and trills; multiphonics producing several notes at once, with a list of the resulting tone quality; humming to produce double stops; and two note tremolos with added fingering, producing a color change.[14]

---

[11] Rehfeldt, ibid., 99.

[12] Eric Salzman, review of Smith recital, *New York Herald Tribune*, March 14, 1964; cited by Bish, ibid., 52.

[13] Smith, "Master Class," 4; William O. Smith, "Preface," in *Variants for Solo Clarinet* (London: Universal Edition, 1967), [4]; Nicholas J. Valenziano, "Twenty-One Avant-Garde Compositions for Clarinet Published Between 1964 and 1972: Notational Practices and Performance Techniques" (D.M.A. diss., University of Missouri–Kansas City, 1973), 46, 48–49.

[14] Smith, "Preface," 1–3.

Each of the six miniatures makes skillful use of new (at the time and presently for many clarinetists and listeners) techniques, sounds, and colors, and may be heard as a series of contrasting sounds and timbres.[15] The length of *Variants* varies from five to eight minutes, but within this time there are a number of technical challenges for the player. Smith recorded this work and it is invaluable to hear his musical approach, fine tone quality, and controlled technique.[16]

The first movement, "Singing," is six phrases separated by breath marks that are grouped into an arch form, ABCDB¹A¹. Phrases one (A) and six (A¹) are similar in melodic movement and use key tremolo and multiphonics; phrases two (B) and five (B¹) both use multiphonics in the fourth and fifth notes of their phrases; and phrases three (C) and four (D) are the mid-point of the movement.[17] It begins *pp*, includes key vibrato (indicated by trilling the key in parentheses) and multiphonics, shown by two bracketed notes with a fingering below, even though other pitches may be heard within these bracketed notes (Ex. 29.1). Smith writes that key vibrato is both, "an easy and effective technique.... [it] can be used throughout most of the clarinet range and consists simply of finding a note approximately a quarter tone lower than the main pitch. Trilling between these two pitches produces a vibrato quite unlike normal vibrato."[18] Crescendos and decrescendos are notated with graphs. Throughout the work, phrases are indicated by breath marks.[19]

EXAMPLE 29.1. Smith, *Variants for Solo Clarinet*, first movement, Singing.

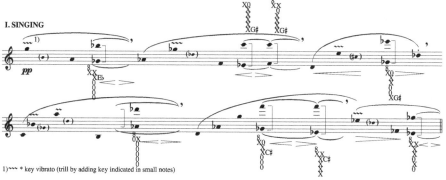

---

[15] Ian Mitchell, "William O. Smith—Musical Pioneer: A Look at the Work of One of America's Most Inventive Musicians," in *The Versatile Clarinet,* ed. Roger Heaton (New York: Routledge, 2006), 80–81.

[16] The recording is accessible though Smith's website. [Online] Available: http://faculty.washington.edu/bills/index.html. [October 24, 2015].

[17] Herbert A. Matthys, Jr., "New Performance Techniques in Selected Solo Clarinet Works of William O. Smith, John Eaton, Donald Martino, and Paul Zonn" (D.M. diss., Indiana University, 1982), 2.

[18] Smith, "Contemporary Clarinet Sonorities," 14.

[19] Dean William Turner, "A Survey of Four Clarinet Compositions by William O. Smith: As an Introductory Source of Contemporary Clarinet Performance Techniques" (Ph.D. diss., Michigan State University, 1975), 30.

The second movement, Aggressive, is nine phrases written in ternary form with a codetta, A (phrases 1–3), B (phrase 4), A¹ (phrases 5–7), and codetta (phrases 8–9). The A¹ section combines techniques played in the A and B sections.[20] The A section begins with a *fp* and while the clarinetist plays one note he or she hums or sings another to create a multiphonic, notated in B♭ on a second line below the first. Two multiphonics are written with crescendo and decrescendo graphs. The multiphonics are rougher and louder here than in the first movement, but at the end of the movement are soft. Smith observes that, "Care should be taken that the played note does not predominate over the sung pitch. Listen carefully to both sounds in order to avoid the tendency for the hummed note to be too weak in volume. The player will find that when the two notes form a small interval, rough beats will result, producing an effect resembling flutter tongue."[21] Smith suggests, "If the voice range is too low, it may be sung up an octave."[22] Matthys suggests practicing humming and playing each line separately before combining them.[23]

The third movement, "Nervous," is fifteen phrases in three sections, A (phrases 1–3), B (phrases 4–9), and A¹ (phrases 10–15). "The melodic movement is primarily half steps or major seconds with octave displacement except for muted high notes which exhibit cadential qualities."[24] "The movement alternates between quiet events such as muted altissimo notes, *f* repeated tongued notes, and large leaps between registers."[25] All of the muted notes are produced by fingering a B4.[26] A cork mute is in the bell throughout the movement. It starts *f* on a legato tongued E_6 resolving to a muted D_6 produced by using the fingering for B4. Other effects are: grace notes in the high register to chalumeau notes, *fp* interrupted tones or tongued legato notes, and several harmonics all fingered as D_6, but sounding an octave higher at D7, E7, and B7. At the end of the movement, each of the D_6s have a different fingering, producing a different timbre. The glissandi between these notes vary in length, becoming progressively wider, played with the throat and lips only.[27]

Smith notes, "A cork large enough to fit snugly into the bell works well for me. It is necessary to devise fingering covering a maximum number of holes in order to obtain the best effect from the mute. In addition to producing changes of color, the

[20] Matthys, ibid., 2.

[21] Smith, ibid., 13. For suggestions on producing multiphonics, see Smith, "Master Class," 4; Elsa Ludwig-Verdehr, "A Practical Approach to New and Avant-Garde Clarinet Music and Techniques," *The Clarinet* 7, no. 2 (Winter 1980): 13–14.

[22] Smith, "Master Class," 4.

[23] Mathys, ibid., 6.

[24] Mathys, ibid., 2.

[25] Matthys, ibid., 2.

[26] Smith, ibid., 5.

[27] Smith, ibid., 6.

mute facilitates extremely high notes. Also, it may prove useful to place the teeth directly on the reed."[28] Smith uses, "a cork about 2½" in diameter with two or three small slits along the sides to allow a bit of air to escape. It should go into the bell far enough to produce the D_6 when fingering B4. It should also produce C5 when fingering that note. It may be necessary to lip the C down a bit. It is also possible to obtain the muted effect by stopping the bell against the calf of the leg or against the top of a table or chair seat."[29]

The fourth movement, "Tranquil," uses trills with the register key, multiphonics, and trilled multiphonics. There are two types of trilled multiphonics. The first uses trills on the highest note of the multiphonic; the second uses trills on the lowest note of the multiphonic. Turner provides performance advice on producing these trills, including, "relax the embouchure more than usual; maintain a very relaxed throat position; use a forward jaw placement; make air pressure as light as possible."[30] The combination of trills and multiphonics creates an eerie quality. This movement is nine phrases in ABA[1] form. The A section (phrases 1–4) includes the bottom trill with multiphonics and the top trill with multiphonics; the B section (phrases 5–7) alternates the top trill with multiphonics and the bottom trill with multiphonics; and the A[1] section (phrases 8–9) highlights the bottom trill with multiphonics.

The fifth movement, "Brilliant," is *f* and fast throughout, with upward and downward glissandi, and two multiphonics. It is twelve phrases in ternary form with a coda. The A section includes a multiphonic followed by glissandi sweeps (phrase 1); B has two and three slurred notes (phrases 2–3); AB has two and three slurred notes (phrases 4–9); and the coda (phrases 10–12) ends with three slurred and three tongued notes to a multiphonic, upward glissando, and a multiphonic. The phrases include ascending and descending ninths, and ascending and descending sevenths.[31] Smith remarks in a footnote in the score, "In this piece all notes slurred in groups of two or three should be played very fast."[32] It is virtuosic and remarkable.

The sixth movement, "Dramatic," uses flutter tongue, upward glissandi, color changes, tremolos with keys depressed, tremolos with double notes, harmonics producing D7 and F7, and (while playing tremolos), the performer depresses touches rapidly enough to create key clicks. The movement's form is tripartite, ABA[1] with eight phrases, A (phrases 1–4), B (phrase 5), and A[1] (phrases 6–8). None of the phrases is repeated; the tremolo is used frequently on different notes. The A[1] section is varied by pitch level, rearranging the phrases, and producing additional key

[28] Smith, "Contemporary Clarinet Sonorities," 14.
[29] Smith, "Master Class," 5–6.
[30] Turner, ibid., 47–49, here 48.
[31] Matthys, ibid., 3.
[32] Smith, "Variants for Solo Clarinet," [7].

clicks.[33] Key clicks are an easy and effective technique, especially using the low F3 and E3 keys, producing a percussive effect. In order to make the clicks audible, the third finger may be used instead of the little finger.[34] A color change occurs when a tremolo is played between F♯4 and E4 and keys depressed for low F3 and E3.[35] The unusual sounds and effects are striking.

In a 1984 interview, Smith stated that *Variants* cannot be played exactly as written each time it is performed, but hoped that in the future it would be easy to perform, and clarinetists could play it as printed. He mentioned that, "he would put a Brahms sonata and his *Variants* in the same program without thinking about it."[36]

Smith's *Variants for Solo Clarinet* is an early work which includes a number of compositional techniques that are commonly written during the late twentieth and early twenty-first centuries. It is a classic of the early avant-garde clarinet literature, musically interesting, and well written. It presents many challenges of technique for the advanced clarinetist, which, with study, can be learned and performed reliably. The student will profit by studying Smith's recording of this work, which is a superb example of a musical and convincing performance. It is best played in a small room rather than a large hall to facilitate hearing the softer multiphonics and subtle quality of the sonorities.

---

[33] Mathys, ibid., 4.

[34] Smith, "Contemporary Clarinet Sonorities," 14; Smith, "Master Class," 7.

[35] Smith, "Variants for Solo Clarinet," [7].

[36] Ian Mitchell, "Profile of William O. Smith," *Clarinet and Saxophone* 9, no. 1 (1984): 10, 14.

30 Louis Spohr, *Concerto for Clarinet and Orchestra, op. 26*

Date of composition: 1808

First edition/ modern editions: Louis Spohr, *Premier Concerto pour la Clarinette*, Leipzig: A. Kühnel, 1812; Louis Spohr, *Orchester, op. 26*, ed. Friedrich Leinert, Kassel: Bärenreiter, 1957 (piano and clarinet), 1985 (orchestral score)

Dedicatee/first performer: Johann Simon Hermstedt; Johann Simon Hermstedt, clarinet

Date/place of first performance: June 16, 1809; Sondershausen, Germany

Orchestral instrumentation: First and second violins, violas, cellos, basses, two flutes, two oboes, two bassoons, two E♭ horns, two C trumpets, and timpani in C and G

LOUIS SPOHR (1784–1859), a German composer, violinist, and conductor, was regarded by many of his contemporaries as on the same level as Haydn, Mozart, and Beethoven. "Later judgments place his works at a lower status and Spohr's works are understood to have embraced classical forms with the structural and harmonic experiments of nineteenth century Romanticism."[1] Spohr's harmonic and compositional technique is known to have influenced several prominent Romantic composers, including Richard Wagner, Frédéric Chopin, and Felix Mendelssohn.[2]

Spohr wrote significant works in several genres: violin concertos; opera; oratorio; chamber music for strings, harp, winds, and piano; piano solos; lieder; part songs; solo songs; and choral works. He wrote four clarinet concertos for Johann Simon

---

[1] Clive Brown, "Spohr, Louis," *Grove Music Online*.
[2] Stephen K. Johnston, "The Clarinet Concertos of Louis Spohr" (D.M.A. diss., University of Maryland, 1972), 97; Clive Brown, *Louis Spohr: A Critical Biography* (Cambridge: Cambridge University Press, 1984), 262–63.

Hermstedt (1778–1846): *Concerto no. 1 in C Minor, op. 26* (1808), *Concerto no. 2 in Eb Major, op. 57* (1810), *Concerto no. 3 in F Minor, WoO. 19* (1821), and *Concerto no. 4 in E Minor WoO. 20* (1828). He wrote three works for clarinet and piano, *Variations on a Theme from Alruna*, WoO. 15 (1809), *Potpourri on Themes from P. von Winter*, op. 80 (1811), and *Fantasia and Variations on a Theme of Danzi*, op. 81, *for string quartet and clarinet or clarinet and piano* (1814).[3]

In 1796, Spohr studied music and violin in Brunswick, was appointed chamber musician at the Brunswick Court in 1799, and 1802–1804, studied violin with Franz Eck. In 1805, Spohr was appointed Konzertmeister in Gotha. The next year, he married the harpist Dorothea Scheidler. In 1808, Duke Günther Friedrich Karl I of Sondershausen commissioned a clarinet concerto from Spohr for Hermstedt, the leader of the Duke's wind band or Harmoniemusik. Spohr's reaction appears in his two volume *Autobiography* (1860–1861):

> In one of these concerts [in Gotha], Mr. Hermstedt, director of music to the Duke of Sondershausen, performed on the clarinet and caused a sensation by his virtuosity, already at that time highly developed. He [the Duke] had come to Gotha to commission a clarinet concerto, for which the Duke was willing to pay a considerable sum on the condition that Hermstedt became the owner of the manuscript. I was very willing to agree, especially as Hermstedt's great skill, as well as his beautiful tone and perfect intonation, gave me the opportunity to give full rein to my imagination. After Hermstedt had helped me to familiarize myself with the technique of the instrument, my work proceeded rapidly and was completed within a few weeks. That was the origin of the C minor concerto which Kühnel engraved some years later [1812] as op. 26, and with which Hermstedt was so successful on his tours that it is not too much to say that he owes much of his reputation to it. I myself handed it to him on a visit to Sondershausen at the end of January [1809] and gave him some hints as to how it should be performed.[4]

In the preface to the Kühnel edition, Spohr states that the clarinetist must own an eleven-key instrument and provides insight into his relationship with Hermstedt and his view of the clarinet:

---

[3] Brown, "Spohr, Louis, Works" *Grove Music Online*; Stephen K. Johnston, "The Clarinet Concertos of Louis Spohr: Some Notes on Performance and Importance," *The Clarinet* 5, no. 4 (1978): 25; Folker Göthel, *Thematisch-bibliographisches Verzeichnis der Werke von Louis Spohr* (Tutzing: Schneider, 1981), 135–36.

[4] Louis Spohr, *Lebenserinnerungen. Erstmals ungekürzt nach den autographen Aufzeichnungen*, ed. F. Göthel (Tutzing: H. Schneider, 1968), 1:121–22; trans. Eric Hoeprich, *The Clarinet* (New Haven, CT: Yale University Press, 2008), 147–48.

I herewith present clarinetists with a concerto, composed two years ago for my friend, musical director Hermstedt of Sondershausen. At that time my knowledge of the instrument was more or less confined to its compass, so that I took too little account of its weaknesses and wrote some passage which, at first glance, may seem impossible of execution. However, Mr. Hermstedt, far from asking me to make changes, sought rather to perfect his instrument, and by constant application, soon attained such mastery that his clarinet produced no more jarring, muffled or uncertain notes. In subsequent compositions for him I was able, therefore, to give free rein to my pen and had no need to fear that anything might be impossible to him.... May this concerto induce other composers for the clarinet (surely the most perfect of all wind instruments if played in the way that Mr. Hermstedt does) to avoid the monotony of most existing clarinet compositions, which largely consist of the repetition of technically simple and terribly trite soloistic passages, and to look for wider fields for an instrument so rich in compass and expression.[5]

Spohr later gained fame for his violin concertos, operas, oratorios, and chamber music, particularly for stringed instruments. He was a kapellmeister in Frankfurt 1817–1820 and in Kassel 1825–1857. In later years he was also highly regarded as a conductor of music festivals.[6] By that time, Hermstedt was a renowned soloist and one of the greatest nineteenth-century clarinetists.

Hermstedt worked with a clarinet maker, probably Heinrich Grenser of Dresden, who by 1809 was making eleven-key clarinets. In 1821, Hermstedt contacted the maker, Johann Heinrich Gottlieb Streitwolf of Göttingen, who made a fourteen-key ebony clarinet with a tuning slide between the upper joint and ivory barrel, and a silver mouthpiece with a gold inlay.[7] The friendship between Spohr and Hermstedt, and Hermstedt, Grenser, and Streitwolf, highlights the important relationships among composer, player, and instrument makers and how their associations influenced the development of the clarinet and its music.[8] Spohr was able to extend the clarinet's technical and musical possibilities because of Hermstedt's talent and willingness to perfect the technical and musical hurdles of this concerto.

[5] Oskar Kroll, *The Clarinet*, rev. and with a repertory Diethard Riehm, trans. Hilda Morris, ed. Anthony Baines (New York: Taplinger, 1968), 72–73. German text reproduced in Göthel, *Thematisch-Bibliographisches Verzeichnis der Werke von Louis Spohr*, 42.

[6] Clive Brown, "Louis Spohr," *Grove Music Online*.

[7] Hans Eberhardt, "Johann Simon Hermstedt 1778–1845: Seine Bedeutung als Klarinettenvirtuose," *Mitteilungen des Vereins für deutsche Geschichte und Altertumskunde in Sondershausen* 10 (1940): 135–37. Hermstedt's fourteen-key B♭ clarinet (ca. 1830), attributed to Johann Gottlieb Heinrich Streitwolf of Göttingen, has survived; Heike Fricke, "Johann Simon Hermstedt und seine Klarinetten," *Rohrblatt* 29, no. 3 (2014): 136–39.

[8] Albert R. Rice, *The Clarinet in the Classical Period* (New York: Oxford University Press, 2003), 5.

The *Concerto for Clarinet and Orchestra, op. 26* is a fascinating example of an early Romantic clarinet concerto. A notable feature is the use of a single melodic cell played by the strings, repeated throughout by the solo clarinet and orchestra (Ex. 30.1).[9] The first movement has a modified sonata-allegro form with an orchestral introduction, episode 1, and episode 2–coda. (See Chart 30.1.) An introspective fourteen-measure Adagio orchestral introduction begins with a timpani roll, followed by a solo oboe playing four measures of a yearning A theme in a slow tempo. Spohr skillfully builds on this A theme in the faster exposition and replaces the usual double exposition of the typical Classical concerto.[10] At the exposition, Allegro (m. 15), quarter note = 108,[11] the strings play eight measures of the A^1 theme, answered by the solo clarinet (mm. 23–40) with an expanded A^1 theme. This theme expertly uses mixed staccato and slurred triplet eighth and sixteenth notes within a clarinet compass of A3 to G_6. Played frequently are sixteenth note chromatic scales, arpeggios, and diatonic scales. Stretto occurs in the exposition among the orchestral flute, oboe, cello, and clarinet (mm. 61–66). A particularly beautiful effect is achieved in measures 69–72 when the flute and horn play part of the A^1 theme while the clarinet plays a soft chromatic run in the clarion register.[12] A striking moment arises after a diminuendo on a downward sixteenth note chromatic run, with triplet-eighth-note arpeggios from E3 to C7 (mm. 78–80), the highest practical note for the clarinet at the time. The first horn plays the A^1 theme in canon with the clarinet (mm. 101–105), and episode 1 presents part of the A^1 theme with strings and winds, alternating solos between horn, flute, and oboe (mm. 131–150). This slows the rhythmic activity and prepares for the development section.

EXAMPLE 30.1. Spohr, *Concerto for Clarinet and Orchestra, op. 26,* first movement, violin part, mm. 15-18; clarinet solo, mm. 67-70.

[9] Brown, *Louis Spohr: A Critical Biography,* 51.

[10] Maurice F. Powell, "Spohr's Music for the Clarinet," *Spohr Journal* 1, no. 3 (Spring 1972): 6.

[11] Suggested by the author.

[12] Wen-Mi Chen, "An Analysis of Sonata Form in Clarinet Concertos by Wolfgang Amadeus Mozart, Louis Spohr, and Carl Maria von Weber" (D.M.A. diss., University of Cincinnati, 2012), 35–36.

Section:	Orchestral introduction	Exposition	Episode 1
Starts at m.	1 Adagio	15 Allegro	131
No. of mm.	14	116	20
Tonalities	C, Ab, c	c, Ab, Eb, C, Gb, Eb	Eb
Themes	A	A¹, fig.	episode 1 (A¹)

Section:	Development	Recapitulation	Episode 2-Coda
Starts at m.	151 (E)	202 (H)	295–314
No. of mm.	51	93	20
Tonalities	Eb, Bb, Eb	c, C, Eb, c, C	C
Themes	B	A²	episode 2-coda

CHART 30.1 Spohr, *Concerto for Clarinet and Orchestra, op. 26*: Structural analysis, first movement, Adagio-Allegro.

The development section (**E**, Bärenreiter edition) states the calm and expressive B theme in Eb major, modulating to the dominant Bb major, and back to Eb major. The B theme is varied by sixteenth-note arpeggios and articulated notes. Thematic development also occurs in transition and closing passages.[13] The recapitulation in C minor at **H** states the A² theme (mm. 202–219), then modulates to a variety of tonalities as clarinet chromatic scales and arpeggios play to high A_6. Episode 2–coda begins with a *f* orchestral section (mm. 295–307) that decrescendos to *p* followed by *mf* clarinet downward chromatic eighth-note triplets (mm. 308–309) from D_6 to D4, and arpeggios in the chalumeau register quieting to a *pp* F♯3 half note (mm. 310–314).[14]

The second movement is a calm, Adagio, quarter note = 60,[15] in ternary form with an eloquent clarinet solo accompanied only by strings. (See Chart 30.2.) The orchestral writing is subordinate to the solo throughout the movement. Its intimate A theme is beautifully varied with thirty-second note and sixteenth note passages in the clarion register, and the chalumeau register is briefly and sensitively used.[16] The thirty-second notes and ornamentation are similar to their use in an operatic, coloratura soprano aria. It is the shortest second movement of Spohr's four clarinet concertos and is a lovely contrast to the virtuosic first and third movements.[17]

---

[13] Johnston, ibid., 80–82.

[14] Johnston, ibid., 77–84, 99; Chen, ibid., 41–42, 113.

[15] Suggested by the author.

[16] Colin Lawson plays the second movement on a Daniel Bangham copy of a ten-key Heinrich Grenser clarinet with the Hanover Band, BMG Entertainment International UK & Ireland Ltd, 1998.

[17] Johnston, ibid., 77, 83.

Section:	A	B	A¹
Starts at m.	1 Adagio	9	23–39
No. of mm.	8	14	17
Tonalities	A♭	E♭	A♭
Themes	A	B	A¹

CHART 30.2 Spohr, *Concerto for Clarinet and Orchestra, op. 26*: Structural analysis, second movement, Adagio.

The third movement, Vivace, quarter note = 116,[18] is a modified rondo with a coda. (See Chart 30.3.) It begins with two sixteenth-note pickups to a quick eight-measure A theme in C minor, consisting of sixteenth and eighth notes, varied throughout the movement. Several wide leaps of over an octave in eighth notes (mm. 28–32) add virtuosity to the melody. After a fermata (m. 72), the clarinet presents an E♭ major dolce *p* B theme in measure 73 at B. In section B and throughout, the winds play thematic material while the clarinet solo plays arpeggios, sixteenth notes, and leaps (mm. 92–96). After a one measure ritardando (m. 100), the clarinet turns to a cheerful B¹ theme at C, leading to virtuoso sixteenth-note triplets up to high A_6 (mm. 112–124). In section A¹, the clarinet briefly plays the C minor A¹ theme at **E** (mm. 150–158), answered by the orchestra's A¹ theme and after a one measure rest at **F** (m. 168), the clarinet plays the C theme. The C section features mixed staccato and slurring, and a rhythmic figure, effectively combining sixteenth, triplet eighth notes, and syncopation (mm. 170–171, 174–175). After a fermata (m. 193) the *p* B² theme in measure 194 at **G**, plays in C major. After the B³ theme at **H** (m. 221), virtuoso triplets play several wide leaps up to a high $F\sharp_6$ (mm. 234–245) and wide eighth-note staccato leaps (mm. 269–273). In the A² section (m. 277), there are two sixteenth pickups to the eight measure A² theme in C minor (mm. 277–285) repeated by the orchestra (mm. 285–293). After a one-measure rest, the coda (**K**) begins with a sprightly clarinet *pp* C¹ theme for four measures; the orchestra answers, and the clarinet plays motives from the A theme. A poco a poco ritardando (m. 310) slows the tempo, ending the movement after a cello solo sixteenth-note run echoed by the clarinet in the chalumeau register.

The composer Carl Maria von Weber reviewed a concert in which Hermstedt played Spohr's first concerto on October 3, 1812. His comments reveal a high opinion of Hermstedt's playing and of the *concerto*:

---

[18] Suggested by the author.

Section:	A	B	A¹		
Starts at m.	1 Vivace	73 (**B**)	150 (**E**)		
No. of mm.	72	77	18		
Tonalities	c, E♭, c, D	E♭	c, E♭		
Themes	A	B, B¹	A¹		

Section:	C	B¹	A²	Coda	
Starts at m.	168 (**F**)	194 (**G**)	277	295 (**K**)–320	
No. of mm.	26	83	18	26	
Tonalities	C, G	C	c	c	
Themes	C	B², B³	A²	C¹, (A)	

CHART 30.3 Spohr, *Concerto for Clarinet and Orchestra, op. 26*: Structural analysis, third movement, Vivace.

[Romberg's D major Overture] was followed by a performance of Spohr's superb C minor Clarinet Concerto played by the justly admired Hermstedt, to whose reputation no words of mine can add anything. It must be said that perhaps on this occasion he seemed to outshine himself particularly in the Adagio; and when he has traveled a little and heard outstanding singers, he may well give a little additional roundness to his own tone, after which perfection will be within his grasp. As far as the composition was concerning, it was the Rondo that the present writer most admired.[19]

Spohr's *Concerto for Clarinet and Orchestra, op. 26*, represents the most technically advanced concerto of its time; it is musically sensitive, and has a well-balanced orchestration. An excellent recital piece, it remains a technical and musical challenge, and is among the most important and musically satisfying concertos of the early nineteenth century.

---

[19] Carl Maria von Weber, *Writings on Music*, trans. Martin Cooper, ed. John Warrack (Cambridge: Cambridge University Press, 1981), 120.

31 Johann Stamitz, *Concerto for Clarinet and Orchestra*

Date of composition: 1754–1755

Modern editions: Johann Stamitz, *Concerto in B-flat major for Clarinet and Strings*, ed. Peter Gradenwitz (piano and clarinet), New York: MCA Music, 1953; Johann Stamitz, *Konzert für Klarinette B-dur mit Streichorchester und zwei Hörnern*, ed. Walter Lebermann, Mainz: B. Schott's Söhne, 1967 (piano and clarinet; orchestral score)

Dedicatee/first performer: Not indicated; Not known

Date/place of first performance: Not known; not known

Dates/places/performers of first modern performances: 1936, London, Frederick Thurston, clarinet (clarinet with string quartet); April 3, 1951, New York, Wallace Shapiro, clarinet, Little Orchestra Society, Thomas K. Scherman, conductor (clarinet and orchestra)[1]

Orchestral instrumentation: First and second violins, violas, cellos, string basses, two flutes, and two optional B♭ horns

JOHANN STAMITZ (1717–1757) was a German composer, violinist, and teacher. He was one of the earliest composers of the Classical symphony and important in establishing the Mannheim Court Orchestra as a leading center for orchestral music. He wrote at least fifty-eight symphonies, sixty-five orchestral trios, and numerous concertos for violin, flute, oboe, clarinet, and harpsichord.[2]

---

[1] Peter Gradenwitz, "Concerto Find: Story Behind the Uncovering of Stamitz Work for Clarinet and Orchestra," *New York Times* (April 1, 1951), section 7, 103; Ronald Thomas Lee, "Background Studies for an Authentic Performance of Johann Stamitz's Concerto in B-flat Major for Clarinet and Strings" (M.M. thesis, University of Michigan, 1966), 62; Peter Gradenwitz, *Johann Stamitz: Leben-Umwelt-Werke* (Wilhelmshaven: Hinrichshofen, 1984), 2: 318.

[2] Eugene K. Wolf, "Stamitz, Johann," *Grove Music Online*.

Stamitz attended school in Německý Brod, the Jesuit Gymasium in Jihlava, and Prague University. He established himself as a violin virtuoso and was engaged by the Mannheim Court Orchestra in 1741. He performed on the violin, viola d'amore, cello, and string bass. In 1745 or early 1746, Stamitz was made Konzertmeister, and in 1750, was appointed director of instrumental music. His main duties were composing and performing orchestral and chamber music, and leading and developing the Mannheim Orchestra. Stamitz was also an important teacher.[3] In 1754 and 1755, Stamitz was in Paris where he appeared at the Concert Spirtuel; he lived at Passy in the palace of Alexandre Jean-Joseph Le Riche de la Pouplinière, a wealthy amateur whose orchestra he conducted; and he appeared at other pubic concerts in Paris including the Concert Italien. Many of his orchestral and chamber works were published in Paris during the 1750s and 1760s, and some in London during the 1770s.[4]

Stamitz was well-known for his successful recruiting and training of fine orchestral players at the Mannheim Court as mentioned by the English music historian, Charles Burney, in 1775, "Indeed there are more solo players, and good composers in this, than perhaps any other orchestra in Europe, it is an army of generals, equally fit to plan a battle, as to fight it."[5]

Stamitz' contribution as a composer, particularly in his symphonies and orchestral trios, is summarized by Burney:

He [Stamitz], like another Shakespeare, broke through all difficulties and discouragements; and, as the eye of one pervaded all nature, the other, without quitting nature, pushed art further than anyone had done before him; his genius was truly original, bold, and nervous; invention, fire, and contrast, in the quick movements; a tender, graceful, and insinuating melody, in the slow [movements]; together with the ingenuity and richness of the accompaniments, characterise his productions; all replete with great effects, produced by an enthusiasm of genius, refined, but not repressed by cultivation.[6]

In 1933, while a student in Berlin, Peter Gradenwitz (1910–2001) discovered parts for a clarinet concerto marked, "Sign. Stamitz" in music parcels sent to him from the

---

[3] Wolf, ibid.

[4] Wolf, ibid.; Eugene K. Wolf, *The Symphonies of Johann Stamitz: A Study in the Formation of the Classic Style with a Thematic Catalogue of the Symphonies and Orchestral Trios* (Boston: M. Nijhoff, 1981), 362–437.

[5] Charles Burney, *The Present State of Music in Germany, the Netherlands, and United Provinces. Or, the Journal of a Tour through these Countries, Undertaken to Collect Materials for a General History of Music*, 2nd ed. (London: T. Becket, J. Robson, G. Robinson, 1775), 1:95.

[6] Burney, ibid., 2: 12–13.

Thurn and Taxis archive in Regensburg, Germany.[7] In a 1936 article, he produced a short style analysis of each movement and compared the work to concertos by Carl Stamitz written during the 1770s and by Michel ca. 1800, concluding that this concerto was written by Johann Stamitz.[8] This attribution has subsequently been accepted; it is the earliest concerto known for the B♭ clarinet.[9] Newhill suggested that Stamitz wrote this concerto for Jean Gaspard Procksch,[10] a Czech clarinetist, employed 1751–1762 by La Pouplinière and the Paris Opèra; 1763–1771 by the Prince de Conti; at the Paris Opèra 1771–1775; and as clarinet teacher 1775–1783.[11] The *Concerto for Clarinet and Orchestra* may have been played during the 1750s by a woodwind player at the Mannheim court who doubled on the clarinet.[12]

The early date of this concerto suggests that it may have been performed on a two- or three-key clarinet. However, the solo clarinet's use of D♯5 or E♭5 nine times, and C♯5 three times, including one leap, indicates that a four- or five-key clarinet with keys for these notes is technically a more likely choice. Evidence for the existence of these instruments is the fact that the earliest extant four-key clarinet (ca. 1760–1765) was constructed by a German maker living in Paris from 1750, Jean Godeffroy Geist; in addition, other makers advertised clarinets during the 1750s, such as Heinrich Carl Tölcke in Braunschweig (1751) and Jeremias Schlegel in Basel (1759). Thus, it is possible that a four- or five-key clarinet was available to players during the 1750s in Paris.[13]

---

[7] Gertraut Haberkamp, *Die Musikhandschriften der Fürst Thurn und Taxis Hofbibliothek Regensburg: Thematischer Katalog* (Munich: Henle, 1981), 329, Ms. Rtt Stamitz 9.

[8] Peter Gradenwitz, "The Beginnings of Clarinet Literature: Notes on a Clarinet Concerto by Joh. Stamitz," *Music & Letters* 17, no. 2 (April 1936): 147–49.

[9] Jiří Kratochvíl, "Koncertantní Klarinet v Českém Klasicismu," *Ziva Hudbá* 9 (1968): 317–18; John P. Newhill, "The Contribution of the Mannheim School to Clarinet Literature," *Music Review* 40, no. 2 (May 1979): 111–12; Wolf, *The Symphonies of Johann Stamitz*, 343; Wolf, "Johann Stamitz works," *Grove Music Online*; Albert R. Rice, *The Clarinet in the Classical Period* (New York: Oxford University Press, 2003), 150–52; Eric Hoeprich, *The Clarinet* (New Haven: Yale University Press, 2008), 78–79.

[10] Newhill, ibid., 111.

[11] Bernadette Gérard, "Inventaire Alphabétique des Documents Repertories Relatifs aux Musiciens Parisiens Conserve aux Archives de Paris," *Recherches sur la Musique Française Classique* 13 (1973): 209; Albert R. Rice, *The Baroque Clarinet* (Oxford: Clarendon Press, 1992), 153–54; Richard J. Viano, "By Invitation Only: Private Concerts in France During the Second Half of the Eighteenth Century," *Recherches sur la Musique Française Classique* 27 (1991–1992): 139–40; Joseph James Estock, "A Biographical Dictionary of Clarinetists Born Before 1800" (Ph.D. diss., University of Iowa, 1972), 276.

[12] Gomer J. Pound, "A Study of Clarinet Solo Concerto Literature Composed Before 1850: with Selected Items Edited and Arranged for Contemporary Use" (Ph.D. diss., Florida State University, 1965), 198–99. The Mannheim court orchestra hired two clarinetists in 1758, officially installing them in 1759. Rice, *The Clarinet in the Classical Period*, 150.

[13] Rice, ibid., 25–28, 37, 59, 150–52 Two modern players have recorded the Stamitz concerto playing original five-key clarinets: Alan Hacker in 1975 on a clarinet by George Miller, London (ca. 1780) and Hans Rudolf Stalder in 1979 on a clarinet by Henry Kusder, London (ca. 1762).

This three-movement *concerto* is written in a galant style; it exhibits recurring phrases with numerous cadences; a refined, light texture; highly ornamented and witty melodies; simple harmony; and an easy treatment of dissonance.[14] Gradenwitz observed that Stamitz uses two-part contrasting themes in many works which are also found throughout the *clarinet concerto*.[15] The Allegro moderato, first movement, quarter note = 60,[16] is in sonata-allegro form with an introduction, two episodes, and a coda. (See Chart 31.1.) It features prominent use of notes above C_6, and selective but effective use of the chalumeau register. It begins with a heroic gesture in the strings, followed by a contrasting sighing phrase.[17] The twenty-five measure introduction features terraced or immediate dynamics, dotted rhythms, triplets, and sixteenth notes. The exposition's clarinet A^1 theme, measure 26 (Schott edition), is initially accompanied by two violin parts and varied by triplet sixteenth notes. There is a rhythmic shift of the A^1 theme from the first to the third beat of measure 29 (also occurring on the third beat in episode 2, m. 81). This late Baroque device is also found in Johann Melchior Molter's D *clarinet concertos* (1750s).[18] A lyrical contrast at measure 39 occurs in the clarinet's syncopated tune with leaps, immediately varied

Section:	Introduction	Exposition	Episode 1	Development
Starts at m.	1 Allegro moderato	26	47	57
No. of mm.	25	21	10	18
Tonalities	B♭	B♭	F	F, g, F
Themes	A	A^1, fig.	A^2	B, fig.

Section:	Episode 2	Recapitulation	Coda
Starts at m.	75	85 (3rd beat)	107–114
No. of mm.	10	22	8
Tonalities	g, F	F, B♭	B♭
Themes	C, B^1	A^3, fig.	cadenza, A^4

CHART 31.1 Stamitz, *Concerto for Clarinet and Orchestra*: Structural analysis, first movement, Allegro moderato.

[14] Eugene K. Wolf, "Galant Style," *The Harvard Dictionary of Music*, 4th ed. (Cambridge: Belknap Press, 2003), 341.

[15] Gradenwitz, *Johann Stamitz*, 23, 315; Robert Austin Titus, "The Solo Music for the Clarinet in the Eighteenth Century" (Ph.D. diss., State University of Iowa, 1962), 151–52.

[16] Suggested by the author.

[17] Gradenwitz, "The Beginnings of Clarinet Literature," 147.

[18] Gradenwitz, ibid., 148; Titus, ibid., 152–53.

with sixteenth and triplet sixteenth notes. This leads into an unusual rapid flourish of thirty-second notes in measures 44–45, reminiscent of the Molter concertos.[19] An F major A^2 theme appears at episode 1 (m. 47). The development (m. 57) begins on D$_6$ with an ornamented, lyrical B theme continuing with triplet sixteenth notes. The six measure episode 2 (m. 75) uses a C theme, followed by a clarinet B^1 theme at measure 81, third beat. The recapitulation on the third beat of measure 85 begins with the A^3 theme. Arpeggios are played in the chalumeau register from G3 (m. 88), and include leaps of up to two octaves and one-third, B3 to D$_6$, at measures 98–101. In the coda, a cadenza is indicated (m. 107), and the orchestra concludes the movement with eight measures of the stately sounding A^4 theme.[20]

Gradenwitz did not find wind parts for this concerto but noted that Stamitz usually added oboes or clarinets and horns to his orchestral works to support the ensemble in tutti passages, but not in solo passages or in the second movement.[21] Lebermann in his edition, reconstructed appropriate parts for two horns but specified they are optional.

The serene-sounding Adagio second movement, quarter note = 66,[22] is in ternary form, with an introduction and coda. (See Chart 31.2.) It exhibits clear phrasing in E♭ major with short and skillful modulations to B♭ and F major, returning immediately to E♭. The strings begin in unison with a formal-sounding four-measure introduction of an eighth-note, dotted-sixteenth-note trill, thirty-second note, and two eighth notes. In section A, the clarinet A theme (m. 5) begins with a half note C$_6$

Section:	Introduction	A	B	A^1	Coda
Starts at m.	1 Adagio	5	31	38	55–58
No. of mm.	4	26	7	17	4
Tonalities	E♭	E♭, B♭, F	B♭	E♭	E♭
Themes	intro.	A	B	A^1, cadenza	coda

CHART 31.2 Stamitz, *Concerto for Clarinet and Orchestra*: Structural analysis, second movement, Adagio.

---

[19] Titus, ibid., 159; Rice, *The Baroque Clarinet*, 109–10.

[20] The author believes that the cadenza written by Gradenwitz in his edition is overtly virtuosic and out of character for this work. A more appropriate approach should emphasize scales and arpeggios.

[21] Gradenwitz, ibid., 149. Clarinet (or oboe) and horn parts in three symphonies by Stamitz are initially found in a 1758 collection of *Six Simphonies* published by Venier in Paris. Wolf, *The Symphonies of Johann Stamitz*, 36–37, 293–94; Rice, *The Clarinet in the Classical Period*, 177.

[22] Suggested by the author.

held for two measures, and accompanied by *p* strings.[23] An ornamented twenty-measure conjunct melody in the clarion register (mm. 5–24) is followed by the introductory music a fifth lower (mm. 24–30). In section B, the clarinet introduces a seven-measure B theme in B♭ major at measure 31. The clarinet A^1 theme (mm. 38–42) is elaborated with thirty-second notes and trills and followed by an endearing melody (mm. 43–50). At the fermata (m. 54) a cadenza is expected,[24] and afterward, the orchestra plays a lyrical four-measure coda.

The third movement, Poco presto in 3/8, dotted quarter note = 72,[25] is a jaunty tune using a sonata-allegro form consisting of an introduction, exposition, episode, development, recapitulation, and coda.[26] (See Chart 31.3.) The orchestral introduction introduces the A theme with two elaborations (mm. 1–28, 29–56) in a convincing and flowing manner. In the exposition (m. 57), the clarinet plays four measures of the A^1 theme, introduces some changes, and presents an impressive series of sixteenth notes in measures 87–94, with a limited compass of B4 to E$_6$. A lyrical B theme in F minor begins at measure 104, modulates to F major (m. 112) and is nicely elaborated with eighth and sixteenth notes featuring leaps. The A^2 theme in the orchestral episode in F major (m. 134) is developed with short cantabile phrases. In the development

Section:	Introduction	Exposition	Episode
Starts at m.	1 Poco presto	57	134
No. of mm.	56	77	36
Tonalities	B♭, F, B♭	B♭, f, F	F
Themes	A	A^1, fig., B, fig.	A^2

Section:	Development	Recapitulation	Coda
Starts at m.	170	213	287–314
No. of mm.	43	74	28
Tonalities	F, f, d, F, B♭	B♭, F, b♭, B♭	B♭
Themes	C	A^3, fig., B^1	A^4

CHART 31.3 Stamitz, *Concerto for Clarinet and Orchestra*: Structural analysis, third movement, Poco presto.

---

[23] Gradenwitz, *Johann Stamitz*, 315.

[24] The author believes that Gradenwitz's cadenza is romantic in character with large leaps, sforzandos, and changes in dynamics not appropriate for this work. Johann Stamitz, *Concerto in B Flat Major for Clarinet and Strings*, ed. Peter Gradenwitz (New York: MCA Music, 1953), 5.

[25] Suggested by the author.

[26] Gradenwitz, *Johann Stamitz*, 315.

(m. 170), a lyrical, conjunct eight-note C theme in F major is played by the clarinet. There is no second episode and the clarinet continues playing until the recapitulation (m. 213). The clarinet is showcased with widely spaced sixteenth-note arpeggios of almost two octaves, from clarion to chalumeau registers (mm. 226–223, 243–249), and with repeated eighth-note leaps of between one and two octaves (mm. 265–268). The B^1 theme in B♭ minor (m. 257) modulates to B♭ major. At the coda (m. 287), the orchestra joyously closes with twenty-eight measures of the A^4 theme.

Stamitz's familiarity with the compass and technique of the clarinet is remarkable. In this movement, he writes in a fluid manner taking full advantage of the beauty of the clarion register, B4 to D$_6$. In the recapitulation, his use of the chalumeau register is brief but idiomatic and effective, writing E5–C5–C4–G3 in sixteenth-note arpeggios (mm. 243–250), and in eighth notes, E3–E5–C5, F3–E5–C5; G3–E5–C5, and A3–E5–C5 (mm. 265–268).

Stamitz's *Concerto for Clarinet and Orchestra* is expertly written and musically charming. It includes some moderate technical demands, requires a solid technique, and is an excellent choice to pair with Romantic and modern works. Historically important as the earliest *concerto* for B♭ clarinet, it was likely written for a four- or five-key instrument. The galant style and assured writing makes this a pleasant and enjoyable work on the modern Boehm-system clarinet.

32 Karlheinz Stockhausen, *Der kleine Harlekin* für Klarinette, no. 42½

Date of composition: 1975

First edition: Karlheinz Stockhausen, *Der kleine Harlekin für Klarinette Werk Nr. 42½*, Kürten: Stockhausen-Verlag, 1978

Dedicatee/first performer: Suzanne Stephens; Suzanne Stephens, clarinet

Date/place of first performance: August 3, 1977; Aix-en-Provence, Centre Sirius

KARLHEINZ STOCKHAUSEN (1928–2007) was the leading German composer of the post-1945 avant garde. A pioneer in electronic music and an innovator in acoustic music, his serial compositions have redefined serialism's musical use.

In 1947, Stockhausen attended the Cologne Music School, graduating in 1951; he studied piano with Hans-Otto Schmidt-Neuhaus and composition with Frank Martin. In August 1951, Stockhausen attended the Darmstadt Summer Course for new music where he became friends with Karel Goeyvaert, a former student of Olivier Messiaen. In 1952, he studied with Messiaen in Paris and met Pierre Boulez and Pierre Schaeffer, who directed the *musique concrete* studios. Stockhausen studied percussion sounds and wrote his first tape work, *Konkrete Etüde*. In 1953, he returned to Cologne as assistant to Herbert Eimert in the electronic music studio of the West German Radio and became director in 1963. He studied phonetics and communications theory with Werner Meyer-Eppler at Bonn University 1954–1956.

By 1953, Stockhausen was established, along with Boulez and Luigi Nono, as one of the leading figures in the serialist avant garde, and from 1956 taught regularly at the Darmstadt International Summer Courses for New Music. In 1958, Stockhausen gave an extended lecture tour in the United States, and during the 1960s his work was being widely performed in Europe. He founded an instrumental ensemble which performed throughout the world until the early 1970s.[1] After *Mantra* (1970), almost all Stockhausen's works used a theme for composing that he called a formula, modified by transposing and reordering the melodies into separate moments.[2] He also adopted a personal religious-spiritual conception of music and influenced several composers after his appointment as professor of composition at the Cologne Music School 1971–1977.

Stockhausen continued to travel widely and worked at home in Kürten on a seven-part operatic cycle, *Licht* (*Light*), each part named for a day of the week. He established a publishing firm, Stockhausen-Verlag, and printed meticulous scores, including excerpts of sketches, and detailed explanations and photos pertaining to performance. These scores earned eight awards by the Deutsche Musikverlegerverband 1992–2005. In 1992, Stockhausen produced a corresponding CD of his works, and acquired the rights to earlier recordings and published scores from other companies.[3]

Stockhausen composed for the American clarinetist, Suzanne Stephens, starting in 1974 and collaborated with her in over forty compositions requiring clarinet, basset horn, or bass clarinet. These include, *Harlekin for Clarinet, no. 42* (1975); *Der kleine Harlekin for Clarinet, no. 42½* (1975); *Amour for Clarinet, no. 44* (1976); *In Freudschaft for Clarinet, no. 46* (1977); *Michaels Jugend, no. 49* (1979); *Tierkreis for Clarinet and Piano, no. 41 8/9* (1981); *Traum-Formel for Basset Horn, no. 51⅔* (1981–1982); *Evas Spiegel for Basset Horn, no. 58½ ex. 1* (1984); *Susani for Basset Horn, no. 58½ ex. 2* (1984); *Xi for Basset Horn, no. 55 ex. 2* (1986); *Ypsilon for Basset Horn, no. 59 ex. 2* (1989); and *Freia for Basset Horn, no. 64 ex. 9⅔* (1991).[4] It was one of the most fruitful collaborations between a clarinetist and composer.[5] Hoeprich notes that:

> This collaboration drew on many aspects of the composer's career (as a wind player [oboe] and *répétiteur* for dance and opera), and demonstrated his urge to encourage performers to take musical ideas and develop them in their own way. As a partner he could have had none better than Stephens, an outstanding performer and tireless promoter of the clarinet and basset horn. Her willingness

[1] Richard Toop, "Stockhausen," *Grove Music Online;* "Stockhausen, Karlheinz," *The Oxford Dictionary of Music, Oxford Music Online.*

[2] Paul Griffiths, *Modern Music and After*, 3rd ed. (Oxford: Oxford University Press, 2010), 249–50.

[3] Toop, "Stockhausen," *Grove Music Online.*

[4] Pamela Weston, *Clarinet Virtuosi of Today* (Baldock: Egon Publishers, 1989), 283; Pamela Weston, "Stockhausen's Contribution to the Clarinet and Basset Horn," *The Clarinet* 25, no. 1 (November–December 1997): 61; Richard Toop, "Karlheinz Stockhausen, Worklist," *Grove Music Online.*

[5] Pamela Weston, "Players and Composers," in *The Cambridge Companion to the Clarinet*, ed. Colin Lawson (Cambridge: Cambridge University Press, 1995), 104–105.

to explore all the dimensions of performance in these works includes new playing techniques, and special choreography and costumes.[6]

In 1975, Stockhausen adapted "The Passionate Dance" from the second section of part 6 called "Harlekin's Dance," in *Harlekin, no. 42* (about 44 minutes long) for *Der kleine Harlekin, no. 42½* (about 9 minutes long).[7]

In *Der kleine Harlekin, no. 42½*, the clarinetist wears a costume to represent a harlequin or joker (Fig. 32.1)[8] wearing dance shoes with metal plates on the soles to produce a tap when struck on the floor.[9] The clarinetist dances, moves, and beats a rhythm percussively by the feet in dialogue with the clarinet line.[10] The eight-page score is a manuscript reproduction in Stockhausen's hand. Five pages of instructions in German with English and French translations provide choreographic instructions, including movements on stage, movements of the clarinet while playing, body movements, breath marks, and where to use circular breathing. The score has a second line indicating the foot rhythm, and has nine photographs of Stephens in a harlequin leotard in dance positions, playing and holding her clarinet.[11] Alternately, this work may be performed by a clarinetist and a drummer or a clarinetist and a dancer.[12]

Stockhausen describes the little harlequin as, "a roguish, exuberant dance musician and a bubbly performing artist, who could inspire a more versatile kind of musician for the future."[13] There are many humorous and tongue-in-cheek movements that establish the harlequin's character. It is a remarkable and unique example of a performer combining the skills of clarinet playing, dance, movement, and mime in a very effective work.[14]

---

[6] Eric Hoeprich, *The Clarinet* (New Haven, CT: Yale University Press, 2008), 218.

[7] Karlheinz Stockhausen, *Harlekin: für Klarinette, Werk Nr. 42* (Kürten: Stockhausen-Verlag, 1978); David H. Odom, "A Catalog of Compositions for Unaccompanied Clarinet Published Between 1978 and 1982, with an Annotated Bibliography of Selected Works" (D.M. thesis, Florida State University, 2005), 85. Because the technical demands are very high in *Harlekin, Nr. 42*, it is not performed often. Odom, ibid., 85.

[8] This photo shows Suzanne Stephens in a costume designed by Mary Stockhausen-Bauermeister, illustrating a dance step in Stockhausen's *Der kleine Harlekin, Werk nr. 42½* on August 4, 1977, the day after its premiere. It appears in color on the cover of *The Clarinet* 26, no. 1 (December 1998), with permission of the editor, James Gillispie. The same photo appears on the cover of Stockhausen's *Der kleine Harlekin* (Kürten: Stockhausen-Verlag, 1978). Reproduced with permission from Stockhausen-Verlag.

[9] Stockhausen, *Harlekin für Klarinette, Werk nr. 42*, VII.

[10] Stockhausen's concept of the instrumentalist-actor, performing in costume, was later introduced into his opera, *Licht* (1987–1991), where the main characters are instrumentalists rather than singers. Griffiths, *Modern Music and After*, 202.

[11] Stockhausen, *Der kleine Harlekin für Klarinette, Werk nr. 42½*.

[12] Stockhausen, *Der kleine Harlekin für Klarinette, Werk nr. 42½*, i. There is also a version available for flute.

[13] Stockhausen, *Der kleine Harlekin, Werk nr. 42½*, i.

[14] Winston Stone, "The Onstage Instrumental Musician as Theater Performer" (Ph.D. diss., The University of Texas at Dallas, 2008), 257–58.

FIGURE 32.1 Stockhausen, *Der kleine Harlekin, Werk Nr. 42½*. Suzanne Stephens in costume illustrating a dance step in 1977.

In *Der kleine Harlekin, no. 42½*, Stockhausen uses a theme or formula (his preferred term) from the third section of *Harlekin, no. 42*, called "the enamoured lyrist" ("Der verliebte Lyriker").[15] Elements from this formula play in different registers and in different tempi throughout *Der kleine Harlekin, no. 42½*.[16] Abad divides the work into five sections:

Introduction, first two staffs of page 1

Section 1, third staff, page 1 to second staff, page 4

Cadenza, third staff, page 4 to sixth staff, page 5

Section 2, seventh staff, page 5 to the end of page 7

Section 3, or Coda, page 8.[17]

These sections vary musical material, tempi, and the physical gestures corresponding to changes in pitch or character.[18]

In the introduction, the costumed harlequin (clarinetist) enters from the right side of the stage, playing a very long *f* trill on high $A\flat_6$ using circular breathing and two different trill fingerings, while dancing in circular movements to the right. The clarinetist then plays repeated arpeggios varying among *f* and *ff* and *p*. When the harlequin faces the audience he/she plays a forceful, brief *ff* introduction in a march tempo, quarter note = ca. 112, while a dance rhythm is taped as a bridge between melody and rhythm. As the clarinet plays a sixteenth-note arpeggio from E_3 to $A\flat_6$, an upward sweeping hand movement is made above the keys and he/she slaps the clarinet up from the bell. After a brief pause, the clarinet plays a sixteenth-note arpeggio from C_7 to $G\sharp_3$ making a downward head movement. At each of the four repeats, the pause in the middle is made shorter as the left lower leg makes a light snapping movement up to the back of the knee. Then, the harlequin stands stiffly and with upward and downward head movements, plays two arpeggios of twelve sixteenth notes up and down, from E_3 to $A\flat_6$ and C_7 to $G\sharp_3$, nine times. At the second arpeggio, the left lower leg is bent up as high as possible. After an eleven-note arpeggio, a C_7 is held as a fermata and the left leg is suspended in the air, bent backward like a stork. While playing the C_7, irregular air accents are made as the left lower leg whips in the air. This is followed by a downward arpeggio of nine notes to $D\sharp_4$ as the left leg is lowered (Ex. 32.2).

---

[15] Reproduced in Robin Maconie, *Other Planets: The Music of Karlheinz Stockhausen* (Lanham, MD: Scarecrow Press, 2005), 374; Karlheinz Stockhausen, *Texte zur Musik 1970–1977, Band 4* (Köln: DuMont Buchverlag, 1978), 294.

[16] Maconie, ibid., 374.

[17] Santiago Martínez Abad, "The Little Harlequin," *The Clarinet* 38 no. 4 (September 2011), 60-63.

[18] The description is based on Abad's observations and Stockhausen's English translation of his German instructions in the music. Stockhausen scores and CDs may be ordered at www.karlheinzstockhausen.org.

EXAMPLE 32.1. Stockhausen, *Der kleine Harlekin, Werk Nr. 42½*, p. 1. Copyright, K. Stockhausen, 1978, reproduced with permission of Stockhausen-Verlag.

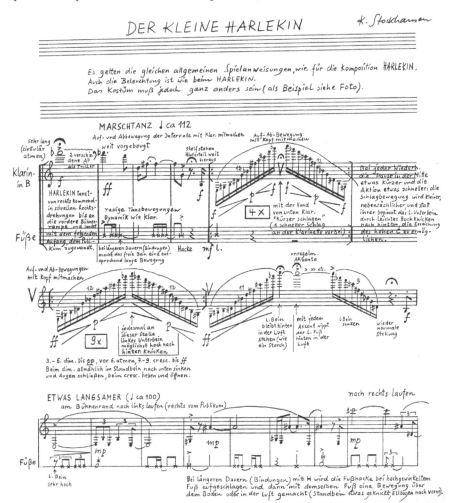

Section 1 begins somewhat slower (etwas Langsamer), quarter note = ca. 100 and the harlequin runs to stage right along the edge of the stage, lifts his/her left leg high, stands, and plays a lyrical, calm melody based on the formula (p. 1). The foot taps a percussive rhythm and for longer taped notes, the heel of the foot is raised at a sharp angle then hits the floor, and a corresponding long movement is made over the floor or in the air. The melody becomes more expansive and intense on page 2, while the harlequin taps a rhythm and moves to the center of the stage. At a third broad section, the harlequin holds a B_6 while creating vibrato and glissando accents heard as triplets, eighth notes, and quarter-note triplets. At the same time, a leg is stomped and the other is bent back. After a leg is stomped down, a free section is played, followed by a molto ritardando to a quasi A tempo, quarter note = ca. 94. After one measure of a broader section, and return of the A tempo, a triplet pattern is played with tapped and played triplets (end of p. 2). The harlequin thrusts his/her rear from side to side at each accented downbeat of eighth- and quarter-note triplets, accelerating throughout up to an A tempo (upper part of p. 3), when the rear end is thrust far out. The foot taps a rhythm and the material from section 1 appears. After wide intervals are played somewhat legato to a tapped rhythm, A$\sharp_6$ to A3 are played in triplets, eighth notes, triplet quarter notes, and quarter notes. The harlequin moves in dance-like steps in a circle to the back center stage, stopping with his/her left profile to the audience, standing on the left leg. The harlequin hops on the left leg, is still for a short time, slowly raises the right leg, and pivots the left foot 90° to the right, now with his/her back to the audience.

At the somewhat slower (etwas Langsamer, middle of p. 3), the foot taps a rhythm and the clarinet plays *ff* in phrases from previous sections. Suddenly, the harlequin turns toward the audience and stands stiffly, then, suddenly turns his/her back to the audience. At the broad (Breit) section, one foot is stamped down, the other is bent to the back, and a *ff* D_6 glissando plays down and up to D_6 over two beats with an eighth-note rhythm punctuated by the foot. This continues to an A tempo, a broad section, an accelerando leading to a fast (Schnell) tempo, and a high B_6 with a foot stomp as the other foot is raised. A tongued tremolo plays B_6 to G$\sharp_6$ for five beats, and the foot that is raised is whipped upward. The broader (Breiter), quarter note = ca. 80 section (upper part of p. 4), includes earlier phrases while the harlequin sways back and forth stilted on his/her toes with knee very high and leg arched. A slow (Langsam) section includes held notes while the harlequin takes three large steps toward the back wall of the stage. Then, while playing *pp* with a poco accelerando, the harlequin takes three steps back again, the third slow. At an A tempo, the harlequin plays two *f* sixteenth notes, C5 to E$\flat_6$, answered by three tapped eighth notes while making three small steps, and turning 45 degrees to the right. After a long, silent fermata, the harlequin plays the same *f* two sixteenth notes, tapping three eighth notes, and moves another 90 degrees to the right. After a long quarter note fermata, the harlequin plays the same two *ff* sixteenth notes, then an eighth note rest, and two eighth notes, answered by eighth-note foot taps.

The cadenza, fiery (Feurig), is a repeated ten line pattern with varying sixteenth notes of wide leaps; each line ends with a trill, vibrato, flutter tongue, or fermata, all played with rubato (pp. 4–5). The clarinetist plays each line as if it is a speaker's questioning exclamatory sentence and calmly moves in large loops upward, downward, to the left, and to the right. As the lines are played, the harlequin slowly turns to the left as seen by the audience, with small tripping steps, eyes closed, holding head and clarinet upward as high as possible.

Section 2 begins in a broader tempo with the two sixteenth notes C_5 to $E\flat_6$, answered by three and four foot eighth-note taps, and a fermata, two times. After the third time, sixteenth notes lead to a high C_7 (end of p. 5) on tip toes, with shoulders held high, head down to chest, shaking the entire body. The C_7 is played low in pitch and tied to a whole note fermata (beginning of p. 6). After the fermata, a very broad (sehr Breit) section begins with a thirty-second note scale from F_5 to $A\flat_6$ while moving the clarinet upward and raising the right leg. It leads back to the humorous march Tempo, quarter note = ca. 90, and the formula. Here, the harlequin walks a large spiral, breast pushed far forward, walking quite rapidly bent forward, almost falling over. Many changes of dynamics are required as is use of vibrato on C_6 and F_6. This leads to a broader section, where a high $B\flat_6$ is held as four half notes with vibrato. Now, the harlequin turns in a circle, lifts the legs very high as an upbeat comes to an A tempo, where the theme plays and the harlequin continues in a spiral, ducking in a secretive manner. After a molto ritardando, and an A tempo, the harlequin plays with circular breathing a trill from D_6 to $C\sharp_6$, varying the speed of the trill and the height and rotation of the bell for about thirty seconds. The harlequin turns in circles forming a spiral, runs off stage with the clarinet held close to the floor, to come back on stage and play, pointing the bell toward the wall.

After the trill ends on D_6 staccato quarter note and a short fermata, the A tempo, quarter note = ca. 90 (top of p. 7), begins with a tapped eighth note and downbeat. The harlequin ducks, moving in a secretive manner in a spiral and begins with p eighth notes to a ppp vibrato half note on $F\sharp_6$, accompanied by a tapping rhythm. A thirty-second note riff from B_5 to $F\sharp_6$ is followed by a down and upward thirty second note run, $G\sharp_6$ to E_3, up to a quarter note A_6. The harlequin taps a rhythm and moves with shoulders and arms pulled up, walking on stilt-like legs. A march dance (Marschtanz), quarter note = ca. 112, sounds a melody in the altissimo and chalumeau registers, the high notes played with the clarinet pointed to the left, the low notes to the right. When the harlequin reaches the center of a spiral, he/she moves quickly with small steps to the front of the stage, playing repeated sixteenth note leaps from high A_6 to E_4, to $G\sharp_4$, $A\sharp_4$, D_5, F_5, A_5, B_5, $D\sharp_6$, $F\sharp_6$, and $G\sharp_6$, to A_6, slowing at the end.

After a short fermata, section 3 begins with the harlequin moving to the middle of the stage in a very fast (sehr Schnell) tempo, quarter note = ca. 170 (p. 8). The repeated foot taps sound like tap dancing while the clarinet plays in the high and clarion registers with varying dynamics and vibrato. At the very broad (sehr Breit) section, the clarinet plays a glissando from $F\sharp_6$ to D to $F\sharp_6$ over six beats as a triplet rhythm is tapped. An immediate decrescendo to a pp $F\sharp_6$ is followed by ff leaps C_5 to $F\sharp_6$, $G\sharp_6$ to A_6; the latter played for five quarter notes with vibrato. Two measures of tapped quarter and eighth note triplets are followed by eighth note and quarter note triplets, as the harlequin turns his/her head to the right looking at the audience, with his/her body facing the exit, then moves behind a curtain. After the last note, a staccato quarter note A♭3, the clarinet is rapidly lifted high from behind the curtain, with the harlequin's hands visible to the audience. For a moment, the harlequin is completely stiff then quickly pulls the clarinet away.

The performance challenges require a close study of every detail written by Stockhausen in the score.[19] Its musical content is difficult but written with an understanding of the instrument's capabilities. The music, which must be memorized, requires a high level of dynamic control while playing runs throughout the register to C7, large leaps throughout, and circular breathing. Facial expression, visual communication, and lighting of the harlequin are important aspects.[20] Stockhausen requires the clarinetist to become the harlequin, performing every choreographed nuance and movement including the coordinated foot tapping and clarinet playing.[21]

Stephens recommends learning Stockhausen's clarinet works by starting with earlier solos, such as *In Freundschaft*, the latter having more limited movements. Most clarinetists who perform these works memorize the notes first and then add the movements.[22] These works are very well written and are effective in performance.[23] Stockhausen suggested studying Stephens' DGG recording of *Der kleine Harlekin* published in 1978.[24] In addition, many musicians have gone to Kürten for two-week sessions for the interpretation and composition courses on the works of Stockhausen.[25]

Stockhausen's *Der kleine Harlekin für Klarinette, Werk nr. 42½* presents many challenges in its music, choreography, dancing, and acting. After overcoming these obstacles, one will be rewarded with an impressive and memorable performance.

---

[19] Marcelo Daniel González emphasizes the intense concentration required when studying *Harlekin* in 1998 with Stephens and Stockhausen, in "Harlekin von Karlheinz Stockhausen: Wie Ich das 45 minütige Stück auswendig Spielen und Tanzen Lernte," *Rohrblatt* 22, no. 1 (March 2007): 35–37.

[20] Abad, "The Little Harlequin," 60.

[21] Stockhausen believed his formula had both mathematical and magical characteristics, and after *Der kleine Harlekin*, he used a triple formula to control all aspects of performance, Richard Dufallo, *Trackings: Composers Speak with Richard Dufallo* (New York: Oxford University Press, 1989), 218–19.

[22] Mary Jungerman, "The Single-Reed Music of Karlheinz Stockhausen: How Does One Begin?" *The Clarinet* 27, no. 1 (December 1999): 57.

[23] The author heard excellent performances of *In Freundschaft* by Suzanne Stephens at the 1980 International Clarinet Congress at the University of Denver. The light was dimmed and a spotlight, controlled by Stockhausen, highlighted Stephens' motions.

[24] Stockhausen, *Der kleine Harlekin für Klarinette*, i. Several excellent performances may be studied on YouTube.

[25] See Richard Faria, "Master Class: *In Freundschaft* by Karlheinz Stockhausen," *The Clarinet* 29, no. 3 (June 2002): 9.

33 Igor Stravinsky, *Three Pieces for Clarinet Solo*

Date of composition: October 6–November 15, 1918

First edition/other editions: Igor Stravinsky, *Trois Pièces pour Clarinette Solo*, London: J. & W. Chester, 1920; Igor Stravinsky, *Three Pieces for Clarinet Solo*, London: J. & W. Chester, 1920; Igor Stravinsky, *Three Pieces for Clarinet (A or B♭) Solo*, ed. Gerard Alphenaar, New York: Omega Music, 1949

Dedicatee/first performer: Werner Reinhart; Edmondo Allegra, clarinet

Date/place of first performance: November 8, 1919; Lausanne, Switzerland, Conservatoire de Lausanne[1]

IGOR STRAVINSKY (1882–1971) was a distinguished Russian composer who later acquired French (1934) and American (1945) citizenship. He is one of the most widely performed and influential twentieth century composers. His works encompass almost every important genre, including nationalism, neoclassicism, and serialism.

Stravinsky's father, Ignaty Stravinsky, studied singing in 1876 at the St. Petersburg Conservatory and became a fine bass-baritone who sang opera at the Marinsky Theater. Because of his father's success, during his youth, Igor met Nikolai Rimsky-Korsakov, Alexander Borodin, and Modest Mussorgsky, the prominent music journalist, Nikolay Findeyzen, and the conductor, Eduard Nápravnik. Igor studied piano as a boy and became a fluent accompanist. He entered St. Petersburg University as a law student but wanted to study music. In 1901, he had private lessons in harmony and theory with Fedir Akimenko, a student of Rimsky-Korsakov, and later with Vasily Kalafaty. In

---

[1] Stephen Walsh, "Stravinsky, Igor, Works," *Grove Music Online*; Clifford Cæsar, *Igor Stravinsky: A Complete Catalogue* (San Francisco: San Francisco Press, 1982), 29.

1902, Stravinsky visited Rimsky-Korsakov, who was staying in Hamburg for the summer, and showed him some of his compositions. Rimsky-Korsakov advised him to continue theory lessons and that he would later supervise his composition lessons. He worked with Rimsky-Korsakov until the latter's death in 1908.[2]

In 1909, two of Stravinsky's orchestral pieces, *Fireworks* and *Scherzo fantastique*, were performed in St. Petersburg, and heard by Sergei Diaghilev, who led the Ballets Russes in Paris. Diaghilev invited Stravinsky to compose a ballet based on a Russian legend of the *Firebird*. Its success made Stravinsky famous, and led to additional music for the Ballets Russes, *Petrushka* (1911) and *The Rite of Spring* (1913). The first performance of the latter caused a riot. At this time, Stravinsky was considered the leader of the musical avant-garde. After the Russian Revolution in 1917 and the loss of his property, Stravinsky formed a small touring theater ensemble to present inexpensive productions. He wrote *L'histoire du soldat* (*A Soldier's Tale*) for his ensemble; the ballet, *Pulcinella*, 1919–1920, using music attributed to Pergolesi in a neoclassical style; the ballet, *Les Noces* (*The Wedding*); and the opera, *Mavra*. In 1920, he and his family moved to France where he wrote works based on eighteenth-century forms with twentieth century harmonies and rhythms.[3]

By 1939, Stravinsky came to New York and Cambridge, Massachusetts, moving the next year to West Hollywood, California, where the climate was beneficial for his health. The *Symphony in Three Movements* (1945) was his first major American work, followed by the ballet, *Orpheus* (1947), based on Stravinsky's study of Monteverdi. Stravinsky met the American conductor Robert Craft, who was enthusiastic about Stravinsky's works, and interested in Baroque music and the Second Viennese School of Schoenberg. With Craft's encouragement, Stravinsky began writing serial music as composed by Webern in the following, *Canticum Sacrum* (1955), *Threni* (1958), the ballet *Agon* (1953–1957), and *Movements for Piano and Orchestra* (1958–1959). In 1962, Stravinsky, his family, and Craft were invited to Russia, ending a successful tour with a reception hosted by Nikita Khrushchev at the Kremlin. His last works were the *Requiem Canticles* (1966), and a setting for soprano and piano of Lear's *The Owl and the Pussy-Cat* (1965–1966). Stravinsky died in 1971. After the funeral in New York, his wife, Vera, requested that he be buried in Venice. The formal ceremony was April 14 on the island of San Michaele, close to the grave of Sergei Diaghilev.[4]

Stravinsky wrote a total of 109 works in the categories of stage or dramatic works, orchestral, large ensemble or band, choral, solo vocal, chamber and solo instrumental,

[2] Walsh, ibid.
[3] Walsh, ibid.; Walsh, "Stravinsky, Igor," *The Oxford Dictionary of Music, Oxford Music Online.*
[4] Walsh, "Stravinsky, Igor," *Oxford Music Online*; "Stravinsky, Igor," *The Oxford Dictionary of Music.*

piano, reductions of his own works, and arrangements of works by other composers.[5] Aside from the larger orchestral and dramatic works, other works for the clarinet are *Berceuse du chat for Contralto and Three Clarinets* (*Cat Lullaby*, 1915–1916), *Ragtime for Eleven Instruments* (1918), *L'histoire du soldat* (1918), *Symphonies of Wind Instruments* (1920), and the *Octet for Wind Instruments* (1922–1923).

The first piece of the *Three Pieces for Clarinet Solo* was composed in Morges, Switzerland, October 6–19, 1918; the second, October 11–24; and the third, November 2–15.[6] On November 19, Stravinsky asked Edwin Evans to contact a publisher in London for his newest works, *L'histoire du soldat*, *Three Pieces for Clarinet Solo*, four a cappella choruses, and children's songs.[7] The first performance of *L'histoire du soldat* was on September 28, 1918. Stravinsky wrote in his autobiography:

> I have kept a special place in my memory for that performance, and I am grateful to my friends and collaborators, as well as to Werner Reinhart, who, having been unable to find any other backers, generously financed the whole enterprise himself. As a token of my gratitude and friendship, I wrote for, and dedicated to him, *Three Pieces* for Clarinet Solo, he being familiar with that instrument and liking to play it among his intimates.[8]

Stravinsky dedicated *L'histoire du soldat* as well as a trio reduction of this work to Reinhart.[9] Reinhart deposited the autographs of *L'histoire du soldat*, *Les Noces* (*The Weddings*), and *Three Pieces for Clarinet Solo* in the Rychenberg Stiftung of the Stadtbibliothek, Winterthur, Switzerland.[10] In October 1918, the Italian clarinetist, Edmondo Allegra, active in Zurich, wrote to Stravinsky probably regarding the clarinet parts for *L'histoire du soldat* or the *Three Pieces for Clarinet Solo*, both of which

[5] Eric Walter White, *Stravinsky: The Composer and his Works*, 2nd ed. (Berkeley: University of California Press, 1979), 174–551; Stephen Walsh, "Stravinsky, Igor, Works."

[6] Maureen A. Carr, *After the Rite: Stravinsky's Path to Neoclassicism (1914–25)* (Oxford: Oxford University Press, 2014), 142, note 42.

[7] Robert Craft, ed., *Stravinsky, Selected Correspondence*, ed. Robert Craft (New York: Knopf, 1984), 2:120. The last two works were published as *Three Tales for Children* and *Four Russian Peasant Songs* by J. & W. Chester in 1920 and 1932; White, *Stravinsky: The Composer and His Works*, 246–47.

[8] Igor Stravinsky, *Stravinsky: An Autobiography* (New York: Simon and Schuster, 1936), 121.

[9] Reinhart helped several composers and as a result they dedicated works to him including, Adolf Busch, *Suite for Solo Bass Clarinet, op. 37a* (1926); Paul Hindemith, *Quintet for Clarinet and Strings, op. 30* (1923); Arthur Honegger, *Sonatine for Clarinet and Piano* (1922); Ernst Krenek, *Kleine Suite for Clarinet and Piano* (1929); Othmar Schoek, *Sonata for Bass Clarinet and Piano* (1928); and Richard Strauss, *Sonatina no. 2 for Sixteen Winds* (1944–1945). Pamela Weston, "Werner Reinhart: Philanthropist Extraordinaire," *The Clarinet* 28, no. 3 (June 2001): 64, 66.

[10] Autograph, MN_768, Rychenberg Stiftung of the Stadtbibliothek, Winterthur, Switzerland; Craft, ed., *Stravinsky, Selected Correspondence*, 3:139; Miles Mitsuru Ishigaki, "A Study of Comparative Interpretations of the *Three Pieces* for Clarinet Solo by Igor Stravinsky" (D.M.A. diss., University of Oklahoma, 1988), 10.

he performed in Zurich in November. A second letter from Allegra to Stravinsky and Stravinsky's response on the back, dated October 8, 1918, were sent to the author, Charles Ferdinand Ramuz, who wrote the spoken text for *L'histoire du soldat*, which was, "read, played and danced."[11] In a December 27, 1918 letter, Vera Stravinsky and Robert Craft mention that Allegra asked Stravinsky several questions about accidentals in the *Three Pieces* and stated that he intended to play the works soon for Reinhart and Stravinsky.[12] Stravinsky's December 29, 1918 response in a recently found letter provides answers and examples for all three movements.[13] Allegra premiered the *Three Pieces for Clarinet Solo*. He played it again along with the trio version of *L'histoire du soldat for clarinet, violin, and piano* with José Porta, violin, and José Iturbi, piano, in Zurich on November 20, and in Geneva on December 17.[14]

Stravinsky mentioned the influence of jazz improvisation on the *Three Pieces for Clarinet Solo* and other works of the same period:

In 1918 Ernest Ansermet, returning from an American tour, brought me a bundle of ragtime music in the form of piano reductions and instrumental parts, which I copied out in score. With these pieces before me, I composed the *Ragtime* in *Histoire du soldat*, and, after completing *Histoire*, the *Ragtime* for eleven instruments. The *Histoire* ragtime is a concert portrait, or snapshot of the genre—in the sense that Chopin's *Valses* are not dance waltzes, but portraits of waltzes. . . . If my subsequent essays in jazz portraiture were more successful, that is because they showed awareness of the idea of improvisation, for by 1919 I had heard live bands and discovered that jazz performance is more interesting than jazz composition. I am referring to my non-metrical pieces for piano solo [*Piano-Rag-Music*] and clarinet solo, which are not real improvisations, of course, but written-out portraits of improvisation.[15]

Carr writes, "By the time he wrote the Clarinet pieces, Stravinsky was moving beyond the idea of 'portrait' toward a higher level of abstraction."[16]

[11] Stravinsky to Ramuz, Craft, ed., ibid., 3:44.

[12] Vera Stravinsky and Robert Craft, *Stravinsky in Pictures and Documents* (New York: Simon and Schuster, 1978), 175–76.

[13] The letter and a manuscript copy of the *Three Pieces for Clarinet Solo* were sold on April 26, 2014, at the Hôtel de vente in Vichy. The author thanks Jean-Marie Paul and Jean Jeltsch for sending a copy of the letter and pages from the copy of the *Three Pieces*.

[14] White, ibid., 70; Pamela Weston, *Yesterday's Clarinetists: A Sequel* (Haverhill: Panda Group, 2002), 20.

[15] Igor Stravinsky and Robert Craft, *Dialogues and a Diary* (London: Faber and Faber, 1968), 54. Allegra immigrated to the United States on August 31, 1925 to play principal clarinet in the Boston Symphony Orchestra, and E♭ clarinet, 1926–1929. Bruce Creditor, "The Clarinet Section of the Boston Symphony Orchestra 1987," *The Clarinet* 14, no. 2 (Winter 1987): 37; Pamela Weston, *Yesterday's Clarinetists*, 21.

[16] Carr, ibid., 140.

Stravinsky insisted that performers interpret his work exactly; the first page of the *Three Pieces* includes the admonition, "The breath marks, accents and metronome marks indicated in the 3 Pieces should be strictly adhered to."[17] Guy Deplus, who recorded the *Three Pieces* under Stravinsky's supervision, told the audience before a 1980 performance that Stravinsky insisted he play the work exactly as written.[18] The first and second of the *Three Pieces* are marked, preferably for the A clarinet, the third piece, preferably for the B♭ clarinet.

The first piece, Sempre piano e molto tranquillo, quarter note = 52, consists of a calm melody of eighth and quarter notes written with constant meter changes from 2/4 to 5/8 to 7/8 to 5/8 to 2/4 to 3/8, etc. throughout. Although confusing at first, it is most easily performed by counting eighth notes. The first movement has four sections in ternary form with a coda, A (mm. 1–9), B (mm. 10–21), A¹ (mm. 21–28), coda (29–30). It is to be played, "*p* and expressively throughout in an introspective manner."[19] "Even though there are many meter changes, the constant flow of eighth notes eliminates any rhythmic pulse other than the eighth notes."[20] The compass is restricted, E3 to A4, in the chalumeau register. "The A clarinet was chosen for its darker coloring and more somber character than the B♭."[21] The melodic elements are often connected by grace notes that support the line.[22] Breath marks in this movement are often intended to be a slight suspension of sound and not a clear break. Stravinsky described these breath marks to the clarinetist, Rosario Mazzeo, in this way: "Each breath is not just so much exact time; its length depends on the moment in the music."[23] The last two measures are an expressive coda marked, poco più *f* e poco più mosso, ending on a fermata with a long diminuendo.

Craft suggests that the unpublished sketch for a duo for two bassoons (1916), titled in 1949, "Lied ohne Name," ("Song without a name") was the source for the first piece of the *Three Pieces for Clarinet Solo*.[24] Although there are similarities in the use of half step intervals in the first bassoon, and the ostinato pattern of the second

[17] Igor Stravinsky, *Three Pieces for Clarinet Solo* (London: J. & W. Chester, Ltd., 1920).

[18] The author heard this performance on August 15 at the 1980 International Clarinet Congress at the University of Denver.

[19] Julie DeRoche, "Master Class: *Three Pieces* by Igor Stravinsky," *The Clarinet* 32, no. 1 (December 2004): 4.

[20] Lyle Clinton Merriman, "Solos for Unaccompanied Woodwind Instruments: A Checklist of Published Works and Study of Representative Examples" (Ph.D. diss., State University of Iowa, 1963), 82.

[21] André Boucourechliev, *Stravinsky*, trans. Martin Cooper (New York: Holmes & Meier, 1987), 136.

[22] Boris Asaf'yev, *A Book about Stravinsky*, trans. Richard F. French (Leningrad: Triton, 1929, reprint, Ann Arbor: UMI Research Press, 1982), 251.

[23] Rosario Mazzeo, "Mazzeo Musings Series II, no. 23 [Igor Stravinsky, *Three Pieces for Clarinet Alone*]," *The Clarinet* 18, no. 3 (May–June 1991): 9.

[24] Craft, ed., ibid., 1:409–10; Ishigaki, "A Study of Comparative Interpretations of the *Three Pieces* for Clarinet Solo," 15–18. This duo is in Stravinsky's sketchbook VI in the Paul Sacher Foundation, Basel; Ishigaki, ibid., 15.

bassoon, to the patterns played in the first movement of the *Three Pieces*, the connection seems remote, and it is not mentioned in Stravinsky's writings.[25]

The second piece, eighth note = 168, is written without bar lines and makes a dramatic contrast to the first piece in its rapid tempo and exploitation of the clarion register up to G_6.[26] It consists of a bipartite form with a coda, A (up to the double bar line), B (chalumeau register to clarion register and fermata), and coda (after the fermata to the end). The compass is wide, from E3 and G_6, and the technically demanding passages should be counted in eighth notes. Stravinsky purposely indicated at the beginning that eighth = eighth, sixteenth = sixteenth, and three sixteeenths = one eighth. This is an important aspect for "accurate rhythmic performance."[27] The thematic "ribbon" produced at the beginning of the piece is in an "improvisatory mood,"[28] likely resulting from Stravinsky's recent study and exposure to jazz, and the breath marks act as slight suspensions of sound. Mazzeo notes that, after the double bar, an arresting *pp* section begins in the chalumeau register with odd leaps of a seventh, many grace notes, and expressive *mp* responses. The subito ending is surprising in its abrupt darkening of tone (sombrer le son), change of volume, and poco ritardando.[29] In comparison to the first movement, the second movement provides a stronger feeling of rhythmic organization because of the predominance of triplet sixteenth notes.[30]

The third piece, eighth note = 160, requires sixteenth = sixteenth, and *f* from beginning to end. It is written in a bipartite form, A (mm. 1–13), B (mm. 13–61), improvisatory in construction, based on the material of the first six measures, and the rhythm of the first measure.[31] The compass is entirely in the clarion register, B♭ to F♯$_6$, and "requires differentiation between two staccato markings, the dot and the wedge."[32] Played on the brilliant sounding B♭ clarinet, "it requires constant propulsion throughout, energetic accents, and clear definition of rhythm."[33] The use of

[25] Crystal Hearne Reinoso, "Sources and Inspirations for Stravinsky's *Three Pieces* for Clarinet Solo, part II," *The Clarinet* 23, no. 4 (July–August 1996): 27–28.

[26] Stravinsky wrote only one earlier work, the *Piano-Rag-Music* (1919), excluding meter and bar lines in four sections. White, *Stravinsky: The Composer and His Works*, 280; Barbara B. Heyman, "Stravinsky and Ragtime," *The Musical Quarterly* 68, no. 4 (October 1982): 560.

[27] DeRoche, ibid., 6, 8.

[28] Asaf'yev, ibid., 251.

[29] Mazzeo, ibid., 9.

[30] Merriman, ibid., 84.

[31] Asaf'yev, ibid., 252; Kenneth Radnofsky, "Portraits of Improvisation," *Winds Quarterly* 1 (1980): 20; Anton Swensen, "Applications of Selected Analytical Techniques to Twentieth Century Works for Solo Clarinet and Their Implications for Interpretation and Performance" (Ed.D. diss., Teachers College, Columbia University, 1969), 217–56.

[32] DeRoche, ibid., 8.

[33] Mazzeo, ibid., 9.

numerous time signatures is confusing at first, but becomes clear when the eighth note is counted throughout (Ex. 33.1). At the end of measure 13, beginning of measure 37, and the end of measure 52, the tone darkens immediately. Stravinsky recommends that at the end, "the fermata on B♭4 is to be held until the performer is sure the audience understands you have arrived at the end, then surprise them by playing a glib and soft B♭5, preceded by its grace note."[34]

EXAMPLE 33.1. Stravinsky, *Three Pieces for Clarinet Solo,* third piece, mm. 1–8.

Several authors have commented on the similarity of syncopated ragtime rhythms in the Ragtime and Tango movements of the *L'histoire du soldat.*[35] Others stated that Stravinsky used syncopated rhythms from popular ragtime music in the third movement.[36] Carr identifies a specific motive in Stravinsky's sketchbook V with a pattern in the third movement of the *Three Pieces for Clarinet Solo* (mm. 25–27), "that emphasizes an intervallic twist by opposing thirds and minor seconds."[37]

Stravinsky's *Three Pieces for Clarinet Solo* is the earliest work for clarinet alone from the twentieth century, and remains one of the most important and valuable in the repertory. It is a fascinating and virtuosic work that remains as fresh in the twenty-first century as it was in the twentieth. The *Three Pieces* is among the most important works studied by undergraduate and graduate clarinetists.[38] It is memorable to hear, useful on any program, a technical challenge in the second and third movements, and musically absorbing to learn.

---

[34] Mazzeo, ibid., 9–10.

[35] Asaf'yev, ibid., 252; Radnofsky, ibid., 19; White, ibid., 282; Stephen Walsh, *The Music of Stravinsky* (London: Routledge, 1988), 91.

[36] Heyman, ibid., 545–46; Ishigaki, ibid., 16, 18; Reinoso, ibid., 30–31.

[37] Carr, ibid., 134, 140.

[38] Cecil Gold, *Clarinet Performing Practices and Teaching in the United States and Canada,* 2nd ed. (Moscow, ID: University of Idaho, 1973), 4–6.

34 Antoni Szałowski, *Sonatina for Clarinet and Piano*

Date of composition: 1936

First edition/second edition: Antoni Szałowski, *Sonatina for Clarinet and Piano*, ed. Simeon Bellison, New York: Omega, 1948; Antoni Szałowski, *Sonatina for Clarinet and Piano*, London: Chester Music, 1986

Dedicatee/first performers: Ludwik Kurkiewicz; Louis Cahusac, clarinet, Antoni Szałowski, piano

Date/place of first performance: May 25, 1937; Paris, École Normal de Musique

ANTONI SZAŁOWSKI (1907–1973) was a Polish composer who studied violin with his father, an accomplished violinist and teacher. In 1930 he graduated from the Warsaw Conservatory where he studied piano with Paweł Lewiecki, composition with Kazimierz Sikorski, and conducting with Grzegorz Fitelberg. He won a scholarship from the National Culture fund and 1931–1936, studied composition with Nadia Boulanger in Paris. In 1936, the Warsaw Conservatory extended an invitation to be a professor. He would have to return to Poland; he declined in order to stay in Paris.[1] In a 1973 interview, Szałowski mentioned that in Poland, "one made music...almost in secret, hardly anybody was interested, and some regarded it with contempt, considering composition as a totally useless activity." In Paris, he met several composers including Igor Stravinsky, Sergei Prokofiev, Maurice Ravel, and Albert Roussel, and was attracted to neoclassicism.[2]

---

[1] Bogusław Schäffer, "Szałowski, Antoni," *Grove Music Online*; Elźbeta Szczurko, "Antoni Szałowski—the Essence of his Creativity." [Online] Available: http://files.musicologytoday.hist.pl/files/Musicology_Today/Musicology_Today-r2011-t8/Musicology_Today-r2011-t8-s61-85/Musicology_Today-r2011-t8-s61-85.pdf. [October 25, 2015].

[2] Szczurko, ibid., 62–63

Szałowski initially composed chamber music, including a *Suite for Violin and Piano* (1931) and *String Quartet no. 2* (1935), lauded by the French critic, Maurice Imbert, in 1935. *Sonatina for Clarinet and Piano* (1936) was written during the last part of this period. Szałowski's *Overture* (1936), his last composition written in Boulanger's class, was performed by the Polish Radio Symphony Orchestra, conducted by Grzegorz Fitelberg at the Théâtre de Champs Élysées during the Festival of Polish music. It was widely praised in 1937 and received the Gold Medal at the Paris World Exhibition. In 1938, when Szałowski visited Poland, several concerts were played and his works were critically praised. The critic Mateusz Gliński, wrote:

> Szałowski has fully mastered that which is the greatest attraction of the French tradition: the classical moderation of form, nobility and purity of contours, as well as clarity and grace of color. In this style the traditional *clarté* of texture becomes at the same time synonymous with the most refined artistic taste, providing a guarantee of total absence of brutal or sterile effects. These clear, expressive forms, measured with mature moderation, provide the outlet for Szałowski's individual creativity.[3]

Overture was played around the world but Szałowski was convinced that his future was in Paris. Szałowski belonged to the Paris Association of Young Polish Musicians as treasurer, vice-president, and president 1938–1950. During World War II, he carried the essential pieces of the association's archive, and relocated to the south of France with the musicians, Michal Spisak, Henryk Szeryng, and Sewern Rozycki. He had money and health issues and did not compose much. Boulanger communicated that his *String Quartet no. 3* (1936) was played at the International Festival of Contemporary Music in New York in 1941, and his *Symphony* (1938–1939) and *Sinfonietta* (1940) were successfully played. Boulanger took scores of the *Symphony* and *Sinfonietta* with her when she traveled in order to promote his music.[4]

Szałowski went back to Paris in 1945. There, with the help of friends, he worked hard to have his works played. His *Sonatina for Oboe and Piano* (1945–1946) was performed in Amsterdam in 1948, and the concert version of his ballet, *The Enchanted Inn*, premiered in Frankfurt in 1951. From the 1950s, Szałowski composed only on commission; many were forthcoming during his last twenty years. In France his publishers were Éditions Françaises de Musique and Max Eschig; in Great Britain, Chester, Augener, and Allegro Press; and in the United States, Omega

---

[3] Szczurko, ibid., 64–66, 68; Elżbieta Szczurko. *Antoni Szalowski: Person and Work*, trans. Zofia Weaver (Frankfurt am Main: PL Academic Research, 2013), 48–49.

[4] Szczurko, "Antoni Szalowski," 68–69; Boguslaw Maciej Maciejewski, *Twelve Polish Composers* (London: Allegro Press, 1976), 20.

Music Corporation.[5] Szałowski did not adopt a serial technique or change his compositional approach so his works became unfashionable in some circles. Nevertheless, his orchestral, chamber, and solo works, including the *Suite for Orchestra* (1953) and the *Violin Concerto* (1948–1954), were well received. The Polish premiere of Szałowski's last composition, *Six Sketches for Chamber Orchestra* (1971–1972), occurred in 1976 at the sixteenth Music Spring in Poznań. It was successful.

Szałowski's compositions include: orchestral works, ballets, instrumental chamber music, works for voice and one instrument, cello solo and piano music, harpsichord music, ondes martenot music, and music for radio and plays.[6] Szałowski won the music award of the Polish Guard Company (attached to the American Army in Europe) for artistic achievement (1955); a first prize from the French RTV for the radio ballet, *La femme têtue* (*The Stubborn Woman*, 1960); and the lifetime achievement music prize of the Alfred Jurzykowski Foundation in New York (1972).[7] Szczurko's summary of Szałowski's style is appropriate for the *Sonatina for Clarinet*:

> His compositions, logically constructed and restrained in expression, are at the same time light and cheerful, marked with humor, calm and lyrical subtlety. All these features are part of the concept of *sérénité* as an expressive category, which results from a harmonious combination of intellect and feeling.... The attractiveness of motion and timbre which is characteristic of his work and which links them to the French tradition results from the composer's particular fondness for, and sensitivity to, color qualities.[8]

The Omega Music Company in New York published Szałowski's *Sonatina for Clarinet and Piano* in 1948, edited by Simeon Bellison and dedicated to Ludwig Kurkiewicz, a distinguished Polish clarinetist and professor at the Academy of Music, Frederick Chopin Society in Warsaw.[9] It was recorded in the United States in 1957 by the most famous classical music clarinetist of the first half of the twentieth century, Reginald Kell, on an LP for Decca.[10] Tuthill's assessment of the sonatina was very positive, "Very attractive, a modern classic. Not difficult, but most musical.

[5] Maciejewski, ibid., 26.

[6] Maciejewski, ibid., 207–9.

[7] Szczurko, "Antoni Szałowski," 70–71, 74, 78–79; Szczurko, *Antoni Szałowski: Person and Work*, 64–65.

[8] Szczurko, "Antoni Szałowski," 82–83; Szczurko, *Antoni Szałowski: Person and Work*, 191.

[9] George Townsend, "The 22nd National Polish Concours for Young Instrumentalists: May 1989," *The Clarinet* 17, no. 1 (December 1989): 40–41.

[10] Lee Gibson, "Reginald Kell: The Artist and his Music," *The Clarinet* 5, no. 1 (Fall 1977): 8–9; Anne McCutchan, "Reginald Kell, A Selected Discography," *The Clarinet* 9, no. 2 (Winter 1982): 11.

A good concert number. Recorded by Kell."[11] Heim is also positive in describing Szałowski's *sonatina* as significant:

> Both the legato and staccato characteristics of the clarinet are exploited in the first and third movements, while the melancholy and melodic character of the instrument is emphasized in the second movement. While this can be used as a good work for the college level clarinetist, the music can be used successfully on a professional recital.[12]

Szałowski's *Sonatina for Clarinet and Piano* is in three movements that are structurally similar to Darius Milhaud's earlier *Sonatine* (1922).[13] The first movement, Allegro non troppo, quarter note = 92, is in sonata-allegro form. (See Chart 34.1.) The writing is polytonal and chromatic with, "a tonal center that vacillates between E♭ minor and C major, but clearly returns to E♭ minor at prominent cadences in the recapitulation, and [the] end of the movement."[14] The clarinet's compass, F3–F$_6$, requires a flexible technique with good control of staccato and dynamics. The A theme is conjunctly chromatic, light hearted in mood, and includes leaps of a fifth, fourth, third, and an octave. The development (m. 16, five measures after **A**) begins as the clarinet holds a C4 and the piano right hand plays an ostinato of sixteenth notes on the second beat that constantly changes chromatically. The piano and clarinet answer each other with accented *f* and staccato phrases (mm. 27–31); a softer syncopated phrase plays from measure 32, alternating with *f* accented passages from piano to clarinet. There is a ritardando two beats before the Tempo I (m. 48). The A^1

Section:	Exposition	Development	Recapitulation
Starts at m.	1 Allegro non troppo	16 (5 mm. after **A**)	48–73
No. of mm.	15	32	26
Tonal Centers	e♭, C	e♭	e♭-E♭-e♭
Themes	A	B	A^1

CHART 34.1 Szałowski, *Sonatina for Clarinet and Piano*: Structural analysis, first movement, Allegro non troppo.

---

[11] Burnet C. Tuthill, "The Sonatas for Clarinet and Piano," *Journal of Research in Music Education* 14, no. 3 (Autumn 1966): 211.

[12] Norman M. Heim, "Sonatinas for Clarinet and Piano," *NACWPI Journal* 39, no. 2 (Winter 1990–1991): 12.

[13] Heim astutely observed that, "The Sonatine by Milhaud is probably the role model for the sonatine repertory"; Heim, ibid., 10.

[14] Szczurko, *Antoni Szałowski: Person and Work*, 175.

Section:	A	B	A¹	Coda
Starts at m.	1 Larghetto	12 (**F**)	28 Tempo I (six mm. after **G**)	41–45
No. of mm.	11	16	13	5
Tonal Centers	c	C-c	C	c-C
Themes	A	B	A¹	coda

CHART 34.2 Szałowski, *Sonatina for Clarinet and Piano*: Structural analysis, second movement, Larghetto.

theme, until measure 65, has the same material as the A theme in the exposition as the piano plays up to measure 70, and an E♭ minor dyad at the end.

The second movement, Larghetto, quarter note = 54, is in ternary form with a coda. (See Chart 34.2.) After a six-beat introduction of piano eighth notes, the clarinet A theme is a plaintive tune in C minor. It features *pp* sustained quarter and eighth notes, and a dotted eighth sixteenth-note motive. At **F** a *ppp* sixteenth note ostinato in the pianist's right hand accompanies the clarinet B theme in the chalumeau and throat registers. A high point is reached (m. 20) with a *f* half note on G♯5 before a downward run to G4 and a dotted rhythm. At **G** (m. 25), the clarinet returns to a dotted rhythm, also played by the pianist's left hand (m. 25) before turning to Tempo I and the A¹ theme (m. 28, six measures after **G**). This theme is the same as the A theme up to measure 39, where eighth-note major dyads and triads are played by the pianist's right hand. The coda (m. 41) begins with an expressive solo clarinet line of twisting eighth notes that ends on a long held D5, and a cadence in C major.

The third movement, Allegro, quarter note = 144, in ternary form with a coda, begins *ff* with a forceful downward piano run in B♭ major answered by a quick clarinet flourish. The A theme at measure 4 is "a quirky melody of eighth notes in minor and major thirds, accompanied by E♭ and B♭ major chords, creating familiar tonal uncertainty."[15] (See Chart 34.3.) After several upward clarinet runs, chromatic passages, and clarinet flourishes, the A theme reappears one eighth note before measure 27 (**I**). This leads to the B theme, played *pp* (mm. 47–57, three measures after **J**, Ex. 34.1). This theme reappears twice, two octaves higher on E₆ (**K**, m. 72) and a sixth lower on A3 (8 mm. after **K**, m. 79). The A¹ theme appears at the last eighth note

---

[15] George Washington Knight, "A Comparative Study of Compositional Techniques Employed in Instructional Materials and Twentieth-Century Solos for the Clarinet" (D.M.A. diss., University of Illinois at Urbana–Champaign, 1973), 191–92.

(m. 96) in the piano's right hand. Imitation between piano and clarinet appears in sixteenth-note runs, constant sixteenth notes are played by the piano from measure 119, and the clarinet has a sixteenth note run up to a trill from D_6 to $E\flat_6$ at **N** (m. 126). From **N** to the end is a brilliant coda, with constant sixteenth piano notes, imitation between clarinet and piano, and repeated clarinet sixteenth notes, followed by several grace notes to D3 on E♭ seventh piano chords ending with a clarinet flourish to a high G_6.

EXAMPLE 34.1. Szałowski, *Sonatina for Clarinet and Piano*, third movement, theme B, mm. 47–54.

Section:	A	B	A¹	Coda
Starts at m.	1 Allegro	47 (3 mm. after **J**)	96 (2 mm. after **L**)	126(**N**)–166
No. of mm.	46	49	30	41
Tonal Centers	B♭, E♭-E	E♭-E	E♭	c, F
Themes	A	B	A¹	coda

CHART 34.3 Szałowski, *Sonatina for Clarinet and Piano*: Structural analysis, third movement, Allegro.

Szałowski's *Sonatina for Clarinet and Piano* is an attractive and brilliant work, particularly successful in utilizing different colors throughout the clarinet's compass, and is interesting musically. Technically, it is within the scope of most college players, but requires careful attention to articulation in the first and last movements. It is an excellent recital piece and will balance other works of a heavier musical quality.

35 Carl Maria von Weber, *Grand Duo Concertant for Clarinet and Piano, op. 48*

Date of composition: July 1815–November 1816

First edition/early editions/modern edition: Charle Marie de Weber, *Grand Duo Concertant pour Pianoforte et Clarinette*, Berlin: Schlesinger, 1817; Charle Marie de Weber, *Grand Duo Concertant pour Pianoforte et Clarinette*, Berlin: Schlesinger, 1830; Carl Maria von Weber, *Grand Duo Concertant op. 48, ed.* Carl Baermann, Berlin: Schlesinger'sche Buch u. Musikalienhandlung, 1869; Carl Maria von Weber, *Grand Duo Concertant for Clarinet (in B♭) and Piano = für Klarinette (in B) und Klavier, opus 48* (JV 204, WeV P. 12), ed. Knut Holtsträter, Mainz: Schott, 2005

Dedicatee/first performers: Not indicated; Heinrich Baermann, clarinet, Carl Maria von Weber, piano (two movements); H. Baermann, C. M. von Weber (two movements); Johann Gottlieb Kotte, clarinet, Julius Benedikt, piano (three movements)

Date/place of first complete performance: August 2, 1815; Hoftheater, Munich; August 8, 1815, Augsburg; April 1824; Dresden, Quartet Academy concerts.

CARL MARIA VON WEBER (1786–1826) was a composer, conductor, pianist, and critic. He was an influential nineteenth century musician whose work and writings as a performer and conductor contributed to the appreciation of music by middle-class audiences. With the great success of *Der Freischütz* (*The Freeshooter*) in 1821, he became the leading figure of German opera during the 1820s, and influenced several later composers such as, Heinrich Marschner, Felix Mendelssohn, Richard Wagner, Giacomo Meyerbeer, Hector Berlioz, and Franz Liszt.[1]

---

[1] Paul Corneilson, et al. "Weber, Carl Maria von," *Grove Music Online*.

Weber was a weak child with a congenital hip disorder that caused a limp. In 1796, the family settled in Hildburghausen where Weber took piano and thoroughbass lessons. In 1797, when the family moved to Salzburg, Weber studied counterpoint with Michael Haydn, and wrote his first compositions. From 1798 to 1800, Weber and his father moved to Munich where his father promoted his son as a prodigy. Carl studied singing, piano, and composition. By 1799, he had composed an opera, a Mass, and piano works. In 1800 in Freiburg, Weber composed a second opera staged in November but it was later lost. By late 1801, Weber moved back to Salzburg, and under Michael Haydn's supervision, composed his third opera, *Peter Schmoll und seine Nachbarn* (*Peter Schmoll and His Neighbors*), staged in 1803 in Augsburg. In 1803, Weber went to Vienna to study with Joseph Haydn, but instead became a pupil of Georg Joseph Vogler. Through Vogler's influence, he became kapellmeister at the Breslau Municipal Theater, 1804–1806. In Karlsruhe, 1807–1809, he wrote two symphonies and incidental music for an opera.

For three years, Weber traveled through Germany giving and organizing concerts, writing articles, meeting people, and composing. In 1811 in Munich he wrote two clarinet concertos for Heinrich Baermann and finished his opera, *Silvana*. In 1813, in Prague, he accepted the directorship of the Prague Opera until 1816. In December 1816, he was appointed kapellmeister in Dresden. Weber worked on his opera, *Der Freischütz* (*The Freeshooter*), 1817–1820. It was first performed at a spectacular premiere in Berlin in 1821. In 1824, Covent Garden Theatre in London commissioned a new opera. He worked on *Oberon* in London in 1826, with a very successful premiere in April. His health was poor and he died in June, the day before he planned to return home.[2]

Weber wrote over 300 compositions: stage works, incidental music, insertion arias and duets, concert arias and duets, sacred and other choral works, vocal ensembles with piano, unaccompanied vocal ensembles, canons, solo songs, orchestral works, concertos and concertante works, wind ensemble works, chamber works, solo piano, works for piano four hand, miscellany, and arrangements of other composers' works.[3] His solo clarinet works are generally considered the finest of the early nineteenth century, *Concertino for Clarinet and Orchestra, op. 26* (April 2, 1811), *Concerto no. 1 for Clarinet and Orchestra, op. 73* (May 17, 1811), *Concerto no. 2 for Clarinet and Orchestra, op. 74* (July 17, 1811), *Seven Variations for Clarinet and Piano, op. 33* (December 14, 1814), and *Grand Duo Concertant for Piano and Clarinet, op. 48* (November 8, 1816).[4] All of these works were dedicated to Weber's good friend,

---

[2] Corneilson, et al., ibid.; Clive Brown, "Weber, Carl Maria von," *The New Grove Dictionary of Opera*; "Weber, Carl Maria von," *The Oxford Dictionary of Music, Oxford Music Online*.

[3] Corneilson et al, ibid.; John Warrack, *Carl Maria von Weber*, 2nd ed. (Cambridge: Cambridge University Press, 1976), 379–390.

[4] Friedrich Wilhelm Jähns, *Carl Maria von Weber in seinen Werken: Chronologisch-Thematischer Verzeichniss seiner sämmtlicher Compositionen* (Berlin: Schlesinger'schen Buch und Musikhandlung, 1871), 132–33, 137–38, 141–42, 151–52, 216–17.

Heinrich Baermann, principal clarinetist at the Munich Court Orchestra and one of the greatest clarinetists of the nineteenth century.

Weber first met Baermann in Munich in 1811, and wrote three works for him in quick succession. He also toured and concertized with Baermann during 1811. Although Weber's Tagebuch (day book) for September 28, 1812 reported that, "Hermstedt wants to have a concerto from me and for the sole rights for two years will give me 10 Louis d'or; I promised him to write one,"[5] and on February 4, 1815, "Composed Savoyard song and a clarinet concerto for Hermstedt."[6] Neither work has been found although Hermstedt has been associated with the *Grand Duo Concertant*.[7] During summer 1815, Weber visited Munich staying in Baermann's home. Here he began work on the *Grand Duo Concertant* which he called at first a Sonata. By July 22nd Weber had finished two of the movements that Weber and Baermann had rehearsed earlier, and the third movement, which became the first, was finished on November 8.[8] Baermann and Weber never performed the three movement version of the work, but Johann Gottlieb Kotte, the principal clarinetist of the Dresden Court Orchestra, and Julius Benedict, piano, were probably the first to perform all three movements, described in the concert report as Weber's *Concertante für Klarinette* in Dresden, April 1824.[9]

Rochlitz wrote a positive review of the published music of the *Grand Duo Concertant* in the *Allgemeine musikalische Zeitung* (June 17, 1818):

> The work consists of a fiery, continual stream in an Allegro in E♭; and an exceedingly tender but by no means effeminate Andante in C minor. The third movement is a merry and partly piquant Rondo in E♭, in which the entire movement mixes with manly cheerfulness, a deep seriousness and melancholy reminiscences that are wonderful and richly effective.[10]

---

[5] "Hermstedt will ein Concert von mir haben und für 2 Jahr Eigentum 10 Louisdor geben: ich versprach ihm, eins zu schreiben," Jähns, *Carl Maria von Weber in seinen Werken*, 434, trans. Weston, *Clarinet Virtuosi of the Past*, 86.

[6] "[C]omp. Savoysches Lied und am Clarinette 'Concert für Hermstedt,'" Jähns, *Carl Maria von Weber in seinen Werken*, 434.

[7] Oscar W. Street, "The Clarinet in Chamber-Music," *Chamber Music* 7, no. 9 (1914): 19; Oskar Kroll, "Weber und Baermann," *Zeitschrift für Musik* 103, no. 12 (December 1936): 1141–42; Hans Eberhardt, "Johann Simon Hermstedt 1778–1845: Seine Bedeutung als Klarinettenvirtuose." *Mitteilungen des Vereins für deutsche Geschichte und Altertumskunde in Sondershausen* 10 (1940), 109; Oskar Kroll, *The Clarinet*, rev. Diethard Riehm, trans. Hilda Morris, trans. and ed. Anthony Baines (New York: Taplinger Publishing Co., 1968), 75, note 3; Albert R. Rice, *The Clarinet in the Classical Period* (New York: Oxford University Press, 2003), 189.

[8] Carl Maria von Weber, *Complete Works, Chamber Music with Clarinet, Series VI: Chamber Music*, vol. 3, ed. Gerhard Allroggen, Knut Holtsträter, Joachim Veit (Mainz: Schott, 2005), XVII-XVIII, 143-47.

[9] "Nachrichten," *Allgemeine musikalische Zeitung* 26, no. 24 (June 10, 1824), 390; Kotte was principal clarinetist of the Dresden Court Orchestra; Pamela Weston, *Clarinet Virtuosi of the Past* (London: Hale, 1971), 89; Pamela Weston, *More Clarinet Virtuosi of the Past* (Corby: Fentone Music, 1977), 143.

[10] "Das werk bestehet aus einem feurigen, in Einem Gusse forströmenden Allegro aus Es, einem ungemein zarten, aber keinesfalls weichlichen Andante aus C moll; und einem heitern, zum Theil sehr pikanten Rondo

In this work, thematic and melodic balance between the clarinet and piano is unique. The clarinet part is as demanding as the most difficult concertos of the time, including leaps of over two octaves, with a compass of E3 to A_6. In the third movement, it is a technical challenge for the pianist to play in rapid thirds and sixths.[11]

The twentieth-century reception of the *Grand Duo Concertant for Piano and Clarinet* was positive. Ward (1957) writes:

> It is an exhibition piece...on the grand scale, with a rather too long first movement, but it has some of the loveliest and most lyrical sweeping phrases for the clarinet that Weber wrote, which are sheer joy to play.... The *andante* also has a wonderfully delayed cadence and makes moving use of the clarinet's range of expression. The rondo is an excellent example of how to be wildly funny without losing that elusive quality, good taste. Take it as fast as you can (but no faster) and the *scherzando* second subject fairly dances along. The rippling chromatic phrases and runs are most carefully marked *grazioso* and *delicatamente*, and if played thus sparkle with a truly disarming humour, while the gaiety of those syncopated leaps down to low E♭ is irresistible. The bravura has a splendid extravagance, and I do not think trills have ever been used to better effect.[12]

Tuthill's 1966 assessment was enthusiastic:

> A very brilliant piece in sonata form, the best show piece in the literature for both clarinet and piano. It uses all the resources of the clarinet and is fun to play. This Opus is Weber's best music for the clarinet, better than the two concertos, the quintet with strings, or the variations.[13]

Weber's *Grand Duo Concertant for Clarinet and Piano, op. 48* is in three movements. The first movement, Allegro con fuoco, half note = 108,[14] is in sonata-allegro form.[15] (See Chart 35.1.) It has many brilliant piano scales in unison of thirds or

---

aus Es, in welchem sich ganz besonders männliche Fröhlichkeit mit tiefem Ernst und sogar wehmüthigen Anklängen, gar wunderbar und effectreich mischt," Johann Friedrich Rochlitz, "Anzeigen," *Allgemeine musikalische Zeitung* 20, no. 24 (June 17, 1818): 443.

[11] Rice, *The Clarinet in the Classical Period*, 189.

[12] Martha Kingdon Ward, "Weber and the Clarinet," *The Monthly Musical Record* 87, no. 982 (July–August 1957): 145–146.

[13] Burnet C. Tuthill, "The Sonatas for Clarinet and Piano," *Journal of Research in Music Education* 14, no. 3 (Autumn 1966): 212.

[14] Suggested by the author.

[15] Wolfgang Sandner, *Die Klarinette bei Carl Maria von Weber* (Wiesbaden: Breitkopf & Härtel, 1971), 126–28.

sixths throughout.[16] The piano introduction of three eighth-note pickups proceeds to a twelve measure A theme of a *ff* E♭ major scale in octaves, answered by the clarinet with a *ff* downward arpeggio. The clarinet plays a *pp* F major arpeggio in eighth notes accompanied by the piano, with longer notes answered by the piano, ending with an eighth-note fermata. The piano begins again with three eighth-note pickups to a *ff* E♭ major scale, and the clarinet answers. A disjunct eighth-note clarinet B theme is answered by the piano, ending with a piano scale in thirds (mm. 25–33), presented with accented imitation between both hands of the piano (mm. 33–38). The piano plays the B^1 theme, a variation of the B theme, and the excitement builds to a high C$_6$, followed by accented clarinet notes and trills in the piano, and a long-held clarinet F5 fading away (perdendosi, m. 64). The piano plays eighth notes to arrive at the beautiful C clarinet theme, marked coaxing (lusingando, mm. 70–88, Ex. 35.1). This nine measure theme includes a repeated clarinet sequence of quarter, half, and quarter notes (G5, F♯5, F5), which is the basis for the themes in the development section.[17] The piano plays accented quarter notes to eighth notes to which the clarinet responds, leading to a poco ritardando (mm. 104–105), and a tempo I (m. 106). At measure 130 the exposition is repeated.

EXAMPLE 35.1. Weber, *Grand Duo Concertant for Piano and Clarinet, op. 48,* first movement, Allegro con fuoco, mm. 70–88.

[16] Warrack, ibid., 178.
[17] Sandner, ibid., 126.

Section:	Exposition	Development	Recapitulation
Starts at m.	1–130, 1–129 Allegro con fuoco	130	207–309
No. of mm.	259	77	103
Tonalities	E♭, B♭	g, G, c	E♭
Themes	A, B, A^1, B^1, C	D, (A)	A^2, C^1, A^3

CHART 35.1 Weber, *Grand Duo Concertant for Piano and Clarinet, op. 48*: Structural analysis, first movement, Allegro con fuoco.

The development moves through several tonalities including G minor, G major, to C minor with fragments of the A theme as the clarinet and piano play in imitation, con passione (m. 174), and sempre *f* (m. 187). The development has unusual imitation in three parts between the piano's left and right hands, and the clarinet (mm. 197–200).[18] The recapitulation in E♭ major (mm. 207–309) presents the A^2 theme of the piano and clarinet, similar to the exposition but subtlely changed (mm. 207–222), such as, the extension of clarinet notes in an arpeggio and two whole notes (mm. 219–221) before the clarinet coaxing C^1 theme (lusingando, mm. 223–241), played a sixth higher. The A^3 theme at m. 279 continues in momentum and intensity until the end of the movement.

The second movement, Andante con moto, quarter note = 60,[19] is a ternary form. (See Chart 35.2.) The clarinet plays a meditative *p* melody with an elegant *pp* chordal accompaniment in a Schubertian style which contrasts with the virtuosity of the first movement.[20] An expressive *f* A theme of eight measures is marked, with sorrow (con duolo, mm. 5–12). The clarinet part quickly becomes theatrical with a crescendo leading to C$_6$ and a rapidly tongued thirty-second note run from F3 to F$_6$, leading to a highly expressive four measure phrase (mm. 20–24) with a chromatic scale from B♭4 to a *fp* F$_6$ and a cadence to C minor (Ex. 35.2). The piano replies in the B section in an operatic manner with an urgent melody and a crescendo to thundering chords (mm. 24–36). At measure 37, the clarinet plays a soft melody in G major as the piano plays *pp* delicately in its highest register. At measure 53, the piano plays *ff* with accents modulating to F minor and C minor at the A^1 theme (m. 67). The con duolo melody returns and builds to a dramatic climax on F$_6$ (m. 80), slowly fading away (morendo) to a *pp* low sustained F3.

---

[18] Sandner, ibid., 127.
[19] Suggested by the author.
[20] Sandner, ibid., 127.

EXAMPLE 35.2. Weber, *Grand Duo Concertant, for Piano and Clarinet, op. 48*, second movement, Andante con moto, mm. 20–24.

CHART 35.2 Weber, *Grand Duo Concertant for Piano and Clarinet, op. 48*:
Structural analysis, second movement, Andante con moto.

Section:	A	B	A¹
Starts at m.	1 Andante con moto	24	67–90
No. of mm.	23	43	24
Tonalities	c	c, G, f	c
Themes	A	B	A¹

Section:	A	B	C
Starts at m.	1 Allegro	42	65
No. of mm.	41	23	24
Tonalities	E♭	E♭	E♭
Themes	A	B	C

Section:	A¹	D	A²	Coda
Starts at m.	89	125	176	254–267
No. of mm.	36	51	78	14
Tonalities	E♭, D♭	D♭, E♭	E♭	E♭
Themes	A¹	D, A²	A³, C¹	C²

CHART 35.3 Weber, *Grand Duo Concertant for Piano and Clarinet, op. 48*: Structural analysis, third movement, Rondo, Allegro.

The third movement, Rondo, Allegro, dotted quarter note = 69,[21] has six sections and a coda. (See Chart 35.3.) It begins in a comfortable 6/8 counted as two beats per measure played con grazia, the piano and clarinet answering each other in sixteenths and seamlessly joined. The piano plays a flowing series of sixteenth notes (mm. 26–33) and a brief fanfare, answered by the clarinet (mm. 34–41) which introduces a jolly scherzando B theme with sixteenth and staccato eighth notes (mm. 42–64). After a quick piano scale, the clarinet plays the C theme, a grazioso sixteenth-note melody that the piano ingeniously joins in thirds (mm. 65–73). The piano introduces a *p* sixteenth note C theme delicately with accents on the first and second beats, answered by the clarinet, two measures later (mm. 73–80); *ff* piano sixteenth note passages lead to a virtuoso *pp* scale in thirds (mm. 87–88). The clarinet plays the A¹ theme (m. 89), later to a staccato passage in sixths with the piano (mm. 109–110). This is followed by a dramatic piano passage with scales that modulate to D♭ (mm. 111–124), and the clarinet ushers in a *f* operatic D theme with much passion (con molto affetto) and a swelling tremolo accompaniment (mm. 125–145).[22] After the excitement dies down, the rondo A² theme is recalled *pp* in the piano's right hand but just for two measures (mm. 145–146), and the clarinet returns with the *pp* D theme (m. 147). A high point is reached with a crescendo to measure 159 on an E♭₆, with a decrescendo to a clarinet E♭5 accompanied by tremolos. The rondo A² theme played *pp* appears again in the piano's left hand modulating to E♭ major

---

[21] Suggested by the author.
[22] Sandner, ibid., 127.

(m. 164). At measure 176, the A^3 theme plays *pp* in the clarinet's chalumeau register on F3; this gradually builds to a *ff* restatement of the A^3 clarinet theme on F5 (m. 186) with brilliant piano arpeggios, octaves, scales, and scales in thirds. The C^1 sixteenth note *grazioso* theme appears (m. 205), including the addition of trills and repeated leaps from eighth notes to quarter note low F3s (mm. 219–220, 223–224). Chromatic scales in sixths and scales in unison lead to two *ff* downward clarinet arpeggios (mm. 243–244), a thirty-second-note run to high A_6 in thirds with the piano (m. 247), and a high point of a two-measure trill on E_6 resolving to F_6 (mm. 253–254, beats 1 and 2). The coda (mm. 254–267) consists of a *pp* C^2 theme, scales, arpeggios, and a crescendo to a brilliant ending.

Weber's *Grand Duo Concertant* is one of the finest works for clarinet and piano and the most outstanding of the early nineteenth century. It presents a number of interpretive and performing goals for the clarinetist. The staccato tonguing in the first and especially the third movement needs careful attention, as does the musical interpretation and coordination with an excellent pianist.

Bibliography

Abad, Santiago Martínez. "The Little Harlequin," *The Clarinet* 38, no. 4 (September 2011), 60–63.

Adelson, Robert. "The Autograph Manuscript of Brahms' Clarinet Sonatas Op. 120: A Preliminary Report." *The Clarinet* 25, no. 3 (May–June 1998): 62–65.

———. "New Perspectives on Performing Mozart's Clarinet Concerto." *The Clarinet* 25, no. 2 (February–March 1998): 50–55.

———. "Too Difficult for Benny Goodman: The Original Version of the Copland Clarinet Concerto." *The Clarinet* 23, no. 1 (November–December, 1995): 42–45.

Adorno, Theodor. *Alban Berg, Master of the Smallest Link*. Trans. J. Brand and C. Hailey, Cambridge: Cambridge University Press, 1968.

Albèra, Philippe. "Introduction auf Neuf Sequenzas." *Contrechamps* 1 (1983): 91–122.

Aleksander, Elisabeth R. "Gustav Jenner's *Clarinet Sonata in G Major, opus 5:* An Analysis and Performance Guide with Stylistic Comparison to the *Clarinet Sonatas, opus 120* of his Teacher, Johannes Brahms." Doctor of Musical Arts thesis, University of Nebraska, 2008.

Amet, Franck. "Rediscovery of a Jean Françaix Piano Score." *The Clarinet* 39, no. 4 (September 2012): 61.

Amore, Adriano. *Il clarinetto in Italia nell'Ottocento*. Pesaro: Accademia Italiana del Clarinetto, 2009.

———. *La letteratura Italiana per clarinetto: storia, analisi, discografia e curiosità*. Frasso Telesino: printed by author, 2011.

Anbari, Sara. "The Clarinet Concertos of Franz Krommer." Master of Music thesis, University of Kansas, 1996.

Anderson, John Edward. "An Analytical and Interpretive Study and Performance of Three Twentieth Century Works for Unaccompanied Clarinet." Doctor of Education diss., Teachers College, Columbia University, 1974.

Antolini, Bianca Maria, ed. *Dizionario degli Editori Musicali Italiani 1750–1930*. Pisa: Edizioni ETS, 2000.

Archibald, Bruce. "Berg's Development as an Instrument Composer." In *The Berg Companion*, ed. Douglas Jarman, 91–122. Boston: Northeastern University Press, 1990.

Arnold, Ben. "Tradition and Growth in the Concertos of Nielsen." In *The Nielsen Companion*, ed. Mina F. Miller, 350–78. Portland: Amadeus Press, 1994.

Asaf'yev, Boris. *A Book about Stravinsky*. Leningrad: Triton, 1929, trans. Richard F. French, Ann Arbor: UMI Research Press, 1982.

Avins, Styra. "Performing Brahms's Music: Clues from his Letters." In *Performing Brahms: Early Evidence of Performance Style*, eds. Michael Musgrave and Bernard D. Sherman, 11–47. Cambridge: Cambridge University Press, 2003.

Bailey, Kathryn. "Berg's Aphoristic Pieces." In *The Cambridge Companion to Berg*, ed. Anthony Poole, 83–110. Cambridge: Cambridge University Press, 1997.

Banfield, Stephen. *Gerald Finzi: An English Composer*. London: Faber and Faber, 1998.

Baron, John Herschel. *Intimate Music: A History of the Idea of Chamber Music*. Stuyvesant, NY: Pendragon Press, 1998.

Będkowski, Stainsław and Stainsław Hrabia. *Witold Lutosławski: A Bio-Bibliography*. Westport, CT: Greenwood Press, 2001.

"Benjamin, Arthur," *Baker's Biographical Dictionary of Musicians*. Centennial ed., eds. Nicholas Slonimsky and Laura Diane Kuhn. New York: Schirmer Books, 2001.

Berg, Alban. *Letters to His Wife*. Ed., trans., and annotated Bernard Grun. London: Faber and Faber, 1971.

Berlász, Melinda. "Preface." In Franz Vinzenz Krommer, *Konzert Es-dur für Klarinette und Orchester Op. 36*, ed. Melinda Berlász, n.p., Zürich: Edition Eulenburg, 1975.

Bernsdorf, Eduard. "Für Pianoforte und Clarinette, Rob. Schumann, Op. 73. Phantasiestücke für Pianoforte und Clarinette (ad libitum Violine oder Violoncell.)." *Neue Zeitschrift für Musik* 32, no. 13 (February 12, 1852), 59–60.

Berry, Wallace. *Musical Structure and Performance*. New Haven, CT: Yale University Press, 1989.

Bingham, Ann Marie. "Carl Nielsen's Koncert for Klarinet og Orkester, opus 57 (1928): A Performance Guide." Doctor of Musical Arts diss., University of Kentucky, 1990.

Bish, Deborah F. "A Biography of William O. Smith: The Composition of a Life." Doctor of Musical Arts diss., Arizona State University, 2005.

Blazich, Joan Michelle. *Original Text, English Translation, and a Commentary on Amand Vanderhagen's Méthode nouvelle et raisonnée pour la clarinette (1785) and Nouvelle Méthode de clarinette (1799): A Study in Eighteenth-Century French Clarinet Music*. Lewiston, NY: Edwin Mellen Press, 2009.

Blotner, Linda Solow, ed. *The Boston Composers Project: A Bibliography of Contemporary Music*. Ed. Linda Solow Blotner, Cambridge, MA: MIT Press, 1983.

Bok, Henri. "The Bass Clarinet." In *The Versatile Clarinet*, ed. Roger Heaton, 91–100. New York: Routledge, 2006.

Bonnerot, Jean. *C. Saint-Saëns (1835–1921): Sa Vie et son Oeuvre*. New ed., rev., and augmented, Paris: A. Durand et fils, 1923.

Boros, James. "A Conversation with Donald Martino." *Perspectives of New Music* 29, no. 2 (1991): 212–78.

Boucourechliev, André. *Stravinsky*. Trans. Martin Cooper. New York: Holmes & Meier, 1987.

Bozarth, George. "Two Sonatas for Clarinet and Piano in F minor and E♭ Major, Opus 120." In *The Compleat Brahms: A Guide to the Musical Works of Johannes Brahms*, ed. Leon Botstein, 101–103. New York: W. W. Norton, 1999.

Bradshaw, Susan. "The Instrumental and Vocal Works." In *Pierre Boulez: A Symposium*, ed. William Glock, 127–239. London: Eulenburg Books, 1986.

Brahms, Johannes. *Sonaten für Klarinette (oder Viola) und Klavier, Neue Ausgabe sämtlicher Werke*. Eds. Egon Voss and Johannes Behr, Serie II, Band 9. Munich: G. Henle, 2010.

Brand, Juliane, Christopher Hailey, Donald Harris, eds. *The Berg-Schoenberg Correspondence: Selected Letters*. New York: W. W. Norton, 1987.

Brisbois, Aaron. "Jean Françaix's Clarinet Concerto: An Examination of Performance Practices." Doctor of Musical Arts diss., University of Oklahoma, 2012.

Briscoe, James R. *Claude Debussy: A Guide to Research*. New York: Garland Publishing, 1990.

———. "Debussy and Orchestral Performance." In *Debussy in Performance*, ed. James R. Briscoe, 67–90. New Haven, CT: Yale University Press, 1999.

Brodbeck, David. "Medium and Meaning: New Aspects of the Chamber Music." In *The Cambridge Companion to Brahms*, ed. Michael Musgrave, 98–133. Cambridge: Cambridge University Press, 1999.

Brody, Martin. "Liner Notes." Donald Martino, *A Jazz Set*. New World Records 80518, 1996, booklet, 1–9. Online. Available: http://www.newworldrecords.org/liner_notes/80518.pdf. October 17, 2015.

Brown, Clive. *Louis Spohr: A Critical Biography*. Cambridge: Cambridge University Press, 1984.

Brown, John Herschel. *Intimate Music: A History of the Idea of Chamber Music*. Stuyvesant, NY: Pendragon Press, 1998.

Brown, John Robert. "Gervase de Peyer in his 80th Year, part II." *The Clarinet* 33, no. 2 (March 2006): 62–64.

Brymer, Jack. *Clarinet*. New York: Schirmer Books, 1977.

Bylander, Cindy. *Krzysztof Penderecki: A Bio-Bibliography*. Westport, CT: Prager, 2004.

Burney, Charles. *The Present State of Music in Germany, the Netherlands, and United Provinces. Or, the Journal of a Tour through these Countries, Undertaken to Collect Materials for a General History of Music*. 2nd ed., 2 vols. London: T. Becket, J. Robson, G. Robinson, 1775.

Butterworth, Neil. *The Music of Aaron Copland*. London: Toccata Press, 1985.

Cæsar, Clifford. *Igor Stravinsky: A Complete Catalogue*. San Francisco: San Francisco Press, 1982.

Cain, Peter L. "A 'Farewell' to his Past: Krzysztof Penderecki's *Clarinet Quartet and Sextet*." Doctor of Musical Arts diss., University of Cincinnati, 2012.

Campbell, David, "Master Class: Five Bagatelles for Clarinet & Piano by Gerald Finzi." *The Clarinet* 26, no. 3 (June 1999): 8–10.

Carlucci, Joseph B. "An Analytical Study of Published Clarinet Sonatas by American Composers." Doctor of Musical Arts diss., Eastman School of Music, 1957.

Carner, Mosco. *Alban Berg: The Man and the Work*. 2nd rev. ed. New York: Holmes & Meier, 1983.

Carr, Maureen A. *After the Rite: Stravinsky's Path to Neoclassicism (1914–25)*. Oxford: Oxford University Press, 2014.

Carse, Adam. *The Orchestra from Beethoven to Berlioz*. Cambridge: W. Heffer & Sons, 1948.

Cawein, Diane Carolyn. "A Comparative Study of Nineteenth-Century Works for Clarinet Based on Motives from the Operas by Vincenzo Bellini." Doctor of Music diss., Florida State University, 1999.

Cellier, Frédéric. "La Musique avec Clarinette de Jean Françaix." *Clarinette Magazine*, no. 28 (1998): 7–11.

Chen, Wen-Mi. "An Analysis of Sonata Form in Clarinet Concertos by Wolfgang Amadeus Mozart, Louis Spohr, and Carl Maria von Weber." Doctor of Musical Arts diss., University of Cincinnati, 2012.

Chen, Yu-Chien. "An Analytic Interpretation of the Clarinet Concerto by Jean Françaix." Master of Music thesis, California State University, Northridge, 2013.

Chłopicka, Regina. "Stylistic Phases in the Works of Krzysztof Penderecki." *Studies in Penderecki* 1 (1998): 51–64.

Childs, Barney. "Young Performers & New Music." *Music Educator's Journal* 51, no. 1 (September–October 1964): 40–42.

Clive, Peter. *Brahms and His World*. Lanham, MD: Scarecrow Press, 2006.

Cohn, Arthur. *The Literature of Chamber Music*. 4 vols. Chapel Hill, NC: Hinshaw Music, 1997.

Collaer, Paul. *Darius Milhaud, With a Definitive Catalogue of Works Compiled from the Composer's own Notebooks by Madeleine Milhaud*. Rev., trans., and ed. J. H. Galante, San Francisco: San Francisco Press, Inc., 1988.

Collier, James Lincoln. *Benny Goodman and the Swing Era*. New York: Oxford University Press, 1989.

[Collis, James]. "Copland's Clarinet Concerto." *The Clarinet* 1, no. 3 (Fall 1950): 24–25.

Connor, D. Russell and Warren W. Hicks, *BG on the Record: A Bio-Discography of Benny Goodman*. New Rochelle, NY: Arlington House, 1969.

Conrad, Doda. *Dodascalies: Ma Chronique du XXᵉ siècle*. Arles: Actes Sud, 1997.

Constaple, Britta. *Der Musikverlag Johann André in Offenbach am Main: Studien zur Verlagstätigkeit von Johann Anton André und Verzeichnis der Musikalien von 1800 bis 1840*. Tutzing: H. Schneider, 1998.

Copland, Aaron. *Copland on Music*. Garden City, NY: Doubleday and Co., 1960.

Copland, Aaron and Vivian Perlis. *The Complete Copland*. Hillsdale, NY: Pendragon Press, 2013.

———. *Copland: Since 1943*. New York: St. Martin's Press, 1989.

Craft, Robert, ed. *Stravinsky, Selected Correspondence*. 3 vols. New York: Knopf, 1982–1985.

Creditor, Bruce. "The Clarinet Section of the Boston Symphony Orchestra 1987." *The Clarinet* 14, no. 2 (Winter 1987): 36–37.

Cremaschi, Andrea. "*Sequenza IX* for Clarinet: Text, Pre-Text, Con-Text." In *Berio's Sequenzas*, ed. Janet K. Halfyard, 153–70. Aldershot: Ashgate, 2007.

Crist, Elizabeth Bergmann and Wayne D. Shirley, eds. *The Selected Correspondence of Aaron Copland*. New Haven, CT: Yale University Press, 2006.

Cuper, Philippe. "Le Concerto pour Clarinette de Jean Françaix." *Clarinette Magazine*, no. 28 (1998): 12–13. Trans. P. Cuper, "Jean Françaix *Clarinet Concerto*." *The Clarinet* 40, no. 3 (June 2013): 42–43.

Cuper, Philippe and Jean-Marie Paul. "The Paris Conservatoire Supérieur: 'Solo de Concours' and Prize Winners from the Origins to the Present Day." *The Clarinet* 15, no. 3 (May–June 1988): 40–48.

"Cyclic Form," *The Harvard Dictionary of Music*, 4th ed., ed. Don Michael Randall, Cambridge, MA: Belknap Press, 2003, 231.

Dahlström, Fabian. "B. H. Crusell à Paris en 1803." *Finnish Music Quarterly*, Numéro Spècial en Français 6 (1990): 54–58.

———. *Bernhard Henrik Crusell: Klarinettisten och hans Store Instrumentalverk*. Helsingfors: Svenska Litteratursällskapet i Finland, 1976.

———. "Preface," to Bernhard Henrik Crusell, *Konsert för Klarinett och Orkester f-moll = Concerto for Clarinet and Orchestra, F minor, op. 5, Monumenta Musicae Svecicae*, 16, eds. Fabian Dahlström and Margareta Rörby, Stockholm: Edition Reimers, 1995.

Dangain, Guy. "Debussy et la Rhapsodie pour Clarinette." *Journal d'Informations Selmer Paris*, no. 15 (December 2003): supplément, 1–4. Online. Available: http://www.selmer.fr/media/action/partitions/Debussy_site.pdf. September 18, 2015.

Daniel, Keith W. *Francis Poulenc, His Artistic Development and Musical Style*. Ann Arbor, MI: UMI Research Press, 1982.

———. "Poulenc's Choral Works with Orchestra." In *Francis Poulenc: Music, Art and Literature*, eds. Sidney Buckland and Myriam Chimènes, 48–86. Aldershot: Ashgate, 1999.

Darmstädter, Beatrix. "Clarinets and Tárogatós used in the Viennese Court Opera under the director Gustav Mahler," *Proceedings of the Clarinet and Woodwind Colloquium 2007: Celebrating the Collection of Sir Nicholas Shackleton*, ed. A. Myers, 225-36. Edinburgh: Edinburgh Collection of Historic Musical Instruments, 2012.

Davenport, David. "Carl Nielsen's *Clarinet Concerto*: Specific Interpretation Approach/Part II." *Percussive Notes* 31, no. 5 (June 1993): 52–60.

Daverio, John. "'Beautiful and Abstruse Conversations': The Chamber Music of Schumann." In *Nineteenth-Century Chamber Music*, ed. Stephen E. Hefling, 208–41. New York: Schirmer Books, 1998.

———. *Robert Schumann: Herald of a "New Poetic Age."* New York: Oxford University Press, 1997.

Debussy, Claude. "Première Rhapsodie pour Clarinette et Piano," *Dans le salon d'Emma Bardac*, Ligia, CD 2010.

DeFotis, William. "Berg's Op. 5: Rehearsal Instructions." *Perspectives of New Music* 17, no. 1 (Autumn–Winter 1978): 131–37.

Del Rosso, Charles Francis. "A Study of Selected Solo Clarinet Literature of Four American Composers as a Basis for Performance and Teaching." Doctor of Education diss., Teachers College, Columbia University, 1969.

De Peyer, Gervase. "Arthur Benjamin's *Le tombeau de Ravel*." *The Clarinet* 18, no. 2 (February–March 1991): 16.

DeRoche, Julie. "Master Class: *Three Pieces* by Igor Stravinsky." *The Clarinet* 32, no. 1 (December 2004): 4, 6, 8–9.

Denman, John. "English Clarinet Music (continued)." *The Clarinet* 8, no. 1 (Fall 1980): 12–13.

Deutsch, Otto Erich. *Musikverlager's Nummern: eine Auswahl von 40 datierten Listen, 1710–1900*. Berlin: Merseburger, 1961.

Devriès, Anik and François Lesure. *Dictionnaire des Éditeurs de Musique Français*. 2 vols. Genève: Minkoff, 1979–1988.

Dickinson, A. E. F. "The Chamber Music." In *Schumann: A Symposium*, ed. Gerald Abraham, 138–75. Oxford: Oxford University Press, 1952.

Draheim, Joachim. "Preface." In Robert Schumann, *Fantasiestücke für Klarinette (Violin, Violoncello) und Klavier op. 73*, ed. Joachim Draheim. Wiesbaden: Breitkopf & Härtel, 2006.

Dressler, John C. *Gerald Finzi: A Bio-Bibliography*. Westport, CT: Greenwood Press, 1997.

Dufallo, Richard. *Trackings: Composers Speak with Richard Dufallo*. New York: Oxford University Press, 1989.

Eberhardt, Hans. "Johann Simon Hermstedt 1778–1845: Seine Bedeutung als Klarinettenvirtuose." *Mitteilungen des Vereins für deutsche Geschichte und Altertumskunde in Sondershausen* 10 (1940): 95–143.

Einzeldrucke vor 1800, International Inventory of Musical Sources. Series A/1, 15 vols. Kassel: Bärenreiter, 1971–2012.

Ellsworth, Jane. *A Dictionary for the Modern Clarinetist*. Lanham, MD: Rowman & Littlefield, 2015.

Erismann, Guy. *Martinů, un Musicien à L'éveil des Sources*. Arles: Actes Sud, 1990.

Estock, James. "A Biographical Dictionary of Clarinetists Born Before 1800." Ph.D. diss., University of Iowa, 1972.

Evans, David H. "Franz Krommer (1759–1831) and His Music for Clarinet: A Stylistic Analysis and Interpretive Study of Selected Works." Doctor of Music diss., Indiana University, 1986.

Fabbri, Mario. "Ignoti Momenti Rossiniani: Contributo all'indagine sul 'Lungo Silenzio' di Rossini e alla Conoscenza dell' Attività Creative Minore del Maestro; Le Segrete Confessioni a Ferdinando Giorgetti e le Sconosciute 'Variazioni' per Alessandro Abate (1817)." *Chigiana* 25 (1968): 265–85.

Faria, Richard. "Master Class: *In Freundschaft* by Karlheinz Stockhausen." *The Clarinet* 29, no. 3 (June 2002): 4–9.

Ferguson, Howard and Michael Hurd, eds. *Letters of Gerald Finzi and Howard Ferguson*. Woodbridge: Boydell Press, 2001.

Fétis, François-Joseph. *Biographie Universelle des Musiciens et Bibliographie Générale de la Musique*. 2nd ed., 8 vols. Paris: Didot Frères, 1883–1889.

———. "Nécrologie. Notice sur J. X. Lefèvre." *Revue Musicale* 6 (November 20, 1830): 399.

Finzi, Gerald. "List of Complete Works, Boosey & Hawkes." Online. Available: http://www .boosey.com/cr/catalogue/ps/powersearch_results.asp?search=Finzi. October 9, 2015.

Firestone, Ross. *Swing, Swing, Swing: The Life & Times of Benny Goodman*. New York: Norton, 1993.

Fleischmann, Ernst. "Full of Phantasy, Uncompromising—Boulez the Conductor and Impresario." In *Pierre Boulez: eine Festschrift zum 60. Geburtstag am 26. März 1985*, ed. Josef Häusler, 16–21. Vienna: Universal Edition, 1985.

The French Clarinet School—Revisited. Harrington Park, NJ: Grenadilla RGP-1008, CD, 2000.

Fricke, Heike. *Catalogue of the Sir Nicholas Shackleton Collection: Historic Musical Instruments in the Edinburgh University Collection*. Ed. Arnold Meyers, Edinburgh: Edinburgh University Collection of Historic Musical Instruments, 2007.

———. "Johann Simon Hermstedt und seine Klarinetten." *Rohrblatt* 29, no. 3 (2014): 136–39.

Frisch, Walter. *Brahms and the Principle of Developing Variation*. Berkeley: University of California Press, 1984.

Gee, Harry. *Clarinet Solos de Concours, 1897–1980: An Annotated Bibliography*. Bloomington: Indiana University Press, 1981.

Gérard, Bernadette. "Inventaire Alphabétique des Documents Repértoriés Relatifs aux Musiciens Parisiens Conservè aux Archives de Paris." *Recherches sur la Musique Française Classique* 13 (1973): 181–213.

Gétreau, Florence. *Aux Origines du Musée de la Musique: Les Collections Instrumentales du Conservatoire de Paris 1793–1993*. Paris: Klincksieck, 1996.

Gibson, Lee. "Reginald Kell: The Artist and his Music." *The Clarinet* 5, no. 1 (Fall 1977): 8–9.

Gilbert, Richard. *The Clarinetists' Discography III*. Harrington Park, NJ: RG Productions, 1991.

Gillespie, James E. Jr. *Solos for Unaccompanied Clarinet: An Annotated Bibliography of Published Works*. Detroit: Information Coordinators, Inc., 1973.

———. "The International Clarinet Congress London, England—August 12–17, 1984." *The Clarinet* vol. 12, no. 1 (Fall 1984): 6–17.

Gold, Cecil. *Clarinet Performing Practices and Teaching in the United States and Canada*. 2nd ed., [Moscow, Idaho]: University of Idaho, 1973.

Goldbach, Felix Constantin. "'Prelude' for Solo Clarinet (1987) by Krzysztof Penderecki." In *Recent Researches in Mechanics, Transportation & Culture. Vouliagmeni, Athens, Greece December 29–31, 2010*, 62–66. Online. Available: http://www.wseas.us/e-library/conferences/2010/Vouliagmeni/MECH/MECH-08.pdf. October 20, 2015.

Goltz, Maren and Herta Müller. *Richard Mühlfeld der Brahms-Klarinettist, Einleitung, Übertragung, und Kommentar der Dokumentation von Christian Mühlfeld*. English trans. Mona Lemmel. *Richard Mühlfeld, Brahms' Clarinettist: Introduction, Transcription, and Commentary of the Documentation by Christian Mühlfeld*. Balve: Artivo, 2007.

González, Marcelo Daniel. "Harlekin von Karlheinz Stockhausen: Wie ich das 45 minütige Stück auswendig Spielen und Tanzen Lernte." *Rohrblatt* 22, no. 1 (March 2007): 35–37.

Göthel, Folker. *Thematisch-Bibliographisches Verzeichnis der Werke von Louis Spohr*. Tutzing: Schneider, 1981.

Gradenwitz, Peter. "The Beginnings of Clarinet Literature: Notes on a Clarinet Concerto by Joh. Stamitz." *Music & Letters* 17, no. 2 (April 1936): 145–50.

———. "Concerto Find: Story Behind the Uncovering of Stamitz Work for Clarinet and Orchestra." *New York Times* (April 1, 1951), section 7, 103.

———. *Johann Stamitz: Leben-Umwelt-Werke*. 2 vols. Wilhelmshaven: Hinrichshofen, 1984.

Graulty, John. "Debussy for Clarinet: The Music and the Conservatoire Context." ClarinetFest 2001 Archives, International Clarinet Association.

Grenser, Heinrich. Eleven-key clarinet owned by Bernhard Crusell. Scenkonst Museet, Swedish Museum of Performing Arts, N.43554. Online. Available: http://instrument.musikverket.se/samlingar/detalj.php?l=sv&iid=288&v=2009-08-25%2014:19:28&str=. September 17, 2015.

Griffiths, Paul. *Modern Music and After*. 3rd ed., Oxford: Oxford University Press, 2010.

Grimley, Daniel. "Analytical and Aesthetic Issues in Carl Nielsen's Concerto for Clarinet and Orchestra." *Carl Nielsen Studies* 1 (2003): 27–41.

The Grove Dictionary of Musical Instruments, 2nd ed., ed. L. Libin, 5 vols. (New York: Oxford University Press, 2014); also on *Grove Music Online*.

Grove Music Online published by *Oxford Music Online*.

Haase, Heribert. *Clarinet Bibliography ClarLit 55000 Data Records, Version 2012 E*. 3rd update, [Germany]: printed by author, 2012. Available: CD-ROM.

Haberkamp, Gertraut. *Die Musikhandschriften der Fürst Thurn und Taxis Hofbibliothek Regensburg: Thematischer Katalog*. Munich: Henle, 1981.

Hacker, Alan and Richard Platt. "Preface." In Robert Schumann, *Soiréestücke for Clarinet and Piano, opus 73*, eds. Alan Hacker and Richard Platt. London: Faber Music, 1985.

Halbreich, Harry. *Bohuslav Martinů: Werkverzeichnis und Biografie*. 2nd rev. ed., Mainz: Schott, 2007.

Halfyard, Janet K., ed. *Berio's Sequenzas: Essays on Performance, Composition and Analysis*. Aldershot: Ashgate, 2007.

Harbaugh, Justin Martin. "The Clarinet B.C. Program Notes for a Masters Clarinet Recital of Works of Brahms' *Clarinet Trio*, Françaix's *Tema con varizioni*, Muczynski's *Time Pieces*, and Carter's *Gra* and *Hiyoku*." Master of Music thesis, Kansas State University, 2009.

Harding, James. *Saint-Saëns and his Circle*. London: Chapman & Hall, 1965.

Harkins, Elizabeth R. "The Chamber Music of Camille Saint-Saëns." Ph.D. diss., New York University, 1976.

Heaton, Roger. "Contemporary Performance Practice and Tradition." *Music Performance Research* 5 (2012): 96–104. Online. Available: http://mpr-online.net/Issues/Volume%205%20 [2012]/Heaton.pdf. July 20, 2016.

Heim, Norman M. "Sonatinas for Clarinet and Piano." *NACWPI Journal* 39, no. 2 (Winter 1990–1991): 10–16.

Heinemann, Ernst-Günter. "Comments." In Claude Debussy, *Première Rhapsodie and Petite Pièce for Clarinet and Piano*. Ed. Ernst-Günter Heinemann, 18–20. Munich: G. Henle, 2004.

Helgert, Lars Erik. "Jazz Elements in Selected Concert Works of Leonard Bernstein: Sources Reception, and Analysis." Ph.D. diss., Catholic University of America, 2008.

Hell, Henri. *Francis Poulenc: Musicien Français*. Paris: Fayard, 1978.

Henderson, Michael. "Some Past and Present Reactions to Martinů and His Music." In *Bohuslav Martinů Anno 1981: Papers from an International Musicological Conference, Prague, 26–28 May, 1981*. Ed. Jitta Brabcová, 255–60. Prague: Česká Hudební Sploečnost, 1990.

Herttrich, Ernst. "Preface." In Robert Schumann, *Fantasiestücke Opus 73 für Klavier und Klarinette*, ed. Ernst Herttrich. Munich: G. Henle, 2005.

Heyman, Barbara B. "Stravinsky and Ragtime." *Musical Quarterly* 68, no. 4 (October 1982): 543–62.

Hilmar, Ernst, ed. *Arnold Schönberg: Gedenkausstellung 1974*. Vienna: Universal Edition, 1974.

Hilmar, Rosemary. *Alban Berg: Leben und Wirken in Wien bis zu seinen Ersten Erfolgen als Komponist*. Vienna: H. Böhlaus, 1978.

———. *Katalog der Musikhandschriften, Schriften und Studien Alban Bergs im Fond Alban Berg und der Weiteren Handschriftlichen Quellen im Besitz der Österreichischen Nationalbibliothek*. Vienna: Universal Edition, 1981.

Hindemith, Paul. "Foreword." In *French Secular Music of the Late Fourteenth Century*. Ed. Willi Apel. Cambridge, MA: Medieval Academy of America, 1950.

Hoeprich, Eric. *The Clarinet*. New Haven, CT: Yale University Press, 2008.

———. "Notes." In Bernhard Crusell, *Klarinettenkonzerte*, Ars Produktion, 2006.

Howells, Herbert. "Arthur Benjamin 1893–1960." *Tempo* 55/56 (Autumn–Winter 1960): 2–3.

"Intégrale des *Sequenze* de Luciano Berio." Dimanche 8 décembre 2013, program at the Cité de la Musique, Paris. Online. Available: http://content.citedelamusique.fr/pdf/note_programme/np_13688.pdf. September 10, 2015.

Ishigaki, Miles Mitsuru. "A Study of Comparative Interpretations of the Three Pieces for Clarinet Solo by Igor Stravinsky." Doctor of Musical Arts diss., University of Oklahoma, 1988.

Jähns, Friedrich Wilhelm. *Carl Maria von Weber in seinen Werken: Chronologisch-Thematischer Verzeichniss seiner Sämmtlicher Compositionen*. Berlin: Schlesinger'schen Buch und Musikhandlung, 1871, reprint ed., Berlin: R. Lienau, 1967.

Jameux, Dominique. *Pierre Boulez.* Trans. Susan Bradshaw. Cambridge: Harvard University Press, 1991.

Jarman, Douglas. *The Music of Alban Berg.* Berkeley: University of California Press, 1979.

Jeltsch, Jean. *La Clarinette à Six Clés: Un Jeu de Clarinettes du Facteur Parisien Jean-Jacques Baumann.* Trans. in English Emer Buckley; in German Susi Möhlmeier; in Japanese Haru Yamagami. Courlay: J. M. Fuzeau, 1997.

———. "Introduction." In *Trois Grandes Sonates: pour Clarinette et Basse 1793.* Courlay: J. M. Fuzeau, 1998.

Jennings, Vance Shelby. "Selected Twentieth Century Clarinet Solo Literature: A Study in Interpretation and Performance." Doctor of Music Education diss., University of Oklahoma, 1972.

Johnson, Madeline LeBaron. "An Examination of the Clarinet Works of Luigi Bassi." Doctor of Musical Arts diss., University of North Texas, 2007.

Johnston, Stephen K. "The Clarinet Concertos of Louis Spohr." Doctor of Musical Arts diss., University of Maryland, 1972.

———. "The Clarinet Concertos of Louis Spohr: Some Notes on Performance and Importance." *The Clarinet* 5, no. 4 (1978): 25–26, 28.

Jones, Timothy Rhys. "Variation Form." *The Oxford Companion to Music, Oxford Music Online.*

Julliard Manuscript Collection, Aaron Copland, "Concerto for Clarinet and String Orchestra (and Harp)." Online. Available: http://juilliardmanuscriptcollection.org/manuscript/ concerto-clarinet-string-orchestra-harp-piano/. September 12, 2015.

Jungerman, Mary. "The Single-Reed Music of Karlheinz Stockhausen—How Does One Begin?" *The Clarinet* 27, no. 1 (December 1999): 52–57.

Kagan, Susan. *Archduke Rudolph, Beethoven's Patron, Pupil, and Friend: His Life and Music.* Stuyvesant, NY: Pendragon Press, 1988.

Keck, George R. *Francis Poulenc: A Bio-Bibliography.* New York: Greenwood Press, 1990.

Keller, Hans. "Arthur Benjamin and the Problem of Popularity." *Tempo* 15 (Spring 1950): 7–9.

Kelly, Barbara L. *Tradition and Style in the Works of Darius Milhaud 1912–1939.* Aldershot: Ashgate, 2003.

Kidd, James C. "Aspects of Mensuration in Hindemith's Clarinet Sonata." *Music Review* 38, no. 3 (August 1977): 211–22.

Klarinette Konzerte des 18. Jahrhunderts, Das Erbe Deutscher Musik, Band 41, ed. Heinz Becker, Wiesbaden: Breitkopf & Härtel, 1957.

Kleppinger, Stanley V. "On the Influence of Jazz Rhythm in the Music of Aaron Copland." *American Music* 21, no. 1 (Spring 2003): 74–111.

Knight, George Washington. "A Comparative Study of Compositional Techniques Employed in Instructional Materials and Twentieth-Century Solos for the Clarinet." Doctor of Musical Arts in Music Education diss., University of Illinois at Champaign-Urbana, 1973.

Kohlhase, Hans. *Die Kammermusik Robert Schumanns.* 3 vols. Hamburg: Wagner Musikalienhandlung, 1979.

Koons. Keith. "A Guide to Published Editions of Mozart's Clarinet Concerto, KV622, for Clarinet and Piano." *The Clarinet* 25, no. 3 (May–June 1998): 34–43.

Koukal, Bohumír. "Franz Vincenc Krommer (Kramář) and His Solo Works for Clarinet." *The Clarinet* 12, no. 2 (Winter 1985): 18.

Kratochvíl, Jiří. "Koncertantní Klarinet v Českém Klasicismu." *Ziva Hudbá* 9 (1968): 285–372.

Kroll, Oskar. *The Clarinet*. Rev. and with a repertory Diethard Riehm, trans. Hilda Morris, ed. Anthony Baines. New York: Taplinger, 1968.

———. "Weber und Baermann." *Zeitschrift für Musik* 103, no. 12 (December 1936): 1439–43.

Kuhn, Laura Diane and Nicholas Slonimsky. *Music since 1900*. 6th ed. New York: Schirmer Reference, 2001.

Laird, Paul R. *Leonard Bernstein: A Guide to Research*. New York: Routledge, 2002.

Lawson, Colin. *Brahms: Clarinet Quintet*. Cambridge: Cambridge University Press, 1998.

———. "The C Clarinet." In *The Cambridge Companion to the Clarinet*. Ed. C. Lawson, 38–42. Cambridge: Cambridge University Press, 1995.

———. *Mozart: Clarinet Concerto*. Cambridge: Cambridge University Press, 1996.

———. "Playing Historical Clarinets." In *The Cambridge Companion to the Clarinet*. Ed. C. Lawson, 134–49. Cambridge: Cambridge University Press, 1995.

Lawson, Jack. *Carl Nielsen*. London: Phaidon Press, 1997.

Layton, Robert. "Nielsen and the Gramaphone." In *The Nielsen Companion*, ed. Mina F. Miller, 116–50. Portland: Amadeus Press, 1994.

Lee, Douglas. *Masterworks of 20th-Century Music: The Modern Repertory of the Symphony Orchestra*. New York: Routledge, 2002.

Lee, Ronald Thomas. "Background Studies for an Authentic Performance of Johann Stamitz's *Concerto in B-flat major for Clarinet and Strings*." Master of Music thesis, University of Michigan, 1966.

Leeson, Daniel N. and David Whitwell, "Concerning Mozart's *Serenade in B♭ for Thirteen Instruments, K. 361 (370a)*," *Mozart Jahrbuch* 1976/1977, 97–130.

Le Fèvre, Xavier. *Méthode de Clarinette*. Paris: L'Imprimerie du Conservatoire, [1802], facsimile ed., Genève: Minkoff Reprint, 1974.

Lesure, François. *Catalogue de L'oeuvre de Claude Debussy*. Geneva: Minkoff, 1977.

———. "Deux Lettres de Gabriel Fauré à C. Debussy (1910–1917)." In "Claude Debussy (1862–1962) Textes et Documents Inédites." *Revue de Musicologie* XLVIII (July–December 1962): 75–77.

Lesure, François. Ed. and trans. Roger Nichols. *Debussy Letters*. Cambridge, MA: Harvard University Press, 1987.

Lewis, David S. "Nielsen's Concerto for Clarinet: Discrepancies between Part and Score." *The Clarinet* 2, no. 1 (December 1974): 9–10.

Lindner, Adalbert. *Max Reger: Ein Bild seines Jugendlebens und Künstlerischen Werdens*. Stuttgart: J. Engelhorns Nachf., 1922.

Link, Dorothea. *The National Court Theatre in Mozart's Vienna: Sources and Documents, 1783-1792*. Oxford: Clarendon Press, 1998.

Litzmann, Berthold. *Clara Schumann; Ein Künstlerleben. Nach Tagebüchern und Briefen. Band 2: Ehejahre 1840–1856*. 3rd expanded ed. Leipzig: Breitkopf & Härtel, 1907.

———. ed. *Letters of Clara Schumann and Johannes Brahms, 1853–1896*. 2 vols. London: Longmans, Green and Co., 1927.

Lockspieser, Edward. *Debussy, His Life and Mind: Vol. II, 1902–1918*. New York: Macmillan Co., 1962.

———. "Review of Gerald Finzi, *Five Bagatelles for Clarinet and Piano*." *Music & Letters* 27, no. 3 (July 1946): 201.

Longyear, Rey M. *Nineteenth-Century Romanticism in Music*. 2nd ed., Englewood Cliffs, NJ: Prentice-Hall, 1973.

Ludewig-Verdehr, Elsa. "A Practical Approach to New and Avant-Garde Clarinet Music and Techniques." *The Clarinet* 7, no. 2 (Winter 1980): 13–14.

———. "Master Class: Witold Lutoslawski's *Dance Preludes*." *The Clarinet* 24, no. 4 (July–August 1997): 4–8.

Lurie, Mitchell. "Master Class: Robert Schumann's *Fantasiestücke, Op. 73*." *The Clarinet* 22, no. 1 (November–December 1994): 6–7.

MacDonald, Calum. "Notes." In Arthur Benjamin, *Violin Sonatina & Viola Sonata*, Hyperion, CDA67979, 2014. Online. Available: http://www.hyperion-records.co.uk/dc.asp?dc= D_CDA67969. September 12, 2015.

Maciejewski, Boguslaw Maciej. *Twelve Polish Composers*. London: Allegro Press, 1976.

Maconie, Robin. *Other Planets: The Music of Karlheinz Stockhausen*. Lanham, MD: Scarecrow Press, 2005.

Mandat, Eric and Boja Kraguli. "Performance Analysis: Intersection and Interaction of Motives in the Brahms Op. 120 Sonatas." *The Clarinet* 40, no. 1 (December 2012): 66–70.

———. "Performance Analysis: Debussy's *Première Rhapsodie*—Motivic Permutations and Interactions." *The Clarinet* 40, no. 4 (September 2013): 42–46.

Mason, Colin. "The Chamber Music of Milhaud." *Musical Quarterly* 43, no. 3 (July 1957): 326–41.

Mason, Daniel Gregory. *The Chamber Music of Brahms*. New York: MacMillan Co., 1933.

Mazzeo, Rosario. "Mazzeo Musings, Series II, no. 23 [Igor Stravinsky, *Three Pieces for Clarinet Alone*]." *The Clarinet* 18, no. 3 (May–June 1991): 8–10.

Matthys, Herbert A. Jr. "New Performance Techniques in Selected Solo Clarinet Works of William O. Smith, John Eaton, Donald Martino, and Paul Zonn." Doctor of Music diss., Indiana University, 1982.

Mawer, Deborah. *Darius Milhaud: Modality & Structure in Music of the 1920s*. Aldershot: Scolar Press, 1997.

Maxey, Larry. "The Copland Clarinet Concerto." *The Clarinet* 12, no. 4 (Summer 1985): 28–32.

McClelland, Ryan. *Brahms and the Scherzo: Studies in Musical Narrative*. Farnham: Ashgate, 2010.

McCorkle, Margit L. *Johannes Brahms: Thematisch-Bibliographisches Werkverzeichnis*. Munich: G. Henle, 1984.

———. *Thematisch-Bibliographisches Werkverzeichnis*. Ed. Robert-Schumann-Gesellschaft, Düsseldorf, *Robert Schumann Neue Ausgabe Sämtlicher Werke*. Serie VIII: Supplement Band 6, Mainz: Schott, 2003.

McCutchan, Anne. "Reginald Kell: A Selected Discography." *The Clarinet* 9, no. 2 (Winter 1982): 11.

McDermott, Vincent. "Current Chronicle, United States, Milwaukee." *Musical Quarterly* 54, no. 4 (October 4, 1968): 524–31.

McDonald, Lawrence. "Master Class: *Sonatina* by Bohuslav Martinů." *The Clarinet* 27, no. 1 (December 1999): 4–10.

McVeigh, Diana. *Gerald Finzi: His Life and Music*. Woodbridge: Boydell Press, 2005.

McVeigh, Simon. "The Professional Concert and Rival Subscription Series in London, 1783–1793." *Royal Musical Association Research Chronicle* 22, no. 1 (1989): 1–135.

Mellers, Wilfred. *Francis Poulenc*. Oxford: Oxford University Press, 1993.

Meredith, William. "Sound Recording Essay-Review: Archduke Rudolph's Sonata for Clarinet and Piano and Trio for Clarinet, Cello, and Piano." *Beethoven Journal* 12, no. 1 (Spring 1997): 22–26.

Merriman, Lyle Clinton. "Solos for Unaccompanied Woodwind Instruments: A Checklist of Published Works and Study of Representative Examples." Ph.D. diss., State University of Iowa, 1963.

Michaels, Jost. "Preface" to Bernhard Henrik Crusell, *Concerto F minor for Clarinet and Orchestra*, op. 5, Hamburg: H. Sikorski, 1962.

Minor, Janice L. "'Were They Truly Neoclassic?' A Study of French Neoclassicism Through Selected Clarinet Sonatas by 'Les Six' Composers: Arthur Honegger, Germaine Tailleferre, Darius Milhaud, and Francis Poulenc." Doctor of Musical Arts diss., University of Cincinnati, 2004.

Mitchell, Ian. "Profile of William O. Smith." *Clarinet and Saxophone* 9, no. 1 (1984): 10, 14.

———. "An American Attitude of Adventure." *Clarinet and Saxophone* 21, no. 3 (1996): 41.

———. "Toward a Beginning: Thoughts Leading to an Interpretation of *Domaines* for Solo Clarinet by Pierre Boulez." In *The Versatile Clarinet*, ed. Roger Heaton, 109–32. New York: Routledge, 2006.

———. "William O. Smith—Musical Pioneer: A Look at the Work of One of America's Most Inventive Musicians." In *The Versatile Clarinet,* ed. Roger Heaton, 75–84. New York: Routledge, 2006.

Morgan, Robert P. "Aleatory Music." In *The New Harvard Dictionary of Music,* 4th ed., ed. Don Michael Randel, 28–29. Cambridge, MA: Belknap Press, 2003.

Muczynski. Robert. Theodore Press Company. Online. Available: http://www.presser.com/composer/muczynski-robert/. October 19, 2015.

Musgrave, Michael. *The Music of Brahms.* Oxford: Clarendon Press, 1994.

"Music in the Making: Notes and News about Composers Associated with Boosey & Hawkes." *Tempo* 6 (February 1944): 8–13.

"Nachrichten." *Allgemeine Musikalische Zeitung* 17, no. 27 (July 5, 1815): 451.

"Nachrichten." *Allgemeine Musikalische Zeitung* 20, no. 31 (August 5, 1818): 560.

"Nachrichten." *Allgemeine Musikalische Zeitung* 26, no. 24 (June 10, 1824): 390.

Nectoux, Jean-Michel, ed., J. Barrie Jones, trans. *The Correspondence of Camille Saint-Saëns and Gabriel Fauré: Sixty Years of Friendship.* Aldershot: Ashgate, 2004.

Nelson, Eric. "The Danish Performance Tradition in Carl Nielsen's *Koncert for Klarinet og Orkester,* Opus 57 (1928)." *The Clarinet* 14, no. 2 (Winter 1987): 30–35.

Nestler, Gerhard. "Dreimal Penderecki." *Melos* 35, no. 12 (December 1968): 469–70.

Neumeyer, David. *The Music of Paul Hindemith.* New Haven, CT: Yale University Press, 1986.

New Grove Dictionary of Opera, Grove Music Online.

Newhill, John P. "The Contribution of the Mannheim School to Clarinet Literature." *Music Review* 40, no. 2 (May 1979): 90–122.

———. "Further Information on Rossini's Works for Clarinet." *The Clarinet* 11, no. 3 (Spring 1984): 2.

Nichols, Christopher Robert. "138 Years of the Clarinet: Program Notes for a Master's Clarinet Recital of Works by Reger, Smith, Donizetti, Muczynski, and Schumann." Master of Music thesis, Kansas State University, 2007.

Nikolska, Irina. *Conversations with Witold Lutosławski: (1987–1992).* Trans. Valeri Yerokbin. Stockholm: Melos, 1994.

Noss, Luther. *Paul Hindemith in the United States.* Urbana: University of Illinois Press, 1989.

Notley, Margaret. *Lateness in Brahms: Music and Culture in the Twilight of Viennese Liberalism.* New York: Oxford University Press, 2007.

Nygren, Dennis. "The Music for Accompanied Clarinet Solo of Claude Debussy: An Historical and Analytical Study of the *Première Rhapsodie* and *Petite Pièce*." Doctor of Music diss., Northwestern University, 1982.

———. "Debussy's Works for Clarinet—Part I." *The Clarinet* 12, no. 1 (Fall 1984): 40–42.

———. "Debussy's Works for Clarinet—Part II." *The Clarinet* 12, no. 2 (Winter 1985): 19–21.

———. "The Chamber Music of Berg." *The Clarinet* 13, no. 3 (Spring 1986): 26–31.

"Obituary, Arthur Benjamin." *The Musical Times* 101, no. 1408 (June 1960): 380.

Odom, David H. "A Catalog of Compositions for Unaccompanied Clarinet Published Between 1978 and 1982, with an Annotated Bibliography of Selected Works." Doctor of Music diss., Florida State University, 2005.

Osmond-Smith, David. *Berio*. Oxford: Oxford University Press, 1991.

Osmond-Smith, David, ed. and trans. *Two Interviews/Luciano Berio: Rossana Dalmonte; Bálint András Varga*. New York: Marion Boyars, 1985.

Oxford Companion to Music, Oxford Music Online.

Oxford Dictionary of Music, Oxford Music Online.

Oxford Music Online.

Page, Tim and Vanessa Weeks Page, eds. *Selected Letters of Virgil Thomson*. New York: Summit Books, 1988.

Paja-Stach, Jadwiga. "The Stylistic Traits of Lutosławski's Works for Solo Instrument and Piano." In *Lutosławski Studies*, ed. Zbigniew Skowron, 269–86. Oxford: Oxford University Press, 2001.

Park, Raymond Roy. "The Later Style of Claude Debussy." Ph.D. diss., University of Michigan, 1967.

Parks, Richard S. "Music's Inner Dance: Form, Pacing and Complexity in Debussy's Music." In *The Cambridge Companion to Debussy*, ed. Simon Trezise, 197–231. New York: Cambridge University Press, 2003.

Paul, Jean-Marie with Eric Perrier. "Jacques Lancelot: A Tribute." *The Clarinet* 34, no. 1 (December 2006): 43–49.

Paul Hindemith: Werkverzeichnis = List of Works. Mainz: Schott, 1985.

Pay, Tony. Berio *Sequenza IXa*, Klarinet Archive posting, 13 January 2000. Online. Available: http://test.woodwind.org/Databases/Klarinet/2000/01/000392.txt. September 10, 2015.

———. Alternative fingering for Berio's *Sequenza IXa*. Online. Available: http://www.woodwind .org/clarinet/Study/Berio.html. September 10, 2015.

Payne, Dorothy Katherine. "The Accompanied Wind Sonatas of Hindemith: Studies in Tonal Counterpoint." Ph.D. diss., University of Rochester, 1974.

Pearson, Ingrid. "Playing Historical Clarinets." In Colin Lawson, *The Early Clarinet: A Practical Guide*, 41–62. Cambridge: Cambridge University Press, 2000.

Penderecki Awards. Online. Available: www.music-unites.com/krzysztof_penderecki/awards/. October 20, 2015.

Peruzzi, Elio. "Preface." In Gioacchino Rossini, *Variazioni per clarinetto e pianoforte*, Padova: G. Zanibon, 1968.

Petersen, Kirsten Flensborg. "Foreword." In Carl Nielsen, *Koncerter = Concertos*. Series II. Instrumental Music 9, eds. Elly Bruunshuus Petersen and Kirsten Flensborg Petersen. Copenhagen: W. Hansen, 2002.

Peyser, Joan. *To Boulez and Beyond: Music in Europe Since The Rite of Spring*. New York: Billboard Books, 1999.

Pierce, Linda J. "William O. Smith I.C.S. 1987 Commission." *The Clarinet* 14, no. 4 (Summer 1987): 26–28.

Pierre, Constant. *Histoire du Concert Spirituel: 1725–1790*. Paris: Société française de musicologie, 1975.

———. *Le Magasin de Musique à L'usage des Fêtes Nationales et du Conservatoire*. Paris: Fischbacher, 1895.

Place, Adélaïde de. "Luciano Berio." In *Guide de la Musique de Chambre*, eds. François-René Tranchefort, Adélaïde de Place, Pierre-Emile Barbier, Harry Halbreich, et al., 115–21. Paris: Fayard, 1989.

Pollock, Daniel. *Aaron Copland: The Life and Work of an Uncommon Man*. New York: Henry Holt and Company, 1999.

Pope, Kathy. "Master Class: *Introduction, Theme, and Variations* by Giocchino Rossini (1792–1868)." *The Clarinet* 31, no. 4 (September 2004): 6–9.

Popelka, Iša, ed. trans. Ralph Slayton, English version eds. Martin Anderson and Aleš Březina. *Martinů's Letters Home: Five Decades of Correspondence with Family and Friends*. London: Toccata Press, 2012.

Poulenc, Francis. *Selected Correspondence, 1915–1963: Echo and Source*. Trans. and ed. Sidney Buckland, research consultant Patrick Saul, London: Victor Gollancz Ltd., 1991.

Poulin, Pamela. "Anton Stadler's Basset Clarinet: Recent Discoveries in Riga." *Journal of the American Musical Instrument Society* 22 (1996): 110–27.

Pound, Gomer J. "A Study of Clarinet Solo Concerto Literature Composed Before 1850, with Selected Items Edited and Arranged for Contemporary Use." Ph.D. diss., Florida State University, 1965.

Powell, Maurice F. "Spohr's Music for the Clarinet." *Spohr Journal* 1, no. 3 (Spring 1972): 5–10.

Prod'homme, Jacques Gabriel. "Camille Saint-Saëns." *Musical Quarterly* 8, no. 4 (October 1922): 469–86.

Radnofsky, Kenneth. "Portraits of Improvisation." *Winds Quarterly* 1 (1980): 17–21.

Rae, Charles Bodman. *The Music of Lutosławski*. London: Faber and Faber, 1994.

"Rapport fait pour la Commission chargée d'examiner la Nouvelle Clarinette Propose par M. Muller, et la Clarinette Alto Perfectionnée par la Même Artiste." *Gazette Nationale, ou le Moniteur Universel* 152 (1812): 593–94.

Ratner, Sabina Teller. *Camille Saint-Saëns 1835–1921: A Thematic Catalogue of his Complete Works. Vol. 1, The Instrumental Works*. Oxford: Oxford University Press, 2002.

Reed, Philip. "Poulenc, Britten, Aldeburgh: A Chronicle." In *Francis Poulenc: Music, Art and Literature*, eds. Sidney Buckland and Myriam Chimènes, 348–62. Aldershot: Ashgate, 1999.

Rees, Brian. *Camille Saint-Saëns: A Life*. London: Chatto & Windus, 1999.

Rees-Davies, Jo. "The Development of the Clarinet Repertoire." In *The Cambridge Companion to the Clarinet*, ed. C. Lawson, 75–91. Cambridge: Cambridge University Press, 1995.

Reger, Max. *Briefe eines Deutschen Meisters: Ein Lebensbild*. Ed. Else von Hase-Koehler, Leipzig: Koehler & Amelang, 1928.

Rehfeldt, Phillip. *New Directions for Clarinet*. Rev. ed. Berkeley: University of California Press, 1994.

———. "Master Class: Donald Martino, *A Set for Clarinet (Unaccompanied)*." *The Clarinet* 23, no. 3 (May–June 1996): 6–7.

Reinoso, Crystal Hearne. "Sources and Inspirations for Stravinsky's *Three Pieces for Clarinet Solo, Part I*." *The Clarinet* 23, no. 3 (May–June 1996): 28–32.

———. "Sources and Inspirations for Stravinsky's *Three Pieces for Clarinet Solo, Part II.*" *The Clarinet* 23, no. 4 (July–August 1996): 26–29.

Reissenberger, Benjamin. "Schumann und die Klarinette." *Rohrblatt* 25, no. 2 (June 2010): 63–65.

Rendall, F. Geoffrey. *The Clarinet*. 3rd ed., rev. P. Bate. London: E. Benn, 1971.

"Review of Alban Berg, *Vier Stücke für Klarinette und Klavier.*" *Le Ménestrel* 83, no. 23 (June 10, 1921): 244.

"Review of Aaron Copland, *Concerto for Clarinet and String Orchestra.*" *Music & Letters* 33, no. 4 (1952): 366.

"Review of Bernhard Crusell, *Concerto, op. 5.*" *Allgemeine Musikalische Zeitung* 20 (August 1818): 560–61.

Rice, Albert R. *The Baroque Clarinet*. Oxford: Clarendon Press, 1992.

———. "Clarinet Fingering Charts, 1732–1816." *Galpin Society Journal* 37 (March 1984): 16–41.

———. *The Clarinet in the Classical Period*. New York: Oxford University Press, 2003.

———. "The Development of the Clarinet as Depicted in Austro-German Instruction Sources, 1732–1892." In *Tradition und Innovation im Holzblasinstrumentenbau des 19. Jahrhunderts*, ed. Sebastian Werr, 81–112. Augsburg: Wissner, 2012.

Ringer, Alexander J. "Schoenbergiana in Jerusalem." *Musical Quarterly* 59, no. 1 (January 1973): 1–14.

Rischin, Rebecca. "The Thinking Clarinet: Berio's *Sequenza* (1980)." *The Clarinet* 40, no. 1 (December 2012): 51–57.

Robinson, Ray. *Krzysztof Penderecki: A Guide to His Works*. Princeton, NJ: Prestige Publications, Inc., 1983.

———. "Penderecki's Reception in the United States of America." In *The Music of Krzysztof Penderecki: Poetics and Reception: Studies, Essays and Materials*, eds. Mieczysław Tomaszewski and Władysław Chłopicki, 163–83. Kraków: Akademia Muzyczna, 1995.

Rochlitz, Johann Friedrich. "Anzeigen." *Allgemeine musikalische Zeitung* 20, no. 24 (June 17 1818): 443.

Rosenberg, Herbert. "The Concertos." In *Carl Nielsen: Centenary Essays*, ed. Jürgen Balzer, 47–55. London: D. Dobson, 1966.

Rossi, Luis. "Clarinetto alla Italiana." *The Clarinet* 28, no. 4 (September 2001): 66–69.

Rossini, Gioachino. *La donna del lago, Edizione critica della opera di Gioachino Rossini*, vol. 2, ed. H. Colin Slim, vol. 24. Pesaro: Fondazione Rossini, 2002.

———. *Mosè in Egitto, Edizione critica della opera di Gioachino Rossini*, ed. Charles S. Brauner, vol. 24. Pesaro: Fondazione Rossini, 2004.

Rybka, F. James. *Bohuslav Martinů: The Compulsion to Compose*. Lanham, MD: Scarecrow Press, 2011.

Sacchini, Louis Vincent. "The Concerted Music for the Clarinet in the Nineteenth Century." Ph.D. diss., University of Iowa, 1980.

Sachania, Millan. "Preface." In Francis Poulenc, *Sonata for Clarinet and Piano*, rev. ed., ed. Millan Sachania, 2. London: Chester Music, 2006.

Šafránek, Miloš. *Bohuslav Martinů: His Life and Works*. Trans. Roberta Finlayson-Samsourová, London: Allan Wingate, 1962.

Sanderson, Roy Victor. "Luciano Berio's Use of the Clarinet in *Sequenza IXa.*" M.A. thesis, California State University, Long Beach, 1986.

Sandner, Wolfgang. *Die Klarinette bei Carl Maria von Weber*. Wiesbaden: Breitkopf & Härtel, 1971.

Schmidt, Carl B. *The Music of Francis Poulenc (1899–1963): A Catalogue*. Oxford: Clarendon Press, 1995.

———. *Entrancing Muse: A Documented Biography of Francis Poulenc*. Hillsdale, NY: Pendragon Press, 2001.

Schmidt, Christian Martin. *Verfahren der Motivisch-Thematischen Vermittlung in der Musik von Johannes Brahms, Dargestellt an der Klarinettensonate f-moll, op. 120, 1*. Munich: Emil Katzbichler, 1971.

Schreiber, Ottmar. *Max Reger in seinem Konzerten. Teil 1. Reger Konzertiert*. Bonn: Dümmler, 1981.

Schumann, Robert. *Robert Schumann's Werke, Serie V für Pianoforte und andere Instrument*, ed. Clara Schumann. Leipzig: Breitkopf & Härtel, 1885.

———. *Tagebücher, Band III Haushaltbücher, Teil 2 1847–1856*, ed. Gerd Nauhaus. Leipzig: Deutscher Verlag für Musik, 1982.

Schwinger, Wolfram. *Krzysztof Penderecki: His Life and Work: Encounters, Biography and Musical Commentary*. Trans. William Mann. London: Schott, 1989.

Scott, Shannon M. "Two Late Clarinet Works by Max Reger: Historical Perspective, Analysis, and Performance Considerations." Doctor of Music thesis, Northwestern University, 1994.

Seggelke, Jochen. "Richard Mühlfeld's Clarinets." In Goltz and Müller, *Richard Mühlfeld der Brahms-Klarinettist, Einleitung, Übertragung, und Kommentar der Dokumentation von Christian Mühlfeld*. Trans. Mona Lemmel, *Richard Mühlfeld, Brahms' Clarinettist: Introduction, Transcription, and Commentary of the Documentation by Christian Mühlfeld*, 332–57. Balve: Artivo, 2007.

Seitz, Barbara Joan. "The History and Significance of the Concert Series Evenings on the Roof, 1938–1954." Master of Music thesis, Indiana University, 1971.

Servières, Georges. *Saint-Saëns*. Paris: Félix Alcan, 1923.

Shackleton, Nicholas and Keith Puddy. "Mühlfeld's Clarinets." *The Clarinet* 16, no. 3 (May–June 1989): 33–36.

Shapiro, Amy. "Bernstein and the Clarinet: Stanley Remembers Lenny, Part I." *The Clarinet* 33, no. 1 (December 2005): 66–69.

———. "Bernstein and the Clarinet: Stanley Remembers Lenny, Part II." *The Clarinet* 33, no. 2 (March 2006): 66–68.

Simeone, Nigel, ed. *The Leonard Bernstein Letters*. New Haven: Yale University Press, 2013.

Simon, Eric. "The Clarinet Works of Max Reger." *The Clarinet*, no. 20 (Fall 1955): 12–14.

———. "Robert Schumann's *Fantasy Pieces*, Op. 73: Remarks About the Composer's Manuscript . . . Suggestion Regarding Interpretation, and Some Thoughts." *The Clarinet* 11, no. 1 (Fall 1983): 11.

Simmons, Walter. Record Review of "Muczynski, *Time Pieces for Clarinet and Piano, op. 43. Sonata for Flute and Piano, Op. 14. Three Preludes for Flute Solo, Op. 18. Six Duos for Flute and Clarinet, Op. 34*." *Fanfare* 8, no. 4 (1985): 265–66.

Simms, Bryan R. "The Society for Private Musical Performances: Resources and Documents in Schoenberg's Legacy." *Journal of the Arnold Schoenberg Institute* 3, no. 2 (October 1979): 126–49.

Simpson, Robert. *Carl Nielsen, Symphonist*. New York: Taplinger, 1979.

Skelton, Geoffrey. *Paul Hindemith: The Man Behind the Music; A Biography*. London: V. Gollancz, 1977.

Skelton, Geoffrey, ed. and trans. *Selected Letters of Paul Hindemith*. New Haven: Yale University Press, 1995.

Skowron, Zbigniew, ed. and trans. *Lutosławski on Music*. Lanham, MD: Scarecrow Press, 2007.

Skowronski, Joann. *Aaron Copland: A Bio-Bibliography*. Westport, CT: Greenwood Press, 1985.

Sluchin, Benny and Mikhail Malt. "Open Form and Two Combinatorial Musical Models: The Cases of *Domaines* and *Duel*." *Mathematics and Computation in Music, Third International Conference, MCM 2011 Paris, France, June 15–17, 2011: Proceedings* in *Lecture Notes in Artificial Intelligence* 6726, eds. Carlos Agon, et al., 255–69. New York: Springer, 2009.

Smith, Joan Allen. *Schoenberg and His Circle: A Viennese Portrait*. New York: Macmillan, 1986.

Smith, Richard Langham. "More Fauré than Ferneyhough: Françaix at 80." *The Musical Times* 133, no. 1797 (November 1992): 555–57.

Smith, William O. "Contemporary Clarinet Sonorities." *Selmer Bandwagon*, no. 67 (1973): 12–14.

———. "Master Class: *Variants for Solo Clarinet*." *The Clarinet* 28, no. 3 (June 2001): 4–7.

———. *Variants for Solo Clarinet*. Recording. Online. Available: http://faculty.washington.edu/bills/index.html. October 24, 2015.

Snavely, John Albert. "Benny Goodman's Commission of New Works and Their Significance for Twentieth-Century Clarinetists." Doctor of Musical Arts diss., University of Arizona, 1991.

Sparks, Dan. "Max Reger, a Brief Look at His Life and Clarinet Works." *The Clarinet* 10, no. 2 (Winter 1983): 32–33.

Spicknall, John Payne. "The Solo Clarinet Works of Bernhard Henrik Crusell (1775–1838)." Doctor of Musical Arts diss., University of Maryland, 1974.

Spohr, Louis. *Lebenserinnerungen; Erstmals ungekürzt nach den autographen Aufzeichnungen*. Ed. F. Göthel, 2 vols. Tutzing: H. Schneider, 1968.

Stein, Fritz. *Thematisches Verzeichnis der im Druck erschienenen Werke von Max Reger einschließlich seiner Bearbeitungen und Ausgaben*. Leipzig: Breitkopf & Härtel, 1953.

Stein, Leonard. "The Privataufführungen Revisited." In *Paul A. Pisk, Essays in his Honor*, ed. John M. Glowacki, 98–105. Austin: University of Texas Press, 1966.

Stevensson, Kjell-Inge. Trans. W. Jewson, "Carl Nielsen's Clarinet Concerto, Op. 57 (1928)." *The Clarinet* 4, no. 4 (Summer 1977): 27–29.

Stier, Charles. "Editions and Misprints: Copland Concerto for Clarinet." *The Clarinet* 19, no. 2 (February–March 1992): 48–50.

Stirzaker, Thomas D. "A Comparative Study of Selected Clarinet Works by Arthur Honegger, Darius Milhaud, and Francis Poulenc." Ph.D. diss., Texas Tech University, 1988.

Stockhausen, Karlheinz. *Texte Zur Musik 1970–1977. Band 4*. Köln: DuMont Buchverlag, 1978.

Stoll, Peter. "Penderecki . . . by Penderecki!" *The Clarinet* 37, no. 4 (September 2010): 56–60.

Stone, Winston. "The Onstage Instrumental Musician as Theater Performer." Ph.D. diss., University of Texas at Dallas, 2008.

Stravinsky, Igor. *Stravinsky: An Autobiography*. New York: Simon and Schuster, 1936.

Stravinsky, Igor and Robert Craft. *Dialogues and a Diary*. London: Faber and Faber, 1968.

Stravinsky, Vera and Robert Craft. *Stravinsky in Pictures and Documents*. New York: Simon and Schuster, 1978.

Street, Oscar W. "The Clarinet in Chamber-Music." *Chamber Music* 7, no. 9 (1914): 19–25.

Stucky, Steven. "Change and Constancy: The Essential Lutosławski." In *Lutosławski Studies*, ed. Zbigniew Skowron, 127–62. Oxford: Oxford University Press, 2001.

———. *Lutosławski and His Music*. Cambridge: Cambridge University Press, 1981.

Studd, Stephen. *Saint-Saëns: A Critical Biography*. London: Cygnus Arts, 1999.

Sulzer, Peter. *Zehn Komponisten um Werner Reinhart: Ein Ausschnitt aus dem Wirkungskreis des Musikkollegiums Winterthur, 1920–1950*. 3 vols. Winterthur: Stadtbibliothek, 1979–1983.

Suther, Kathryn Hallgrimson. "Two Sides of William O. 'Bill' Smith," Part II, Interview Conclusion and Admirer Tributes." *The Clarinet* 25, no. 1 (November–December 1997): 42–48.

Švalbe, Erika. "Looking for David Oppenheim." *The Clarinet* 25, no. 3 (May–June 1998): 44–45.

Swensen, Anton. "Applications of Selected Analytical Techniques to Twentieth Century Works for Solo Clarinet and Their Implications for Interpretation and Performance." Doctor of Education diss., Teachers College, Columbia University, 1969.

Szczurko, Elżbieta. *Antoni Szałowski: Person and Work*, trans. Zofia Weaver. Frankfurt am Main: PL Academic Research, 2013.

———. "Antoni Szałowski—the Essence of His Creativity." (2014). Online. Available: http://files.musicologytoday.hist.pl/files/Musicology_Today/Musicology_Today-r2011-t8/Musicology_Today-r2011-t8-s61-85/Musicology_Today-r2011-t8-s61-85.pdf. July 24, 2016.

Thurmond, Anne Marie. "Selected Woodwind Compositions by Robert Muczynski: A Stylistic and Structural Analysis of Muczynski's *Sonata, opus 14, for Flute and Piano, Sonata opus 29, for Alto Saxophone and Piano, Time Pieces, opus 43, for Clarinet and Piano*, and *Moments, opus 47, for Flute and Piano*." Doctor of Musical Arts diss., University of Georgia, 1998.

Titus, Robert A. "The Solo Music for the Clarinet in the Eighteenth Century." Ph.D. diss., State University of Iowa, 1962.

Townsend, George. "The 22nd National Polish Concours for Young Instrumentalists: May 1989." *The Clarinet* 17, no. 1 (December 1989): 40–41.

Tuthill, Burnet C. "The Sonatas for Clarinet and Piano." *Journal of Research in Music Education* 14, no. 3 (Autumn 1966): 197–212.

Turner, Dean William. "A Survey of Four Clarinet Compositions by William O. Smith: As an Introductory Source of Contemporary Clarinet Performance Techniques." Ph.D. diss., Michigan State University, 1975.

Valenziano, Nicholas J. "Twenty-One Avant-Garde Compositions for Clarinet Published Between 1964 and 1972: Notational Practices and Performance Techniques." Doctor of Musical Arts diss., University of Missouri–Kansas City, 1973.

Viano, Richard J. "By Invitation Only: Private Concerts in France During the Second Half of the Eighteenth Century." *Recherches sur la Musique Française Classique* 27 (1991–1992): 131–62.

Vojtech, Ivan. "Der Verein für musikalische Privataufführungen in Prag." In Ernst Hilmar, ed., 83–91. *Arnold Schönberg: Gedenkausstellung 1974*. Vienna: Universal Edition, 1974.

Walsh, Stephen. *The Music of Stravinsky*. London: Routledge, 1988.

Walzel, Robert L. Jr. "Bohuslav Martinů: An Examination of Selected Chamber Music Involving the Clarinet, with Three Recitals of Selected Works by Rossini, Sutermeister, Castelnuovo-Tedesco, Weiner, Bowen, Beethoven, Brahms, and Others." Doctor of Musical Arts thesis, University of North Texas, 1997.

Wanderley, Marchelo M. and Bradley W. Vines. "Origins and Functions of Clarinettists' Ancillary Gestures." In *Music and Gesture*, eds. Anthony Gritten and Elaine King, 165–91. Aldershot: Ashgate, 2006.

Ward, Martha Kingdon. "Weber and the Clarinet." *The Monthly Musical Record* 87, no. 982 (July–August 1957): 141–47.

Warrack, John. *Carl Maria von Weber*. 2nd ed. Cambridge: Cambridge University Press, 1976.

Waskowska, Teresa. "Clarinet Concerto Opus 57, FS129." In *Carl Nielsen, Mennesket og Musikken = Carl Nielsen: The Man and the Music*, Denmark: AM Production Multimedia, 1998, CD-ROM.

Waterhouse, William. *The New Langwill Index: A Dictionary of Musical Wind-Instrument Makers and Inventors*. London: T. Bingham, 1993.

Weber, Carl Maria von. *Sämtliche Werke = Complete Works, Series VI: Chamber Music*. Vol. 3, eds. Gerhard Allroggen, Knut Noltsträter, and Joachim Veit, Mainz: Schott, 2005.

———. *Writings on Music*. Trans. Martin Cooper, ed. John Warrack, Cambridge: Cambridge University Press, 1981.

Weber, William. *The Great Transformation of Musical Taste: Concert Programming from Haydn to Brahms*. Cambridge: Cambridge University Press, 2008.

Weinstock, Herbert. *Rossini: A Biography*. New York: Alfred A. Knopf, 1968.

West, Charles. "Master Class: *Time Pieces for Clarinet and Piano, op. 43* by Robert Muczynski." *The Clarinet* 26, no. 4 (September 1999): 6–8.

Weston, Pamela. *Clarinet Virtuosi of the Past*. London: R. Hale, 1971.

———. *More Clarinet Virtuosi of the Past*. Corby: Fentone Music, 1977.

———. *Clarinet Virtuosi of Today*. Baldock: Egon Publishers, 1989.

———. "Players and Composers." In *The Cambridge Companion to the Clarinet*, ed. Colin Lawson, 92–106. Cambridge: Cambridge University Press, 1995.

———. "Stockhausen's Contributions to the Clarinet and Basset Horn." *The Clarinet* 25, no. 1 (November–December 1997): 60–61.

———. "Werner Reinhart: Philanthropist Extraordinaire." *The Clarinet* 28, no. 3 (June 2001): 64, 66.

———. *Yesterday's Clarinettists: A Sequel*. Haverhill: Panda Group, 2002.

White, Eric Walter. *Stravinsky: The Composer and His Works*. 2nd ed., Berkeley: University of California Press, 1979.

Whitwell, David. "Franz Krommer: Early Wind Master." *Journal of Band Research* 10 (Spring 1974): 21–24.

———. "Improvisation in Harmoniemusik literature." In *Kongressbericht Abony/Ungarn 1994*, ed. W. Suppan, 435–39. *Alta Musica*, vol. 18. Tutzing: H. Schneider, 1996.

Willett, Charles. "A Conversation with Michel Arrignon." *The Clarinet* 16, no. 4 (July–August 1989): 32–36.

William O. Smith/Bill Smith. Online. Available: http://faculty.washington.edu/bills/wos_excerpts.html. October 24, 2015.

Wolf, Eugene K. "Galant Style." In *The Harvard Dictionary of Music*, 4th ed., 341. Cambridge: Belknap Press, 2003.

———. *The Symphonies of Johann Stamitz: A Study in the Formation of the Classic Style with a Thematic Catalogue of the Symphonies and Orchestral Trios*. Boston: M. Nijhoff, 1981.

Worthen, John. *Robert Schumann: Life and Death of a Musician*. New Haven: Yale University Press, 2007.

Wunch, Rebecca Lynn. "The Merger of Jazz and Twentieth Century: A Performance Analysis of Donald Martino's *A Set for Clarinet*." Master of Music thesis, Bowling Green State University, 2007.

Young, Phillip T. *4900 Historical Woodwind Instruments: An Inventory of 200 Makers in International Collections*. London: T. Bingham, 1993.

Zimmermann, Reiner. "Concluding Remarks." In Claude Debussy, *Première Rhapsodie pour Orchestre avec clarinette principale en Sb*, Leipzig: Peters, 1975, 50–52.

Index

CPSIA information can be obtained
at www.ICGtesting.com
Printed in the USA
BVHW031321210620
581838BV00006B/19

9 780190 205218